HIGHER EDUCATION

HIGHER EDUCATION
Quality and Management

Editors

S.M. Paul Khurana and P.K. Singhal

GYAN

Higher Education: Quality and Management

Rs. 750

ISBN: 978-81-212-1058-4

Published in 2010 in India by
Gyan Publishing House,
23, Main Ansari Road, Darya Ganj,
New Delhi-110002
Phones : 23282060, 23261060
Fax : 011-23285914
E-mail: books@gyanbooks.com
Website: www.gyanbooks.com

Lasser Type Setting: Quick Media, Delhi
Printed at : Chawla Offset Printers, Delhi

Contents

SECTION: III — COMPETENCE AND LEADERSHIP DEVELOPMENT

SECTION: IV — GLOBALIZATION, INNOVATION AND ENTREPRENEURSHIP

SECTION: V — RE-ENGINEERING AND REFORMS FOR GENERATION OF KNOWLEDGE CAPITAL

SECTION: VI— STRATEGIC ALLIANCE BETWEEN ACADEMIA AND INDUSTRY

Dr. Bal Ram Jakhar

Raj Bhawan
Bhopal- 462 003

Foreword

In the present era of liberalization and globalization, when the world is going through its fourth major transition as it develops from an industrial to a knowledge society, the Indian system of higher education is facing many challenges. Foremost is the inadequate coverage of youth to avail higher education. The other one is lack of quality in human resources, which is aggravating the problem of unemployment. There is, accordingly, an urgent need to review the existing models of management and delivery of higher education in India, for generation of globally competitive and employable human resources.

The benefits of liberalized economic growth, scientific and technological developments and the spiritual progress of India should percolate down to the coming generations. This may require alternative models of higher education management, strategic alliance among various stakeholders by re-engineering the curricula, evaluation methods etc. The articles incorporated in this volume are thought-provoking and call for serious consideration at decision-making levels.

I hope the publication will not only be useful to teachers and students but also provide critical inputs to all other stakeholders of the system, including the administrators, potential employers, policy makers, planners, etc.

June 8, 2009

(Bal Ram Jakhar)

Phone: 0755-4080170, 4080180 FAX: 0755 4080172

Preface

Under the present era of globalization and liberalization where the world society is already undergoing its fourth major transition from Industrial to Knowledge society, the Indian system of higher education is facing many formidable challenges. The first challenge is its grossly inadequate coverage of the relevant age group – hardly 8% in contrast to about 30 to 40% in developed nations. Then is the lack of required quality in the human resource, which most of the national and international employers find hardly employable. Finally, there is an acute shortage of excellent faculty across the institutions. This is leading to a significant mismatch between the quality and quantity of the human resource that should hamper the future national GDP growth, if not corrected soon or in a short period.

There is a need to review the existing models of delivery, management and regulation of higher education in India with a focus on generation of globally competitive and employable human resource from our institutions. Such a review should also ensure that the benefits of liberalized economic growth, scientific and technological developments, and spiritual progress and enlightenment percolate down to the masses making them sufficiently empowered to alleviate problems of corruption, illiteracy, inequitable growth and poverty. This may entail huge investments hardly affordable to the nation and re-engineering of our curricula and evaluation methods already being messed up by plethora of the regulatory agencies always at crossroads. These require alternate models of higher education management, strategic alliance among various stakeholders including the industry, and introduction of innovative modules of higher learning.

We therefore, undertook the task to bring out a book "Higher Education – Quality and Management" on the following themes (sections);

1. Infrastructure, Norms and standards
2. Accreditation and Quality Audit

3. Competence and Leadership Development
4. Globalization, Innovation and Entrepreneurship
5. Re-engineering and Reforms for Generation of Knowledge Capital
6. Strategic Alliance between Academia and Industry
7. Corporate Governance and Social Responsibility
8. Environment and Ethics
9. Emerging Models.

We approached renowned experts, in the field, i.e., the academicians, administrators, policy makers and researchers, to enrich the target audience with their views and synthesis for shaping the Indian Higher Education to meet the formidable challenges from within and outside. It is matter of great satisfaction that these experts made a wholehearted contribution that would significantly help and catalyze the ongoing process of revamping higher education in the country. We are grateful to Professors H.P. Dikshit, Bhopal, S.P. Thyagarajan,Chennai, C.P.S. Chauhan, New Delhi and K.K. Panda, New Delhi for their articles in the Section I – Infrastructure, Norms and Standards. Section II – Accreditation and Quality Audit includes contributions from Professors P. Ramalingam, Puducherry, N.K. Jain, Jaipur and R.M. Mathew, Abu Dhabi. Section III – Competence and Leadership Development has the enlightening article from the former President of the country His Excellency Dr. A.P.J. Abdul Kalam and Fr. D. George, Jabalpur. Section IV – Globalization, Innovation and Entrepreneurship has excellent synthesis by Professors P.H. Trivedi, Ahemdabad and Dr. Panjab Singh, Varanasi (now New Delhi). Section V – Re-engineering and Reforms for Generation of Knowledge Capital has thought provoking articles by the editors. Section VI – Strategic Alliance between Academia and Industry, includes a visionary article by Prof. I. Fagoonee and associates from Mauritius. Section VII – Corporate Governance and Social Responsibility, has benefited from the excellent synthesis by Professors Pankaj Mittal, Sonepat, A.K. Kapoor, Gwalior, K. Sudharao, New Delhi and V.K. Arora, Jaipur. Section VIII – Environment and Ethics includes articles by Dr. R. Rajarathinam, Tiruchirappalli, Fr. D. George, Jabalpur, Usha Rao, Mumbai and G.S. Mishra, Jabalpur. Finally, Section IX – Emerging Models has some very interesting and futuristic ideas by Professors Sukhadeo Thorat, New Delhi,

M.M. Salunkhe, Kolhapur, P.N. Srivastava, New Delhi, Kamlesh Joshipura, Rajkot and Fr. Xavier Alphonse, Chennai.

We place on record our deep gratitude to each of above-mentioned authors of the articles for their readiness to be an active partner of this odyssey of bringing together various stakeholders on a single platform in bringing processes and products of Indian Higher Education at par with that of the World.

Heartfelt gratitude and sincere thanks are also due to Dr. Ashok K Chauhan, Founder President, RBEF and Chairman, AKC Group of Companies for his encouragement and kind permission for use of Amity University, Campus Noida pictures on the cover.

The pattern used in preparation of MSS by various authors, have not been changed, to retain their originality despite the variations in style in the book. It is pertinent to mention here that a few chapters, viz. Mentoring, Creating excellence, Value education, Motivation, Ethics of environment, Community college in this book are only indirectly related to the Quality and Management yet they influence both of them hence have been included to provide material for ready reference/ information to all the readers such as teachers, higher education industry (college owners) and even students as well as University Administrators, serving / aspiring Registrars / Deans / Principals/ HODs.

We are optimistic that the visionary ideas and thoughts of these renowned scholars will benefit the country in its stated objectives of having the appropriately knowledgeable human resource for future economic, social and technological growth of our society.

Dr. S.M. Paul Khurana
Vice-Chancellor
R.D. University, Jabalpur
1st March 2009

Dr. P.K. Singhal
Professor in BioScience

Contributors

A.K. Kapoor, Former Vice-Chancellor, Jiwaji University Gwalior 474011, India.

A.P. J. Abdul Kalam, Former President of India, New Delhi 110001, India. <apj@abdulkalam.com>

Anjana Daiboo, University of Mauritius, Mauritius.

Brij Kishore Baguant, University of Mauritius, Mauritius.

C.P.S. Chauhan, National University of Education Planning and Administration, New Delhi 110016, India.

Davis George, Principal, St. Aloysius College, Jabalpur 482001, India. <dgeorge55@gmail.com>

G.S. Mishra, Former Dean, Faculty of Education, Rani Durgavati University, Jabalpur 482001, India.

H.P. Dikshit, Director General, School of Good Governance and Policy Analysis, Bhopal 462001, India.

K. Sudha Rao, National University of Educational Planning and Administration, New Delhi, 110016, India.

K.K. Panda, Former Director, Institute of Constitutional and Parliamentary Studies, New Delhi.

Kamelsh Joshipura, Vice-Chancellor, Saurashtra University, Rajkot, India. <kpjoshipura@yahoo.com>

M.K. Singh, National University of Educational Planning and Administration, New Delhi, 110016, India.

M.M. Salunkhe, Vice-Chancellor, Shivaji University, Kolhapur 416004, India.

N.K. Jain, Former Vice-Chancellor, University of Rajasthan, Jaipur 302004, India.

P.K. Singhal, Head, Department of BioScience, Rani Durgavati University, Jabalpur 482001, India.

<pksinghalvdvv@gmail.com>

P.N. Singh, Delhi School of Professional Studies and Research, Rohini, Delhi, India.

P.N. Srivastava, Former Chairman, All India Council of Technical Education and Vice-Chancellor, Jawaharlal Nehru University, New Delhi, India.

P. Ramalingam, UGC-Academic Staff College, Pondicherry University, Puducherry 605 014, India.

<panchramalingam@hotmail.com>

Panjab Singh, Former Vice-Chancellor, Banarasi Hindu University, Varansi, India.

Pankaj Mittal, Vice-Chancellor, Bhagat Phool Singh Mahila Vishwavidyalaya, Khanpur Kalan, Sonepat, India.

Parimal H. Trivedi, Vice-Chancellor, Gujarat University, Ahemdabad, India.

R. Rajarathinam, Principal, St. Joseph's College, Tiruchirappalli, India.

Raju M. Mathew, Al Ain University of Science and Technology, Abu Dhabi, UAE.

S.M. Paul Khurana, Former Vice-Chancellor, Rani Durgavati University, Jabalpur 482001, India.

<smpkhurana@amity.edu>

S.P. Thyagarajan, Former Vice-Chancellor, University of Madras, Chennai, India. <profspt@gmail.com>

Sukhadeo Thorat, Chairman, University Grants Commission, New Delhi 110002, India.

Usha Rao, Former Principal, College of Education, Mumbai, India.

V.K. Arora, Former Director, UGC Academic Staff College, University of Rajasthan, Jaipur 302004, India.

Xavier Alphonse, Director, ICRDCE, Chennai 600008, India.

<macrdce@vsnl.com>

SECTION : I - INFRASTRUCTURE, NORMS AND STANDARDS

1

Quality and Management of Higher Education in India

H.P. Dikshit

ABSTRACT

It seems, we are passing through a very important, dynamic and turbulent phase of development of higher education in our country. There are a lot of new opportunities being explored for increasing access of quality higher education by setting up new IITs, IIMs, IIITs, Central Universities. There is an unprecedented steep rise of 900% in 11th Plan financial allocation for higher education. Also there are serious challenges arising from our longstanding concerns to bring in qualitative changes in one of the world's largest systems of higher education that we have today. There is urgency in expanding the quantity and quality of the talent pool of India. We are looking ahead to a revolution in higher education to achieve our cherished goal similar to the Green Revolution in Agriculture Sector which was responsible for quantum jump in our food production. We have to encounter and succeed in global and cross border competitiveness.

INTRODUCTION

The title of this article is indicative of some recent trends and new approaches appearing in our system of higher education which were not prominently visible when I joined as a faculty member in one of the premier universities of India more than 46 years ago. Except for new universities which had started showing up at that time, generally, universities were considered as centres of advanced learning and research of the highest level. This is evident from the fact that as a Post-Graduate student, I had shared the class room with quite a few students from developed countries from North America and Europe. The word management never appeared in academic or administrative transactions in the University system. Gradually, we started getting introduced to new titles for institutions of higher learning like Indian Institute of Technology (IIT) and later Indian Institute of Management (IIM) and subsequently many others. Although, universities and as a unique exception the Indian Institute of Science Bangalore retained the old nomenclature for the apex statutory bodies, the IITs started having Senate and Board of Governors in place of Academic Council and Executive Council respectively. Further following this trend, even new universities like Indira Gandhi National Open University (IGNOU) started having Board of Management in place of the Executive Council and limited membership of the Academic Council.

Thus the word Management started appearing more prominently in the higher education system of the country. This was indicative of a beginning of a paradigm shift in our approach to higher education in the country, which gradually became more dominant. Much before this, internationally also some of the countries developed a new perception of treating higher education as a commodity which could be marketed and exported for generating new sources of funding for higher education. This forced higher education to become very competitive and market oriented within the countries and globally. These developments lead many of us in higher education to believe that well tried and successful techniques of management, its Quality Principles etc. of corporate sector could be successfully applied for better management of higher education. I have some reservations for such a belief. However, a transformed and appropriately interpreted version suitable to the Indian context may be useful. I will elaborate on this view subsequently in this article. In corporate sector the main parameter for measuring quality is in terms of the ratio between the costs involved and profits which could be easily quantified. How do you measure quality of education? Do we make any consistent study of the outcome of education imparted in terms of inputs of quality of students admitted, costs involved in educating them and tracer studies about the students coming out of the system? In most of the scholarly articles on quality of education I hardly find any significant effort on examining the tracer studies.

2. The unfulfilled tasks. I would like to remind all sectors of our civil society and especially those managing education system in the country about the following most farsighted and important observation made by Swami Vivekanand, when India was about to become an independent country after the British Rule. I quote ***"If we are to rise again we shall have to do it by spreading education among the masses"***. Incidentally, this observation and the following are in consonance with the observation of Plato viz.*"Those who have mastered the art of Governance of their empires (their nations in the present day context) know the importance of education in it"*. In his famous speech delivered to the nation on the eve of the Independence of India, in 1947, Pt. Jawaharlal Nehru our first Prime Minister, essentially promised to the nation that one of our premier commitments was to educate our people to liberate them from illiteracy, ignorance and exploitation. These important pronouncements and directions were soon followed by appearance of the report of the "University Education Commission" of 1948-49 (Radhakrishnan Commission Report) and a little later appeared the Laxmanaswamy Mudaliyar Committee on Secondary Education (1952-1953). The University Education Commission report contained the following very important directions for development of education and its goals in India.

> *"The most important and urgent reform needed in education is to transform it, to endeavor to relate it to the life, needs and aspirations of the people and thereby make it the powerful instrument of social, economic and cultural transformation necessary for the realization of the national goals. For this purpose, education should be developed so as to increase productivity, achieve social and national integration, accelerate the process of modernization and cultivate social, moral and spiritual values."*

Let us look back in retrospect and examine as to how much we have succeeded in implementing recommendations of the

University Education Commission about some very important and fundamental dimensions of education in general and higher education in particular. It is not that these recommendations have become obsolete even today but it is our failure and inability to implement them, for unexplained and unjustified reasons.

I do not mean to suggest even remotely that there has been no progress in the development of education in the country but perhaps, we could not continue to attach due importance to quality of the content and its delivery system. In 1947, we had only 18% men and 2% women in the country who were literate whereas the same percentages have increased to 75.85% and 54.16% by the year 2001. Average literacy rate rose to 65.38% but a disturbing variation of averages between different regions is 35% to 96%. In fact we could not place any robust system of expansion and management of education that matched the challenges arising from pressures of increase in population and even worst the high rates of dropouts. *Quality of education of course suffered in such a lopsided development.*

The recommendations of the "Education Commission" of 1964-66, (popularly known as Kothari Commission) again remained only partly implemented and there are enough evidences of major deficiencies in implementation of some of these which adversely affected the quality of higher education. The commission had drawn up a long-term enrolment plan based on study by a joint team of the London School of Economics and the Indian Statistical Institute. We are not aware of such periodical studies on a continuous basis on this very important issue related to expansion of education maintaining its quality. Further, while submitting the report to the Union Education Minister on June 29, 1966 Prof. D.S. Kothari noted *"the future shape of things is unpredictable. This emphasizes all the more the need for an educational policy which contains a built-in flexibility so that it can adjust to changing circumstances. It underscores the importance of experimentation and innovation."* It is on these accounts that we are witnessing a series of contemporary initiatives at national level to revisit the recommendations of the Kothari Commission after nearly a period of 40 years to learn lessons from lapses in its implementation and their contemporary interpretations for improvement in quality of education and other aspects related to it [18] (see also [2]).

I happened to be a contributor to a national conference organized by the National University for Education and Planning (NUEPA) on 40 years of Kothari Commission (see [10], [11] and [18] for conference proceedings). In order to fulfill the important task and commitment to remove the disturbing gap between the provision and requirement of higher education, we achieved greater access often sacrificing quality. There are of course very few exceptions to this, but in a country like ours with large student population, we cannot be satisfied with such a situation. It is tragic to note that we have not learnt lessons from the failures of the past and as we would examine, a little later, this trend of decline in quality at the cost of increased access is likely to continue unless some important long term and short term measures are ensured along with midterm reviews and modifications in our projections for expansion.

3. Analyzing decline in quality with increased access. The importance of increase in access to higher education cannot be denied but it is equally important to maintain its quality. It is even more important to create an ambience for continued aspirations for enhancement in quality of education. In this section we would like to analyze the present status of quality in the traditional and nontraditional systems of higher education in the country as a prelude to some subsequent sections.

3.1 The traditional system: As I mentioned earlier at the time the Kothari Commission report was being written there existed quite a few universities in the country which provided education of the highest quality comparable with some of the leading universities of the world. Two of such universities were often referred to as the Oxford and Cambridge of the East. Eminent scientist and educationist Dr. D.S. Kotahri was a product of one such university and had received education of the highest quality in the Department of Physics which had Prof. Meghnad Saha and Prof. Krishnan as teachers and student prodigies like Harish Chandra, who later became an illustrious Professor at the Princeton University. Thus the Kothari Commission envisaged more universities of this category and therefore while recommending creation of new universities it was specifically mentioned that adequate care should be taken to ensure appropriate infrastructure in terms of buildings, Libraries, Laboratories etc. and sufficient faculty positions. *Following this recommendation a large number of universities started being set up mostly by state legislation without ensuring the essential preconditions mentioned in the Kothari Commission Report. Unfortunately this trend gained momentum and the process continues even today at the cost of quality of education.*

The number of universities has increased from 20 in 1947 to 400, colleges from 500 to 18064, teaching staff from a meager 15,00 to nearly 480 thousand. Student population in higher education increased from 100 thousand in 1950 to over 11.2 million in 2005. From 1% of population of relevant age group in 1950 in higher education, it has risen in the range of 7%-10% by around 2007. In the letter of the Chairman of the National Knowledge Commission (NKC) addresses to the Prime Minster dated 29th November 2006 a figure of 7% is indicated. 90% of institutions of education are in urban areas [12]. There is great variation in crucial statistical figures about higher education in the country available from different sources like Selected Education Statistics (SES), National Sample Survey (NSS), Population Census (PC), Association of Indian Universities (AIU), University Grants Commission (UGC) and few others [21] also provide data on number of student enrolment.

The technical education institutions have increased from about 96 in 1950 to 7000 institutions in 2008 with an annual intake of 1.3 million students. As in other cases there are even more serious regional imbalances and variations in spread of these institutions and quality of education imparted by them. Technical Education Institutions located in just four states of the country are providing education to nearly 910 thousand students that is, 70% of the total number of students receiving technical education. There is a great variation in free structure of these institutions which generally do not seem to be quite dependent on quality of education but other factors. According to the Chairman of the All India Council of Technical Education (AICTE), these factors are leading to commercialization of technical education in the country. Several institutions in the country which do not fulfill even the minimum norms prescribed by the AICTE and are not recognized continue to conduct Degree, Diploma and Certificate Programmes in Technical Education [22]. *This is yet another instance of our failure in maintaining quality while expanding access.*

3.2. The nontraditional system: Kothari Commission realized that opening of new universities with the prerequisites prescribed by the Commission may not be enough to meet the increasing demand for education. Therefore, the Commission suggested as a supplementary measure the introduction of the Correspondence Courses. This was a major improvement over the system of what we called private, non-collegiate or non-regular and non-campus students in whose case the only obligation of the universities, with a few exceptions, was generally limited to collecting fees from students and then conducting examination and declaring results. In spite of this there were instances where some of the students in this category faired equally well as those who received regular inputs of classroom teaching. We may ponder if this has any reflection on the quality of teaching. It is very sadly observed that this system or even further degraded systems exist in higher education even today. For brevity, we would like to refer to a detailed analysis of these issues in a very recent paper of the author [18]. All the foregoing facts and figures remind us of the following very important observation made in the Kothari Commission. ***"...no report, however good, can be a substitute for action"***. It seems we were found lacking in full implementation of the Kothari Commission Report.

4. Quality and Excellence in NPHE 1986. The National Policy on Higher Education (NPHE) of 1986 identified the following principle goals for higher education:

- Greater Access,
- Equity in Access,
- Quality and Excellence,
- Relevance and
- Promotion of social Values.

The policy document was perhaps the most widely discussed across the country with different stake holders, Vice-Chancellors, Teachers and other Educationists, Student Organizations and the Civil Society. Thus the Programme of Action, 1992 further developed the details of the policy and processes of its implementation. I had the privilege and opportunity to participate in this massive exercise. The importance and significance of this document is still realized and the Association of Indian Universities chose the topic on Quality and Relevance of Higher Education for their Annual conference of Vice-Chancellors held in 2008 [3].

There was a very significant recommendation in the Programme of Action, 1992 to the effect that *the Universities and other Academic Institutions of Higher Education should play a leading role in all developmental activity of the country.* This placed great confidence and challenging responsibilities on the academia and institutions of higher education in the country. Meeting the important task emanating from the foregoing recommendation of course required as prerequisites for high quality education and academic excellence in our institutions of higher education.

I was aware of the Oxford Study Group consisting of a few faculty members of the Oxford University who took the initiative of developing contacts with Industries to study and propose solutions for industrial problems. It did not take long before the Industries realized the importance of this Group and the demand for consultancies from this group for industries increased many fold. The Oxford Study Group had some eminent academics willing to look around for applications of their knowledge. Thus, in the background of the foregoing recommendations contained in the Programme of Action, 1992, I looked forward to Academic Institutions playing a central role by sharing their knowledge and expertise in different sectors of our society.

In retrospect, I realize that this did not happen except in a few cases in spite of a large number of conferences, workshops, special schemes etc. There are many reasons for our having missed this great opportunity. Some of the reasons for our failure seem to be *i) the rigidity in our educational system, which unfortunately continues even today, ii) misapprehensions about success of academic inputs in other sectors, iii) general reluctance in academia to encourage and support serious dialogues and interaction beyond their disciplines and campuses and iv) weakness in our system of education, in not being able to sufficiently motivate our students in problem solving and accepting new challenges with confidence.* Some of the foregoing dimensions are important components for achieving quality, relevance and general acceptance of the credibility of education by society. Expectations of the society from us are well reflected in the following extract from the recent quote from the address by the Chief Justice of India, Justice K. G. Balakrishnan, delivered at the 18th Convocation of IGNOU in 2007, *"Education is central to addressing the paradoxes and inequities that challenge our society today."*

In order to further strengthen the point raised in the beginning of this section about quality and relevance of higher education, I would like to cite the examples of two internationally recognized institutions imparting education and research of highest quality and great national significance in our country. These are our institutions setup by the pioneering atomic scientist Dr. H. J. Bhabha and pioneering space scientist Dr. Vikram Sarabhai in the area of Atomic Energy and Space research and its applications respectively. Besides his outstanding contributions to scientific research Dr. Bhabha established the Atomic Energy Establishments including the famous Tata Institute of Fundamental Research which continue to produce intellectuals and engineers of highest merit and quality even today. This was not without personal sacrifices and great efforts made by him. It may be relevant to refer to the following very sharp reaction of the Nobel Prize winning scientist Prof. S. Chandrasekhar to a remark that one fails to understand as to how Dr. Bhabha could have given up research to build up institutions [24].

"Science, he said could be served in many ways. All of these are important and one should choose the path best suited to one's ability and according to what is most needed. He also gave example of Hermann Bondi, who relinquished active research to become the scientific adviser to the British Government." The message is clear and is of far-reaching significance and importance. Institution building for high quality education and research is indeed a noble cause which serves the ultimate goal of education that effects generations after generations.

The other illustrious example is of initiatives taken by Dr. Vikram Sarabhai the pioneer in development of Indian Space Research Programme, which resulted in internationally acknowledged capacity, capability and grand success of the country in the area of Space Research and its Applications. These developments of which the nation is proud of emanated from the following visionary statement of Dr. Vikram Sarabhai: "*We are to play a meaningful role nationally, and in the* community *of nations, we must be second to none in the application of advanced technologies to the real problems of man and society.*" This visionary statement and pioneering efforts and establishment of institutions propelled our country to the status of one of the top six countries in the world in capabilities like development and launch of satellites for different useful applications including successful recent achievement of the mission of landing on the moon.

I would like to conclude this section by referring to the following two more recent observations that emerged from the NKC and more recently by UGC. In a recent letter of the Chairman of the NKC to the Prime Minister of India dated 5th July, 2007 it was observed that "*Systematic reform of the higher education system (including skill based marketable vocational education) in India is essential to develop the required intellectual capital as well as generate effective synergies among industry, government, the educational system, the R&D environment and the consumer*".

As another important recent initiative to revisit and re-examine our systems of higher education, UGC-AICTE Review Committee has been appointed under the Chairmanship of Prof. Yash Pal to consider restructuring of UGC - AICTE to enable them to meet the globally emerging and dynamic changes and challenges arising in higher education. The UGC-AICTE Review Committee met on the 30th April, 2008 at the UGC Office in New Delhi. In his opening remarks Prof. Yash Pal observed as follows [22]: "*... a university symbolizes a universe of knowledge; this should be place where new knowledge keeps growing often crossing the boundaries of established disciplines*".

5. Quality Assessment and Accreditation. The NPHE identified quality and relevance as focused areas for development of higher education in the country. As follow up action three major initiatives for determining and assessing quality of education in institutions of higher education were initiated by the AICTE, IGNOU and UGC. National Board for Accreditation (NBA), Distance Education Council (DEC) and National Assessment and Accreditation Council (NAAC) respectively were set up by the AICTE, IGNOU and UGC. NBA was set up as a constituent unit of AICTE; DEC was set up under the Act of IGNOU (which had similar provisions for distance education as those in UGC Act) and NAAC as an Inter University Centre for performance evaluation, assessment and accreditation of the Universities and Colleges in the country. The approach to assessment and accreditation of these systems are quite different. NBA focused its assessment and accreditation on the quality of Programmes of Study which seems to be more precise and measurable. Since DEC was an outcome of IGNOU Act and the institution was itself delivering distance education programmes therefore the process of assessment and accreditation by DEC got delayed. NAAC based its assessment and accreditation on overall performance of various departments and units of institutions of higher education. We would also discuss more recent demand driven trends of assessment of quality of higher education and competence. The assessments by NASSCOM and World Bank which we will discuss are essentially driven by economic competitiveness related to Knowledge Economy.

5.1. Quality Assessment and Accreditation by NBA: It started assessment of programmes from the session 1996-1997 and the growth in assessment up to 2003-2004 (source: AICTE website) is indicated in the following Table 1.

Table 1. Number of Programmes Accredited by NBA 1996-2004

Year	*Number of Programmes accredited by NBA*	*Year*	*Number of Programmes accredited by NBA*
1996-97	73	2000-01	21
1997-98	93	2001-02	202
1998-99	72	2002-03	344
1999-00	24	2003-04	190

Thus, a total 1019 Programmes only had been accredited in the period 1996-2004. The steep decline in the number of Programmes accredited to the extent of 45% from the year 2002-2003 to 2004, while the number of technical education institutions increased considerably is disturbing. This proportionate decline seems to have continued up to 2006 but it is satisfying to note that the number of programmes accredited by NAB increased substantially during 2007 and 2008. In the following Table 2, state wise numbers of institutions which got at least some of their programmes accredited by NAB up to July 19, 2008 are given (*source official website of AICTE*).

Table 2. Number of Institutions that got Programmes accredited by NBA up to 2008

Year	*Number of Institutions accredited by NBA*	*State*	*Number of Institutions accredited by NBA*
Tamil Nadu	135	Uttar Pradesh	56
Maharashtra	133	Gujarat	26
Andhra Pradesh	68	Madhya Pradesh	27
Karnataka	68	All others	138

Thus, out of nearly 7000 institutions of technical education that exist today only 651 that is just 9.3% institutions have got at least one Diploma /Undergraduate degree /Postgraduate Programme accredited by NBA for a period of 3 or 5 years since its inception in 1996. In order to have a reasonable estimate of the percentage of programmes accredited by NBA so far, we make moderate assumption of five programmes per institution as average. As of today there are about 7000 technical education institutions in the country [22], therefore we arrive at the conclusion that 35,000 programmres are being conducted by various technical education institutions out of which it is reasonable to infer from Table 2 that only 3255 proogrammes could be accredited by NAB. *Thus, only 9.5% of total programmes being conducted by technical education institutions in the country could be accredited by NBA so far.* A natural implication is that fairly large percentage of our students is not able to receive quality technical education and yet they have to pay unduly high fees. It is in this undesirable state of our institution that the Supreme Court of India was constrained through a judgment to step in and order setting up of State Fees Committees to decide reasonable fees structure for Technical and Professional Programmes.

5.2. Distance Education Council: DEC started recognition of those Open Universities in the initial years 1994-1999, which were set up by State or Central Legislation and were also approved by the UGC under section 12(b). Since the year 2000, DEC started recognizing State Open Universities without the requirement of recognition of UGC under 12(b), in spite of serious objections raised by the UGC. Notwithstanding the provisions of the Act of IGNOU, confusion persisted about empowerment of DEC to assess and accredit institutions and programmes delivered through Distance Education. The problem became even more complicated with growth of distance education programmes spanning the jurisdiction of the general higher education, technical education and even beyond. Thus, the confusion which arose from questioning the authority of DEC, a large number of highly substandard distance education programmes emerged and most unfortunately the momentum gained during that period is still perpetuating.

In 2004, the Ministry of Human Resource Development (MHRD), Government of India started contemplating setting up DEC as an organization not dependent on IGNOU through a new act of Parliament. The first draft was developed by 2005, which went through several revisions and the final draft was put up by MHRD for consideration of the Union Cabinet in October, 2008. However it is reported that it could not be approved by the Union Cabinet and all that happened was to refer it to a Committee of Group of Ministers (GoM). Thus responsibility of Assessment and Accreditation of Distance Education Programme in spite opposition from different quarters is still with DEC under IGNOU. In my view misinterpretations of decisions of DEC continue unabated. There is a Global Open University with its office in Amsterdam and we now have a new Global Open University Nagaland set up under a State act of Nagaland. DEC has given provisional recognition for one year with certain conditions about quality of student support services and course content. The new Global Open University Nagaland has progressed with terrific speed and it has advertised one year M. Phil. Degree programme in any discipline or group of disciplines which one can think of, with delivery centres spread over all parts of the country (*source website of the university, in January,* 2009) In order to ensure quality, in January 2009, DEC has come out with a Hand Book on the processes of Assessment and Accreditation of Distance Education Programmes.

5.3. National Assessment and Accreditation Council: The development of NAAC has been similar to that of NBA with the exception that NAAC assesses and accredits institutes as whole rather than individual programmes of study, departments and units of institutions. Recognition of quality of Departments and other units is done through several Schemes of UGC like Departments of Special Assistance, Centres of Advanced Studies etc. Besides, these, two fairly general criteria with minimum requirement adopted by the UGC are (i) recognition of temporarily affiliated colleges under section 2(f) and (ii) recognition of universities and permanently affiliated colleges under section 12(b). The universities and colleges in the latter category become entitled for financial support by the UGC. By the year 2006, out of a total of about 14,000 colleges coming under the purview of the UGC, 40% were recognized under 2(f) and 38% under 12(b). 22% Colleges were not recognized by the UGC due to deficiencies even in the minimal requirement prescribed by it. Similarly out of 317 universities that existed in 2006 only 50% were recognized under 12(b) by the UGC and the other 50% remained unrecognized even under 12(b). More elaborate assessment done by NAAC covered 140 universities out of a total of nearly 400 universities that exist today. This accounts for 35% of the universities. However, it is seen from the following Table 3 that only negligible percentages of universities have found place in top grades of **A^{++}, A^{+}, 5 or 4 star.**

Table 3. Accreditation of Universities Region Wise with Higher Grades

Region	*Total Number of Universities accredited*	*Numbers under grades :*			
		A^{++}	5 Star	A^{+}	4 Star
North Eastern	08	0	0	0	2
Eastern	16	0	2	0	1
Western	31	1	4	1	9
Northern	41	0	6	1	5
Southern	44	1	7	2	5
Total	140	2	19	4	22
Category wise percentages out of a total of 400 universities existing in 2008		0.05	0.5	0.1	0.55

UGC has also introduced the concept of potential for academic excellence and under this category. 9 Universities, 12 Centers with specific specialization in 12 universities 477 Centers/Departments and 97 Colleges have been identified as having potential for excellence [21]. We had an occasion to closely examine the working of NAAC and the progress made by it in assessing and accrediting institutions of higher education during the first 12 years of its existence in the year 2004 when the Ministry of Human Resource Development (MHRD), Government of India appointed a committee to review the functioning of NAAC. Our report after an extensive study and interaction with different stakeholders including the officials of NAAC was submitted to the MHRD in 2005 [6].

5.4. Demand driven assessment of quality: External evaluation of quality of institutions by established News Publications and user agencies, which is common in developed countries, has also started emerging in our country during the last few years. However, this seems to be in the process of getting stabilized as different news agencies provide grading of top ten or twenty institutions of higher education in the country and often there is significant variation in the ordering of the institutions. For instance, according to one source IIT-Kanpur was on the top of the ordering while another put IIT-Bombay on the top. Perhaps among the world class institutions fine tuning of grades may not be possible. Nevertheless such grading by outside agencies is a welcome step.

Studies about knowledge economy and knowledge work force have also given rise to some robust models for assessment. Thus a transformation of the following model could be considered for dynamic assessment and evaluation on a massive scale with greater transparency and speed. The World Bank Institute's Knowledge for Development Program has developed the *Knowledge Assessment Methodology* (*KAM* - www.worldbank.org/kam), which is an Internet-based tool that provides a basic assessment technique. It is a user-friendly interactive diagnostic and benchmarking tool that is designed to help individual countries understand their strengths and weaknesses. The *KAM* is therefore useful for identifying problems and opportunities. The unique strength of the *KAM* lies in its approach that allows a holistic view of the wide spectrum of factors. Comparisons in the *KAM* are made on the basis of 80 structural and qualitative variables. Currently, there are 128 countries and 9 regional groupings that are available in the *KAM*. The data on which the *KAM* is based are all published by reputable institutions that are at the forefront of gathering and producing country statistics that is reliable and internationally consistent. The data are continuously updated [4].

The National Association of Software and Service Companies (NASSCOM) have been responsible for many very successful initiatives to project India's capability in IT sector world over. One of the objectives of NASSCOM which is relevant to higher education reads as follows. *Expand the quantity and quality of the talent pool of India.* Various studies including NASSCOM-McKinsey Study 2005 [17] made by NASSCOM throws up some interesting insights to validate India's positive human-power status and some serious concerns. One of these reports mentions that *only 30% of our graduates are employable*. This of course reflects on quality of our education system and its disconnection from employment needs of the country. See also [8] and [19].

NASSCOM's Education initiatives which have developed very useful partnerships with the Government, academia that aim to bring positive changes to the Higher Education system of our country and its orientation towards employable students. NASSCOM has launched *Assessment of Competence* **(NAC)** as an industry standard assessment and certification programme to ensure the transformation of a "trainable" workforce into an "employable workforce". NAC Test and job fair conducted in collaboration with the Department of Information Technology & Communication, Government of India and Government Rajasthan have received considerable attention and interest.

5.5. Issues arising from Assessment and Accreditation processes for quality: It is very important to analyze the impact of the whole process of assessment and accreditation being followed in the country. It seems two parallel processes are in practice in the country each being managed by three different apex level statutory organizations viz. AICTE, IGNOU (DEC) and UGC. There is variation in approach and even under the same organization two different methods are adopted to evaluate performance of academic institutions of the country. Very rigorous processes adopted by NAB and NAAC which have been practiced during the lat nearly 15 years have been modified with effect from January, 2009 and April 2007 respectively. There is uncertainty about assessment and accreditation agency for Distance Education programmes as the draft bill for setting up DEC by an act of parliament is pending for a final decision of the Union Cabinet. However, a Hand Book on assessment and accreditation of Distance Education Programmes issued in January 2009 may be helpful.

In view of the fact that NBA, NAC and DEC taken together have been able to assess and accredit quality of a very small percentage of institutions since their inception and that some of the leading institutions, which enjoy the status of highest credibility and quality by all stake holders like teachers, students, parents and others have not cared for assessment and accreditation, the whole exercise seems to be not of any great significance. Further, most of the processes of assessment and accreditation rely on infrastructural inputs like building, laboratory, and number of faculty irrespective of their quality but not in terms of outputs which provide more significant and relevant parameters. Even more disturbing are the facts that AICTE and UGC admit the existence of a large number of unrecognized Universities and Institutions including those identified as Fake Universities. UGC of course puts the names of such universities in its website but that is not enough. In such a situation quality of education is the worst victim.

The foregoing observations indicate the state of confusion which exists today. Serious self assessment and retrospection of our systems by all concerned is very important for ensuring reforms and improvements. Thus, the Chairman, UGC observed the following in the Nehru Memorial Lecture delivered at the University of Mumbai on 24th November 2006 which describes the present status of Quality and Excellence in the higher education system in the country [21]: *"There is limited literature on the estimate of quality and excellence of our university and collages system. In the absence of the studies I wish to present the status of quality and excellence with the help of conceptual and methodological framework developed"*.

5.6. Emerging approaches to ensure quality of teaching and research: There are several critical reports and comments on the quality of higher education but that should not deter us from accepting the challenges and finding a way out to bring in a revolution in higher education to ensure highest quality. All stake holders that is students, parents, teachers, organizations like UGC, AICTE and DEC, education departments of Governments both at the Centre and States all have to work together to ensure an environment in which gradually we could ensure quality of higher education. *A historic initial step was taken by us (Prof. Arun Nigavekar and the author as the Chairpersons of UGC and DEC respectively) along with the Chairperson of AICTE in issuing a letter jointly signed by us with the monograms of all the three organizations laying some minimal checks to stop substandard distance education programmes and exploitation of students. This did make an impact in improving quality of distance education programmes in the country.* Following this communication addressed to various stake holders, the Governor and Chancellor of the universities in Tamil Nadu convened a meeting of all the Vice-Chancellors in which Prof. Nigavekar, the

Chairman UGC and the author in his capacity as the Chairman of DEC were invited to participate. Some important decisions to implement quality measures for Distance Education Programmes were taken. Coordinated approach initiated by formation of UGC-AICTE Review Committee in 2008 is a welcome beginning in this direction.

NKC has made strong critical remarks about existing status of higher education and research in their reports and letters sent to the Prime Minister. The following extracts from the report on higher education submitted by the Chairman, NKC along with his letter dated 29th November 2006 express urgency in reforms which is very relevant and important for future development of the country. *"We will continue to think about the next steps in higher education. But we must emphasize the urgency of the situation, because our future depends on it. We are convinced that it is important to act here and now. At the same time, we believe that there is an opportunity in this crisis."* It is satisfying to note that besides commitment for thinking about next steps there is stress on acting here and now. I wish that we in education system could bring in a revolution for quality similar to the Green Revolution in agriculture sector, which gave a quantum jump to our food production.

Since the radio communication had played a key role in the success of the Green Revolution a lot of hope for a revolution in education system arose from the unique initiative taken by the Department of Space, Government of India in launching a dedicated satellite *EDUSAT* to meet point to point communication requirement of the country for education. The Government of India constituted a Steering Committee for utilization of *EDUSAT* in which I had the privilege of serving as the Chairman. Several meetings of State Ministers of Education and Secretaries were convened by the HRD Minister, Government of India. This was followed by organization of Workshops by the Department of Space, Government of India. We had fixed first meeting of the Steering Committee on 2nd December, 2004 for taking a decision about sharing of available bandwidth between all major organizations dealing with education across the Ministries. But the disinterest of some of our major organizations can be sensed from the fact that when I took charge as Chairman, AICTE on 1st December,

2004, to discover that no proposal for use of *EDUSAT* capability had been forwarded till then from AICTE. Indian Council of Agriculture Research (ICAR) could not take any decision about usage of *EDUSAT* capability for a long time. *Nearly 4 years out of 13 years of life of EDUSAT have already passed and I believe we lost a great opportunity of providing quality inputs in education on a very large scale at low costs even to the most distant and least developed locations of the country.*

6.1 Academic freedom and quality: We would examine a very recent trend on the part of some of the best institutions imparting quality education and research. Many of these had to depend on the existing universities for award of Degrees including Ph.D. and other Research Degrees. There was a great mismatch between the academic freedom enjoyed by scholars in these institutions and the rigid university systems. The quality of teaching and research transactions in these intuitions were well recognized and in my opinion the universities should have taken a more flexible approach in reaching out to these institutions to encourage and support quality of research and teaching. I would like to mention a small beginning in this direction made by one university and how this has gained momentum in the last few years.

The National Board for Higher Mathematics (NBHM) under Department of Atomic Energy, Government of India has been taking several initiatives to attract and nurture bright young students to take up Science as a career. Success of NBHM in organizing training of brilliant young students is reflected in their success in earning medals at the International Mathematics Olympiad through tough international competition. As a member of NBHM for nearly 13 years I have participated in serious deliberations within the NBHM and beyond on how to encourage these brilliant students to pursue science as a career. Indeed this is an important but difficult task as these students have many options to choose which are more attractive in terms of financial gains. Any *loss of brilliant students, from the education stream, after schooling means, loss of brilliant future researchers and teachers who would have ensured highest standards of quality in research and teaching.*

I would like to cite the example of one very successful and pioneering initiative which made a visible dent to attract some of the most brilliant students to pursue higher studies and research as a career and which can be viewed as a prelude to the following statement of Prof. Manmohan Singh, Prime Minister of India while speaking on the occasion of a function organized by the CSIR on January 10, 2009. *"A greater synergy and collaboration between CSIR laboratories and the university system is absolutely necessary — these two parallel systems have largely remained disconnected. I do believe that our scientific enterprise and research activity should be rooted in the university system. Universities must be more open to the free flow of talent so that research and teaching activity can develop together"*

A very distinguished scholar of international recognition and repute Professor C. S. Seshadri, FRS, who was also a member of the NBHM had initiated of his own a small centre to motivate some brilliant young students to take up scientific research as a career. His vision, which turned out to be very successful in years to come, needed initial recognition of some statutory university without sacrificing academic standards and autonomy. He was greatly disappointed with our rigid university systems, which did not allow freedom in academic matters to enable him to implement his vision. In this background emerged our plan to identify his Centre as a Special Centre under a new university which I was setting up as its Vice-Chancellor. We developed a new statute with lot of academic flexibility, which was duly approved by a statutory committee chaired by the Governor of the State and Chancellor of the university and attended by the Chief Minister, Education Minister, Principal Secretary Education of the State Government and all Vice-Chancellors of the universities in the state. The provisions of this statute were very different than those existed in other universities of the state or the country.

This gave momentum to Prof. Seshadri's vision and a world class institution emerged which produced graduate students worthy of getting selected for Ph.D. Programmes of some of the finest institutions of the world with fellowships in France, Germany and USA. I would say that the name of this new university became known internationally through the work of these students. The Centre continued to be with the university until recently when in 2007, the Centre viz. Chennai Mathematical Institute (CMI) was declared a deemed university and more recently

MHRD has sanctioned Rs. 100 million for its development. CMI of course had been receiving grants from the DAE and Indian Space Research Organization (ISRO). This is an excellent example of developing a world class institution around a well known scholar by accommodating flexibility and greater autonomy in the approach of our university systems. I wish more of such initiatives materialize to provide capable researchers and teachers.

Chairman DAE and Chairman ISRO both were deeply impressed by the quality of teaching and research at the CMI. The success of the foregoing initiative drew attention of many others and in year 2004, the Director of Harish Chandra Research Institute (HRI), another DAE supported Institute met me at IGNOU and we signed an MOU for a joint HRI-IGNOU teaching cum research Programme. Meanwhile, a Committee consisting of Prof. S.K. Joshi, former Director General of Council of Scientific and Industrial Research (CSIR) and the author visited the Tata Institute of Fundamental Research (TIFR) to recommend the inclusion of the Institute as a Deemed university, which gave them more academic freedom than that they enjoyed by association with the University of Bombay.

The foregoing pace setting trend continues and now Homi Bhabha National Institute (HBNI) has emerged as another prestigious deemed university of the country. It provides academic freedom for design and development of new courses and programmes under a single research-driven framework, with the authority to award Degree / Diploma by the university. DAE runs four (4) major Research Centers: Bhabha Atomic Research Centre (BARC), Mumbai, Indira Gandhi Centre for Atomic Research (IGCAR), Kalpakkam, Raja Ramanna Centre for Advanced Technology (RRCAT), Indore and Variable Energy Cyclotron Centre (VECC), Kolkata and seven (7) grant-in-aid institutions: Tata Institute of Fundamental Research (TIFR), Mumbai, Saha Institute of Nuclear Physics (SINP), Kolkata, Institute of Plasma Research (IPR), Gandhinagar, Institute of Physics (IOP), Bhubaneswar, Harish-Chandra Research Institute (HRI), Allahabad, Tata Memorial Centre (TMC), Mumbai and Institute of Mathematical Science (IMSc), Chennai.

The upcoming Advanced Institute of Science and Technology (AIST) of Council for Scientific and Industrial Research (CSIR) will be an autonomous university offering interdisciplinary and innovative undergraduate and postgraduate courses. Dr. Samir Brahmachari, Director General of CSIR recently announced that the AIST will offer global participative courses like Abrasion Engineering, Fabrionics etc. The university will be spread across CSIR's 39 laboratories in the country. Five (5) of these are in Physical Sciences, seven (7) in Chemical Sciences, 11 in Biological Sciences, 13 in Engineering Sciences, and three (3) in Information Sciences. The interest of the scientists working in some of the leading R&D institutions in setting up new universities is well reflected in the following observation of Dr. Raghunath Mashelkar, former Director General of CSIR. *"It's always doctoral and post doctoral students who do all the research work. So lack of students means lack of research,"* The CSIR system believes that CSIR- AIST University will greatly facilitate and encourage research and from the present level of 400 Ph.Ds per year CSIR would be able to produce 1500 quality Ph.Ds per year.

A very unique model of developing an international university of highest quality is focused on reviving the glory of the ancient Nalanda University of India. A Nalanda Mentoring Group (NMG) with the Nobel Prize Winner Prof. Amartya Sen as its Chair and members like the Foreign Minister of Singapore has been deliberating on setting up of Nalanda University near its ancient site in Bihar. Five meetings of the NMG have been held: July 2007 in Singapore; December 2007 in Tokyo; May 2008 in New York, August 2008 in New Delhi and February 2009 at Bodh Gaya. The framework and structure of international cooperation and partnership governing the establishment of Nalanda University (NU) that would facilitate continued international support and engagement and help initiate funding arrangements have been finalized. Choice of the Inaugural Rector to be appointed for NU has been finalized. The NMG discussed and favoured the idea of having affiliations with academic institutions of distinction in other countries such as Chulalongkorn University of Thailand and The Institute of Southeast Asian Studies, Singapore.

6.2. Quality of Research: It seems that we have ignored proper assessment of quality of research, its adequate recognition and promotion, which are directly related to the availability of quality teachers. *Quality of faculty is the single most important factor for ensuring quality of education.* I have been associated with the apex statutory bodies of some of the finest institutions of the country like IISc, Bangalore, IIT-Bombay, a few Central Universities and have realized the immense difficulty that we encounter due to great scarcity of qualified faculty in the country. The situation has led us to insurmountable proportions, which was described by the Chairman AICTE in following words [22]. *"A crucial problem in ensuring quality of technical education and even elsewhere is the non-availability of qualified teachers. Unplanned expansion in the system has led to severe faculty shortage and in about 65% of the institutes imparting technical education, faculty with B. Tech. degree are teaching B.Tech, Faculty with even M. Tech. degree are not available for teaching.* What could you say about quality of programmes delivered by such teachers? In this scenario the analysis of NASSCOM that nearly 70% of our graduates are not employable seems to be justified. Attention to this issue was drawn by the Secretary to Government of India in Higher Education Department of MHRD in the first meeting of the UGC-AICTE Review Committee [22].

Some of the best institutions are now organizing selection processes by conducting them abroad. A large number of faculty positions remain vacant which is a serious road block in maintaining quality with enhanced access. The growth in the number of doctorates has only been 20% in India in the period 1991-2001 compared to 85% in China. Not more than 1% of those completing undergraduate degrees currently opt for doctoral studies in India, and a substantial number of students prefer to go abroad. Analyzing these facts the Chairman NKC in his letter to the Prime Minister dated 6th November, 2008 observed as follows. *"...the transition to a Knowledge economy, it is therefore vital that research and development within the country be dramatically improved. There is ample evidence that India is not well-placed for this future transformation. For example, in many disciplines, there is already a severe shortage of well-trained young doctorates to fill in existing posts in research institutes and universities. This problem is likely to be even more acute in the envisaged elite new universities.* NASSCOM also came out with the following observations about research in the country. *"One of the biggest human-power challenges being faced at the level of higher-end education is the paucity of Ph.Ds and research scientists. Currently, post-graduate education is lagging behind undergraduate learning, with barely a handful of takers for the top-of-the-line Ph.D programmes".* Both the above observations and comments from those who are outside the main stream of education are driven by global competitiveness and operational market forces and concerns for development of Knowledge Societies. According to a World Bank Paper [4], in 2005, the majority of technical knowledge was being produced in the developed countries: more than 70 percent of patenting and production of scientific and technical papers were accredited to researchers in industrialized countries. It is disturbing to note that *the disparity in the production of technical knowledge per capita between developed and developing countries is even greater than the disparity in income* [4].

In the emerging scenario of global competitiveness, UGC posted on 17th February, 2009 its official website a draft notification which included a very elaborate system of measuring quality of research and weights attaf it to ched to it to various aspects assess performance of faculty in the university and college system of the country. In order to give a flavor of these proposed assessments of research publication we would like to refer to the following Table 4 based on the contents, which use Impact Factor (IF) of journals [1, 4, 15].

Table 4. Research Publications and Weights Attached to Different Categories of Journals

Points/paper	*Categories of journals*
10	Refereed Journals with IF 1.0 or above / or indexed as international publication
05	Refereed Journals with IF less than 1.0 / not indexed
03	National level research papers in non-refereed journals but having ISBN/ISSN numbers.
02	Full papers not abstracts in conference proceedings, etc.

I would like to discuss about IF a little later and international debate going on its reliability or otherwise. Initially the draft envisaged to link this with the new pay scales of the teachers. However by a notification dated 19th February, 2009 it was delinked from implementation of the new pay scales. Such sudden declarations have a value to the extent that they arouse debates and discussions for a positive change but unless they are deliberate and discussed extensively they lead to counterproductive effects. I believe teachers would be quite willing to accept reforms for quality provided these are discussed with them and a reasonable time is given to prepare them for desired orientation and changed approach. If we have never questioned them about quality of journals where they publish their research papers and suddenly ask them after several years of working that their publications will be assessed by using Impact Factors (IF) of journals where papers are published. Many of them may find it difficult even to draw implications of various formulae connected with IF in the beginning. A glance at the IF of journals shows significant variation across the different disciplines. Thus measuring quality by uniform requirement of IF of journals is not justified. In support of this I would like to refer to the following observations of Dr. Eugene Garfield, Founder and Chairman Emeritus, Institute for Scientific Information [14]. *"The impact factor is a very useful tool for evaluation of journals, but it must be used discreetly. Considerations include the amount of review or other types of material published in a journal, variations between disciplines, and item-by-item impact."*

It needs to be emphasized that measuring quality of research only on the basis of citation data is strongly disputed. Robert Adler, Technion–Israel Institute of Technology, John Ewing (Chair), American Mathematical Society and Taylor, Peter, University of Melbourne in their joint Report [1] observe as follows: *"But citation data provide only a limited and incomplete view of research quality, and the statistics derived from citation data are sometimes poorly understood and misused. Research is too important to measure its value with only a single coarse tool. If we set high standards for the conduct of science, surely we should set equally high standards for assessing its quality".*

To begin with we could look to the system of Research Assessment Exercise (RAE), which is an exercise undertaken approximately every five years on behalf of the four UK Higher Education Funding Councils to evaluate the quality of research undertaken by British higher education institutions. RAE submissions from each subject area (or *unit of assessment*) are given a rank by a subject specialist peer review panel. The rankings are used to inform the allocation of quality weighted research funding (QR) each higher education institution receives from their national funding council. Previous RAEs took place in 1986, 1989, 1992, 1996 and 2001. The most recent results were published in December 2008. Under RAE system of assessment the faculty knows in advance the level of journals for a period of five years and they could plan publication of their papers accordingly [15]. In a country with 480 thousand teachers imparting higher education through over 400 universities and nearly 18,000 Colleges there has to be a continuous dialogue and discussion aimed at improving quality.

6.3. Maintaining quality with expansion: There cannot be any disagreement on the recommendations made by Kothari Commission, NPHE, MHRD and NKC about expansion of Higher Education to meet the ever increasing requirements and demand especially of our youth to receive quality education in the country. However, one very important lesson that we have to draw from our failures in the past is to take all necessary steps to ensure quality as we proceed to increase access. Therefore, it would be necessary to closely examine projected expansion of higher education in the next few years especially by the MHRD and NKC and others and their actual implementation in the first two years of the 11th Plan (April 2007-March 2011) and future developments during the remaining three years of the Plan and even beyond for sustained quality of education.

6.4. MHRD's recent initiatives: It is well understood that Costs, Quality and Expansion of education to increase access are closely interrelated and interdependent. If you decrease funding of education and increase expansion quality is bound to decline. It is from this point of view that MHRD, Government of India has taken unprecedented decision of earmarking 19.8% of the 11th Plan outlay for education. Thus financial support for higher education is set on a steep growth curve during the 11th Plan period. In contrast to the 10th plan outlay for higher education of Rs. 89285 million, the 11th plan proposes outlay of Rs. 847430 million that is an increase by 900%. With this steep upward out lay, the MHRD proposes to set up – 30 new Central Universities, eight new Indian Institute of Technology (IITs), six new Indian Institute of Management (IIMs), 10 new National Institute of Technology (NITs), five new Indian Institute of Science Education and Research (IISERCs), 20 new Indian Institute of Information Technology (IIITs), and two Schools of Architecture. Besides these new institutions intake capacity is proposed to be doubled in many institutions like that of existing IITs. MHRD also proposes to especially support institutions with potential for excellence for achieving higher levels of quality and excellence.

During the presentation of Interim Budget before the Parliament in February, 2009 the following appreciable success made by the MHRD was reported on behalf of the Government of India. *"Higher education is of vital importance for the country in consolidating its comparative advantage in skill and knowledge intensive services and in building knowledge based society... An Ordinance has been promulgated for establishing 15 Central Universities. Six new IITs have started functioning ... during 2008-09. Two more IITs in Madhya Pradesh and Himachal Pradesh are expected to commence their academic sessions in 2009-10. All five IISERs are now functional. Two new Schools of Planning and Architecture at Vijayawada and Bhopal have already started functioning. Teaching is expected to commence in four of the six new IIMs from the academic year 2009-10".*

Another important initiative for Public Private Participation; *"National Skill Development Corporation in July 2008 with an initial corpus of Rs.10 thousand million has been set up to stimulate and coordinate private sector participation in skill development"* was announced. There was no mention of the 20 new IITs but according to NASSCOM, MHRD with support from NASSCOM and the IT industry has recommended the launch of five new IIITs, based on the Public-Private Partnership model, by the year 2008. The process of announcing new institutions continues and it is reported that in the Union Cabinet meeting held on February 23, 2004 a decision has been taken to set up a National Institute of Biomedical Genomics at Kalyani.

The progress made in the first two years of the 11th Plan is impressive but it has to be continued with greater vigour and consistency. At best we may be able to initiate the beginning of all the new institutions projected above during the 11th Plan but major financial support will be required as they become fully functional in the next 5-year Plan. I am afraid even the increased allocation by 900% will fall short of the requirements of funds for developing new world class institutions and quality will be forced to be compromised from the beginning unless we undergo midterm review of our plan of expansion and modify it if there is paucity of funds. In view of the experiences of the past we fear that history may not get repeated and just as even some world class universities lost their glory and credibility in imparting highest quality education and research, some of the brand name institutions like IITs and IIMs may not lose their world class ranking. Thus while maintaining momentum of the process of implementation of the 11th Plan projections, we have to be especially careful about the quality of education and research expected of these institutions. It is this fear that has perhaps recently deterred existing IIMs from mentoring new IIMs. A few existing IITs, however have taken up the responsibility of mentoring new IITs and IIITs. From my personal experience of closely watching the mentoring system in case of one of the IITs mentoring a new IIIT, I can say that it is very difficult to attract qualified faculty comparable with the existing IITs in the institutions mentored. Consequently quality of teaching and research both suffer with excessive teaching pressures on a few core faculty members.

There are other reasons to worry about shortage of funds in fulfilling our commitment for the noble and fully justified projections of MHRD to increase access of quality education. New pay scales for university and college teachers which have been revised after 10 years are rightly pitched at a much higher level. MHRD had announced these scales on 31st December 2008 which will be effective from 1st January, 2006. The backlog of arrears and increased pays would need additional expenditure in the 11th Plan. Further, a substantial portion of the enhanced funding would be required for improving existing facilities of 18,000 colleges and 400 universities with 480 thousand teachers imparting higher education. To make a rough estimate of additional funds required for up-grading our Libraries alone, we examine the following statistics [15]. The average price of an academic journal rose by 58% between 1998 and 2003. For the different period between 1990 and 2000, Blackwell's Periodical Price Indexes show an increase in average journal price of 184.3% in medical journals and 178.3% in science and technology journals. Similarly additional investments on several other items will have to be increased many folds.

7. Management in higher education system. From the foregoing analysis it becomes very apparent that we have a very heterogeneous system and class conscious system of higher education. On one hand we have a large number of institutions which do not fulfill even the minimum prescribed requirement and on the other hand we have institutions which prefer to attach the adjective "World Class" with their institutions to distinguish their institutions from others. There is also a great variation in funding of the institutions. We had an occasion to estimate a rough idea for per student expenditure on one really World Class institution and it turned out to be nearly Rs. 300 thousand per year per student.

The World Class institutions like IITs, IIMs, National Centres, and some Central Universities etc. are funded liberally and over the years, norms of management of these institutions have evolved under which they have been working and it is not easy to bring any substantial change in the management of the institutions. But even there one often finds deficiency in flexibility to introduce new courses and programmes. The concept of transfer of credits is mostly nonexistent. The management of these institutions is also not generally subjected to level of external pressures and constraints common to many other institutions. The faculty and Directors or Vice-Chancellors also have freedom in selection of new faculty. Subject to availability of qualified academics appointments can be made from a pool of positions. The Chairman of Board of Governors or the Visitor or the Chancellor is also very eminent person like President or Vice President of India, eminent educationists, or technocrats and well known industrialists.

I may say with due apologies that the most difficult systems to manage are the universities different than those in the foregoing category. The management of these institutions also is related to the management of a large number of colleges affiliated to them. Thus majority of the students in the country undergo their education under this system of institutions and we may discuss the management of these in a greater details. Management of such institutions will vary from institution to institution, state to state, region to region and it would be almost impossible to categorise all of them and then give prescription for qualitatively improved system of managing these institutions. In this complex situation lot of experiment with some successes and some failures also take place. In view of this factual situation the Chairman NKC in his letter to the Prime Minister dated 29.11.2006, observed the following.*"In conclusion, it is important for us to recognize that there is a quiet crisis in higher education in India which runs deep. And the time has come to address this crisis in a systematic, forthright manner."* The complexities of such systems do suggest that practices of crisis management may work [5]. Nevertheless there has been a gradual shift in our national approach to management of higher education system. It seems some basic ideas of "Quality Principle" have started getting in to the management systems of Higher Education.

The components of the Quality Principle have been discussed [5, 7, 13 & 16].

- Vision, mission, and outcomes driven
- System dependent
- Leadership creating a quality culture
- Systematic individual development
- Decision based on fact
- Delegation of decision making
- Collaboration
- Planning for change
- Leadership supporting a quality culture

The components of the principle and other ideas from management of the corporate sector have been extensively used in management of higher education institutions in developed countries. Higher education environments across the globe are frequently described as turbulent and dynamic. In such a scenario various models for economics and marketing of higher education have emerged and are being practiced. In some universities of USA and Europe important components like salaries of teachers depended on the total tuition and consulting fees earned by the faculty. There were instances where salaries even got slightly reduced. This trend continues and several dialogues and discussions on applications of well practiced concepts of corporate sector like Quality Management (QM) or even Total Quality Management (TQM) of Higher Education are taking place world over.

In this article we would not focus on QM or TQM but quality and workable practices in management of Higher Education keeping in view the Indian context. It is to be understood by all stake holders that the main objective of a university or institution is to aspire for excellence in quality of education. The system has to be student centric and their performance after the pass out from the institutions of higher learning should be given prime importance. Excellence in education is an outcome of a continuous process of achieving higher and higher levels of quality in terms of the content and the delivery system.

In our country some measures based on the Quality Principles are being developed. I may mention the following efforts and initiatives taken by MHRD, UGC, AICTE, DEC and other similar organizations. With the turn of the century it was impressed on various institutions on defining their Vision and Mission. For example evolving Vision and Mission for DEC and IGNOU very interesting discussions and dialogues took place and the same were finalized around 2004. Around that time many institutions did a similar exercise. The UGC appointed a committee with Sri T.N. Seshan, former Chairman Election Commission of India (see [20]) on a very vital issue of revamping the university system with special focus on Visva-Bharti University at Shantiniketan. We were amazed to see as to how much the university dreamt by the Great Poet Gurdev Rabindra Nath Tagore who was one of the first nobel prize awardees in literature from Asia had deviated from the noble vision of Gurdev which had attracted students from all over the world.

Leadership creating a quality culture was not uniformly followed but it was certainly encouraged in many institutions. Systematic individual development did happen to some extent mainly for teachers but hardly for other staff, that is, those involved in the actual management of the institutions. For officials of course some effort has been made by NUEPA but that covers a very small percentage of the concerned population. We in the School of Good Governance and Policy Analysis arranged self evaluation and retrospection programmes for the members of the State Cabinet of the Government which were found to be very useful. We are now conducting sessions for attitudinal and behavioural change for the staff of the secretariat and the participants find them very useful. Such initiatives for officers and other staff involved in managing the higher education system should be quite useful in bringing a positive change in management. We deal with large number of students and precise and reliable statistical data about various relevant parameters of students like their back ground, economic status etc. institution wise; state wise and even at the country level is not available [21]. We therefore base our decisions on approximate projections with minimal information.

Weakness in Delegation of decision making and collaboration are the two processes well settled in our systems which adversely affect our management systems in Education. Decision makers hesitate to take bold decisions even if they are confident of their benefits to the institutions due to lack of confidence reposed on them. There are universities which have statutory provisions to summarily remove the Executive and Academic Head of the institution viz. the Vice Chancellor. I would suggest that one could apply very strict norms and conditions for selection of Vice-Chancellors but once they are chosen they have to be allowed to develop confidence and respectability in the institutions and the society around them. I had the opportunity of having worked in universities which had top class Indian Civil Service (ICS) bureaucrats who had held the highest administrative positions like that of the Cabinet Secretary in Government of India or Chief Secretary in a State and Secretary in Government of India but could not prove to be successful. Two of them confided with me that University Administration was the most challenging administrative job that they ever had. We have experimented with Officials of the Defense Forces, Police Forces and Judges as Vice-Chancellor without arriving at any conclusion about relative quality in managing the University system. Such experiments continue.

Collaboration is another very important area where we have failed to take even some basic steps like converting our programmes in to credits and facilitating education of our students by allowing transfer of credits at least between groups of universities. I participated in meetings that discussed this issue at the highest level but our resolves to have uniform credit system with facility for transfer of credit could not materialize as yet. Even inter-department or inter-faculty collaboration is mostly not visible.

The Planning for change is another important area where much is required to be done. At one stage the UGC had introduced the statutory Planning and Evaluation Board which was a mix of internal faculty and external experts besides a nominee of the UGC. This was vigorously pursued and got implemented in almost all the universities by making efforts for nearly 10 years. The objectives of the Board were laudable and it did involve a process of assessment of Departments and continuous process for change but then it has now become a matter of history under the shadow of the new systems just focused on assessment. Since the higher education has to be quality oriented support of leadership for quality is another very important parameter.

It is clear that the success in managing higher education depends on precise estimation of a fairly heterogeneous target group of learners and clear understanding of the complexions and complexities involved in assessing their ability and capability, and their need and expectations for higher education. There are several examples of first rate scholars who accomplished their best work at a very young age. It is commonly said that innovations in research are more games of young men and women. Therefore, we have to take special care to nurture them and enable their talent to bloom as they work in our institutions of higher learning. Prof.

Manmohan Singh, Prime Minister of India while speaking in a function organized by the CSIR on January 10, 2009 observed as follows."*We must devise ways in which younger scientists and researchers feel free to pursue their work and secure remuneration without being hindered by administrative constraints.*

It is also very crucial for us to foresee the emerging future demands and needs for higher education especially in the background of a fast transformation of the system which has become highly competitive, especially in the background of increasing interventions of cross border education and global economy. In order to sustain and survive such pressures, we have to continuously upgrade, invent and encourage innovations in our courses and programmes with main focus on the prospective learners.

Identification of emerging areas of knowledge, however, depends on our capacity and ability to keep ourselves abreast with front line areas of academic development and active research. It is also very well understood that the new knowledge is growing at a very fast rate and it is extremely important to have very dynamic systems for course design and development and dissemination of the content for the benefit of learners. We may have to, therefore, review our existing systems of design and development of curriculum which are quite often very slow and are not suited to catch up with contemporary trends and advances. In view of the multidimensional complexion of the capacity and ability to assimilate new inputs of education on the part of the different target group of learners, it is important that the system should be flexible and modular. This is why I preferred to highlight continuous aspirations for excellence in our systems of higher education.

A large group of students who just miss entrance in to some of the finest institutions of the country by a narrow margin may be perhaps at least comparable or in some cases even better than those who get entry in these intuitions. Such reasonably brilliant young minds get highly unmotivated and disillusioned about their dreams and aspirations to pursue higher education. Many of them turn up to the University or College system which has to nurture them through quality education to bring in confidence in them.

Denying access to quality education for such capable young boys and girls in our country cannot be justified and we have to evolve some special measures to nourish the ambitions and aspirations of this category of students through existing systems or even by adopting alternative approaches to education [9].

On 17th February, 2009 UGC posted a draft notification on revision of pay scales and other measures for maintenance of standards in universities and colleges [23], with the objective of introducing Performance Appraisal Scoring System (PASS) based on Weight Points (WP) for faculty. Activity wise proposed weights are as under. Teaching and contribution to professional related activities 150 points. Points for Research publications have ben given in Table 4. Submission of M.Phil. and Ph.D. Theses under the guidance of the faculty 5 and 10 points respectively per Thesis. Participation in orientation and refresher courses of Academic Staff Colleges of duration of not less than 3 weeks: 20 points. Extension, Co-curricular work and student mentoring activities etc. 200 points. These and similar other recommendations have just appeared only a week ago and it may be too early to make overall comments on these. But I am sure that UGC will encourage a thorough discussion and dialogue on this draft before arriving at a final decision about implementation of parameters and processes for self appraisal by teachers.

REFERENCES

1. Adler, Robert, Ewing, Taylor, John. 2008. Joint IMU/ICIAM/IMS Committee on Quantitative Assessment of Research, *A report from the International Mathematical Union (IMU) in cooperation with the International Council of Industrial and Applied Mathematics (ICIAM) and the Institute of Mathematical Statistics (IMS)*
2. Agarwal, Pawan. 2007. HIGHER EDUCATION – I. From Kothari Commission to Pitroda Commission. *Economic and Political Weekly. February 17, 2007.*
3. AIU. 2008. Conference on Quality and Relevance of Higher Education.
4. Chen Derek, H. C. and Dahlman, Carl J. 2005. The Knowledge Economy, the KAM Methodology and World Bank Operations, *The World Bank Washington DC, USA.*

5. Crosby, Philip B. 1979. Quality Is Free, McGraw-Hill, New York.
6. Das, G., Dikshit, H.P. and Mehta, G. 2005. A Report on National Assessment and Accreditation Council, *Submitted to the Ministry of Human Resource Development, Government of India.*
7. Deming, W. Edwards, 1986. Out of the Crisis, *Cambridge Mass. MIT, Center for Advanced Engineering Study,*
8. Dikshit, H.P., Powar, K.B. and Tiwari, M.D. (Eds.) 2002 ICT Enabled Distance Education. *AIU Publication.*
9. Dikshit, H.P. 2005. Prof. G.R. Damodaran *Endowment Lecture delivered at Coimbtore.*
10. Dikshit, H.P., Garg, Suresh, Panda, Santosh and Vijayshri (Eds.) 2002. Access and Equity : Challenges for Open and Distance Learning. *Kogan Page India,* New Delhi.
11. Dikshit, H.P. 2008. The vision of institutionalizing new ideas of the education commission: focus on open and distance learning. In [15].
12. Dongaonkar, Dayanand. 2006. Missing Links in Education System in India, *AIU Occasional paper* p. 13.
13. Freed Jann E., Khugman Marie R. and Fife, Jonathan D. A. 1997. Culture for Academic Excellence: Implementing the Quality Principles in Higher Education, *Higher Education Report Series Volume* 25, *No.* 1.
14. Garfield, Eugene. 2005. The Agony and the Ecstasy—The History and Meaning of the Journal Impact Factor, *Paper presented at International Congress on Peer Review and Biomedical Publication Chicago,* USA
15. House of Commons. 2004. Science and Technology - *Tenth Report,* UK.
16. Juran Joseph M. 1988. Juran on Planning for Quality, *Free Press,* New York.
17. NASSCOM. 2005. Various Studies including NASSCOM-McKinsey Study. *Posted on NASSCOM website.*
18. Prakash, Ved and Biswal, K. (Eds.) 2008 Perspectives on Education and Development: Revisiting Education Commission and After. *Shipra Publications, Delhi.*
19. Roy, Shubhajit. 2007. Higher Education, Lowest Standards, *online paper posted on indianexpress.com,* June 10, 2007.

20. Sheshan, T.N., Joshi, Kireet, Valianathan and Dikshit, H.P. 2003. Report on Revamping of the University System with a Special Reference to Shanti Niketan University, *Report submitted to the Chairman UGC.*

21. Thorat, Sukhadeo. 2006. Higher Education in India Emerging Issues Related to Access, Inclusiveness and Quality. *Nehru Memorial Lecture University of Mumbai, Mumbai.*

22. University Grants Commission-All India Council of Technical Education Review Committee. 2008. *Minutes of the First Meeting held on 30th April,* 2008.

23. UGC. 2009. Draft UGC notification on revision of pay scales, minimum qualifications for appointment of teachers in universities and colleges and other measures for maintenance of standards, *source official website of UGC.*

24. Vishveswara, C. V. 2000. Leaves from an unwritten diary, S. Chandrasekhar: Reminiscences and Reflections, *Current Science, Vol.* 78, *No.* 8, pp. 1025-1031.

2

Governance in Indian Universities: Paper to Practice

S.P. Thyagarajan

PROLOGUE

In the post-independence era, the major concern of the Government of India and the States has been to give increasing impetus to education, including higher education to facilitate expansion, inclusiveness, quality, excellence and value systems etc., to accelerate national progress in economy and security. Several Commissions and committees, notably, University Education Commission (1948-49), Secondary Education Commission (1952-53), Education commission (1964-66), Committee on Governance in Universities and Colleges (1969-70), Committee towards New Educational Management (1990) have given in depth policy guidelines and strategic methodologies. It is of great academic concern to review the extent of translation of the policies and programmes envisaged in the reports of these Commissions and Committees, as deliverable outcomes commensurate with the financial inputs into the educational systems by the Central and State Governments. Compounding to these issues, Higher education in India has witnessed many fold increase in its institutional capacity since independence. During 1950 and 2008, the number of universities has increased from 20 to about 431, colleges from 500 to 20,677 and teachers from 15,000 to nearly 5.05 lakhs. Consequently, the enrolment of students has increased from a mere 1.00 lakh in 1950 to over 116.12. The critical question that still remains to be answered is, whether our governance systems in universities has got modernized proportionately? A validated answer to this question is of paramount importance, since the function of a university today is not only to enable the students to attain excellence in knowledge, but also to contribute directly to national development, to furnish intellectual, economic and moral leadership to the community at large.

2. *UNIVERSITY GOVERNANCE* (*Historical Perspective*)

The colleges in India were autonomous until the establishment of the first three affiliating Universities of Calcutta, Bombay and Madras in 1857. These Universities were formed primarily for the purpose of holding common examination and to ensure common standards. Prior to the establishment of above affiliating Universities, there existed Universities (Takshashila, Nalanda, Vikramshila, Vallabi, Kanchi) and Colleges which were mostly stand-alone institutions with academic independence of their own.

The affiliating system, since 1857, was designed and implemented on the model of University of London at a time when both the number of colleges as well as those of the Universities in the country were small. When the number of colleges in the country increased in order to increase higher education access to the eligible youth, there arose a need to maintain and further improve the standards of higher education in the country. Hence several expert committees, constituted during pre-independence and post-independence periods, provided ways to improve the academic standards in the Universities and affiliated colleges. The most important of these are : (1) The University Education Commission (1948-49) known as Dr. S. Radhakrishnan Commission; (2) Education Commission chaired by Dr. D.S. Kothari (1964-1966), (3) Committee on Governance of Universities and Colleges (1969) headed by Dr. P. Gajendragadkar, and (4) Committee on New Educational Management under the chairmanship of Dr. A. Gnanam (1990).

2.1. The University Education Commission (1948-49) –Dr. S. Radhakrishnan Commission- recommended, among others, that "the Universities should be teaching institutions rather than affiliating ones and recommended the elimination of affiliating Universities. Government colleges should be transformed into constituent colleges to give rise to 'federative Universities'. The aim of affiliated college should be to develop into a unitary University and later into a federative one"

2.2. Education Commission (1964-66) chaired by D.S. Kothari made a realistic suggestion of phasing out the affiliating system. It suggested giving autonomy to some viable / credible colleges with critical potentials. Such autonomous colleges should eventually emerge as deemed Universities. The response in many States / Universities was lukewarm. Even now, many University Acts do not provide autonomous colleges. The number of autonomous colleges (falling far short of the target of 500 anticipated in a five year period by Kothari Commission) is too small to make any perceptible impact. The UGC guidelines on autonomous colleges are found mutilated everywhere, with little autonomy in letter and spirit. Even after over three decades of autonomy, the earliest autonomous colleges (eg. Tamil Nadu) are yet to be facilitated / motivated to become deemed Universities. Other suggestions of Kothari Commission include conferring autonomy to University Departments/Schools as well, which also remain mostly on paper; restriction on the number of affiliated colleges to a University at a manageable level.

In a categorical way, the Education Commission (1964-66) has stated that, "In a traditional society, change is so slow that the conservatism of the educational system does comparatively little harm. In a modern society, on the other hand, change is so rapid that the system must be always alert if it is to keep abreast of the significant changes. The educational system which does not renovate itself becomes out-of-date and hampers progress, because it tends to create a lag between its operative purpose and standards and the new imperatives of development both in quality and quantity".

2.3. Committee on Governance of Universities and Colleges (1969) headed by Dr. P. Gajendragadkar again stressed on "autonomy" as core principles of University / College governance. The University autonomous saddled with growing burden on managing large number of affiliated colleges) was given its due emphasis in order to enable the system for innovation, experimentation and change. The Committee stressed that," The system has to be so framed and evolved as to enable the academics to introduce appropriate changes from time to time in the contents of education and the methods of teaching and evaluation of student performance. The administrative wing of the university has to function in a human and imaginative manner, and the statutory bodies of the university should be so organized as to give to the academics, full freedom and latitude, to meet the changing requirements of modern society. *Inflexibility or rigidity should be foreign to the* organizational *set-up of the university, and flexibility and capacity to change should be its characteristic.*

2.4. Committee "Towards New Educational Management (1990)"

Under the chairnmanship of Dr. A. Gnanam, made an exhaustive study of various dimensions of University Management and recommended *inter alia,* seven alternate models which could be adapted depending on the local conditions and the nature/type of the University some of these have direct bearing on affiliating system.

2.4.1. A modified three tier system of University management in which the traditional three apex authorities of the University are to undergo structural changes: Senate/ Court as an advisory /recommendatory body, with less of electoral politics and also cut to size for serious deliberations; Executive Council as the Chief decision making and administrative authority; and Academic Council having the ultimate authority in all academic matters. The core principle is a clear-cut division / separator of powers / responsibilities.

2.4.2. A "bifurcated system" under which the University Departments shall be relieved of the routine of following the same syllabi / regulations of the affiliated colleges. Evaluation system and methodology would also be different for both. The affiliated colleges would de facto, get de linked from "imposing" themselves on the academics of University campus.

2.4.3 A 'two-tier model" (mostly for small affiliating or deemed /Unitary Universities) with the removal of the traditional Senate (which has outlived its purpose.)

2.4.4. A decentralized model, for "large" affiliating Universities, envisages setting up of Regional Evaluation and Resource Centres (as Phase I) and autonomous regional campuses (as Phase II). This is suggested to effectively manage oversized (unwieldy) handling of hundreds of affiliated colleges in the University jurisdiction.

2.4.5. Presidential system in which the Vice-Chancellor be restyled as President with adequate discretion as well as accountability, almost on the pattern of US Universities.

2.4.6. A new (exclusively) affiliating model wherein the management of affiliated colleges, their curriculum and conduct of evaluation and maintenance of standards would be the only focus; mostly as University enabling/supervising the teaching programmes.

2.4.7. A reconstituted University structure in which, the faculty /school would be the nodal / nucleus center of all academic activities, abolishing the concept of statutory "Departments" (which are almost stumbling blocks in the way of inter-disciplinary approach in teaching and research in most of the Universities).

2.5. National Knowledge Commission on restructuring of University system

The primary recommendation of NKC has been to establish 1500 universities in India. Other specific recommendations on restructure of undergraduate colleges are:

"The system of affiliated colleges for undergraduate education, which may have been appropriate 50 years ago, is no longer adequate or appropriate and needs to be reformed. There is an urgent need to restructure the system of undergraduate colleges affiliated to universities.

2.5.1. The most obvious solution is to provide autonomy to colleges either as individual colleges or as Cluster of colleges, on the basis of criteria that have been stipulated. However, this would provide a solution for a limited proportion, or number, of undergraduate colleges.

2.5.2. Some of these affiliated colleges could be remodeled as Community colleges, which could provide both vocational education and formal education.

2.5.3. A Central Board of Undergraduate Education should be established, along with State boards of Undergraduate Education, which would set curricula and conduct examination for undergraduate colleges that choose to be affiliated with them. These Boards would separate the academic functions from the administrative functions and at the same time, provide quality benchmarks.

2.5.4. New undergraduate colleges could be established as Community Colleges and be affiliated with the Central Board of Undergraduate Education or State Boards of Undergraduate Education or with some of the new universities that are established"

2.6. *Present maladies in the Indian Universities*

Achieving the above goals would have been easier in a time of favorable demographics and freedom of management. The environment has changed now due to interference at every stage of planning, preparation, programme implementation, quality sustenance and quality improvement of the universities across the country by all tiers of university administration, like syndicate, academic senate, academic and administrative staff keeping their personal gains well above institutional attainments. Most institutions have missions, but most are not accustomed to measuring the outcomes of their processes. Most get satisfied with what they preach and not in what they practice; Traditionally, constituents within the higher education institutions act independently rather than interdependently. Leaders are not trained in the tools and techniques used to improve systems and processes. Developing management skills and knowledge is not the norm in higher education management in universities. Although data are collected for a variety of purposes for directing higher education institutions, they are not collatable since they are neither collected systematically before making academic and administrative decisions nor they are systematically analysed. Committees in academe are common; but actually collaborating and working as teams is not usually practiced. In the present day political context, the recommendations of the committees during implementation, are either shelved or delayed or distorted due to political or financial reasons. Presently, the traditional university administration is being run with 19th century tools and personnel without the knowledge and training in modern management techniques and pro-active administrative acumen suited for the 21st century.

Over the years, the number of colleges affiliated to the Universities have multiplied to the present level of over 20,000 affiliated to about 260 Government supported public universities, consequently causing enormous hurdles in the smooth functioning of the very affiliating system. Steep decline in the academic standards, profiteering by the college managements, low level of the quality of teaching, vulnerable examination systems etc were reported from a number of institutions from several States. The overall opinion emerged that the affiliating system stifles academic freedom and innovations in higher education.

Because of these system oriented deficiencies and degradation of value systems in universities which are supposed to be the nurturing ground for such values , present day universities are not able to perform educational functions and financial management proficiently resulting in mis-utilisation or non-utilisation of the resources provided to them by the Central and State Governments, and the funds generated by them through multimodal methodologies, however meager they are.

2.7. Strategies to transform quality in higher education from Paper to Practice

2.7.1. U.S. Experience- 1985-2002 (Michel K. McLendon., et al. The J. Higher Education, 2007;78(9):645-675):

The study has analysed the factors that influenced the enactment of legislation reforming the governance patterns in U.S. Higher Education from 1985-2000. Nine factors have been accounted for governance changes. They were: (i) Year-to-year changes in the control of legislature, (ii) the tenure of governors, (iii) growth in legislative membership, (iv) state economic climates, (v) growth in undergraduate tution levels, (vi) growth in undergraduate enrolment levels, (vii) the presence of a statewide coordinating board, (viii) a state's previous adoption of a performance-funding policy, and (ix) regional diffusion pressures.

Based on the above, it is reported that the US. State governments followed more than 100 measures to modify their higher education governance systems during 1985 and 2002.

It is to be considered whether these case studies and experiences of other countries could be taken worthy of introspection under the indigenous circumstances.

2.7.2. UGC Experience- 2008

The UGC constitute an Expert Committee on "Affiliation Reforms" under the Chairmanship of Dr. S.P. Thyagarajan to look into the genesis, intensity and governace lacunae in the affiliating system of colleges with the Universities in the country and to provide suitable recommendations for making the affiliating system academically productive and administratively rewarding in all spheres. The Committee also taken up the recommendations of National Knowledge commission for deliberation with the stake holders of higher education in the country.

The Committee projected two main options as Reform models for discussion with the stake holders:

(i) Outright replacement of affiliating system with new models or

(ii) a multi-tier system replacing the existing pattern.

2.7.2.1. Methodology adopted to elicit views and Suggestions from stakeholders of Higher Education

1. Interaction meetings with cross section of Vice-Chancellors of Universities and Chairperson/Vice Chairpersons of State Councils of Higher Education.
2. Proforma based information/views collection from universities across the country.
3. Proforma based information/views collection from colleges across the country.
4. Proforma based information/views collection from State Councils of Higher Education/Secretaries of Higher Education departments of State Governments.

In all, 125 Vice Chancellors of Central, Northern, Western, Eastern & North-Eastern and Southern Zones Universities were consulted in small group meetings as detailed below. In addition, Proforma based informations were collected from 348 College Principals across the country by random sampling of Government, Government-aided and Self-financing Colleges across the Country.

Table 1. Details of Interaction Meetings of Vice-Chancellors Conducted by the UGC Committee

S. No.	*Type*	*Venue*	*Date*
1.	National	UGC. HQ, Delhi	30-07-2008
2.	Northern Zone Universities	Punjab University, Chandigarh	08-08-2008
3.	Western Zone Universities	University of Mumbai, Mumbai	04-09-2008
4.	Eastern & North-Eastern Zone Universities	University of Calcutta, Kolkata	31-10-2008
5.	Southern Zone Universities	NAAC, Bangalore	18-12-2008

2.7.2.2. The following are the major suggestions emanated from Vice-Chancellors through these Interaction Meetings:

1. The present affiliating system needs a change with alternate models which can take care of expansion, access and educational effectiveness to be implemented in a time bound manner within the next five years.

   A multi tier system of affiliation system could be thought off in the place of the present system. Outright rejection may result in undesirable confusion

2. The ceiling in the number of colleges to be affiliated to an University may be fixed at 100 at any point of time which need to be objectively worked out using geographic demarcation, students size per University, etc.

3. The bifurcation/trifurcation of large universities could be as constituent colleges and university departments as one category and purely affiliated colleges as the other category; Naming such smaller universities from the parent ones could preserve the history and heritage besides name and fame; e.g., Mumbai University-South; Mumbai University-North etc.,

4. New universities that are to be created should be in rural/tribal areas with Constituent/Community colleges and should provide urban facilities and infrastructure

5. NAAC- 'A' grade can be taken as an index for given autonomous status/degree awarding status /Deemed to be University Status upon their voluntary applications.

6. Quality Assessment and accreditation by National Assessment and Accreditation Council and other approved bodies has to be made mandatory for all Universities and colleges across the country through an UGC regulation.

7. The desirability of Central/State Board of UG education need to be looked into at greater depth. The establishment of Central/State Boards of UG Education would only result in another bureaucratic regulatory structure and hence they may, if established, be given only the

examination conducting functions like the school boards of examinations currently in vogue.

8. The issue of filling up of teacher vacancies and providing the present appointees UGC scales in all the colleges of the country is of paramount importance for inducting quality into the system.
9. A national level affiliation norm in the form of regulation need to be developed by UGC and adopted by all Universities by suitable amendments to their respective Acts & Statutes.
10. The present day problem of conflicts among the Statutory councils, UGC, State governments and the Universities have to be sorted out by a comprehensive Act.
11. with the diversity of political structure and the need of taking the State governments into confidence are to be the guidelines while framing the recommendations.
12. The concept of single faculty university like Medical, engineering, agriculture etc., which is becoming more and more practiced in many States erodes the interdisciplinary nature of the university system. This also has to be looked into while making recommendations.
13. The governance structure of the universities to be made modern using e-governance to make the affiliating/ examination functions transparent, user-friendly, time targeted and efficient so that the suggested reforms are implemented.
14. Since XI Plan financial allocation to State Universities is dismally low, (i) the UGC allocation need to provide (a) the development grant, and (b) bench-marks linked Plan grants, and (ii) the Union Planning Commission has to specifically earmark grants under "High Education" while Plan allocations are made to State Governments which is presently done as a single head, "Education" because of which the State Governments do not provide adequate funds for higher education institutions of the State. A 'National funding model for Universities and colleges

need to be evoled jointly by Central and State governments to achieve the overall goals and objectives of higher education in the country.

15. UGC to provide a Model Act and State University Acts to be amended accordingly;
16. Autonomous colleges and all University departments should be given complete academic, administrative and financial autonomy linked to accountability through Academic, Administrative and financial audits.
17. Newer universities, when established, have to be only multi-disciplinary with separate norms and guidelines for unitary types and affiliating university types.
18. National level guidelines on selection of Vice-Chancellors with regard to their qualifications, credentials, experience, etc. need to be framed by UGC for adoption by the State Governments for their Universities to facilitate efficient leadership and effective governance of the university system in the States.
19. Urgency of introducing multi pronged reform models tuned with regional, cultural and educational diversities of the country to achieve uniform quality in Higher Education.
20. All States should have UGC supported State Councils for Higher Education. TQM Centres, incorporating the IQAC, need to be introduced by UGC in all universities and colleges as a holistic mechanism of quality assurance and improvement.
21. Efforts to develop the new-generation teachers with capacity to use technology enhanced educational tools have to be incorporated in the reforms package.
22. The constituent colleges of the universities should be developed as "model colleges" with full autonomy which should be emulated by other colleges affiliated to that university, eventually evolving as new unitary universities in future.

It could be seen that the U.S. experience quoted above is very much similar to our own research conducted by UGC through this committee.

2.7.3. Transformation strategies for implementation of reform models developed in the past and at present:

2.7.3.1. 'Multi-tier Models' of University governance:

The 'Models' to be evolved at the Central level for adoption by all types of universities in the country may have to satisfy the following redefined approaches of university governance:

(i) Structure of universities and composition of and representation in various university bodies, i.e. senate/ court/executive council/ academic council etc. as per the modern day requirement through updated Acts/Statutes.

(ii) Relationship of universities with affiliated colleges including conditions of affiliation, constitution of the governing bodies, university representation etc to promote academic, administrative and financial freedom with quality benchmark and accountability.

(iii) Student participation in statutory bodies of universities / colleges and in quality assessment of educational delivery by the Higher Education Institutions in the country.

2.7.3.2. Model act(s)/Statute(s) for Indian Universities:

There should not be a single Model Act for all types of Universities in the country. It would be ideal that 'Models are developed at the central level for Central (Unitary), Central (affiliating), State (Unitary), State (affiliating), Deemed-to-be category(UGC funded/ Private-funded), State-Private and Central-Private Universities with the models of Institutes of National Importance acting as a template. All these 'Models' should incorporate legally all the international new generation higher education governance principles.

At the same time, it is equally important that freedom is given to the concerned governments/bodies to have region-specific and category-specific Statutes/Ordinances.

2.7.3.3. E-governance:

Universities have to implement the e-governance programme running on a campus network that will provide a smooth flow of information, commands, requests and reporting between the "University administration" and the "Students, Staff and Public" so as to enhance the speed and quality of internal functioning as well as to provide a "user-friendly" access to outsiders. This should be a layer above the concept of "Office Automation", and would demonstrate how information technology tools can lead to definite improvements in productivity, transparency, efficiency and 'Customer satisfaction' in the environment of a typical Indian university as a measure of Total Quality Management (TQM). A measurable result of this would be substantial reduction in the use and movement of paper, as well as reduced need for the movement of people searching for information, leading to reduced delays, cost savings as well as environmental conservation.

2.7.3.4. Internalisation of Quality assurance and Quality improvement requirements:

There need to be a 5-level quality assurance cycle internalized in all the universities and colleges. They are:

(i) Implementation of all the affiliation requirements by the affiliating university as per the UGC regulation on affiliation norms;

(ii) Setting up of Internal Quality Assurance Cells (IQAC) in all universities and colleges and their annual cycle of internal quality evaluation and implementation of remedial measures through university governance;

(iii) External evaluation by Academic Administrative Audit committees to conduct assessment and report to State and central authorities once in three years;

(iv) State level co-ordination and monitoring of quality issues and accreditation requirements of Universities and colleges of the concerned region through State Level Quality Assurance Cells (SLQAC) and State Level Quality Assurance Coordination Committees of the concerned State governments.

2.7.3.5. Transformation strategies to inculcate quality culture of readiness to accept change among the university community:

Usually, when paradigm shifts, members of the university community begin to ask different questions in search of new answers to the same old issues. For this culture to change, the university members need to shift their thinking about how work is done in international universities. They need to embrace change as a positive value in the cultural system of the institution since **continuous improvement is based on continuous change.** Planning for change is an attitude to be cultivated by the leaders of the higher education institutions so that they can percolate it down the ladder. Further, planning and implementation of academic schemes etc., is an attitude to be cultivated not only by the leaders of higher education institutions, but also by the leadership tiers of the institutions for supporting systems development in administration and systematic individual development among the University community.

It is to be brought into the higher education system that the initial eligibility qualifications for appointment need to be upgraded through systematic, structured, periodic and accountability-linked Faculty Development Programmes, Professional Development Programmes for Educational Administrators of the university system and by Administrative Staff Training Schemes as a dynamic parallel process at every level of academic and administrative career of the university community.

2.8. Professional Development Programmes for educational administrators and University community:

In order to implement all higher education reforms as per modern requirements including e-Governance with full commitment and to bring about Good Governance in the university system, a four level Professional Development Programme need to be built into the system.

2.8.1. Level I Programme for Vice-Chancellors, Pro-Vice Chancellors and Syndicate Members:

The Vice-Chancellor and the above officers have to take strategic decisions about the vision and the future growth of the concerned institution(s). Therefore, wide ranging training inputs are to be imparted to facilitate these officers to develop both short-term as well as long-term vision with associated technology / management, ethics and moral requirements that are considered necessary.

2.8.2. Level II Programme for Registrars, Finance Officers, Controller of Examinations, Deans, Directors of Universities, HODs of University Departments and Principals of Colleges:

The training for this category must emphasize the need to orient them to be service providers. The training must help them in dealing with the students, management of the areas of teaching, research, examination and extension work, curriculum development, computer literacy, behavioral and organizational structure, education policy, finances, auditing requirements, e-governance etc.

2.8.3. Level III Programme for Deputy Registrars of Universities, Bursars and HODs of colleges:

The programme may focus on practical aspects concerning the specialized functions of the university such as general administrative norms, e-governance details of the institution, examination, finance / accounting in much greater depth along with refresher in the hands on use of ICT based technologies. The participants have to be exposed to procedures, rules, ordinances, statutes, Acts and the functioning of the Executive Council, Academic Senate and other statutory bodies besides information on the funding agencies at national and international levels.

2.8.4. Level IV Programme for Assistant Registrars, Section Officers, Assistants, Upper Division Clerks and equivalents in Universities and Superintendents/Assistants of College Office:

A three-stage Staff development programme consisting of an initial basic programme to cover organization analysis, office management, noting and drafting, forms and procedure of communication, editing of files, elements of book keeping and accountancy, file system, writing skills, management system and computer training, IT media, Accounting and Finance systems followed by the second higher-level course may focus more on practical aspects concerning the specialized functions of the university such as examination, finance or accounting in much greater depth. The participants could be exposed to procedures, rules, ordinances and the functioning of the Executive Council/ Syndicate, Academic Senate, and other statutory bodies.

At the third level the emphasis may be on human relations, communication skills and conceptual skills needed for efficient university administration. An advance course on application of computer in the examination and financial/auditing branches could be imparted.

It is important that at every level of promotions in their cadres, a pass / certification in the Staff Development Programmes has to be made mandatory.

2.8.5. Methodology of Logistics:

As a novel methodology, internal governance and professional development of educational administrators could be imparted in a professional way by establishing " **Higher education academy**" in every state to train Levels I-III officials mentioned above. Similarly, "**Adminstrative Training Centres**" are to be established in each university to facilitate continuous Staff Development Programmes of Level IV.

3. EPILOGUE

The major quality principles emerged in the Total Quality Management practices of International Universities have to be adopted for bringing about "Educational Effectiveness" and "Excellence" in the Indian higher education system. These quality principles could be:

- Ø Vision and Mission to be linked to the institutional Goals and Objectives and made accountable to the driven outcomes;
- Ø Leadership trained to create quality culture;
- Ø Leadership tiers chosen and trained for supporting quality culture;
- Ø E-Governace Systems' development in administration through ICT and ITES;

- Ø Systematic individual development among the members of the University community, viz faculty, staff and students through continuous capacity building ;
- Ø Decision to be made based on facts;
- Ø Delegation of decision making power;
- Ø Intra and Inter Institutional collaboration, and
- Ø Planning, Preparation and creation of the culture of receptivity for change(s).

A "Total Quality Management centre" in each of the institution, as an independent body, could anchor this process with qualified and trained personnel.

Only when we achieve all the above in a comprehensive manner through multimodal strategies, the historic statement of Pandit Jawaharlal Nehru, made by him in 1947 to the graduates of Allahabad University as "A university stands for humanism, for tolerance, for reason, for the adventure of ideas and for the search for truth. It stands for the search for the onward march of the human race towards even higher objectives. If the universities discharge their duties adequately, then, it is well with the nation and the people" can become a reality.

3

Higher Education in India: Issues and Challenges

C.P.S. Chauhan

ABSRACT

Acquisition and transmission of knowledge, has been considered a valuable service in Indian society since the ancient days. Buddhist centers of learning at Takshashila and Nalanda were the examples of ancient Indian universities. However, the first three modern universities were set up in 1857 at Calcutta, Bombay and Madras. Now India has a large higher education system with 431 universities, more than 21,000 colleges, about 14 million students and 505,000 teachers. But, gross enrollment ratio is only 12% as compared to average of 23% for the whole world, 55% for developed countries and 11.3% for developing ones. The Government plans to increase the GER to 15% by 2012 and to 21% by 2017, by undertaking large-scale expansion. During the last one decade there is a clear shift of enrollment trends from general education to professional/technical education, but enrollment in research has gone down. Moreover, weaker and marginalized sections have low access to higher education. India's contribution to research is going down because the system does not encourage and reward research. The quality of education imparted is low and our universities hardly find place in the world university rankings. The roll

of NAAC as a quality control mechanism is dubious. The politicized approach to appointment of Vice-Chancellors has converted higher education institutions into hotbeds of politics.

HISTORICAL REVIEW

Knowledge has been one of the greatest virtues of man which is immensely valued in Indian traditions. Acquisition and transmission of knowledge has been considered as a service of highest order since the dawn of civilization. Even during the ancient period, the *rishis* and *munis* of this land showed the world the path of truth, wisdom and peace. These great teachers (called *gurus*) enjoyed high social status and prestige even among the kings and emperors. In the ancient *gurukula* system the students, including princes from ruling families, lived in their teacher's house (called *ashrama)* like members of their family and had a great thrust for knowledge. The term *gurukula* literally means 'the house of the teacher'. The *gurukulas* were mostly located in the distant forests free from noise and disturbance of habitations. The system was privately managed by teachers and students without any interference of state. The *autonomy* was, thus, complete and practical. The concept of a university is close to that of these forest ashrams of the ancient Hindu tradition for adult learning. As far back as 1500 BC, teachers would retire to clearings in the forests, far from the noise of settlements, and attract a group of young men willing to join them in living a life of contemplation and philosophical discussion. The origin of the idea of a *residential university* may be traced in these forest *ashrams* of ancient India, distant away from the disturbance of habitations, where *rishis* – the great teachers, used to assemble their *shishyas* (students) for intellectual discourse. Over a course of time these *ashram* schools grew in number and size and attracted learners from far and wide, and in the process, took the shape of corporate institutions. The Buddhist centers of learning at *Takshashila* (in the 5th Century AD) and *Nalanda* (in the 12th century AD) are the examples of ancient Indian universities. The University of Takshashila was the oldest in the world. It is said that in its good days it had over 10500 students. The city of Takshashila (now in Pakistan) was founded and built by King *Bharata* after the name of his son *Taksha*. It is said that the institution at *Nalanda* was a large establishment and resembled a university setup which had more than 10,000 students on roll and 1500 teachers. It had several library buildings and halls of residence for students. There existed some other similar centers of higher learning also.

But, modern universities came into being during the British period towards the later half of the 19th Century on the recommendations of *Wood's Education Dispatch (1854)* to that effect. The first three universities at Calcutta, Bombay and Madras were established in 1857 exclusively as *examining bodies* for conducting examinations for the students of existing 25 colleges which were till then affiliated to the University of London. These three universities were modeled on the lines of the University of London. Later on, two more universities were set up – Punjab University at Lahore (1882) and University of Allahabad (1887), thus raising the number of universities to 5 with about 190 affiliated colleges and less than 18000 students towards the end of the Century. All these universities were funded and managed by central government, and thus, were central universities. The main function of these universities was to conduct examinations for the students of affiliated colleges which carried out teaching work.

The Indian Universities Commission (1902) appointed during the regime of Lord Curzon as Viceroy made a recommendation suggesting the creation of *teaching universities* in India which formed an important proposal of Indian Universities Act of 1904. Thereafter a few more universities were opened which included Banaras, Patna, Osmania, Lucknow, Mysore and Aligarh universities, and by 1921 the total number of universities rose to 11 most of the new ones being *unitary* in character with teaching departments. After 1921, the national freedom movement gained strength and the process of establishment of educational institutions including universities slowed down. A few institutions of higher learning like Kashi Vidyapeeth, Tilak Maharashtra Vidyapeeth and Jamia Millia Islamia grew out of the philosophy of national system of education developed and propagated during the freedom struggle. By the year 1947, the number of universities increased to 20 (including the Punjab University at Lahore which is now in Pakistan) with about 500 affiliated colleges and less than

300,000 students including those studying in pre university classes – now a part of school education.

After independence, the government of India appointed the University Education Commission in 1948 which was headed by Dr. S. Radhakrishnan – then Vice-Chancellor of Madras University, to suggest measures for development of higher education system in the country and maintenance of its quality. The Commission made several important recommendations including establishment of UGC for funding universities and those related to the general structure of school and college education in the country. Soon after this, more colleges and universities were established, and in 1951, there were 27 universities and 700 colleges having enrolled about 173,000 students (excluding those pursuing pre-university courses). The non-statutory UGC also started functioning in 1953, but the UGC Act was passed by the Parliament in 1956, which entrusted it with the responsibility of disbursement of funds to universities and oversee their functioning in order to ensure that standards of teaching, research and examination are properly maintained.

THE CURRENT SCENARIO

Expansion

The government of India started the process of planned development in 1950-51 with pre-determined developmental targets to be achieved within each plan period of 5 years for each sectors of the economy, including education, and budgeting of requisite funds for them. During the 10 five year plans (1951 – 2007) there has been tremendous development of higher education in the country the maximum pace of development being in 3rd, 4th and 5th plans (1961 -1976). While the overall growth rate of school education has been 4-5 percent per annum, the university education had expanded at the rate of 13-15 percent during 1950s and 1960s, and 3-4% during 1970s and 1980s. Even now the growth rate of university education - about 4.5% per annum, is higher than that of school education. In the process of unplanned expansion in order to meet the growing demand for higher education among the poor and underprivileged sections of the society, we have created a large system of higher education. The period of six decades since independence has witnessed tremendous expansion of higher education. Today, India has one of the largest higher education systems of the world with 431 universities (including 14 open universities), more than 21000 colleges and about 14 million students. These institutions have engaged more than 505,000 academics as teachers. In our country, a person is expected to enter an institution of higher learning at the age of 18 years and may continue in regular institution till the age of 24 years. The system follows a mixed model. There are some UG and PG courses in general and professional education which follow British pattern and there are others which follow integrated patterns followed in the USA.

Although, our higher education system is very *large*, yet it is very *small*. It is large in the sense that about 10% of the total enrollment in higher education in the world is in Indian universities and colleges. It is small in the sense that it caters to the needs of about 12% of the Indian youth in the relevant age-group of 18-24 years. Our youth population in this age group is around 130 million and we have enrolled only 14 million. While GER is 12% at the national level, there is wide state-wise variation with Nagaland and Kerala having GERs between 18-19% and the state of Arunachal Pradesh having only about 3%.

Though, there has been sharp increase in the enrollment figures, raising GER from 6% to 12%, during the past half a decade partly due to expansion in distance education facilities and partly due to phenomenal growth of private education providers, yet we are far behind the developed and developing countries. Our GER of 12% is very low as compared to the world average of 23%. The average GER for developed countries is 55% and that for developing counties is 11.3%. For some countries the figures are: 82 for USA, 72 for Australia, 60 for UK, 58 for Canada, 56 for France, 55 for Japan, 29 for Malaysia, 27% for Iran (UNESCO, 2008) and 19 for China. In terms of number of institutions also we are far behind some developed countries. While we have 431 universities for 1150 million people Japan has about 700 universities for 127 million, USA has about 2400 universities for 276 million, UK has over 100 universities and 230 autonomous institutions for 60 million and Germany has 330 universities for 82 million people.

As per UNESCO estimate at least 20% GER is a prerequisite for rapid socioeconomic development of a country. *The government of India proposes to increase the GER from the present 12% to 15% by the end of XI Plan (2007-2012) and to 21% by the end of XII Plan (2012-2017).* This means that during the next 9 years (2008-17) *about* 7 million additional students will have to be added to the existing less than 14 million - more than 50% increase in 9 years. *But, such a fast linear expansion of the system is likely to tell upon its quality which is already being questioned.* In addition, the government plans to set up set up 8 IITs, 7 IIMs, 5 IISER and 30 Central Universities. A study commissioned by the UGC has predicted that in order to achieve these targets by the end of XII Plan, 735 additional universities and over 2600 new colleges need to be created. *While the number of universities needs to be raised by more than 70%, the additional colleges required are only about 12% of the existing lot. The logic underlying such a prediction is beyond comprehension. If the approach is purely statistical then it assumes that existing set up of institutions provides an acceptable benchmark irrespective of its quality.*

Equity and Relevance

Higher education is a powerful instrument of socioeconomic advancement of a society as a whole in general and a vehicle for upward social mobility for deprived and marginalized sections in particular. First challenge before us is how to expand higher education opportunities so as to make them available to all who deserve and desire. There are many who *desire* higher education because of social prestige attached to it but *do not deserve* it because they do not have capabilities to benefit from it. Nowhere in the world formal higher education is accessible to all those who desire it. *We have to think whether we can afford to divert our scarce resources for providing opportunities of higher education to those who do not deserve it. It is a very emotive and highly politicized issue.* The measures taken or proposed to be taken by the government have to be assessed in the light of their implications for the development of individuals and the society as a whole. *It is said that higher education results in personal benefits to the extent of 99% and social benefits only to the extent of 1%. Can we afford to use public funds for personal benefit of a few, especially, those who do not deserve?* During mid-sixties, the Education Commission (1964-66) suggested that all education *beyond elementary* should be selective and the limited resources that we have should be utilized for developing and nurturing excellence.

If we examine the distribution of students over the faculties we find that it is highly skewed and provides an L-shaped curve with a large majority of students, over 80%, concentrated in the faculties of arts, science and commence pursuing general education. This resulted in the production of graduates and post graduates which not only remained unemployed but also were *unemployable,* because the skills and capabilities that they developed were not relevant to the emerging needs of the employment market. That is why the figure of educated unemployed has gone up to over 50 million. The pattern has almost remained the same throughout the decades since independence with minor shift in recent yours towards professional and technical education due to mushrooming of private institutions largely providing market-oriented technical education. Due to these developments, during the period 2001-2006, enrollment of students in general education at undergraduate level and in research has reduced by 1.4% and 4.1% respectively while enrollment figures in Engineering and Technology, Medicine and Education have increased by 32%, 16% and 10% respectively. Thus, there is a clear shift of enrollment trends from general education to professional/ technical education

We have to examine yet another issue which is sociological in character. At the time of independence, access to education, especially higher, was restricted to a microscopically small section of the people mostly coming of the top 2-3% of the affluent classes, with large majority of the people remaining deprived. The children of disadvantaged groups/castes including women had limited access even to school education. After independence, the government took up the task of expansion of school education in pursuance of the constitutional obligation of providing free and compulsory elementary education to all children of the eligible age-group. The massive expansion of schooling facilities forced the government to expand secondary education, which in turn, built a mounting pressure on higher education due to lack of any other alternative and increased social demand. However, the *representation of weaker sections of the society still remains low as measured against their share in the total population of the country even after enforcement of reservation of seats in all higher educational institutions including those high-profile ones which were exclusively meant for promoting excellence.* The figures quoted by the government say that GER for SCs is 7%, for STs 4.5% and for women it is less than 8%. The figures are even less than half of their share in the total population of the country. The matter is serious and needs to be thoroughly examined in terms of its ramifications for individual benefits and social harmony. *It has been established that main reason for low representation of marginalized sections in higher education is their low pass-percentage at secondary and senior secondary school stages. It appears that there is a need to help them at school stage before promoting their access to higher education level.*

ISSUES AND CHALLENGES

Research

During the recent past the contribution of Indian scholars to the high quality research publications has been dwindling. It has also been observed that enrollment of students (per teacher) in research has been going down along with the increasing reluctance of the faculty to supervise research. Moreover, most of those who join research are not genuinely interested in it. The problem is twofold. *On the one hand talented students with genuine interest in and motivation for research are not available, and on the other, a large majority of faculty is indifferent to research.* We will examine both these issues separately.

These days *market-oriented education having a potential of fetching immediate and handsome monetary returns is valued in the society. That is why the first choice of every secondary school pass-out is to appear in the competitive tests for admission to high- profile institutions of technical and professional education such as IITs, IIMs and AIIMS.* Those (of the second layer) who do not succeed in securing admission to these institutions remain contented with other institutions of professional education such as NITs, government engineering and medical colleges, university colleges of medicine and engineering and other private professional institutions. Those who are left out of this first-stage screening join graduate courses in universities and colleges and try their luck in the admission process of professional courses like MBA, MCA, CA and Teacher Education after graduation. *Those who are still left out have no choice but to join postgraduate courses in Arts, Sciences and Commerce. It is from this lot that we have to look for good researchers. Our choices are limited and expectations are high.* How can we expect quality research in such circumstances? Research as an intellectual endeavor requires talented persons with high levels of interest, aptitude and motivation for it. Experience shows that only 10% of all students enrolled in doctoral research complete their work and there is almost 90% dropout. Recently, the UGC has started giving scholarship to all students enrolled for Ph.D. in central universities in order to increase research output. A handsome amount of Rs. 5000 per month is given as scholarship along with some contingency amount. *This kind of policy is not going to generate ability, aptitude and interest for research automatically. Research requires students with highest intellectual caliber which scholarship cannot ensure.*

The university faculty is also not much interested in conducting and supervising research partly because good research students are not available, but mainly because there is hardly any professional incentive for a genuine researcher. During the first three decades after independence promotions to higher academic positions were based on ones merit and performance in the open competition for limited positions. The quality of research conducted and supervised by a faculty member was valued and was considered a basis for academic rewards. But, after this everything became time-bound. *Once a person enters the university system as lecturer by hook or by crook, he must retire as a professor, or sometimes as a Vice-Chancellor even if he does not have a single article to his credit in a refereed journal. Nowhere in the world, are professors appointed through internal promotions, except in India. Some of our friends, who could not complete their doctoral research work in their lifetime not to talk supervising any research work worth the name, got promoted under CAS as Professors and even rose to the level of Vice-Chancellors due to political connections. The system of higher education in India as it stands today has nothing to offer to a faculty member doing good research work.* That is why, over the years, the contribution of Indian researchers in international publications has been dwindling. The Chaddha Committee appointed by the UGC recently for revision of pay for university teachers had proposed the position of 'Professor of Eminence' for a faculty member having made significant contribution to research in his field *with salary package being equivalent to that of a Vice-Chancellor, but vested interests did not allow the proposal to get through for obvious reasons. The idea has crashed even before it could take off.* Is that how we expect to promote quality research?

Quality

Our universities are facing a grave crisis of standards. An unplanned quantitative expansion of the system has caused deterioration in the quality of education. More and more new universities and colleges were created without matching improvement in physical infrastructure and availability of qualified and motivated faculty. The system of affiliation of colleges, which we borrowed from Britain, is another major reason of downfall in standards. There are universities which have more than 200 colleges affiliated to each of them and the university authorities keep busy in conducting examination throughout the year. Over 55% of the 21000 affiliated colleges are not recognized by the UGC for the purpose of grants because they do not fulfill the required conditions for this purpose. But, over 88% undergraduate and 56% postgraduate and 10% research students are enrolled in colleges. This shows that *we in India do not have a university system rather we have only a colleges system with most of the universities still playing the role of examining bodies. Unless the standard of colleges is raised, quality of higher education can not improve. Opening a few elite institutions here and there is not going to solve the problem.*

The present phase of globalization and the WTO agreements under GATT have already promoted internationalization of higher education in a big way. Foreign universities and *education corporations* (especially from developed countries of the northern world) are attracting our students through their centers or local collaborations or providing education through distance education mode. Our universities must compete with these global players for their own survival, and hence, must improve quality. In a recent ranking (2005) of 500 universities of the world by a Chinese organization on the basis of academic and research performance shows that US is the leader with 53 of the 100 best universities, and 17 of 20 best institutions. The best three Indian universities were IIS, Bangalore (301-400), IIT Kharagpur and University of Calcutta (401-500). Even in the Asia and the Pacific region, these three institutions are laggards. While China has 18 of the top 500 universities, India has just three.

Table 1. Ranking of Universities of Different Countries (2005)

Country	*Top 100*	*Top 200*	*Top 300*	*Top 400*	*Top 500*
USA	53	90	119	140	168
UK	11	19	30	36	40
Germany	5	16	23	33	40
Japan	5	19	23	24	34
China	0	2	6	15	18
India	0	0	0	1	3

According to the world university rankings of 200 universities (2008), conducted and published by *London Times Higher Education Supplement, only one IIT of India figured among the top 200 universities (at rank 41) of the world. Our other elite institutions like IITs, IIMs, AIIMS, and TIFR, which cover only 1% of the entire enrollment in higher education in the country, had no place. About 50% of the pass-outs of these institutions go abroad for higher studies and do not return - the rate of return being only 14%.* The list included three universities of China, three of Hong Kong, three of South Korea, and one of Taiwan. These countries are all Asian and major competitors of India.

The establishment of the National Assessment and Accreditation Council (NAAC) by the UGC was a welcome step in the direction of quality assessment. The NAAC was set up in

1994 to evaluate and grade the performance of universities and colleges and their programs according to the quality of education imparted by them. It is an external Quality Assurance Agency like the Higher Education Quality Control Council of UK and is a member of the International Network of Quality Assurance Agencies in Higher Education (INQAAHE). All institutions of higher education must have gotten themselves assessed and accredited by specified dates. However, as per information available only about 150 institutions have so far come forward for assessment, of which only 10 are universities and the rest, are affiliated/autonomous colleges. The last date specified by the UGC for the assessment of universities was December 31, 2000 and for colleges it was December 31, 2003. According to recent reports only about 25% of the colleges and 45% of the universities have been so far accredited by NAAC on quality parameters. *The NAAC has also not been functioning properly since its inception. It is known that it trained a large number of people for its work, but has identified a handful of them in the academic fraternity for engaging the same persons repeatedly in inspection of institutions which is part of assessment and accreditation work. The underlying story is still unknown.*

Funding

Education has never been a priority area for the purpose of government funding. Quality of education imparted by educational institutions depends on the quantity and quality of human and material resources put in. During 1960s the government of India spent 1.5 – 1.9% of the GDP on education. Education Commission (1964-66), which assessed all aspects of education, recommended that at least 6% of the GDP should be spent on education. *The Commission agreed that it would be costly for a poor country like India, but warned that not spending would be costlier.* The recommendation was accepted by the government and concrete proposals were incorporated in National Policy on Education -1968. But unfortunately, even after more than four decades since the commission's recommendations, the government has not been able to touch the target set up by the commission. In 1965-66, public expenditure on education was 1.69% of the GDP which increased to steadily to 2.11% by 1970-71 and to 2.98% by 1980-81. Through the National Policy on Education-1986, the government reiterated its commitment to increase public expenditure on education to 6% of the GDP as early as possible. During late 1980s, some progress was made in this direction and the figures rose to 3.84% in 1990-91 and to 4.28% in 2000-01 (Govt. of India, 2008). The figure of 4.28% achieved in 2000-01 is the highest figure achieved so far. But after this, the figure started declining and by 2005-06 it came down to 3.46%. Even now the figure is hovering around 3.50%. For the last half a decade *government has been charging extra tax from the public in the name of education-cess, but expenditure on education in terms of percentage of GDP has gone down.* It is just contrary to the expectations.

Private Initiative

During the period of first two decades after independence the government of India, like most other countries, funded higher education sector to the extent of 90-95% of the total expenditure. But, during 1970s the economists put forward the view that *higher education benefited individuals who acquire it more than the society as a whole, and hence, it should be treated as a 'private good' rather than a 'public good'*. It was argued that social benefit of higher education is 1% while that of elementary and adult education is 25%. Professional courses are costlier than general education. An art graduate pays about 15% of the cost of his education as fees, but a graduate in a professional course pays only about 10% of the cost incurred on his education. *The costlier the course, the more it is subsidized. Most of the students in higher education come from top 30% of families in the socioeconomic hierarchy. Why should the other 70% pay for their education by way of taxes? Does it not amount to taking money from the pockets of poor people and spending it for the welfare of rich? Can we do it in democracy?* This view shifted the emphasis of governments of most countries, including India, to *elementary and adult education sectors, which supposedly resulted in greater social benefits.* Even international organizations like the World Bank advised the governments to spend more on school education and gradually encourage private initiative in the higher education sector. An advisory committee, popularly known as Birla-Ambani Committee, appointed by the Prime Minister suggested the government to encourage privatization of higher education and divert funds to elementary and adult/social education. The committee also suggested that the *government should finance courses in social sciences and humanities only and let the beneficiaries pay their cost in market-oriented professional courses.*

One reason of poor quality of education in pour educational institutions is that education here is almost free with a negligible amount of fee charged and high level of subsidy. We can see people queuing up at the windows of high fee-charging private schools, with overfull bags of currency, ready to pay any amount to ensure seats for their wards. But, when government schools enhance fees there is a hue and cry. This means that *people are interested in educating their children and are ready to pay, but they want good quality of education in return.*

Governance

Our institutions of higher learning are characterized by their large size, scarcity of funds and poor governance. Intrusion of politics deep in the academic life influences decision making process at all levels including admission of students, appointment of teachers and conduct of examination. Increased influence of politicians and bureaucrats in campus life has brought the system vitally at a standstill. Some universities, with lakhs of students, are practically unmanageable. Increased dependence on government funds has eroded the university autonomy which is the essence of an academic life. Vice-Chancellors are appointed purely on political considerations whose *voice and pen* are under the remote control of their political mentors and the bureaucracy. *The only one reform of 'de-politicization of appointment of Vice-Chancellors' will go the longest way in upgrading standards.* The *twin-actions of appointing incompetent people as Vice-Chancellors on political considerations and then talking of creation of world class universities are contradictory in terms. Under the present sociopolitical conditions in India, we can never have world class universities.*

SUGGESTED READING

1. NCERT. 1971. *Education and National Development*, Report of the Education Commission (1964-1966), Govt. of India, New Delhi;
2. Govt. of India. 2008. *Eleventh Five-year Plan Document (2007-12)*, Planning Commission of India, New Delhi;

3. Govt. of India. 2008. *Selected Educational Statistics (2005-06),* Ministry of Human Resource Development, New Delhi;

4. UNESCO. 2009. *EFA Global Monitoring Report,* Regional Overview – South and West Asia, Statistical Tables, UNESCO Institute of Statistics, Montreal (Canada);

5. QS World University Rankings. 2007. Times Higher Education – Top 400 Universities, topuniversities.com/worlduniversityrankings/.../top_400_universities;

6. London Times Supplement. 2008. University top 200 in full, www.**timesonline.co.uk**/tol/news/uk/education/article4910798.ece - 14.

4

Higher Education in India: Envisioning a Future

K.K. Panda

ABSTRACT

The vision for higher education in India was provided in the policy statement of India's first Prime Minister, Jawaharlal Nehru. He said", A University stands for Humanism, for Reason, for Advancement of Ideas, and for Search for Truth. If the universities discharge their duties adequately then it is well with the nation and the people inequalities." This spirit was well reflected in the Radhakrishnan Commission Report. On 5 September 1947, in his message to the UNESCO Conference Mahatma Gandhi said that "real security and lasting peace cannot be secured so long as extreme inequalities in education and culture exists as they do among nations of the world. Light must be carried even to the remote homes in the less fortunate countries which are in the comparative darkness, and I think that in this cause the nations which are economically and educationally advanced have a special responsibility."

There cannot be perhaps a better understanding of the basic philosophy of education as a spirit of the concept of creative co-existence for the contemporary human civilization. In the context of globalization and liberalization of world economy, it is pertinent that the institutions of higher education must be made more caring, responsible, and civil. The higher education in India has traveled a long distance from conventional disciplines to inter-disciplinary ones. Despite these entire developments, one often feels that higher education in India is facing a number of critical challenges such as issues of inclusive approach, equitable access to the areas of national empowerment process. It presents a sharp contrast to our surging economy.

Lack of adequate infrastructure, absence of quality as a defining principle of academic approach, increasing intrusion of political process into the areas of higher education, and an absence of a meaningful investment have put higher education in India into the process of disintegration. Any critical analysis of higher education in India must undertake evaluation of challenges, planning and designing of a curriculum that should be professionally relevant and intellectually enriching. In the contemporary world development, no nation can afford to remain in isolation and ignore to take note of emerging developments in the field of higher education in other parts of the world. Indian education system must evolve new skills, entrepreneurial techniques, and strategies that must be in communion with international growth, orientations, and progress. It must acquire a challenging range of skills, moving far beyond the existing ones, to meet the growing economic, political, and social challenges of the coming millennium. It has to be based on a new paradigm-developmental, human centered and inclusive. .

The task of developing creative human resources as the very foundation of higher education has become the most urgent need not only for each nation but also for entire human society. Higher education in India must be a dynamic instrument of transmission process of knowledge, skills, culture, and values. The recommendation of the Lyngdoh Commission to weed out criminal elements from the election process of the student's community in the universities, and the recommendation of the National Knowledge Commission (NKC) to have a more effective regulatory system for higher education are steps in the right direction.

The Yashpal Committee on Higher Education echoed the same spirit and sentiment when it said, "Creation of a few institutions of excellence and some Central Universities, without addressing the issues of deprivation that state-funded universities are suffering from, would only sharpen the existing inequalities."

INTRODUCTION

The vision for higher education in India was provided in the policy statement of India's first Prime Minister, Jawaharlal Nehru. He said, "A university stands for Humanism, for Tolerance, for Reason, for the Advancement of Ideas, and for the search for Truth. It stands for onward march of human race towards ever-higher objectives. If the universities discharge their duties adequately then it is well with the nation and the people". He emphasized that education is meant to free the spirit of man and not to imprison it in set frames. The spirit of this blueprint, reflecting India's role for the Radhakrishnan Commission also highlighted the development of world civilization, set up immediately after the Independence.

Answering a question in 1938 whether it was possible to impart religious values to the students Gandhi strongly advocated the teaching of truth common to all religions. He said, "I do not want my house to be walled in all sides and my windows to be stuffed. I want the cultures of all lands to be blown about my house as freely as possible. But I refuse to be blown off my feet by any". In his message to the UNESCO Conference held in Nanking on 5 September 1947 Gandhi said, " ... real security and lasting peace cannot be secured so long as extreme inequalities in education and culture exists as they do among nations of the world. Light must be carried even to the remote homes in the less fortunate countries which are in the comparative darkness, and I think that in this cause the nations which are economically and educationally advanced have a special responsibility." In the context of globalization of economic, political and social values it is pertinent that the institutions of higher education must be made more caring, responsible and civil, neither instruments of political power nor seats of conspiracy of Higher education in India has travelled a long distance since Independence. The numbers of universities have gone up from 20 in 1950 to 378 and colleges from 500 to 18,064 in 2006. The enrolment into higher education has increased from a mere one lakh in 1950 to over 112 lakhs in 2006. During the same period, the gross enrolment ratio (GER) in higher education has moved from a mere one percent to 10 percent. There has also been a significant change in courses from conventional disciplines to inter-disciplinary ones.

Notwithstanding some of the developments we have witnessed over the decades, one can safely say that neither the nature of the socio-structural demands for higher education nor the socio-economic implications and impacts of higher education have been carefully analyzed and investigated in our political system. Some of the critics are even skeptical of the capacity of our political system to initiate and withstand meaningful reforms in the field of higher education in India. Altbach and Chitnis, two leading authorities on higher education in India, are of the opinion that "We are not optimistic that systemic reform is possible in the Indian context. The system, having grown... to an immense size, leads a life of its own, to basically alter its direction or configuration would require unprecedented political will and the exercise of considerable power, Improvements at the margin are probably all that can be expected."

PROBLEMS OF HIGHER EDUCATION IN INDIA

Higher education in India is now passing through a critical phase. It is, one sometimes feels, that perhaps in the process of disintegration. Unprecedented expansion of institutions of higher education is unfortunately accompanied by lack of effective, transparent and internationally accepted uniform quality assurance instruments. Quality assurance in higher education as an intrinsic instrument of economic and social development is no more a national matter but a matter of global concern.

These developments notwithstanding higher education in India today are facing a number of challenges i.e., the issues of improvement in over-all enrolment, equitable access, and quality education. The current enrolment of 10mn students into higher education, eight percent of our student population, are too low compared with world average of 23 percent and 40 to 60 percent in case of the developed countries.

The state of higher education in India presents a sharp contrast to our surging economy. It is largely over-regulated, under funded, and mis-managed. The state of teaching and research in most of the universities is deeply deplorable. Lack of adequate infrastructure, absence of quality as a defining principle of academic life, increasing intrusion of political process, and an absence of proper investment have put higher education in the process of disintegration. Besides, there are other problems too concerning academic reforms, and advancing access with inclusion and excellence.

INITIATIVES OF GOVERNMENT OF INDIA IN HIGHER EDUCATION

It will not be out of place to refer to certain major initiatives taken by the Government of India in the field of higher education recently. The recommendation of the Lyngdoh Commission to weed out criminal elements from the election process of the students unions in the universities, and the recommendation of the National Knowledge Commission (NKC) to have a more effective regulatory system for higher education are steps in the right direction. Although there is still resistance at various levels in the government to what its Chairperson referred to as "rigid organizational structures and the territorial mindset", some of the recommendations such as on translation, English language, and developing a knowledge net-work are already under implementation. The five-fold increase in allocation on education during 11th Plan period (2007-12) to Rs. 3,00,000 crore, is an indication of the highest priority government accorded to the sector. Unless meaningful steps are initiated and majors taken to meet the crises that ail the university system, an increased outlays may not lead us towards an envisioned social system.

The Prime Minister's Office (PMO) has been emphasizing now to put emphasis on the academic reforms for all higher educational institutions. The Central Universities Bill that was passed by the Lok Sabha on 19 February 2009, referring to the Objects of university said," The objects of the University shall be to disseminate and advance knowledge by providing instructional and research facilities in such branches of learning as it may deem fit; to make special provisions for integrated courses in humanities, social sciences, science and technology in its educational programmes; to take appropriate measures for promoting innovations in teaching-learning process and inter-disciplinary studies and research; to educate and train manpower for the development of the country; to establish linkages with industries for the promotion of science and technology ; and to pay special attention to the improvement of the social and economic conditions and welfare of the people, their intellectual, academic and cultural development." PMO's office has given weightage to the recommendations of the Parliamentary Standing Committee on Education. It has called for the extension of academic reforms across all higher education institutions. According to the report of the Parliamentary committee Report, it "takes note of variety of innovative measures encompassing all conceivable quality aspects of academic programmes as well as better service conditions for teaching community envisaged in this clause. While welcoming these path-breaking innovative measures, the Committee would like to point out that such a provision should find place in all the Acts governing Central Universities. The Committee, therefore, recommends that necessary action may be taken accordingly." The University Grants Commission has been emphasizing gender equity and inclusionary approach through its policies and curriculum design in the XIth Plan of the Commission.

RECOMMENDATION OF THE NATIONAL KNOWLEDGE COMMISSION

The Chairman of the National Knowledge Commission, Sam Pitroda, has urged for a "mission approach" to inspire academic community towards research and academics. He has recommended for the establishment of a national research mission under the National Science and Engineering Research Board. The Commission has also called for a series of academic reforms for more" professional administration of universities such as de-politicization of the appointments of the VCs and registrars, and administrative autonomy. The Commission's recommendation for urgent 'regulatory reforms' in higher education, reducing regulation while improving governance has not been received well by the Ministry of Human Resource Development of the Government of India. Notwithstanding these reservations, the Commission's recommendation for major academic reforms such as greater autonomy for departments within universities to introduce new relevant courses, encouragement and rewards for innovation in teaching and research, greater flexibility and increased funding for university departments to recruit and retain good faculty from across the world, periodic peer review of departments in the universities and encouraging recruitments of capable and talented younger faculty have been widely appreciated.

THE YASHPAL COMMITTEE ON HIGHER EDUCATION

The Yashpal Committee on Higher Education has recommended that the multiple regulatory bodies in the sector be replaced with a Higher Education Commission. The report has called for the scrapping of multiple regulatory bodies like UGC and AICTE. It has also called for removal of the deemed university system, divesting professional course regulators like AICTE and Medical Council of India of all academic functions and expansion of all IITs and IIMs to the status of full-fledged universities, and equal status and benefits to central and state universities. The Report said, "Creation of a few institutions of excellence and some Central Universities, without addressing the issue of deprivation that state-funded universities are suffering from would only sharpen the existing inequalities." The Report was equally critical of "an impoverished undergraduate education". It said," The prospect of six million of first degree holders passing through this system – which has not renewed itself and has not been able to provide opportunities to the students to avail of a variety of curricular experiences which would be of relevance to their real life needs-should lead us focus our attention on revitalizing our undergraduate programmes and prioritise them in our new scheme of higher education."

Although in some universities, the faculty serving undergraduate colleges is given opportunities to participate in the post-graduate teaching at the university, no such arrangements are there for the university faculty to teach in the colleges. This very arrangement reflects not only perceived hierarchy of the PG and UG stages of higher education, treating UG teaching as a 'lower' level of learning, has itself created a psyche of inequity and deprivation, ultimately resulting in intellectual malnourishment in our academic system. Apart from these recommendations, the UGC proposal for a uniform syllabus system across all the Indian universities has been criticized by the wide sections of the academic community. This approach will not only undermine the very integrity of the concept of a university, it will destroy the very creativity university system stands for. The notion of homogenization of all higher education institutions, non-participation of teachers and students from the areas of framing of syllabi, courses of study, and new frontiers of knowledge, and above all, centralization of accountability is bound to destroy the academic creativity.

GLOBALIZATION AND HIGHER EDUCATION

In an information society the comparative advantage of higher education sector lies in its identity as the custodian of knowledge-based net-works that provides it a global mandate and reach. Under the impact of globalization universities across the world are being forced to change from bureaucratic to market-responsive institutions. Under this circumstance, the proposal of the University Grants Commission to insist on a uniform-syllabus and to standardize curriculum, is bound to undermine the basic spirit, idea and integrity of a university system. The higher education and research sector in India is already over-regulated and under-funded, and has been steadily declining behind the world average. If we believe in a knowledge economy and society then we must not duck important questions concerning higher education in the university system. The paradox is that even if we have eminent educationists comparable to the best in the world, we don't have world class institutions, with an ability to innovate, throw-up new ideas, and open up new frontiers of knowledge. We hope that when an independent regulatory authority is created for higher education, it must not operate with a rigid bureaucratic mind-set of an authoritarian political system.

INCLUSIVENESS IN HIGHER EDUCATION

Inclusiveness in higher education is an essential component of an inclusive economic growth process. A combination of compensatory policy for particular social groups and a pro-poor policy is important for inclusiveness in higher education. Irrespective of measures being taken in the name of inclusiveness in higher education, one feels that while there is a need for a massive dose of affirmative action, the acceptance of numerical quotas as the only solution was not the right step. One would have worked out strategies for genuine empowerment than reservations. In order to achieve social justice in a political system one has to combine affirmative actions with an imaginative compensatory program. The absence of any comprehensive strategy might in reality lead to strengthening of caste divisions in our political system. Inclusiveness as an approach is to be understood as context driven and not content driven. Access to empowerment and excellence is the basic spirit of inclusiveness. It offers an approach to the process of creating spaces free of inequities so as to empower marginalized people.

The education in this Information Age raises two sets of issues: contribution of education to the growth of society and expansion and reform of education so as to be able to meet the needs of society. The International Commission on Education for the 21st Century set up by the UNESCO has talked about four pillars of education : learning to know, learning to do, learning to be, and learning to live together. India is in the process of a dynamic transformation : social, political and economic. The very foundation of education is based on a synthesis between national and global structures in education. Any debate on higher education should undertake the evaluation of challenges, planning and design of curriculum that should be professionally relevant and intellectually enriching. No meaningful and responsive system has yet evolved at our university level to inspire students at the middle or lower levels. A culture of non-seriousness has over-taken the whole process of higher education encouraging creation of parallel coaching institutions. Over the years, the colleges and universities have not got the support and initiatives to create the right kind of human resources. According to a report of the World Bank, only ten to 25 percent of general college graduates are 'suitable' for employment. The universities, in particular, instead of developing into vibrant centres of high-quality education and research able to attract both good faculty and students, have become largely moribund. Over-coming this critical situation must be accorded a higher national priority than setting-up new institutions. The Prime Minister, in his recent address to the Goa University said," Our strategy is to widen access to education and improve the quality of education at all levels of the educational pyramid."

HIGHER EDUCATION AND CIVIL SOCIETY

The break-down of the university system has deeply affected our civil society and incapacitated our democratic roots. While we continue to produce large number of engineers and managers, in the more abstract fields of higher education –mathematics, physics, literature, social sciences, and economic theory –we are lagging far behind world standard. The growth of service sectors is intrinsically linked with abstract fields of higher education. There is need for a new relationship between universities, civil society, and emerging global market economy. Another reason that has affected the development of higher education is the creation of a false dichotomy between teaching and research. As the universities are repository of free and critical enquiry there has to be a greater inter-locking of universities with research institutions. The universities have responsibility for the enhancement of social structures of the nation. If the universities fail to become a part of national reconstruction process they will themselves lose relevance. The issue of broadening access is deeply intermingled with process of inclusiveness and maintenance of quality and excellence. Besides, ours being the second largest university system in the world it has to encounter the sweeping changes world over, particularly the communication revolution in the last decade of last century. The universities have to provide not only a new curriculum to meet the needs of our society but also to create a new academic environment to interface with the society. As the society is becoming increasingly knowledge based the institutes of higher education have now to operate as essential components of culture, socio-economic and environmentally sustainable development of communities and nations. The critical issues of size, access, equity, relevance, quality and resource constraints notwithstanding there is need for the adoption of an appropriate strategy for their governance, organization management to respond to the changing needs of society which is becoming more and more information and knowledge sensitive. Higher education institutions have, in order to survive in the competitive world of globalization and liberalization of economy, to perform multiple functions like educational, sponsored research and consultancy, continuing education and extension, development and services, and management.

HIGHER EDUCATION AND UNIVERSITY STRUCTURE

There is also need for a radical reorganization of the systems of governance within and outside the universities. A good and vibrant knowledge system requires that the university administrative structures should be less hierarchical and bureaucratic, and to be de-linked from teaching and research. The system should be so designed that the university departments, faculties and colleges would be in a position to have more autonomy to respond to the changing needs of civil society. Autonomy is not a privilege ; it is the very basis of higher education system. The regulatory bodies are created to operate as buffers between state and universities, and to maintain and coordinate standards, not to put emphasis on having uniformities in curriculums and standardizations. There is, therefore, an urgent need for the authorities of higher education to make these regulatory bodies sensitive to needs of a growing knowledge economy.

It is generally perceived that the institutions of higher education in India in the contemporary phase have been deprived of their autonomous character, and largely operate through various systemic constraints that restrict the very growth of quality education. Autonomous character of an institution is to be understood and analysed as both organizational and managerial requirement for meeting the growing imperatives of an international environment, not as irresponsible stumbling blocks to structural needs. Over the decades since Independence both the political and bureaucratic structures have, often deliberately, misused the basic spirit of the Acts and Ordinances concerning higher education through legislative provisions and conservative interpretation of rules, guidelines, and procedures, even occasionally at the level of universities, without proper understanding of linkages of areas of accountability and autonomy in the matters of academic restructuring and innovations. Lack of proper co-ordination between statutory bodies having financial and regulatory powers concerning educational institutions and statutory bodies that have been entrusted with the responsibility of maintaining standards in the professions has affected the functioning of various statutory organizations and the autonomous character of the universities. The Gajendragadkar Committee Report (University Grants Commission, 1971, pp. 9-10) states that "The concept of University autonomy is often misunderstood. It is not a 'legal concept', not even a 'constitutional concept'. It is an ethical concept and an academic concept. The concept does not question that, in a democratic society like ours, legislatures are ultimately sovereign, and have a right to discuss and determine the question of policy relating to education, including higher education..., The concept of university autonomy, however, means that it would be appropriate on the part of the democratic legislatures not to interfere with the administration of university life, both academic and non-academic. The claim for autonomy is made by the universities not as a matter of privilege, but on the ground that such an autonomy is a condition precedent if the universities are to discharge their duties and obligations effectively and efficiently."

CONCLUSION

The higher education in India is at a crossroad of history.It is torn between a flourishing knowledge society and growing economy on the one hand, and the structures, practices, and regulatory systems of yesteryears. Unless we take steps to foster a new idea of private-public partnership and create new structures of governance to encourage creativity, innovation, and experimentation, we may not be in a position to move towards a global mandate and reach. Way back in the mid-sixties of the last century, the Kothari Commission Report (1964-66) had emphasized that "Education should be related to life, needs and aspirations of the people. The present system of education including college education is too academic. It is not of material help in increasing the national wealth. Teachers and students generally are unaware of the efforts of national reconstruction, remain uncommitted to it and rarely have opportunities to participate in its programmes. The present education does not emphasize character-formation, make little or no effort to cultivate moral and spiritual values." What the Report highlighted nearly four decades is very much relevant even today.

In the light of the rapidly changing globalization process which has had a far-reaching impact on civil society-market-university relationship, it is imperative that we re-think higher education as a repository of free and critical enquiry, tolerance of diversity, and a commitment to transmission of creative and innovative learning from one generation to another. The idea, concept, and relevance of higher education as a good and vibrant knowledge system needs re-examination. If the Indian higher education system needs to be transformed to be more responsive to the challenges the contemporary international community is presenting to the human community. In his address entitled "A Matter of Heart" delivered at the Peking University in 1990 Daisaku Ikeda, a leading peace philosopher said, ". It is people who will pave the way toward the future of our world, and there is no greater influence in the development of an individual than that of solid, human-centered education.

Learning is the fundamental force that builds society and shapesan age. It nurtures and tempers the infinite potential latent in all of us, and it directs our energies towards the creation of values." The basic aim of any education system is to remove a climate of cumulative inequity and to neutralize more tangible grievances, observable injustices, indignities, deprivation, and exclusiveness. The strategy of an integrated higher education system through a cognitive, effective, and evaluative academic process alone can make a society increasingly rational, analytical and empirical, and its articulation process more meaningful. Indeed, the success or the failure of democratic institutions in India could only be judged through right academic institutional arrangements and policies.

SECTION : II - ACCREDITATION AND QUALITY AUDIT

5

Quality Assurance through Professional Development of Teachers

P. Ramalingam

ABSTRACT

The term 'quality assurance' is widely used in educational and industrial sectors. Quality assurance is achieved in different ways by applying various parameters. Professional competencies of teachers are one among the parameters to reach quality education. Effective teaching is the way how a teacher can achieve quality education in classrooms. Mostly, classroom teaching requires effective teaching so as to inspire the students. Effective teaching can be performed by several methods such as interactive lecture, demonstration, role play, and discussion. Choosing a method to teach in an effective way depends upon the teachers concerned. Most of the teachers think that lecturing is easier than employing any other methods. Really, teaching through several approaches helps students to understand the subject clearly. This paper aims at exploring the possibilities of training the teachers with effective teaching skills for the professional development in the Orientation and Refresher Courses conducted by the UGC - Academic Staff Colleges (ASCs). The major objective was to explore the possibilities of introducing various techniques for the professional development of the teachers in the Orientation and Refresher Courses conducted by the ASCs to acquire effective teaching skills in addition to other components. Invariably all the teachers have shown a keen interest to practice as many as skills possible to teach in the classroom and suggested that the Orientation and Refresher Courses are necessary for understanding and developing various skills in teaching and applying recent trends in higher education so as to assure the quality in higher education.

INTRODUCTION

The supreme art of teaching is to awaken joy in creative expression and knowledge - Albert Einstein.

Teaching is a gift of self-born love, nurtured by aspiration and manifested in wisdom, devotion and selfless action. Teaching involves many skills and techniques so as to make the class interesting. Teachers can acquire teaching skills through continuous practice like that of driving a car. Teaching at the higher level is different from teaching at the school level. Developing various skills and abilities are the primary concern of the teachers at the school education, whereas higher education demands application of critical thinking and knowledge input. In the present scenario teachers working in colleges and universities are getting opportunities to develop their professional competencies through Orientation and Refresher Courses conducted by the UGC - Academic Staff Colleges (ASCs).

Teaching is a dynamic and complex process. The teaching-learning process is a challenging one. The classroom teacher has to deal with this teaching task both as an artist and scientist. Teaching is proved to be a complex skill which can be resolved into a number of simple components which may be called as teacher's behaviours or a set of teaching skills, which are effective in bringing about desired behavioural changes in pupils. Teaching skills are specific instructional techniques and procedures that a teacher may use in the classroom. They represent an analysis of the teaching process into relatively discrete components that can be used in different combination in the continuous flow of the teacher's performance (Gage, 1968).

Teaching - learning process is a complex phenomenon. It appears to be an open ended spiral movement as compared to the linear model of conventional teaching. Considering the dynamic status of arts and sciences knowledge today, a teacher has to be a lifelong learner himself to keep up-to-date and be well informed about recent advances in different fields.

Teaching Effectiveness

Smith (1960) defines teaching as "...a system of action intended to induce learning. The success of teaching depends on the teachers, the setting, the students, and how the three factors interact. Teachers do not have complete control over all these variables". The teacher is the first person who stimulates, motivates, guides, directs, tests and evaluates the learning outcome of others. Teaching effectiveness has been defined differently by different authorities taking different criterion variables under study. Generally speaking, effect of ability is observed in the act. An impressive performance indicates the effectiveness of the ability. If teaching ability is teaching potential, teaching effectiveness is the measure of the ability plus the efforts made. Thus, the teaching ability is the potential of a teacher.

Effectiveness cannot be a permanent label to be attached to a teacher because effectiveness is the result of the interaction between teacher and the taught." Teaching effectiveness is a matter of an almost infinite number of inter-relations among teachers, pupils, administrative personnel, colleagues and the community influenced by inherent talent and professional training.

The effectiveness of the teacher is determined by three factors such as the situation, the pupil and the teacher. The two very important reasons why effective and ineffective teacher cannot be described with any assurance are the wide variations in the value concepts underlying descriptions of desirable teaching objectives and the differences in teachers' role at different educational levels in different subjects and with different pupils.

In certain highly specialised disciplines, where qualified and experienced faculty members are scarce, retired teachers from other institutions are hired. In essence, having qualified teachers has not been a serious problem and most of the institutions have adequate qualified faculty (Stella & Gnanam, 2002).

Innovative approaches in teaching and learning process will improve the quality of education and human resources. The behaviourist school of learning believes that learning takes place through stimulus, response and reward. The stimulus is the input and the learned behaviours are the outputs. Behaviourists also consider repeated practice and the use of rewards to help appropriate responses to be important. Whereas, the cognitive school of thought focuses on perception, memory, concept formation and the ability of people to demonstrate their understanding of what they have learned by solving problems.

Several concepts bear consideration when developing a curriculum for learners in higher education. First, learning experiences must be chosen with care. Tyler (1949) recognized that essentially "learning takes place through the experiences which the learner has: that is, through the reactions he makes to the environment in which he is placed". With regard to learners in higher education, Knowles (1980) points out that they have accumulated a "growing reservoir of experience that becomes an increasingly rich resource for learning". In the training of future generations, it was this rich resource of experiences in schools that provided the foundation for much of what we taught. Second, students in higher education have some learning characteristics that influence curriculum choices. Some students may show interest in science subjects and others in social sciences. Knowles (1980) suggests that learner's self-concepts move from one of being a dependent personality toward being a self-directed human being, that their readiness to learn becomes oriented increasingly to the developmental tasks of their social (and professional) roles, and that their time perspective changes from one of postponed application to immediacy of application, which shifts their orientation from one of subject-centeredness to one of performance centeredness. Henson (1995) recognizes the need for connecting new learning to old. "Throughout the twentieth century, connectionist psychologists have insisted that when learning occurs, it occurs in steps, each part building on simpler content learned earlier. Constructivists agree that each part of the content should be tied to prior learning".

Therefore, while we strive to ensure that our curriculum has been built on understandings already gained by the learners, we also design activities that maximize techniques to directly involve the students in the learning itself. A third factor to consider in constructing learning activities for learners in higher education is the environment in which instruction occurs. In recent years, several studies related to brain research have taken place. One such study points out that a "state of flow' which human beings enter when they participate in an activity they find interesting and challenging but not overwhelming" (Mannell, as cited in Williams, 1996). Recognizing the need for non-stressful learning environments, Costa and Liebmann (1997) stated that, "educators need to return to learners their willingness to be playful, courageous, trusting, and risk taking. We need to invite them to reach for their outermost limits at all times. We need to create environments that allow students to practice freely without fear".

In the phase of globalisation changes are taking place in the realm of higher education in different parts of the world. The compelling imperatives of the knowledge society have forced governmental policy makers, the academia and the large body of youth who would like to leave the past behind and plan for a hopeful future, to create a new ethos in the area of higher education (Patil, 2002). In the present system, technical education gets more attraction from the students believing that it creates a lot of job opportunities, whereas social sciences needs special attention to make aware of the students that in the complex society it provides knowledge and development of skills to meet the opportunities and challenges.

In the present globalisation scenario promotion of international understanding and collaboration with foreign educational institutions support the potential to create a common culture and a set of operational norms in which collaboration between progressive education and collaborative arrangements with academically engaged learning environments. It is essential, to form greater motivation and encouragement as a result of promoting their studies so that learning becomes more relevant to their future. There are opportunities for social scientists especially from our country to play a major role to impart value oriented education to the rest of the world. Human values are recognized as the most important educational components even for science education. Therefore, social scientists may have prominent role in teaching Indian traditions and culture (Ramalingam, 2006). There are good chances for higher educational institutions to better coordinate their internal and external relationships within the context of integrating subjects of all disciplines based on the needs of the society.

Role of Academic Staff Colleges

Indian Higher Education system has played a vital role for the economic progress of the nation since Independence. It has helped to promote specialized scientific and technical skills through human resource development. The education commission (1964-66) recognized the importance of teachers in Higher Education for providing quality learning in educational institutions. The role of the teacher is more challenging in the 21st century than before due to global competition. The XI plan guideline of UGC has emphasized the importance of teacher training at the Academic Staff Colleges in various skills including Information Technology and Multimedia to enhance the quality of teaching. The present plan period is encouraging the teachers in all aspects such as teaching, research, extension activities and preparing for e-resources.

The Education Policy of India (1986) recognised the important role of teachers in higher education, as per the recommendations the UGC implemented a scheme in 1987 by establishing Academic Staff Colleges in different universities all over the country, and fifty-seven colleges exist today. They were established with a view to plan, organise, implement, monitor and evaluate Academic Staff Orientation Programmes for newly appointed college and university teachers and Refresher Programmes for senior teachers. The following are the important objectives of the Academic Staff Colleges to enable the teachers in higher education to:

(a) Understand the significance of education in general, and higher education in particular in the global and Indian contexts;

(b) Understand the linkages between education and economic, socio-economic, and cultural development, with particular reference to the Indian polity where democracy, secularism and social equity are the basic tenets of society;

(c) Acquire and improve basic skills of teaching at the college/university level to achieve the goals of higher education;

(d) Be aware of the latest development in their specific subject;

(e) Understand the organisation and management of a college/university and to perceive the role of a teacher in the total system;

(f) Utilise opportunities for development of personality, initiative and creativity.

The major concern of ASCs is to provide training to teachers in higher educational institutions through Orientation and Refresher Programmes. Teachers are to be equipped with recent teaching methodologies and made aware of the present educational system in the country. Teachers need to have adequate knowledge and information about the teaching and learning processes. They need to continuously keep in touch with developments in their subject areas and update their subject knowledge, in addition to improve effectiveness of their teaching. Though several attempts have been made to improve the professional competencies of the teachers and their teaching effectiveness, we do not have adequate investigative methods to prove definitely the relationship between in-service training and professional practice of the teachers. The ASCs are conducting programmes to develop the teachers to achieve optimum level teaching so as to sustain the quality education and professional development of teachers in higher education.

Quality Assurance in Higher Education

In fact, The University Grants Commission is spending a huge amount of funds to develop the professional competencies of teachers in the higher education. The strategies suggested in the XI plan guidelines of the UGC are the product of a wealth of experimentation and experience. The ASCs are considering the introduction of a teaching effectiveness programmes so as to assure the quality of education.

The benchmarks of successful teaching improvement programmes suggested by Eble and McKeachie (1986), Menges (1991), Seldin (1993), and Seldin (1994) are as follows:

- Design it for long-term impact but build it for short- term payoffs.
- Structure it with multiple approaches to meet individual preferences, schedules, and styles.
- Gain clear and visible support from top-level administrators and be sure this support is publicly articulated.
- Use advisory groups to design and manage the programmes.
- Conduct pilot projects targeting specific needs or groups.
- Approach the improvement of teaching positively and offer opportunities for the solid contributors and the stars, not just those who have been ineffective.
- Enable teachers to participate as partners and let them exercise significant autonomy and initiative in shaping their development experiences.
- Enlist substantial numbers of faculty in planning and administering the program.
- Simulate faculty enthusiasm and a high rate of participation in various aspects of the program. See up a feedback mechanism to learn of tangible changes in courses, Beaching strategies and methodologies, or curricula resulting from the program.
- Challenge teachers to screen their individual efforts.
- Reduce resistance to the programme not by fire or muscle but by being willing to listen to others, explain and modify the program, and allow enough time for the program's acceptance.

- Recognize and reward excellence in teaching.

These are some of the points the ASCs are inculcating in their course activities. In addition to various other recommendations related to the promotion of quality concern, the measures like improving the infrastructure, undertaking administrative reforms, using transparent admission criteria, integration of ICT in all the academic activities including the teaching of diverse courses with appropriate ICT related infrastructure, ensuring the quality of teachers and the academic courses are to be considered (Gnanam, 2007).

Effective Teaching Skills

Excellence in universities cannot be achieved by average and mediocre teachers. Here are some factors, which have contributed to the lowering of academic standards in the universities leaving the ultimate hopes for lifting up the standard on the UGC and other policy makers whose decisions, guidelines and directives have always moulded the curricula and destiny of the universities (Paul Khurana, 2007). The teacher endeavours to help the students understand how to play major roles in directing their own education. Teaching involves behavioural transaction within the classroom. It is expected that the teachers must understand the process of teaching and learning so as to ensure the quality education in the country. It will help them to acquire necessary skills in teaching. Effective teaching skills are intertwined with various aspects. Some of them are listed below:

- Dress code is very important for the teachers in the Indian tradition and culture. Wearing of hats, t-shirts with sayings on them, and contrast colour dresses are not good.
- Punctuality is the starting point for any kind of teaching activities.
- Teachers are creative thinkers. They will think and generate new ideas and innovations in the class room.
- Teachers are problem solvers and trouble shooters, not problem makers. They will suggest possible solutions to solve any kind of problem.

- Teach male and female students with equal respect.
- Voice modulation is the most important aspect for the teachers to inspire the learners. Teaching with proper voice modulation allows students to understand the pronunciation clearly.
- Teachers must look at their students. They have not to teach looking on the roof of the classroom or at the blackboard. Eye contact is an important non-verbal teaching skill. Always teachers have to sweep the class with pleasing eyes.
- Use of Information and Communication Technologies in the classroom help better teaching. While lecturing, teachers have to use visuals, transparencies.
- Just passing information in the classroom is not teaching. Teaching must be inspiring.
- Teachers should interact with the students by asking questions related to the topic of the discussion so as to create critical awareness among students.
- Preparation of lesson needs involvement and commitment in the subject.
- Teachers try to teach the lesson without having textbook in the class and also request the students not to bring text book to the classroom so as to create new learning environment.
- Lecturing helps in a large classroom to reach the last row students to hear and learn.
- Teachers should make purposeful movement in the class. Movement in the class will help the teacher to draw attention of students.

It is proved that the ASCs are training the teachers through Orientation and Refreshers courses so as to develop their professional competencies in teaching skills, application of ICT in teaching, preparation of E-contents, effective use of E-resources and upgrading their subject knowledge.

Implications

In the present global scenario of educational implications the present study reveals that the teachers in higher education to bring out the best in their students and themselves by providing opportunities to meet the challenges of the new millennium. The innovative approaches in curriculum designing, uses of various models of teaching, and use of ICT to support teaching- learning process will enhance the quality of learning outcome. It is also suggested that the establishment of national net working of teachers in all disciplines will help in creating new learning environment so as to reach the quality education.

CONCLUSIONS

This chapter explains the possibilities of developing innovative approaches to enhance professional competencies of teachers in higher education. It encourages quality assurance by establishing a national consortium of teachers to bring out the best in their educational institutions. Instead of focusing on teaching methods learner-centered approaches will help to promote a deep learning environment to develop critical and skilled learners. This paper also encourages strategies for preparing faculty wise best teachers in higher education. It helps more effectively at national and international levels weighing the opportunities and challenges in the use of technology to support teaching and learning. It also suggests that the establishment of national networking with various higher educational institutions for Information and Communication Technologies (ICT) will help integrated teaching and learning among teachers in higher education. The Academic Staff Colleges should provide Summer Schools with integrated course structure in various disciplines so that all the teachers can benefit. Necessary exposure to practical skill in all subjects would be arranged with ICT and E-resources. In order to effectively implement the integrated courses for teachers one or two week programmes should be conducted during summer and winter vacations. There are significant implications for creating awareness among the teachers, educational policy makers, educational administrators and those who are interested to implement innovations in their courses of study and teaching methods so as to ensure quality education.

REFERENCES

Antony Stella & Gnanam, A. 2002. *Assuring quality and standards in higher education: The contemporary context and concerns*, New Delhi: Allied Publishers.

Costa, A. L., & Liebmann, R. M. 1997. *Envisioning process as content. Thousand Oaks*, CA: Corwin Press, Inc.

Eble, K.E., & McKeachie, W.J. 1986. *Improving undergraduate education through faculty development*, San Francisco, CA: Jossey-Bass.

Evans, D.R. 1970. Micro-teaching: An Innovation in Teacher Education. *Education in Eastern Africa, 1*, 9-21.

Gage, N.L. (Ed.) (968. *Handbook of Research on Teaching*, Chicago, Rand McNally and Company.

Gnanam, A. 2007. National Knowledge Commission: The third empire, *University News, 45 (48), 21-26.*

Henson, K. T. 1995. Curriculum development for educational reform, New York: Harper Collins College Publishers.

Knowles, M. 1980. The modern practice of adult education: From pedagogy to andragogy. Chicago: Follett.

Menges, R.J. 1991. The real world of teaching improvement. In M. Theall and J. Franklin (Eds.), *New Directions for Teaching and Learning: No. 48. EJfective practices for improving teaching*. San Francisco, CA: Jossey-Bass,

National Policy on Education. 1986. New Delhi: Ministry of Human Resource Development, Govt. of India.

Patil, V.T. 2002. *Studies in higher education*, Pondicherry: Virat Publications.

Paul Khurana, S.M. 2007. Issues in higher education in India, *University News, 45 (48), 63-67.*

Ramalingam, Panch. 2003. Teaching effectiveness through Technological Advancements, *Journal of Technical and Vocational Education*, *20*(2), 6-15.

Ramalingam, Panch. 2006. Innovative Approaches to Enhance Teaching and Learning in Social Sciences. In I. Ramabramam, and Meena Hariharan (Eds), *Globalization: Contextualizing Social Science Research* (pp 129-141), New Delhi: Allied Publishers.

Seldin, P. 1993. Improving and evaluating teaching. Paper presented at the American Council on Education Department Chairs Seminar, Washington, DC.

Seldin, P. 1994. Improving college teaching. Paper presented at Hong Kong University, Hong Kong.

Smith, B.O. 1960. *A concept of teaching*. Teachers College Record, 229-241

Tyler, R. W. 1949. *Basic principles of curriculum and instruction*. Chicago: The University of Chicago Press.

Williams, M. T. 1996. Playing is the thing: Three activities for school leaders. In J. L. Burdin and J. S. Yoon (Eds), *Prioritizing instruction, Fourth yearbook of the National Council of Professors of Educational Administration* (pp. 36-41), Lancaster, PA: Technomics Publishing Co.

6

Accreditation and Quality Audit

N.K. Jain

ABSTRACT

Higher education in India has exhibited phenomenal growth since independence. By the turn of the last century, the Indian university system comprised about 240 universities that has increased to 431 and colleges from 700 to 20,677 by 2008. It currently provides employment to 50.5 lakh teachers as against 15,000 in 1950. It is the second largest system in the world. It is a model of mass education with emphasis on quantitative expansion. Globalization of economy has also led to globalization of higher education. In the new context of globalization, the issue of quality is assuming paramount importance. In 1994, a decision was taken to establish the National Council for Assessment and Accreditation (NAAC) under the section 12CC of the UGC Act of 1956. The accrediting agency, NAAC, after assessing and accrediting universities found that most of these fall in the medium range. There was a high variation in quality of different types of universities and colleges. The unplanned expansion of higher education institutions is leading to its commercialization and delivery of sub-standard education. This scenario points towards the need of having some kind of quality control mechanisms at the national level, which will go a long way in addressing the concern of all the stakeholders, namely, the students, the parents, the higher education community and the accredits. Along with accreditation, academic audit is crucial to ascertain the teaching quality, program delivery and the achievement of learning outcomes.

INTRODUCTION

Accreditation by a commission on colleges and universities signifies that an institution has a well-defined purpose appropriate to higher education and has programs, resources and services sufficient to accomplish and sustain that purpose. Accreditation indicates an institution maintains clearly specified educational objectives that are consistent with its mission, appropriate to the degrees it offers, and that it is successful in achieving its stated objectives. It enhances educational quality throughout the region by improving the effectiveness of institutions of higher education community, and serves as a common denominator of shared values and practices among the diverse institutions. It is, therefore, a product as well a process. Accreditation provides an assessment of an institution facilitating effectiveness in the fulfillment of its mission. It shows the efforts on the part of institution to enhance the quality of students' learning and its programs and services.

The process of accreditation encourages evaluation and improvement. If we look at accreditation as a product, it can be said that the stakeholders come to know about their capacity to provide effective programs and services by the statement of the accrediting agency.

It can be said by analyzing various accreditation processes in the world that:

- Accreditation is self regulatory.
- Accreditation is based on peer review process.
- Accreditation processes and instruments are fine tuned from time to time.
- Accreditation process is broadly used for understanding the 'Quality Status' of an institution.
- Participation in accreditation process is voluntary.

The Accreditation assumes that the programs offered by the institutions are facilitated by the support structures and resources by

- Requiring an institutional commitment to student learning and achievement, and
- Aiming at bringing in excellence in imparting knowledge for high productivity and professional performance in practice.

Accreditation is the process of presentation of certification of competency, authority or credibility.

Benefits of Accreditation

Assessment of performance of institutions of higher learning and grading them according to quality is essential. Accreditation helps the institution to know its strengths, weaknesses and opportunities and threats through an informed review process. It particularly helps an institution to :

- Identify its internal areas of planning and resource allocation,
- Enhance collegiality on the campus,
- Optimize funding agencies' objective data for performance funding,
- Innovate and adopt modern methods of pedagogy,
- Find a new sense of direction and identity,
- Disseminate reliable information on quality of education being offered to the society,
- Access information on the quality of education offered from potential recruiters, and
- Promote intra and inter institutional interactions.

The process of accreditation is answerable to:

- The higher education community itself.
- The students and the public at large.
- The judgment of the accredits about the institution.

Indian Higher Education System

Indian higher education system is the second largest in the world. It has fourteen million students and over half a million teachers on its roll. Higher education in India has exhibited phenomenal growth since independence. By the turn of the last century, university system in India consisted of 240 universities that have expanded to 431 and the colleges from 700 to 20,677 by 2008. The university education had expanded at an average annual rate of 13 to 15% during 1950s and 1960s, and only 3 to 4% during 1970s and 1980s. Even now, the growth rate of University education in India is about 5% per annum. It is higher than that of school education. The Gross Enrollment Ratio has gone up from 11 to 14% during 1991 to 2001. In 1991, 4.89 million students were enrolled in higher education that increased to 11.2 million in 2003-04 and is expected to increase to 14 million in 2011 with a decline thereafter. The challenge before us is to improve access to higher education so as to increase enrollment ratio to 30% of the relevant age group. In order to achieve this goal, we have to expand our system quantitatively. Meticulous planning is the need of the hour otherwise it will affect the quality of the higher education.

Quality Issues in Indian Higher Education System

Globalization of economy has also led to globalization of higher education. Under the present era of globalization, the issue of management of quality has assumed a new facet. The demand for higher education, especially for the profession related courses, is increasing not only in our country but in most of the countries throughout the world. While the demand is growing, the capacity of the public sector to satisfy this need is being challenged by various stakeholders. As a result, private initiatives are coming in the forefront to deliver education. The foreign universities are opening more and more centers in India. Until now the government has gone for quantitative expansion of higher education, but there is a shift from quantity to quality of education during recent times. With the higher education becoming an international service, there is a growing concern on its quality and standard. The concept of educational accreditation came into existence to achieve the said objectives. Earlier the concept was not well developed and it was done by the academic institution itself. But now it is being done by the external body to determine if applicable standards are met. The external agency grants accredited status to an institution that meets the prescribed standards.

In India, the National Assessment and Accreditation Council (NAAC) was established in 1994 on recommendation of the ***National Policy on Education*** (1986) to *"address the issues of deterioration in quality of education"* and the ***Plan of Action*** (1992) to devise *"strategic plans for the policies including the establishment of an independent national accreditation body"*. The NAAC came into existence with an objective of helping higher education institutions under the purview of University Grants Commission to know their strengths, weaknesses and opportunities through an informed review. National Board of Accreditation (NBA) was set up by All India Council of Technical Education (AICTE) in September 1994 for academic auditing, ensuring and promoting quality technical education in Engineering, Management, Pharmacy and Architecture programs. The Distance Education Council (DEC) was established in 1992 with the objective to coordinate, promote and maintain standards in all the open and distance education institutions. The DEC along with setting guidelines for the establishment of state open universities also set up Quality Assurance Panel to recommend necessary measures to ensure acceptable quality standards in distance education.

Accreditation Status of Indian Universities

Out of 369 universities as up to 2001, 111 universities have got themselves accredited by the NAAC (Table 1). A total of only 35 (32%) Universities were placed in Group A (A++, A+ or A rating), another 58 (52%) in Group B (B++, B+ or B rating), and the remaining 18 (16%) in Group C (C++, C+ or C rating). The data indicates that only a few universities got themselves accredited and there is a wide variation in their quality status. The quality status of colleges also tells that there is a large variation.

Table 1. Quality Status of Different Types of Universities as Accredited by the NAAC up to 2001

Type of Universities	*Group AA++, A+, A*	*Group B B++, B+, B*	*Group C CC++, C+, C*	*Total*
Central	01 (25%)	02 (50%)	01 (25%)	04 (100%)
State	23 (27%)	47 (55%)	16 (19%)	86 (100%)
Deemed	11 (52%)	09 (43%)	01 (05%)	21 (100%)
Total	35 (32%)	58 (52%)	18 (16%)	111 (100%)

In the recent past, the growth of higher education institutions was not done in a planned way and the result is that only 2956 colleges could get accreditation by NAAC and a whopping 9875 colleges could neither get recognition nor funds from UGC. The students receiving degrees from these colleges imparting education of an inferior quality remained mostly unemployed. These non-accredited colleges imparting low quality education gave degrees that were recognized as being equivalent to those awarded by the quality institutions. In our country, the quality of institutions is highly variable. We have examples where the public has assessed and accredited the institutions of higher learning. Indian Institute of Management (IIMs), Indian Institute of Technology (IITs) and Birla Institute of Technology and Science, Pilani are some of the Indian premier institutions that are not accredited yet known for quality education not only in India but abroad also.

If we want to be a partner in the global market of higher education, our institutions will be measured by a yard stick for global quality standards. Accreditation seems to be the only answer, and the key to successful accreditation is the quality.

Many colleges are involved in alluring students through aggressive marketing. The students and parents fall prey to them. They even assure them of good employability. Not to be misled by the advertisements, there is a dire need of assessment and accreditation of institutions of higher learning. Different education stakeholders, especially the students, the employers and the public, need to be made aware of accreditation and these degree mills.

In spite of the built-in regulatory mechanism aiming at assurance of satisfactory level of quality in the functioning of the large number of diverse higher education institutions spread over the expense of the country, the quality of education imparted by the institutions must be ensured for global compatibility. The NAAC has been instilling a momentum of quality consciousness and aiming for continuous improvement on one hand, while the new self-financed colleges are springing up without caring for quality on the other hand. There is a dire need to check the growth of such degree mills and discourage commercial approach in education by making accreditation and assessment compulsory by statutory quality bodies.

Academic Audit

In India, the performance of the institutions of higher learning is based on a predetermined frame of reference and that is the accepted methodology of the accrediting agencies world over. But as we know that every university performs the two major functions, i.e., teaching and research, there is a growing feeling among the academia, students and other stakeholders that apart from institutional and programmatic accreditation, academic audit should also be undertaken to complete the process of quality assessment. Teaching and research functions of any institution of higher learning has a direct bearing on its quality. The academic audit process will enhance the quality of academic atmosphere in the institute. The goal of academic audit is continuous quality empowerment to accomplish so that faculty, administrators and staff engage themselves to achieve maturation of education quality process. By adhering to standards of best practices, they can analyze, compare and monitor their progress towards achieving the common goal of quality. The faculty work collegially towards improvement in teaching and learning. It promotes teamwork, collaboration, cooperation, coherence and consensus. It gives an opportunity to revisit ongoing efforts to improve both instructional and research programs. It boosts the morale of the faculty. Academic audit focuses on making improvements without seeking additional budgets.

It is important that institutions of higher education engage in activities that advance both accountability and improvement. The academic audit is an approach that can accomplish both. The academic audit has been adopted by higher education institutions in Australia, China, New Zealand, Sweden and England. Academic audit analyses effectiveness of students' learning to ensure the proficiency needed to compete in the global environment. But a rigorous, well designed assessment process can make this happen. In this direction, Dr. William Massy of the Jackson Hole Group, a widely respected expert and pioneer in the development of Academic Audit, is providing assistance in the Pilot Project. He is exploring the process which will provide the significant improvement in accountability that its stakeholders require.

Dr. William Massy has given five steps of Academic Audit as under:

I. Learning Objectives

II. Curriculum and Co-curriculum

III. Teaching and Learning Methods

IV. Student Learning Assessment

V. Implementation and Quality Assurance

The academic audit process thus solely concentrates on teaching, learning and research.

In the accreditation process employed by NAAC in India, 36 key aspects have been taken in to consideration. Out of which, 6 are denoted to teaching a learning and 6 are related to research. The weightage assigned to these parameters is 450 out of a total of 1000. It shows that these two parameters do not carry that weightage which needs to be given looking to the major output in terms of teaching and research in the highest temples of learning. Therefore, it becomes essential to think of academic audit to bring professionalism in teaching and research. It will put teaching and learning at the centre of the university enterprise.

SUGGESTED READING

Academic Audit for Enhancing Quality. 2008. *The Hindu : Education Plus Chennai*, 8th Sep., 2008 edition.

Educational Accreditation. Internet Source : Wikipedia the free encyclopedia.

Qamer, F. 2008. Status of Quality in Higher Education Varying Perceptions in Higher Education in India- Issues Related to Expansion, Inclusiveness, Quality and Finance. U.G.C. Delhi.

Shafi, S. Zeenat. 2003. Privatization of Higher Education, *AIU*, New Delhi.

Sharma, Rita (Ed.). 2004. Assessment and Accreditation in Higher Education, *AIU*, New Delhi.

Tennessee Board of Regents Academic Affairs Brief, www.tbr.state.tn.us/academic_affairs.

Uvalic-Trumbic, Stamenka. 2009. *Global Higher Education : New Challenges for Quality Assurance* – Paper presented in the Sub-regional Conference of South, South-west and Central Asia on Higher Education, NUEPA, New Delhi.

7

Higher Education in the Age of Great Depression II

Raju M. Mathew

ABSTRACT

Part I of the paper deals with the present Global Crisis–the Great Depression II and formulating the strategies for dealing with it. Education, especially universities have to play a crucial in this regard on a long term basis. Building up the knowledge sector and applying knowledge for solving the basic human problem is the best strategy to deal with such a crisis.

Part II of the paper examines the theoretical and methodological issues of quality and management of higher education. The basic question is how to make higher education relevant, flexible and adaptable. It is high time to formulate New Higher Education Policy in the context of the Great Depression II of 2009.

PART I – THE AGE OF GREAT DEPRESSION II

The present crisis that we are facing can rightly be called as **the Great Depression II of 2009** and it is several times severe than the **Great Depression I of 1929**. It is global. No nation can be made insulated from its lasting impacts, even the richest oil exporting or technology exporting countries. The industrial and military super powers too be turned mere paper tigers. The proverb says, after the great storm, all big trees are uprooted and, the grasses are remained unhurt. India, though not a ' super power', would be one of a handful of countries that could withstand the lasting impacts of the Great Depression II because of its lasting civilization, knowledge bases and intellectually gifted and hardworking young generation and above all its spirituality and way of life, especially of the rural folk.

Who has brought it?

Almost all banks had been lending five to ten times more than what they had, by diluting the principle of 80/20 in the age of electronic cash and e-banking or e-commerce, that ultimately resulted in the credit crisis and crushing of the stock markets. Further, the heavy expenditure on armaments incurred by almost all nations and terrorist organizations had aggravated the crisis. By siphoning off billions from the accounts of the big corporations and governments and also individuals, especially the elderly, the terrorist organizations made money for their operations. Governments borrowed heavily for defense expenditures. Unfair business practices and high level frauds had made everything very complex.

The Basic Reason

After high and fast growth and booms now it is the turn of gloom, recession and depression. There is a limit for speed and growth. Development based on aggressive marketing, consumerism and globalization, ignoring the vast majority, cannot go on very long. Recessions and depressions are self correcting mechanism for the maladies of a society that strives for unlimited growth at a high speed. No human being or economy can run fast for very long. Information Technology and the Modern Management Techniques do not have any answer for the present crisis. These are the basic lessons that the Great Depression II teaches us.

After a period of fast life, everybody has to go back to slow life. In the fast life, nobody has any time even to dream, imagine, think and learn. Knowledge and scholarship are pushed back for data and information; learning is reduced into an exercise for scoring of higher grades or marks; reading is neglected for the sake of scanning and extracting from the internet. Critical thinking and creative ideas or works are denigrated; superfluous analysis and mimicries are dominated in the place of sound theories and strategies. Men of ideas, scholarship, theories and strategies and multi-disciplinary backgrounds could alone solve the present crisis.

In the fast life, even young men and women could not find time for romance and love making other than fast sex, that too without the botheration of child birth. The greatest causality is the family life, the cordial relationships between wife and husband and between parents and children. Even in religion, faith in God and love of human beings are pushed back by the harsh and rigorous practices and rigid interpretations, without any element of mercy and forgiveness.

The Missing Links

The value and importance of rural life, especially agriculture are withered away for the over projection of the glory of urban life and the service sector. But cities could not survive without farming and rural sector. Urban sector is depending too much on the rural sector rather than the villages relaying on cities, because most of the villages could be easily made self sufficient with regard to the basic necessities of life. Service sector of an economy could not flourish when its agricultural or industrial sectors are weak.

For the sake of fancy or glittering subjects or courses centered on IT, Management and Global Trade, most of the universities have pushed back core and basic courses and research works in Science, Social Sciences and Humanities. As a result, we could not find academics and researchers with depth knowledge empowered with theories and strategies and multi-disciplinary background.

The greatest threat faced by humanity is a lack of holistic approach to solve basic human problems that cannot be solved with mere narrow and partial knowledge or massive bundles of data or information retrieved from the web or net with the help of newly emerged powerful search engines. In the midst of the Great Depression II, all our super star academics and intellectuals, who had been acting as advisers and consultants to governments and companies on market, finance, investment and growth, have become warriors without arms.

How long will it be?

The Great Depression II, now in its first phase, would continue for a minimum period of five years, sometimes ten years, in a more rigorous way. It brings about a crisis of faith in technology, money power, managerial talents and the entire banking and insurance sector, besides the money and stock and share markets and the credit system The highly acclaimed economic and business wisdoms and formulas are crushed and shattered. A sense of helplessness and even meaninglessness are to dominate in the thinking and behavior of the common people. Everybody, including the top billionaires and technocrats and the most trusted business houses, has become vulnerable. A good many of them, especially the youth, are in the verge of a suicide or mental brake down.

We have to accept that the age of consumerism and the dominance of the service sector over the agriculture and industrial sectors are over. So also is the case with cities over the villages. The inter-sector imbalances with regard to growth and wage or salary structures and the striking disparities with regard to the standard of living of the people of the various sectors are the basic reason for the present global crisis. The growth of defense industries is possible only jeopardizing all the other industries and sectors.

The only agency to deal with **The Great Depression II** with long term strategies and policies is the Governments that must be strong and duly functioning. No single country or government could tackle it; instead, global efforts and strategies are required. The UN must be made strong enough to act globally for dealing with the Great Depression II, chalking out the area of international cooperation. It must act on a war footing; other wise, almost all nations would go for protectionism, over 80 per cent of the jobs would be wiped out and billions would die out of hunger, epidemics and civil wars.

Ineffectiveness of the Keynesian Strategies

The Great Depression II could not be dealt with a set of conventional monetary and fiscal policies as have been prescribed by the Keynesians or the Post-Keynesians that have reached the saturation level. There is a limit for technology and management techniques, including marketing in this regard. Now what are required are a massive behavioral change and a new way of life, freeing from consumerism and fast life style on the part of the society as a whole. Greater cooperation and mutual support between nations, even at global level, are the only means for survival and growth. All nations must cut their defense expenditure to the extent of seventy or eighty per cent and a joint global strategy against terrorism must be launched as no nation can be made free from it.

Time for Re-creation

This present global crisis, the Great Depression II, brings life slow. This is the time for learning and acquiring knowledge, creative works and above all reinventing the basic human, family and religious values coupled with humanism, spirituality and cooperation. Everybody wants to learn something new and equip him or her to withstand the crisis with strong knowledge base, including our own culture and great literary works besides.

This is the time for baby booms. This is the time for the re-birth of rural and farming sector. People find new meaning in agriculture and country life. Now, it is unproductive to make heavy investments in cities and high technologies and the service sector. Religions have to play a very important positive role in these regards, even by developing mutual respect and cooperation rather than rivalary and aggressive fundamentalism.

Counter Strategies

The best strategy to deal with The Great Depression II is to invest heavily on the rural and farming sector and develop their infrastructures along with making heavy investment in education, especially basic science and engineering, social sciences and humanities. Learning must be encouraged by developing libraries and encouraging the overall reading habits of the people.

Increasing cost of education is a basic threat to the development of humanity. Education must be made coast –effective. Open Learning— Open Schools and Open Universities or Virtual Universities, even in Science and Technology must be set up or developed to make education reach in the hands of millions.

Problem is Global, Solution too...

The above noted strategies could be made applicable on a global basis, to both the East and West, developing and developed nations, including GCC countries, with the necessary variations. Nobody, including the American President, Barrack Obema, has a magic stick to deal with The Great Depression II, other than following the above noted long term strategies and policies. It is high time to realize that no affluent nation can survive by keeping a large number of nations or people poor and depressed and selling arms and defense equipments and following consumerism and aggressive marketing. It is high time to realize that terrorism and religious fundamentalism add miseries and sufferings of the humanity and bring hell on earth.

From Dooms to Booms and Hopelessness to Hopes

When implementing the above policies and strategies, people will come out with innovative ideas, plans and strategies and to apply them in agriculture, industry and the service sector within three years. All these will push up economic activities, including global trade and business. International cooperation between developed and developing or underdeveloped societies and nations would emerge so as to ensure a minimum development and standard of living for all. The people will dictate their terms of peace and co-existence over the Governments and the Terrorist Organizations, including aggressive and fundamentalist religions.

PART II –HIGHER EDUCATION : QUALITY AND MANAGEMENT

It is customary on the part of the politicians and academics to lament about the falling standard or quality of education, especially of universities in India. When we talk about the falling standard or quality, it invariably implies a comparison with the earlier standard or quality. Quality always presupposes a set of criteria or measuring road, some sort of a time tested and fixed one. The basic question is: can we apply such fixed criteria to measure the relevance and effectiveness of a university. Is it true to say that universities about fifty years ago were far better than the present ones? No; not at all.

Quality and Management

The very concept of quality of universities is not a fixed or static one. It varies according to the changing conditions or situations. The so called 'the best universities of yester years' may be the worst universities of today, unless they adapt to the changing situations and become highly flexible. The greatest challenge of higher education in India is the inability of our universities to be flexible and adaptable. They are rigid and highly conventional with outdated by-laws or Acts/ Statues / Regulations and organizational structures well suited for at least fifty years ago. There is nothing like management in universities, but only day to day administration. In such a set up, it is almost impossible to bring about quality control at all.

Relevance and Cost-Effectiveness

It is high time to conduct detailed cost-benefit, cost-effectiveness and demand analyses of the entire university system in India, after identifying its basic goal and objectives and estimating the cost and expenditure and the actual benefits rendered by it on the basis of relevance and adaptability. Now we have to find out the answers for the basic questions: What extent do the universities in India are relevant, adaptable, flexible, competitive and cost-effective? These questions are important because they determine the very survival and growth of higher education in India in the years to come.

Age of the Great Depression II

It is a fact that the present global crisis has its worst impacts on universities all over the world, especially India. It is quite logical on the part of the Government to cut a substantial part of its budget on higher education to meet the other immediate requirements. The basic question is to tide over the impending global crisis. As part of a series of measures, the Government has to stall most of the major expansion programs, starting new universities or courses, cutting the funds for libraries and laboratories and making fresh appointments, both faculty and non-faculty members. In the drive for minimizing the cost of production and cost of living, the Government has to declare a moratorium for any salary revision or at the extreme to cut the salary till the conditions change. Even in such an adverse condition, we have to build up a very effective and successful higher education system in the country to cater the knowledge and skill acquisition needs of the society, especially the young and the unemployed.

Networking and Pooling the Resources

Higher education must be considered as a unified system, well-integrated with the total socio-economic system. It is neither independent nor autonomous. It cannot exist by itself. It is subjected to the ups and downs of the overall economy or society. All institutions or centers of higher learning and research in India must be brought under a common system by building up a national network so as to pool their resources, including facilities, expertise and manpower. Indian Universities must be allowed to concentrate on facilitating learning and conducting teaching, research and extension activities that must be competitive, relevant and cost-effective on a global basis. Unfortunately, most of the universities are wasting a lot of their time and energy for controversies related to the selection and appointment and even the promotion of both the faculty and non-faculty members. If these functions are entrusted with a National or State University Recruitment and Placement Commission, universities could concentrate on genuine academic activities by getting rid of several controversies.

CONCLUSION

In the wake of the Great Depression II, the Government of India must formulate a New National Policy on Higher Education and Research so as to protect the interest of the Country and its people, especially the young. It must strive for a sustainable growth for Higher Education by achieving innovation, adaptability, flexibility and cost-effectiveness and above all social relevance and competiveness. For the realization of the Great Indian Dream, and aspiration of its young, India needs to adopt an ultra modern and highly effective and efficient higher education system so as to withstand the present and any crisis in future.

SECTION : III – COMPETENCE AND LEADERSHIP DEVELOPMENT

8

Mentoring: Paradigm Shift in Academic Leadership

Davis George

ABSTRACT

Leaders make things happen. A visionary leader stands for enhancing and sustaining quality, empowering people and ushering in the required paradigm shift to redefine the vision and mission of the institution and meet the challenges of the times. Institutions flourish or perish depending largely on the leadership qualities of the persons at the helm of affairs. Six Sigma effect of change can be brought about by mentoring and coaching. Words of affirmation and guidance would make the team explore the latent potentials and produce the required synergy to sustain capacity building. Transformational leadership through relationship to achieve the required purpose would be more enduring. When Soft skills compliment hard skills the effectiveness of leadership can be maximized. Personal integrity and authenticity would enhance trust and credibility. "You be the change you want to see in others", said Mahatma Gandhi. Management of change - of self and others, in a positive and proactive way would make the academic leadership effective.

INTRODUCTION

'Leaders Make Things Happen'

As Ralph Nader **Rightly Said,** "I start with the premise that the function of leadership is to produce more leaders, not more followers." According to John Quincy Adams, "If your actions inspire others to dream more, learn more, do more, you are a leader." Leaders make things happen. A visionary leader stands for enhancing and sustaining quality, empowering people and ushering in the required paradigm shift to redefine the vision and mission of the institution and meet the challenges of the times. Institutions flourish or perish depending largely on the leadership qualities of the persons at the helm of affairs, 2 Sigma effect of change can be brought about by mentoring and coaching. Words of affirmation and guidance would make the team explore the latent potentials and produce the required synergy to sustain capacity building. Transformational leadership through relationship to achieve the required purpose would be more enduring. Soft skills when compliment hard skills can maximize the effectiveness of leadership. Personal integrity and authenticity would enhance trust and credibility. "You be the change you want to see in others", said Mahatma Gandhi. Management of change - of self and others, in a positive and proactive way would make the leadership effective.

If you just walk into any bookstore you will find hundreds of leadership books purport to answer all questions concerning leadership. Broadly, the research, thinking, and writing about leadership can be divided into two camps. One camp holds that leadership is all about behavior and that if you want to excel, you should learn and replicate the key behaviors of good leaders. Many companies pursue this view by developing competency models and then rigorously assessing and training their leaders accordingly. The other camp holds that leadership is all about character, values, and authenticity and companies that adhere to this view focus on transmitting company values and orienting leaders to the right way to do things. Stephen Covey advocates principle-centred leadership for effective and sustainable impact.

Leaders who do not succeed tend to be people who lack self-awareness. Daniel Goleman has made this basic truth clear by describing the importance of emotional intelligence as an important component of effective leadership. Ineffective leaders don't understand their own motivations or acknowledge their weaknesses; they don't engage in reflection, especially when they fail and are unwilling to assume accountability. As smart and skilled as these people may be, they don't really know themselves, and this lack of self-knowledge derails them, especially when they face new leadership challenges. High-performing leaders, however, are aware of their strengths *and* their weaknesses; they talk and think about their limitations and failures and try to learn from them.

1.1. *Behavioral perspective*: A behavioral perspective on leadership focuses not on what a leader is, as the trait approach does, it focuses on what a leader does. Two classic series of leadership studies, done primarily in the 1950's and 1960's at the Universities of Ohio State and Michigan, have led to the fundamental distinction between task-oriented and person-oriented leadership behaviour. It seems clear that successful leadership involves both (1) attention to the task and getting the job done, while also (2) attending to people and social processes. A task focus is necessary if a group is going to stay on track and achieve its goals. One aspect of leadership behaviour, therefore, must concentrate on defining roles, providing structures, directing activities, communicating information, scheduling, etc. It is critical that leaders attend to the content of decisions and tasks at hand. These types of activities, however, are all too frequently the sole focus of the leader and the group. The second factor these studies highlighted, of equal importance, relates to consideration of peoples' feelings and the building of mutual trust and respect for people's ideas and attitudes. It is also concerned with how the group goes about achieving what it needs to achieve.

***1.2. Transformational perspective*:** Another, more recently distinguished idea is between transactional and transformational leadership. Transactional leaders attempt to satisfy the current needs of followers by focusing their attention on tasks and interpersonal exchanges. Transformational leaders, on the other hand, attempt to stimulate followers and promote dramatic changes in individuals, groups and organizations.

One critical difference between transactional and transformational leadership is in regards to performance. It has been suggested that transactional leadership provides the basis for expected levels of performance, while transformational leadership builds upon that base resulting in performance beyond expectations. Transformational leaders "motivate subordinates to do more than originally expected. They raise the consciousness of subordinates about the importance and value of designated outcomes and ways of reaching them and, in turn, get subordinates to transcend their own immediate self-interests for the sake of the mission and vision of the organization. Subordinates' confidence levels are raised and their needs are expanded." This increased motivation is linked to three factors of transformational leadership:

1. Transformational leaders are more charismatic and inspiring in the eyes of their followers. They inspire commitment, instill a vision and excite people. They are well trusted and their followers feel confidence in them. 2. Transformational leaders give individual consideration. They pay attention to individual differences in subordinates' needs for growth and development. They coach, mentor and assign tasks that not only satisfy immediate needs, but stretch peoples' capabilities in an effort toward improvement. They also link the individual's current needs to the organization's mission. 3. Transformational leaders provide intellectual stimulation. They raise peoples' awareness of issues and problems. They help people become aware of their own thoughts, imagination, beliefs and values. It is through intellectual stimulation that transformational leaders facilitate the generation of new methods of accomplishing the organizational mission.

2. Visionary Leadership

Vision is what determines what an organization is going to try to accomplish. Without a clear vision the organization will be pulled in many different directions. It is much easier to lead if you have a clear idea of what you want to achieve and your ideas are good. Even if you don't have a tremendous amount of skill as a leader, having a clear vision can help you through your shortcomings. People want to follow someone with a plan. By having a clear vision of what you want to accomplish, you will attract followers and people who want to align themselves with your vision. Individuals realize that one of the cornerstones of success is a clear vision. For this reason they want to align themselves with someone who articulates a vision - they want to join in the success. In fact, a poor leader with a great vision will achieve more than a great leader with an ill-conceived plan. People want to follow someone who will lead them to success. If you appear to be able to do this, people will want to follow you. If you have a track record of success, people will want to follow you. If you are pushing people toward shared success, they will tend to stick with you because they are succeeding. In some cases they may even start mimicking some of your poor leadership habits thinking they are part of the reason for your success. Many people mistake success for good leadership skills. That is because people want to follow people with whom they can be successful. Obviously good leadership skills are very important. It is much better to lead with a solid vision and skillful leadership expertise.

Visionary leaders are the builders of a new dawn, working with imagination, insight, and boldness. They present a challenge that calls forth the best in people and brings them together around a shared sense of purpose. They work with the power of intentionality and alignment with a higher purpose. Their eyes are on the horizon, not just on the near at hand. They are social innovators and change agents, seeing the big picture and thinking strategically. There is a profound interconnectedness between the leader and the whole, and true visionary leaders serve the good of the whole. They recognize that there is some truth on both sides of most polarized issues in our society today. They search for solutions that transcend the usual adversarial approaches and address the causal level of problems. They find a higher synthesis of the best of both sides of an issue and address the systemic root causes of problems to create real breakthroughs.

2.1. What is it that makes a visionary become a visionary leader? : A visionary may dream wonderful visions of the future and articulate them with great inspiration. A visionary is good with words. But a visionary leader is good with actions as well as words, and so can bring his/her vision into being in the world, thus transforming it in some way. More than words are needed for a vision to take form in today's world. It requires leadership and heartfelt commitment. A visionary leader is effective in manifesting his or her vision because s/he creates specific, achievable goals, initiates action and enlists the participation of others.

What is the mysterious inner process within leaders that enables them to work their magic and radiate the charisma that mobilizes others for a higher purpose? Visionary leadership is based on a balanced expression of the spiritual, mental, emotional and physical dimensions. It requires core values, clear vision, empowering relationships, and innovative action. When one or more of these dimensions are missing, leadership cannot manifest a vision. The best visionary leaders move energy to a higher level by offering a clear vision of what is possible. They inspire people to be better than they already are and help them identify with what Lincoln called "the angels of their better nature." This was the power of Martin Luther King's "I have a dream" speech. The creative power of lighted, inspired words can sound a certain inner note that people recognize and respond to. This, then, creates dramatic social change. Like King, visionary leaders have the ability to sense the deeper spiritual needs of the followers and link their current demands to this deeper, often unspoken, need for purpose and meaning.

Visionary leaders often have the ability to see higher spiritual forces at work behind the scenes of events, and they align with the vision of these redemptive forces. Both George Washington and Winston Churchill spoke about the help they received from a "guiding hand." Churchill said, "...we have a guardian because we serve a great cause, and we shall have that guardian as long as we serve that cause faithfully."

3. Leadership in Practice: Empowerment

There are different types of leaders and you will probably encounter more than one type in your lifetime. Formal leaders are those we elect into positions or offices such as the senators, congressmen, and presidents of the local clubs. Informal leaders are those we look up to by virtue of their wisdom and experience such as in the case of the elders of a tribe, or our grandparents; or by virtue of their expertise and contribution on a given field such as Albert Einstein in the field of Theoretical Physics and Leonardo da Vinci in the field of the Arts. Successful leaders are able to motivate, energize and empower others. When people are excited and empowered in this sense, it affects both their task initiation and task persistence. That is, empowered people get more involved, take on more difficult situations, and act more confidently. Empowered people expend more effort on a given task and are more persistent in their efforts.

The central question for us is how can leaders empower, motivate and activate people? Based on Bandura's (1974) classic work on self-efficacy beliefs and their effects on peoples' sense of personal power, we will discuss several means of empowering others. We know that people gain confidence when they take on a new and complex task, receive training if necessary, and complete a task successfully. Therefore, one important set of leadership skills relates to mentoring, coaching and counseling wherein we are concerned with providing employees with the necessary direction, information, skills and support necessary for task mastery. We also know that when people feel more capable, they are empowered intellectually. There is a wealth of evidence that what we believe we are capable of doing is shaped by what others believe us to be capable of. If we expect people to succeed they will be more likely to do so than if we expect them to fail. Therefore, another critical set of leadership skills is related to oral persuasion and motivation. A third process for activating people is to provide a successful role-model from which to observe and learn. This modeling and role-model effect is not as powerful as actually experiencing mastery; however, it does have positive effects. Therefore, a third set of leadership skills is powerful-people skills, related to how you as an individual can feel and behave more powerfully, and can act as a positive leadership role-model. Each of these will be considered in more detail below.

4. Leadership Styles

Leadership style is the manner and approach of providing direction, implementing plans, and motivating people. There are normally three styles of leadership (U.S. Army Handbook, 1973) : Authoritarian or autocratic, Participative or democratic, Delegative or Free Reign. Although good leaders use all three styles, with one of them normally dominate, bad leaders tend to stick with one style.

***4.1. Authoritarian (autocratic)*:** This style is used when the leader tells his/her employees what s/he wants done and how s/he wants it done, without getting the advice of his/her followers. Some of the appropriate conditions to use it are when you have all the information to solve the problem, you are short on time, and your employees are well motivated. Some people tend to think of this style as a vehicle for yelling, using demeaning language, and leading by threats and abusing their power. This is not the authoritarian style...rather it is an abusive, unprofessional style called bossing people around. It has no place in a leader's repertoire. The authoritarian style should normally be used only on rare occasions. If you have the time and want to gain more commitment and motivation from your employees, then you should use the participative style.

***4.2. Participative (democratic)*:** This type of style involves the leader including one or more employees in on the decision making process (determining what to do and how to do it). However, the leader maintains the final decision making authority. Using this style is not a sign of weakness; rather, it is a sign of strength that your employees will respect. This is normally used when you have part of the information, and your employees have other parts. Note that a leader is not expected to know everything - this is why you employ *knowledgeable* and *skillful* employees. Using this style is of mutual benefit - it allows them to become part of the team and allows you to make better decisions.

4.3. Delegative (free reign): In this style, the leader allows the employees to make the decision. However, the leader is still responsible for the decisions that are made. This is used when employees are able to analyze the situation and determine what needs to be done and how to do it. You cannot do everything! You must set priorities and delegate certain tasks. This is not a style to use so that you can blame others when things go wrong, rather this is a style to be used when you have the full trust and confidence in the people below you. Do not be afraid to use it, however, use it wisely! A good leader uses all three styles, depending on what forces are involved between the followers, the leader, and the situation. Some examples include:

- Using an authoritarian style on a new employee who is just learning the job.
- The leader is competent and a good coach. The employee is motivated to learn a new skill. The situation is a new environment for the employee.
- Using a participative style with a team of workers who know their job. The leader knows the problem, but does not have all the information.
- The employees know their jobs and want to become part of the team.
- Using a delegative style with a worker who knows more about the job than you. You cannot do everything! The employee needs to take ownership of her job. Also, the situation might call for you to be at other places, doing other things.

5. Leadership Styles Depend on the Situation

Most of the time, leaders employ a combination of leadership styles, depending on the situation. In emergency situations such as periods of war and calamity, decision-making is a matter of life and death. Thus, a nation's leader cannot afford to consult with all departments to arrive at crucial decisions. The case is of course different in times of peace and order - different sectors and other branches of government can freely interact and participate in governance. Another case in point is in leading organizations. When the staffs are highly motivated and competent, a combination of high delegative and moderate participative styles of leadership is most appropriate. But, if the staffs have low competence and low commitment, a combination of high coaching, high supporting, and high directing behavior from organizational leaders is required. Leadership is not about rulers and subordinates, masters and slaves. It is not about management skills or having the right structure. Leadership is about building a sense of community, ownership, family and accountability. Rank does have privileges, but wise leaders never rely on power to get things done.

6. Mentoring: Awakening the Sleeping Giant

Globalization has ushered in era of competition and impersonal existence with emphasis exclusively on task and results. Persons and their uniqueness have become things of the past. Survival of the fittest has come to stay. Success at any cost seems to have become the maxim. Competencies and talents often remain buried in this world of cut throat competition. And yet when institutions and organizations are ready to embark on a journey of mentoring their protégés and employees, the result would be incomparable. What we do in mentoring is that we awaken the sleeping giant.

Mentoring is not the same as teaching. Very often, people misconstrue mentors to be the same as teachers. Employees can find mentors in professional and personal lives. A mentor is not just a teacher. Nor is he a coach or trainer. The job of a mentor encompasses more than that of a teacher and a coach. A mentor literally takes his mentee under his wing and is morally responsible for the development of the student. A mentor is not just involved in imparting technical knowledge to his students. He is also involved in the emotional and spiritual development of the student. A mentor can have an involved relationship with the mentee than the relationship with a coach.

It is very difficult to nurture and manage a mentor – mentee relationship. Not every senior employee is equipped to play the role of a mentor as the job of a mentor is very demanding. However, organizations that encourage mentorship go a long way in building their human capital. Organizational structures are stronger because of mentors. Corporate mentors can build healthy climates for employees with a positive mentoring program. A mentor participates in the transition of the employee's organizational growth and is actively involved in the establishment of the employee's new organizational roles. A mentor helps the mentee chart out long term career goals with the organization and stimulates the mentee to enhance work competencies.

A mentor is a person who has a vast repertoire of experience in the field that he trains. Mentors have had both experience and professional training in the subject that he has to mentor. For instance, leadership mentors need to have adequate experience as leaders and should have undergone leadership training themselves. What do mentors offer to their students that formal training sessions cannot offer? For one, the mentors can use personal experiences as lessons for students. Moreover, mentors are capable of resolving dynamic issues due to their abundant knowledge and experience in the field. A training program cannot possibly prepare students to face unexpected challenges. Mentors can vary their training depending on the nature of their students and the different levels of complexity faced by the mentee.

A mentor need not be an immediate superior or for that matter belong to the same department. Cross department mentoring is very common and often encouraged. With a mentor from another department, needless office politics don't creep into the relationship. Moreover, the mentee finds a mentor at a similar position of power as that of his boss. The mentor-mentee relationship is often less autocratic, but more compassionate. There could be conflicts of viewpoint between them but it does not hurt their relationship in any way.

A mentor grooms his students to take on higher responsibilities and face all odds that surface in the journey. Mentors have to prepare their students to tackle organizational roadblocks, power games, bad will, subordinate resistance and other such challenges. The relationship of a mentor and a mentee can extend well beyond the mentoring program. Some mentoring relationships end as per the agreement made by organizations. Some could end even more abruptly if the relationship does not work out amicably. In any case, it is the duty of the mentor to formally close the relationship and ensure that the termination of the relationship does not affect the student's achievements.

Mentoring is a relationship where a mentor, through support, counsel, friendship, reinforcement and constructive example, helps another person (usually a young person) reach his or her work and life goals. Although many people may equate mentoring with friendship, mentoring actually has its roots in the professional world. Mentoring principles and practices have perpetuated the continuity of art, craft and commerce dating back to ancient times where masters taught, coached and guided the skills development of apprentices. Mentoring is a relationship built on trust. It is not expensive, and the return on investment of a successful mentoring relationship can be profound and significant.

Mentoring relationships provide valuable support to young people. Mentors can help guide youth through the sometimes awkward developmental stages that accompany the transition into adulthood. Mentoring can offer not only academic and career guidance, but also role models for leadership, interpersonal and problem-solving skills. Many youth with disabilities, like other disadvantaged youth, have not had the same opportunities as their peers for exposure to career preparation options like mentoring. Even today, some youth with disabilities play at best a passive role in their own career-planning process. This may reflect low expectations that either they or others have, learned dependency, or the perceived need for protection and support.

By and large, youth appreciate mentors who are supportive, caring, and willing to assist them with activities that support academic, career, social or personal goals. One common theme is that the longer the relationship continues, the more positive the outcome. Another is that youth are more likely to benefit from mentoring if their mentor maintains frequent contact with them and knows their families. As a general rule, youth who are disadvantaged or at-risk stand to gain the most from mentoring. Youth with disabilities are among these populations.

When we apply mentoring to teaching and teachers, it can improve teaching performance, increase the retention of new teachers, promote the personal and professional well-being of new teachers, and transmit the culture of the educational system to beginning teachers. A mentoring program should provide opportunities for new and experienced teachers to grow professionally and improve their teaching. It is more than just assigning an experienced teacher with a novice teacher. It has been noticed that 30% of new teachers quit during the first two years;

50% leave teaching during the first four years. It costs an institution time and money to recruit, hire and train new teachers.

A mentor can be to provide a new teacher with insight on: motivating students, providing for individual differences of students' assessing student work, relating to parents, organizing class work, obtaining materials and supplies, assistance with discipline and so on. A mentor can provide a new teacher:

- Ideas about instruction
- Personal and emotional support
- Advice on resources and materials
- Information about school, district policies and procedures
- Ideas for additional techniques on classroom management

This suggests that new teachers with a mentor can focus on instructional needs rather than concentrating on classroom management.

6.1 Mentoring: Definition and Explanation

If you touch me soft and gentle, if you look at me and smile at me, if you listen to me talk sometimes, before you talk, I will grow, really grow. - Bradley. "The best mentors are the people in your life who push you just a little bit outside your "comfort zone" - Leigh Curl. "Mentors are guides. They lead us along the journey of our lives. We trust them because they have been there before. They embody our hopes, cast light on the way ahead, interpret arcane signs, warn us of lurking dangers, and point out unexpected delights along the way..." Laurent A Daloz.

Interestingly, the concept of mentoring stems from Greek mythology. Mentor was Odysseus's friend and teacher to his son Telemachus. In Homer's Odyssey, Athena, the goddess, assumed the form of Mentor to proffer advice to Odysseus and Telemachus. Since then, the word Mentor has become synonymous with someone who is a wise advisor. The name is synonymous with a person who guides another toward the path of education, growth, maturity, development, progress and prosperity. An organization can use the art of mentoring as a tool to help bring out the best in their younger employees, leveraging the synergy for individual and organizational growth and success.

Dr Audrey Collin, of the School of Management at Leicester Polytechnic, gathered a number of largely US definitions of mentoring for an article in *Personnel Review* magazine. Mentors were said, for example, to be 'influential people who significantly help you reach your major life goals' (1979). Mentoring is 'a process in which one person [the mentor] is responsible for overseeing the career and development of another person [the mentee] outside the normal manager/subordinate relationship'. Alternatively, mentoring was 'a protected relationship in which learning and experimentation can occur, potential skills can be developed, and in which results can be measured in terms of competencies gained rather than curricular territory covered'.

The basic model of mentoring is that one person passes his/her greater knowledge and wisdom to another. A mentor is a professional person who is a wise, experienced, knowledgeable individual who 'either demands or gently coaxes' the most out of the mentee. "A one-to-one relationship in which a senior manager oversees the development and progression of a more junior manager" (Equal Opportunities Review, 1995). **"Mentoring is to support and encourage people to manage their own learning in order that they may maximise their potential, develop their skills, improve their performance and become the person they want to be"** (*Eric Par sloe, The Oxford School of Coaching* and *Mentoring).* Thus, as said by John C. Crosby, "Mentoring is a brain to pick, an ear to listen, and a push in the right direction."

All of these definitions are valid in the specific context which they were intended to describe. None, however, can truly be said to be generic - equally applicable in all situations. As with most definitions of complex phenomena, the more generic they are, the vaguer they tend to be! Mentoring is a partnership between two people built upon trust. It is a process in which the mentor offers ongoing support and development opportunities to the mentee. Addressing issues and blockages identified by the mentee, the mentor offers guidance, counseling and support in the form of pragmatic and objective assistance. Both share a common purpose of developing a strong two-way learning relationship.

6.2. Coaching: Coaching is a relatively direct means of helping someone develop competence. It is relatively directive because the coach is in charge of the process. Although there are, in turn, four basic styles of coaching, which range from the highly directive to more stimulative, learner-driven approaches, it is common for the learning goals to be set either by the coach or by a third party. In the world of work, coaching goals are most frequently established as an outcome of performance appraisal. The issue of learner commitment (is this really what matters to them?) is therefore relevant. Some of the useful behaviours effective coaches may display include challenging the learner's assumptions, being a critical friend and demonstrating how they do something the learner is having difficulties with.

6.3. Counseling: Counseling - in the context of support and learning, as opposed to therapy - is a relatively non-directive means of helping someone cope. By acting as a sounding-board, helping someone structure and analyze career-influencing decisions, and sometimes simply by being there to listen, the mentor supports the mentee in taking responsibility for his or her career and personal development.

6.4. Networking: To function effectively within any organization, people need personal networks. At the very least they need an information network (How do I find out what I need to know?) and an influence network (How do I get people, over whom I have no direct control, to do things for me?). The same is true for the unemployed young adult in the context of community mentoring, for newly recruited researchers at university and for people in many other situations where mentoring can be applied. Effective mentors help their mentees develop self-resourcefulness by making them aware of the plethora of influence and information resources available to them - people, organizations and more formal repositories of knowledge. They may make an introduction to someone they already know, or talk the mentee through as to how he or she will make his or her own introduction to that person, or help the mentee build entire chunks of virgin network.

6.5. Guiding: Guiding (effectively acting as a guardian) is another relatively hands-on role and is the one most managers find easiest because it is closest to what they do normally. Giving advice comes naturally. It is unfortunate that so many managers who have attended coaching courses or read well-meant books on the developmental role of the supervisor come away feeling guilty, or worse, that they have to constantly restrain themselves from giving straight answers to their direct reports. The reality is that there are many situations where asking 'What do you think you should do?' is not an appropriate response. Using the tools of reflective analysis at inappropriate times is likely to have a far greater de-motivating effect than simply leaving well alone. Equally, however, always providing the answer is not going to help someone grow. Because, being a guide/guardian tends to carry with it a relatively strong element of being a role model - an example of success in whatever field the learner has chosen to pursue - one's behaviours, good or bad, are likely to be passed on to the learner along with more practical support. The aim is to make the person aware of his unique capabilities and to ensure that he maximizes his potential and minimizes his weaknesses.

Finally, mentoring draws on all four other 'helping to learn' styles. Indeed, the core skill of a mentor can be described as having sufficient sensitivity to the mentee's needs to respond with the appropriate behaviors. Thus, the effective mentor may use the challenging behaviors of stretch coaching at one point and the empathetic listening of counseling a short while later.

7. Coaching Vs Mentoring

Given the frequent confusion between these two terms, it is worth drawing out the differences more finely. Although coaching and mentoring share some tools and approaches, coaching are primarily focused on performance within the current job and emphasize the development of skills. Mentoring is primarily focused on longer-term goals and on developing capability.

Coaching	*Mentoring*
Concerned with task	Concerned with implications beyond the task
Focuses on skills and performances	Focuses on capability and potential
Primarily a line manager role	Works best off-line
Agenda set by or with the coach	Agenda set by the learner
Emphasizes feedback to the learner	Emphasizes feedback and reflection by the learner
Typically addresses a short-term need	Typically a longer-term relationship, often 'for life'
Feedback and discussion primarily explicit	Feedback and discussion primarily about implicit, intuitive issues and behaviours

Getting the best from a mentoring scheme, then, involves building in the best aspects of both formal and informal approaches. A formal structure is essential because it provides meaning and direction for relationships and support where necessary. But, individual relationships will flourish best when allowed to operate as informally as possible. Successful formal relationships very frequently go on to become successful informal ones. There is also an increasing body of field evidence that the quality and extent of informal mentoring improves dramatically once a critical mass is achieved of people who have been effective mentors and mentees under formal arrangements. An organization that manages to create a mentoring/coaching culture can increasingly relax the level of formal intervention it imposes. What structures it does provide - in terms of educational materials and training, for example - become regarded as support mechanisms rather than as controls. Meetings between mentors to develop their skills can become informal, self-driven support networks. And the range of people from whom the mentees learn can gradually be extended as they learn to build and manage their own learning nets.

8. Easier Recruitment and Induction

Mentoring cultivates in the mentee an increased sense of commitment and loyalty to the organization. The mentor is the mediator between the mentee and the company. Through close interaction with the mentee, the mentor creates a personal atmosphere in what might otherwise seem a faceless bureaucratic organization. The mentee receives through the mentor a positive perception of the company. The mentee can be made to feel that he or she is participating in the inner operations of the company, and this in turn generates a closer identification with the organization's goals.

8.1. Improved employee motivation: Mentoring can help reduce managerial and professional turnover at other critical stages, too. Young, ambitious people often undergo a period of frustration and impatience when they realize their progress up the company career ladder is slower than they initially expected. If mentees have a mentor who is taking an active interest in their career and who explains the reasons for and ways round current blockages, they are more likely to persevere. The mentor helps them understand and recognize the long-term plans the company has for them, and helps the mentee make the most of the learning experiences inherent in the current job. In this way mentoring lessens the threat that other companies may lure away promising young employees with offers of speedier career advancement.

A mentoring relationship also motivates the middle and senior managers involved and can be a valuable means of delaying 'plateauing'. A manager is less likely to retire mentally in the job if he or she is constantly faced with fresh challenges arising from a mentoring relationship. Mentors are forced to clarify and articulate their own ideas about the company's organization and goals in order to explain them to their mentees. They may feel they have to improve their own abilities to justify the mentees' respect.

8.2. The management of the corporate culture: Instead of preserving cultures, companies are desperately trying to change them. This poses a number of problems - not least that it makes it even more difficult to identify mentors with the 'right' values. Mentor and mentee in an effective developmental relationship are able to explore the differences between espoused corporate values and actual behaviour. At the same time, the mentor helps to clarify in the mentee's mind which aspects of the culture are fixed and not open to challenge, and which are open for dialogue.

8.3. Succession planning: An increasingly common benefit reported by larger companies is an improvement in succession planning. Widespread mentoring, especially where the duration of formal relationships is limited to one or two years, ensures that senior managers are familiar with the strengths, weaknesses and ambitions of a relatively large pool of more junior talent.

8.4. Improved communications: In a traditional senior to junior mentoring relationship, the mentee's unique position in the organization can aid informal communications because he or she straddles several levels. For example, through the relationship with the mentor the junior management mentee has access to and is accepted by middle management. At the same time he or she is accepted in the lower managerial levels. Because the mentee is familiar with the language and mannerisms of both, he or she can efficiently communicate each group's ideas and opinions to the other. Rich informal communication networks improve productivity and efficiency in a company since they lead to more action, more innovation, more learning, and swifter adjustment to changing business needs.

9. The 10 Competencies Needed For Effective Mentoring

9.1. Self-awareness (understanding self): Mentors need high self-awareness in order to recognize and manage their own behaviour within the helping relationship and to use empathy appropriately. The activist, task-focused manager often has relatively little insight into these areas - indeed, he or she may actively avoid reflection on such issues, depicting them as 'soft' and of low priority. Such attitudes and learned behaviours may be difficult to break. Providing managers with psychometric tests and other forms of insight-developing questionnaire can be useful if they are open to insights in those areas. However, it is easy to dismiss such feedback, even when it also comes from external sources, such as working colleagues. SWOT analysis would be an effective means to self understanding. If nothing else, the model helps open up some of the hidden boxes in the Johari Window! An important debate here is whether low self-awareness is the result of low motivation to explore the inner self (disinterest), or high motivation to avoid such exploration, or simply an inability to make complex emotional and rational connections (in which case there may be physiological aspects to consider as well). The approach in helping someone develop self-awareness will be different in each case and is likely to be least effective in bringing.

9.2. Behavioral awareness (understanding others): Like self-awareness, understanding how others behave and why they do so is a classic component of emotional intelligence. To help others manage their relationships, the mentor must have reasonably good insight into patterns of behaviour between individuals and groups of people. Predicting the consequences of specific behaviours or courses of action is one of the many practical applications of this insight. Developing clearer insight into the behaviours of others comes from frequent observation and reflection. Supervision groups can help the mentor recognize common patterns of behavior by creating opportunities for rigorous analysis.

9.3. Business or professional savvy: There is not a great deal to be done here in the short term - there are very few shortcuts to experience and judgment. However, the facilitator can help the potential mentor understand the need for developing judgment and plan how to acquire relevant experience. Again, the art of purposeful reflection is a valuable support in building this competence. By reviewing the learning from a variety of experiences, the manager widens his or her range of templates and develops a sense of patterns in events. The more frequently he or she is able to combine stretching experience with focused reflection - either internally or in a dialogue with others - the more substantial and rapid the acquisition of judgment. A useful method of helping people develop business savvy is to create learning sets, where a skilled facilitator encourages people to share their experience and look for patterns.

9.4. Sense of proportion/good humor: Is good humor a competence? I would argue strongly that it is. Laughter, used appropriately, is invaluable in developing rapport, in helping people to see matters from a different perspective, in releasing emotional tension. It is also important that mentor and mentee should enjoy the sessions they have together. Enthusiasm is far more closely associated with learning than boredom is! In practice, good humor is a vehicle for achieving a sense of proportion - a broader perspective that places the organization's goals and culture in the wider social and business context. People acquire this kind of perspective by ensuring that they balance their day-to-day involvement with work tasks against a portfolio of other interests. Some of these may be related to work - for example, developing a broader strategic understanding of how the business sector is evolving. Others are unrelated to work and may encompass science, philosophy or any other intellectually stimulating endeavor. In general, the broader the scope of knowledge and experience the mentor can apply the better sense of proportion he or she can bring.

9.5. Communication competence: Communication is not a single skill: it is a combination of a number of skills. Those most important for the mentor include:

- Listening - opening the mind to what the other person is saying, demonstrating interest/attention, encouraging him or her to speak, holding back on filling the silences.
- Observing as receiver - being open to the visual and other non-verbal signals, recognizing what is not said.
- Parallel processing - analyzing what the other person is saying, reflecting on it, preparing responses; effective communicators do all of these in parallel, slowing down the dialogue as needed to ensure that they do not overemphasize preparing responses at the expense of analysis and reflection; equally, they avoid becoming so mired in their internal thoughts that they respond inadequately or too slowly.
- Projecting - crafting words and their emotional 'wrapping' in a manner appropriate for the situation and the recipient(s).

- Observing as projector - being open to the visual and other non-verbal signals, as clues to what the recipient is hearing/understanding; adapting tone, volume, pace and language appropriately.
- Exiting - concluding a dialogue or segment of dialogue with clarity and alignment of understanding (ensuring that the message has been received in both directions).

9.6. Conceptual modeling: Effective mentors have a portfolio of models they can draw upon to help mentees understand the issues they face. These models can be self-generated (e.g. the result of personal experience), drawn from elsewhere (e.g. models of company structure, interpersonal behaviours, strategic planning, career planning) or - at the highest level of competence - generated on the spot as an immediate response.

According to the situation and the learning styles of the mentee, it may be appropriate to present these models in verbal or visual form. Or the mentor may not present them at all - simply use them as the framework for asking penetrating questions. Developing the skills of conceptual modelling takes time, once again. It requires a lot of reading, often beyond the normal range of materials that cross the individual's desk. Training in presentation skills and how to make simple diagrams can also help. But the most effective way can be for the mentor to seize every opportunity to explain complex ideas in a variety of ways, experimenting to see what works with different audiences. Eventually, there develops an intuitive, instinctive understanding of how best to put across a new idea.

9.7. Commitment to one's own continued learning: Effective mentors become role models for self-managed learning. They seize opportunities to experiment and take part in new experiences. They read widely and are reasonably efficient at setting and following personal development plans. They actively seek and use behavioral feedback from others. These skills can be developed with practice. Again, having a role model to follow for themselves is a good starting-point.

9.8. Strong interest in developing others: Effective mentors have an innate interest in achieving through others and in helping others recognize and achieve their potential. This instinctive response is important in establishing and maintaining rapport and in enthusing the mentee, building confidence in what he or she could become. While it is possible to 'switch on' someone to the self-advantage of helping others, it is probably not feasible to stimulate an altruistic response.

9.9. Building and maintaining rapport/relationship management: The skills of rapport-building are difficult to define. When asked to describe rapport in their experience, managers' observations can be distilled into five characteristics:

1. Trust - Will they do what they say? Will they keep confidences?
2. Focus - Are they concentrating on me? Are they listening without judging?
3. Empathy - Do they have goodwill towards me? Do they try to understand my feelings, and viewpoints?
4. Congruence - Do they acknowledge and accept my goals?
5. Empowerment - Is their help aimed at helping me stand on my own feet as soon as is practical?

To a considerable extent, the skills of building and maintaining rapport are contained in the other competencies already described. However, additional help in developing rapport- building skills may be provided through situational analysis - creating opportunities for the individual to explore with other people how and why he or she feels comfortable and uncomfortable with them in various circumstances. This kind of self-knowledge can be invaluable in developing more sensitive responses to other people's needs and emotions. The mentor can also be encouraged to think about the contextual factors in creating rapport. Avoiding meeting on the mentor's home ground (e.g. in his or her office) may be an obvious matter, but where would the mentee feel most comfortable? Sensitivity to how the meeting environment affects the mentoring dialogue can be developed simply by talking the issues through, both in formal or informal training and with the mentee.

9.10. Goal clarity: The mentor must be able to help the mentee sort out what he or she wants to achieve and why. This is quite hard to do if you do not have the skills to set and pursue clear goals of your own. Goal clarity appears to derive from a mixture of skills including systematic analysis and decisiveness. Like so many of the other mentoring competencies, it may best be developed through opportunities to reflect and to practice.

10. Mentors as Catalysts and Capacity Builders

10.1. The Mentor who encourages and Motivates: The ability to encourage and motivate is another important interpersonal skill that the mentor must have in abundance if the relationship with the mentee is to reach its full potential. The mentor must be able to recognize the ability of the mentee and make it clear to the mentee that he or she believes in the mentee's capacity to progress within the company. The mentor must be willing to let the mentee turn to him or her for as long as needed, as well as be willing to help the mentee eventually become independent.

The mentor encourages the mentee through recognizing the different roles he or she can play. For a certain period the mentor can be a reassuring parental figure to whom the mentee can turn for support and sympathy. The mentor must also at this stage be willing to let the mentee identify with him or her and use him or her as a role model. At other stages of the relationship, the mentor can encourage the mentee to become more independent and make individual decisions.

10.2. The mentor who nurtures: The mentor must be able to create an open, candid atmosphere that will encourage the mentee to confide in and trust him or her. The mentor is there to draw out the mentee and help discover his or her identity within the organization. With the help of the mentor, the mentee undertakes self-assessment and discovers where his or her skills, aspirations and interests lie. Most importantly, the mentor must be able to listen to the mentee and ask open-ended questions that will draw out the less experienced person.

10.3. The mentor who teaches: This is a skill that the mentor may need to be taught, because being a really good teacher does not come naturally to many people. Highly ambitious, self-motivated people (and the description applies to most people who make it to top management) often lack the patience to teach. Yet the mentor must know how to help the mentee maximize his or her opportunities to learn. The mentor does this by creating a stimulating environment that consistently challenges the mentee to apply theory to the real world of management.

10.4. The mentor who offers mutual respect: An essential ingredient in any mentoring relationship is mutual respect between the two partners. If the mentee does not respect and trust his or her mentor's opinions, advice and influence - and vice versa - the benefits from the relationship will be severely limited. Programme co-ordinators must remember that a mentee's attitude towards the mentor is inevitably influenced by the mentor's general reputation within the company. The emphasis on career outcomes expressed here has now generally been balanced by an equal or greater emphasis on the personal development outcomes, which may or may not have a direct impact on career achievement. Respect within developmental mentoring comes less from an appreciation of what the mentor can do for the mentee than from what he or she can help the mentee do on his or her own.

10.5. Measuring and Monitoring the Programme

- Relationship processes - what happens in the relationship; for example, how often does the pair meet? Have they developed sufficient trust? Is there a clear sense of direction to the relationship? Does the mentor or the mentee have concerns about his or her own or the other person's contribution to the relationship?
- Programme processes - for example, how many people attended training? How effective was the training? In some cases, programme processes will also include data derived from adding together measurements from individual relationships, to gain a broad picture of what is going well and less well.
- Relationship outcomes - have mentor and mentee met the goals they set? (Some adjustment may be needed for legitimate changes in goals as circumstances evolve.)
- Programme outcomes - for example, have we increased retention of key staff, or raised the competence of the mentees in critical areas?

Measuring all four gives you a balanced view of the mentoring programme and allows the scheme co-ordinator to intervene, with sensitivity, where needed. Mentors can redirect their energies into a stimulating and creative role. Mentoring demands a flexible and individual approach rather than applying habitual, well-used formulae. As a result, the mentor finds new self-respect as he or she recognizes, he or she has valuable experiences and knowledge to pass on to the mentee.

11. The Top 10 Qualities of an Inspiring Mentor Relationship

11.1. Mutual respect: The mentor and the learner share a deep respect for the common pursuit as well as for the underlying values driving the pursuit. It is the shared respect that connects and provides the foundation for the work the mentor and the learner will do together.

11.2. Trust: When a deep level of trust exists between the mentor and the learner, the individual is able to take great risks—risks one might not have taken without the trust. The mutual trust between mentor and learner provides a safe space for the latter to step out in faith and achieve what might appear difficult, impossible, or overwhelming. The trust the mentor provides as part of the framework is fundamental for the learning experience to occur.

11.3. Mentor as a conduit: A mentor provides access to learning and growth. It is through the mentor relationship that deep learning occurs. The mentor provides a framework for exploration by creating a context that provides support, encouragement, and growth.

11.4. Space, learning and integration: A mentor creates a space for listening and for helping the person to integrate the learning into their lives. A mentor becomes like an "inner voice"– we borrow the mentor for this guiding voice while we search to find and express our own voice.

11.5. Safe space: Unconditional acceptance is a key ingredient for establishing trust and a safe space. When we experience unconditional acceptance and a sense of belonging, we are able to more clearly reveal and be ourselves. Accepting others for who they are, without apology or explanation, is therefore an essential aspect of mentoring. With total acceptance, one feels trusted and known, and is able to take great risks. In a safe space, nothing is taboo.

11.6. Vision: A mentor holds a vision of what's possible, and leads the way to the vision. A mentor believes in the vision as much as the learner does.

11.7. Shared experience: A mentor relationship is rich with learning through shared experiences. The learning's not just academic and has a vibrancy and depth that goes beyond reflective discussion. The mentor has discussions in "real time"- the interaction and the learning aren't just academic. They are deep and real.

11.8. Challenge: The mentor challenges and stretches the person, and provides inspiration for the person to take on even greater challenges. A mentor stretches a person from within.

11.9. Inspiration: A mentor "walks the talk" and provides inspiration through their very being. A mentor is someone who we aspire to become; the mentor has qualities/skills we want for ourselves. The mentor helps us to see possibility by bringing to life the qualities we aspire for ourselves.

11.10. Sage Advice: A mentor will offer sage advice, will show the learner "the ropes" and will invest time and energy in the development of the individual. The more open the learner is to accessing this wisdom, the more profound the discoveries will be!

How true, "Mentoring is a brain to pick, an ear to listen, and a push in the right direction."- John C. Crosby

CONCLUSION

Mentoring is an Essential Skill which Enhances Academic Leadership

There is a story of a ship builder, Marcus who was given a rough stone by his friend, Barnabas. Marcus examined the odd-looking red stone in his hand. "It's a red-looking rock, Master." Marcus placed the stone on the bench between them.

Barnabas then took out a cut and polished Ruby. He held it up to the light and let the sun sparkle through it, showing off the stone's beauty. "This is one of the most magnificent stones in Athens." He tossed it to Marcus who almost dropped the stone as it bounced off his hand and into his lap. Barnabas laughed and asked Marcus to explain both stones again. "What is the difference between the two stones, Marcus?"

"Well, one seems to be a red rock and the other an exceptional gem. One is available, the other is not, I guess."

Barnabas replied, "On the contrary, son. The rough stone you so casually placed on the bench is soon to become the most valuable Ruby in all Greece. It is Ruby of the finest quality. All it lacks is to be in the hands of a master jeweler. Once he takes the rough edges off and applies some polish, the world will see how beautiful the stone can truly be."

"People are the same as this rough stone, my friend. Put in the hands of a master, they too can become more than the eye can at first perceive. It takes the vision and the skill of a master leader to bring them to their full potential."

"Look at the men on your crew. With your guiding hand, they can each become much more than the eye sees. It will take your hand to guide them and clip away the rough edges. Always see them as they will become, not as they are." Focusing on what one could become, is mentoring.

"The best mentors are the people in your life who push you just a little bit outside your comfort zone" - Leigh Curl. Mentoring is an essential leadership skill. In addition to managing and motivating people, it's also important that you can help others learn, grow and become more effective in their jobs. You can do this through a mentoring partnership, which you can arrange within your organization or through a personal or professional network. Becoming a Mentor can be a rewarding experience for any one, both personally and professionally. You can improve your leadership and communication skills, learn new perspectives and ways of thinking, advance your career, and gain a great sense of personal satisfaction. Soft skills when compliments hard skills, professional competence when compliments personal integrity, management of change compliments management of self, leadership becomes a source of transformation of self, society and institution/Company. Such leadership thus creates, leaders and not followers, which is the prime purpose of visionary leadership. Academic leadership has to focus on mentoring teachers as well as students. If it is done with passion and enthusiasm to awaken the sleeping giant in each one of them, then there would be many more success stories. We need to help each other to discover for themselves their own capabilities and help them to bloom where they are planted. We need to change from looking at everyone as potential threat to potential contributor; from general categorization of people to personal attention to their unique contribution, assessing their talents and willingness to learn. A paradigm shift is needed in capacity building to enhance productivity and personal and professional fulfillment.

SUGGESTED READING

1. Jack, Myrick. 2006. ***Ancient Wisdom For Today's Leadership Challenges, "The Ship-Builder"***, Five Ancient Principles of Leadership. Jaico Publication House, New Delhi.
2. Sharma, Robin. 2003. Leadership Wisdom, from the monk who sold his Ferrari, ***The 8th Ritual of Visionary Leadership.*** Jaico Publication House, New Delhi.
3. Lynch, James. J. 2004. ***Leadership through Integrity- Building the Ethical Company,*** Infinity Books.
4. A Harvard Business Review Paperback on ***Breakthrough Leadership.*** 2001. Harvard Business School Press, Boston, MA.
5. Kumarasamy, Anand. 2006. ***Gandhi on Personal Leadership, Lessons from the life and times of Indian's Visionary Leader,*** Jaico Publication House, New Delhi.
6. Sharma, Robin. 2008. ***The Greatness Guide 2, 101 Ways to Reach The Next Level,*** Jaico Publication House, New Delhi.
7. Covey, Stephen. R. 1992. Principle Centered Leadership, ***The 7 Habits Of Highly Effective People.*** Simon & Schuster Publications, New York.
8. Covey, Stephen. R, Merrill Roger. A, Merrill. Rebecca, R. 1995. ***First Things First,*** Franklin Covey Co.
9. Covey, Stephen, with Merrill Roger. A, Merrill. Rebecca. R. 1990. ***The Seven Habits of Highly Effective People, Powerful***

Lessons in Personal Change, Simon & Schuster Publications, New York.

10. Goleman Daniel, Boyatzis and Mckee, Anne. 2002. ***The New Leader, Transforming The Art Of Leadership Into The Science OF Results.*** Little Brown, London.
11. ALLEMAN E. 1984. ***What's Really True About Mentoring?*** **Mentor**, Ohio, Leadership Development Consultants Inc.
12. ALRED G. and GARVEY R. 1996. ***'Approaching mentoring: becoming a semi-god'***. Proceedings of the Third European Mentoring Conference, London.
13. ANTAL, A. B. 1993. ***'Odysseus' legacy to management development: mentoring'***, *European Management Journal*, Vol. 11, No 4.
14. BARHAM, K. and CONWAY, C. 1998. ***Developing Business and People Internationally - A mentoring approach.*** Berkhampsted, Ashridge Research.
15. BAXTER, A. G. and CLARK, K. M. 1992. ***'Positive and productive mentoring: inside views', Mentoring International***, Vol. 6, No.s 2/3, spring/summer.
16. BENNETTS, C. 1999a. ***'Interpersonal aspects of informal mentor/ learner relationships: a research perspective'***. Proceedings of the European Mentoring Centre Conference, London, November.
17. BENNETTS, C. 1999b. ***'Mentoring relationships and young people: trend and tradition in mentoring'***. National Youth Agency/DfEE/Rowntree, Research, Policy and Practice Forum on Young People, London.
18. BROWN, S. 2000. ***'The keys to successful mentoring in Smith Kline Beecham'***. Proc. Seventh annual European Mentoring Conference, Cambridge, November, 2000.
19. BUREAU OF BUSINESS PRACTICE. 1990. ***'Being a mentor', Management Letter 304***, February
20. CHAO, G. T. 1997 ***'Mentoring phases and outcomes'***, *Journal of Vocational Behavior*, Vol. 51: 15-28.

9

Empowering the Young Minds: Mission of Teachers

A.P.J. Abdul Kalam

"Knowledge is the most powerful Resource for nation building."

The institutes of higher education have a major responsibility in nation building through enriching students in Science, Engineering, Technology, life-sciences, humanities, arts, commerce, management, languages and equally important in values as good citizens. These institutions are not required only to impart knowledge but also motivate the students to develop necessary soft skills to apply the knowledge in the emerging disciplines and domains.

The India 2020 mission and beyond requires the energetic youth to face many challenges and bring glory to the country with greater emphasis on total quality management in the learning process and education system. Indeed Teachers and Vice Chancellors can transform the young minds into role models. Teachers in particular have a vital role in ignition of young minds to innovate and excel in their areas of specialization. In each of my interactions with over two lakh teachers I would have met at various occasions in schools, colleges, universities, award functions and teacher's day functions during the last seven years, I used to administer an eleven point oath to all the teachers. I would like to discuss here the significance of each point in the oath since it has got direct relationship in teaching and learning process of our education system. Let us see what the oath is.

Eleven Point Oath for Teachers

1. First and foremost, I will love teaching. Teaching will be my soul.
2. I realize that I am responsible for shaping not just students but ignited youths who are the most powerful resource under the earth, on the earth and above the earth. I will be fully committed for the great mission of teaching.
3. I will consider myself to be a great teacher for I can lift the average to the best performance by way of my special teaching.
4. All my actions with my students will be with kindness and affection like a mother, sister, father or brother.
5. I will organize and conduct my life, in such a way that my life itself is a message for my students.
6. I will encourage my students to ask questions and develop the spirit of enquiry, so that they blossom into creative enlightened citizens.
7. I will treat all the students equally and will not support any differentiation on account of religion, community or language.
8. I will continuously build the capacities in teaching so that I can impart quality education to my students.
9. I will celebrate the success of my students, with great élan.
10. I realize by being a teacher, I am making an important contribution to all the national development initiatives.
11. I will constantly Endeavour to fill my mind, with great thoughts and spread the nobility in thinking and action.

I was always fortunate and blessed to have one or two great teachers during every phase of my educational period between 1936 and 1957. Evolution of the oath has resulted from what I have experienced and what I have felt and grown through my teachers. The first oath talks about the teacher loving teaching and teaching being the soul of the teacher. What is the significance of this? Here

I would like to give the example of the teacher who really loved teaching.

A. Teacher Loves Teaching

It was the year 1936; I recall my initiation of education at the age of 5 years in Rameswaram Panchayat Elementary School. I had a Teacher Muthu Iyer who took special interest on me mainly because I performed very well in a class exercise. He was impressed and next day he came to my house to tell my father that I was a very good student. My parents were happy and got my favourite sweet from my mother. Another important event while I was in first class, which I cannot forget. One day I did not turn up to my school. Teacher Muthu Iyer noticed my absence and same evening he came to my father to ask what the problem was and why did I not go to school and whether he can do anything to help me. On that day, I was having fever. Another important thing, which he noticed was my hand writing, was very poor. He gave a three page writing exercise and told my father that he should ensure that I do the exercise everyday regularly. By these actions of my teacher Muthu Iyer, my father told me in later years that teacher Muthu Iyer is not only a good teacher to me in teaching but he influenced and shaped me with good habits and he was a noble friend to my family. Even today I realize how my teacher loved teaching and took personal interest to bring up his pupils. Now let me talk about another teacher who taught me in my fifth class.

B. Teacher Encourages Questions from Students

I was studying in 5th class at the age of 10, when I got a vision for my life. I had a teacher, Shri Siva Subramania Iyer. He was one of the very good teachers in our school. All of us loved to attend his class and hear him. One day he was teaching about bird's flight. He drew a diagram of a bird on the blackboard depicting the wings, tail and the body structure with the head. He explained how the birds create the lift and fly. He also explained to us how they change direction while flying. He gave the lecture for nearly 25 minutes providing information about lift, drag and how the birds fly in a formation of 10, 20 or 30 etc. At the end of the class, he wanted to know whether we understood how the birds fly. I said I did not understand how the birds fly. When I said this, he asked the other students whether they understood or not. Many students said that they did not understand. Our teacher was a real teacher and very good teacher. He did not get upset by our response.

In view of this, my teacher said that he would take all of us to the sea shore. That evening the whole class was on the sea shore. We enjoyed the roaring sea waves knocking at the rocks in the pleasant evening. Birds were flying with sweet chirping voice. He showed the sea birds in formation in 10 to 20 numbers, we have seen the marvelous formation of birds with a purpose and we were all amazed. And we were simply looking at the formation. The teacher showed the birds and asked us to see when the birds fly, what it looked like. We saw the wings being flapped. He explained how the birds flapped the wings to generate the lift. He asked us to look at the tail portion with the combination of flapping wing and twisting tail. We noticed closely and found that the birds in that condition flew in the direction they wanted. Then he asked us a question, where the engine is and how it is powered. Bird is powered by its own life and the motivation what it wants. All these aspects were explained to us within 15 minutes. We all understood the whole bird dynamics with practical example. How nice it was? Our teacher was a great teacher; he could give as a theoretical lesson coupled with live practical example. This is real teaching. I am sure, many of the teachers in schools and colleges will follow this example.

For me, it was not merely an understanding of how a bird flies. The bird's flight entered into me and created a feeling on the seashore of Rameswaram. From that day evening, I thought that my future study has to be with reference to something to do with flight. At that time, I did not realize that I have to go towards flight science. I am telling this because my teacher's teaching and the event that I witnessed inspired me to lead to the goal in life. Then one evening after the classes, I asked the teacher, "Sir, please tell me, how to progress further something to do with flight". He patiently explained to me that I should complete 8th class, and then go to high school, and then I should go to college that may lead to education of flight. If I do all these things I might do something connected with flight sciences. This advice and the bird flying exercise given by my teacher really gave me a goal and a mission for my life. When I went to college, I took Physics. When I went to engineering in Madras Institute of Technology, I took Aeronautical Engineering.

Thus my life was transformed as a rocket engineer, aerospace engineer and technologist. That one incident of my teacher encouraging me to ask questions, showing the visual examples proved to be a turning point in my life which eventually shaped my profession. Shri Sivasubramania Iyer was an example for shaping not just students but igniting the youth both average and extraordinary by allowing them to ask questions and answering them till they fully understood.

C. Teacher puts the Students Ahead

Now I would like to discuss about my mathematics teacher Prof Thothatri Iyengar. As a young science student, I had an opportunity at St. Joseph's College to witness a unique scene of divine looking personality walking through the college campus every morning, and teaching Mathematics to various degree courses. Students looked at the personality who was a symbol of our own culture, with awe and respect. When he walked, knowledge radiated all around. The great personalitv was, Prof Thothatri Iyengar, our teacher. At that time, 'Calculus Srinivasan who was my mathematics teacher, used to talk about Prof Thothatri Iyengar with deep respect. They had an understanding to have an integrated class by Thothatri Iyengar for first year B.Sc. (Hons) and first year B.Sc. (Physics). Thus, I had the opportunity to attend his classes, particularly on modern algebra, statistics and complex variables. When we were in the B.Sc first year, Calculus Srinivasan used to select top ten students to the Mathematics Club of St. Joseph's, who were addressed by Prof Thothatri Iyengar. I still remember, in 1952, he gave a masterly lecture on ancient mathematicians and astronomers of India. In that lecture, he introduced four great mathematicians and astronomers of India, which is still ringing in my ears. They are Aryabhata, Srinivasa Ramanujan, Brahmagupta, Bhaskaracharya. Let me discuss one.

Prof. Thothatri Iyengar explained, based on his analysis, that Aryabhata was both an astronomer and mathematician, born in

476 AD in Kusuma-pura (now called Patna). He was known to represent a summary of all Maths at that point of time. Just when he was only 23 years old, he wrote his book ARYABHATIYAM in two parts. He covered important areas like arithmetic, algebra (first ever contributor), trigonometry and of course, astronomy. He gave formulae for the areas of a triangle and a circle and attempted to give the volumes of a sphere and a pyramid. He was the first to give value of pie. He discovered that the earth takes about 365 days to orbit around the sun. Prof. Thothatri Iyengar always puts the student to take a pride in India's contribution in astronomy and mathematics and puts the students ahead. This great teacher combined his knowledge of science with his deep insight into many aspects of our civilizational heritage. Prof. Thothatri Iyengar was an example for continuously building capacities among students and putting the students well ahead in mathematical sciences. He also injected great thoughts in the minds of students and promoted nobility in thinking and action. Now I would like to discuss about the teacher who built the capacity of working together and evolution of integrated system design even during engineering student life.

D. Learning Integrated System Design

While I was studying aeronautical engineering in MIT, Chennai, (1954-57) during the third year of my course, I was assigned a project to design a low-level attack aircraft together with six other colleagues. I was given the responsibility of system design and system integration by integrating the team members. Also, I was responsible for aerodynamic and structural design of the project. The other five of my team took up the design of propulsion, control, guidance, avionics and instrumentation of the aircraft. My design teacher Prof. Srinivasan, the then Director of MIT, was our guide. He reviewed the project and declared my work to be gloomy and disappointing. He didn't lend an ear to my difficulties in bringing together data base from multiple designers. I asked for a month's time to complete the task, since I had to get the inputs from five of my colleagues without which I cannot complete the system design. Prof. Srinivasan told me "Look, young man, today is Friday afternoon. I give you three days time. If by Monday morning I don't get the configuration design, your scholarship will be stopped." I had a jolt in my life, as scholarship was my lifeline, without which I cannot continue with my studies. There was no other way out but to finish the task. My team felt the need for working together round the clock. We didn't sleep that night, working on the drawing board skipping our dinner. On Saturday, I took just an hour's break. On Sunday morning, I was near completion, when I felt someone's presence in my laboratory. It was Prof. Srinivasan studying my progress. After looking at my work, he patted and hugged me affectionately. He had words of appreciation: *"I knew I was putting you under stress and asking you to meet a difficult deadline. You have done great job in system design"*.

Through this review mechanism Prof Srinivasan, really injected the necessity of understanding the value of time by each team member and brought out the best from the system design team. I realized that if something is at stake, the human minds get ignited and the working capacity gets enhanced manifold. That's what exactly happened. This is one of the techniques of building talent. The message is that young in the organization, whatever be their specialization, be trained to systems approach and projects, which will prepare them for new products, innovation and undertaking higher organizational responsibilities. Teacher has to be a coach like Prof. Srinivasan.

Now let me talk about the capacities which are required to be built among the teachers and thereby among the students.

E. Capacity Building

Can we sow the seeds of capacity building among the students? There will be continuous innovation during the learning process. To realize this, special capacities are required to be built in education system for nurturing the students through teaching. The capacities which are required to be built are research and enquiry, creativity and innovation, use of high technology, entrepreneurial and moral leadership.

E.1. Research and enquiry: The 21st century is about the management of all the knowledge and information we have generated and the value addition we bring to it. We must give our students the skills with which they find a way through the sea of knowledge that we have created and continue with life long learning. Today, we have the ability, through technology, to really and truly teach ourselves to become the life-long learners. This is required for sustained economic development

*E.2. **Creativity and innovation***: The management of knowledge in the 21st century is beyond the capacity of a single individual. The amount of information that we have around is overwhelming. The management of knowledge therefore must move out of the realm of the individual and shift into the realm of the networked groups. The students must learn how to manage knowledge collectively. When the information is networked, the power and utility of the information grows as square as stated by Metcalfe's law. Information that is static does not grow. In the new digital economy information that is circulated creates innovation, enriches students leading to his or her contribution to national wealth.

*E.3. **Capacity to use high technology***: Every student in our colleges should learn to know how to use the latest technologies for aiding their learning process. Colleges should equip themselves with adequate computing equipment, laboratory equipment, and Internet facilities and provide an environment for the students to enhance their learning ability. In the midst of all of the technological innovations and revolutions, we cannot think that the role of the teachers will be diminished. In fact the teacher will become even more important and the whole world of education will become teacher assisted and would help in "tele-porting" the best teacher to every nook and corner of the country and propagate the knowledge. In this connection, the universities should make use of the EDUSAT (educational satellite) which has been specifically designed for making education reach the unreached. This system will be primarily for school, college and higher level of education; however it will also support non-formal education. The scope of EDUSAT programme will be realized in three phases. Along with EDUSAT, we need a multi pronged approach to tele-education.

*E.4. **A multi-pronged approach for Tele-Education***: A three-pronged approach is essential to make distance education programme viable and a successful proposition through the universal tele-education system to all remote parts of the country.

The three components may be the Connectivity, Tele-Education System and the Quality Content Generation and deployment.

E.4.1. Connectivity: EDUSAT is expected to provide one-lakh fifty thousand ground terminals in its full capacity. The other parts of the country have to be covered by providing Broadband and Wireless communication network in an integrated fashion. Terrestrial optical communication is becoming cost effective and can complement the space communication with its low cost, high bandwidth and networking capability. An integrated networked system comprising EDUSAT, Broadband and Wireless networks should provide a highway for reaching quality education to all parts of the country.

E.4.2. Tele-Education System: Once we have the connectivity, then there should be a universal tele-education system in place for making full utilization of the connectivity to bring virtual classrooms in a multi class environment with seamless two-way interaction between the teachers and students in a collaborative environment. This system should not only enable the lecture delivered from the Studio at the university to reach any remote corner but also enable a good teacher in the remote area to provide multicast information to other participants of the programme.

E.4.3. A Tele-Education Delivery System: The connectivity is through V-SATs provided by ISRO, Voice Over-IP and Internet. In this platform, the live virtual studio environment is created and it will connect a number of remote locations and provides seamless, one to many connectivity, through multicasting mode in a collaborative environment. This also provides two-way connectivity. I have used a Multimedia Studio to give a presentation and address the remote locations, where the multimedia delivery is possible and also I can interact through various collaborative tools. I can refer any informational website from Internet to all the remote locations and can also delegate the remote expert to give a lecture to all those who are connected. Next element is content generation.

E.4.4. Quality Content Generation: There are three components for education: lectures, laboratory and library. The content includes all the above three. Content can be generated in many ways. The first one is the assimilation of the subject by an expert teacher through research study of many books and articles leading to the generation of quality and creative content in a presentable format. The teacher presents in a unique and innovative way to make the content appealing and easily understandable to the students. The second form of content could be on a self-learning method by breaking down the content into a series of question answer models. Third may be from various books, which can be extracted through a digital library and presented just-in time to all the remote students. Fourth may be from Internet, where wealth of information is available. Teacher may search the information in the Internet and push the content live through the tele-education system. The faculty members assembled here can definitely make important contribution towards content generation.

E.5. Entrepreneurship: The aptitude for entrepreneurship should be cultivated right from the beginning and in the University environment. We must teach our students to take calculated risks for the sake of larger gain, but within the ethos of good business. They should also cultivate a disposition to do things right. This capacity will enable them to take up challenging tasks later.

E.6. Moral leadership: Moral leadership involves two aspects. First it requires the ability to have compelling and powerful dreams or visions of human betterment. Moral leadership requires a disposition to do the right thing and influence others also to do right things. The best way of the engineering education has to be based on "work with integrity and succeed with integrity". Is it possible?

F. Research - Teaching – Research

Good teaching emanates from Research. The teachers' love for research and their experience in research are vital for the growth of the institution. Any University is judged by the level and extent of the research work it accomplishes. This sets in a regenerative cycle of excellence. Experience of research leads to quality teaching and quality teaching imparted to the young in turn enriches the research.

In sum, *inquiry, creativity, technology, entrepreneurial and moral leadership* are the five capacities required to be built through the education process. If teachers develop in all our students these five capacities, we will produce "Autonomous Learner" a self-directed, self controlled, lifelong learner who will have the capacity to both, respect authority and at the same time is capable of questioning authority, in an appropriate manner. These are the leaders who would work together as a "Self-organizing Network" and transform any district as a prosperous district and thereby the nation.

The teachers of the modern society are, therefore, expected to fulfill the following duties:

1. They should encourage inquisitive response by showing visual examples for shaping not just students but igniting young minds for full comprehension and understanding of the concepts.
2. They should combine their knowledge of the subject with deep insight into many aspects of our heritage, injecting great thoughts in the minds of students and promoting nobility in thinking and action.
3. They should train the youth for adopting system approach and projects, which will prepare them for new products, innovation and undertaking higher organizational responsibilities.
4. They should make youth to really and truly understand how to use latest technologies to become life-long learners for sustained economic development.
5. They should invoke the confidence among the students that they can do it.

CONCLUSION

I was reading the two volumes of the book titled 'The Big and the Small' from the Microcosm to the Macrocosm written by Dr. G. Venkataraman. In this book, author establishes fascinating link between particle physics and cosmology in two volumes. I would like to share an incident narrated in the book about Sir CV Raman. Raman was in the first batch of Bharat Ratna Award winners. The award ceremony was to take place in the last week of January, soon after the Republic Day celebrations of 1954. The then President Dr. Rajendra Prasad wrote to Raman inviting him to be the personal guest in the Rashtrapati Bhavan, when Raman came to Delhi for the award ceremony. He wrote a polite letter, regretting his inability to go. Raman had a noble reason for his inability to attend the investiture ceremony. He explained to the President that he was guiding a Ph.D. student and that thesis was positively due by the last day of January. The student was valiantly trying to wrap it all up and Raman felt, he had to be by the side of the research student, see that the thesis was finished, sign the thesis as the guide and then have it submitted. Here was a scientist who gave up the pomp of a glittering ceremony associated with the highest honour, because he felt that his duty required him to be by the side of the student. It is this character that truly builds science. If all the experienced teachers develop this culture, large number of great scientists and technologists will emerge in India.

SECTION : IV – GLOBALIZATION, INNOVATION AND ENTERPRENEURSHIP

10

Globalization of Education: Threat or Opportunity—Lessons from Innovations at Gujarat University

Parimal H. Trivedi

INTRODUCTION

Trade in services was the issue first raised in the Uruguay Round of General Agreement on Trade and Tariff. This issue along with several others like intellectual property rights became very controversial to the extent that it not only took a decade to resolve them but also brought about a metamorphic change in the very structure of GATT by transforming it into the World Trade Organization. Trade in service included the education services in the new charter of WTO.

The provisions of WTO agreement on Trade in services covers trade in educational services also. India, being the original signatory of the WTO charter, is compelled to open up its educational services sector to world trade soon. Already a lot of foreign players have entered the arena. Generally the entry off the foreign players is perceived as a threat to the domestic education system. In this paper I argue that the perception of the threat is over played as the opportunities which have opened up now have neither been identified nor utilized by the education system to take full advantage of the WTO provisions. The arguments are related to trade in higher education only as the opening up of the primary and secondary level education is still at a lower rate compared to the higher education. Further I have used the example of the innovative efforts of Gujarat University to illustrate how alternative strategies can be evolved to combat the threat imposed by the opening up of this sector.

THE INDIAN HIGHER EDUCATION SYSTEM

After independence, the Indian higher education system has been governed by the University Grants Commission which has been following the recommendations of the Radhakrishnan Commission, Mudaliar Commission and the Kothari Commission. In 2005 the National Knowledge Commission has been established under the chairmanship of Shri Sam Pitroda to suggest measures to convert India into a knowledge society through its formal and informal education system. This commission has given two sets of recommendations so far. In both these sets of recommendations, several relate to higher education. But these recommendations have been criticized severely on many grounds. These recommendations may bring about a paradigm shift in the whole education system in India and may lead to a drastic change in the role being played by India in the realm of educational services as and when they are adopted. But till such time the position of India as a world level player in educational services is as follows:

Indian Role in the Trade Related to Higher Education

The role of India can be looked into from two sides. One is from the side of a service provider and the other from the side of a client for these services. The important characteristics of both these roles are outlined below.

As a Service Provider

- Indian Higher education is considerably cheaper compared to that provided by other developed countries.
- Living expenses are also comparatively low for students.
- India has a wide range of institution of higher education. The top ones being the IITs and IIMs to Universities and colleges offering courses in almost all disciplines and subjects with innovative combinations.

- The courses vary in duration and level to suit requirements of the students.
- EDCIL has been promoting these services abroad through the governmental channels.
- The regulation of higher education by UGC and other regulatory bodies ensures quality and authenticity of the degrees.
- Most of the degree courses have gained recognition for their quality in the western world.
- There are many areas such as literature, language, history, jurisprudence where India provides unique courses not available elsewhere.

As a Client

- There has always been a huge demand from India for study abroad since the formal system of higher education expanded faster in the western world along with it socio-economic development.
- The literacy rate has been rising in India so that the demand increases in volume.
- The population pyramid still being bottom heavy in India ensures a continuity of high demand for educational services in the coming decades.
- There has been a fascination for the stamp of a foreign degree which puts an additional artificial value on them, creating an artificial demand.
- The general increase in, the prosperity levels, the easy availability of educational loans has supported the increased demand.
- The active lobbying and massive advertisement campaigns have raised the aspirations of the youth for a foreign degree.

The Threat Perception

Scrutiny of various debates related to opening up of the higher education sector reveals that in India the threat perception is generally related to the client role and competition, because:

- Entry for foreign universities and other service providers will increase supply.
- This will also increase, the competition for Indian Universities and therefore weaken their monopolistic position.
- It will make the service more expensive as the state subsidy will not be available to the foreign players.
- Foreign players may generally take over with increased financial inflows and the existing institutions may become defunct.
- Western education may not fulfill the requirements of the Indian job market.
- There can be no check on quality of foreign players.

THERE HAS BEEN HARDLY ANY ATTEMPT TO IDENTIFY THE OPPORTUNITIES WHICH WILL OPEN UP WITH FREE TRADE IN SERVICE. In fact the first step should have been the identification, assessment and supplying for the global demand for higher services. Then the threats could have been over come by the utilization of the opportunities. I would like to illustrate how this can be done through the innovations made in Gujarat University, Ahmedabad. These innovations cover two diverse fields. One is related to catering of foreign demand while the other is related to catering to the domestic needs. These are described in the following two sections.

Catering to Foreign Demand

Indian universities should realize that they might be much younger compared to some of the universities existing in the western world but in spite of a younger age they have a font of knowledge unavailable in the western world. For example the knowledge of Sanskrit, Indian philosophy and religion, ayurveda, vedic 'philosophy and mathematics to name a few. Slowly the western world has woken up to the fact that traditions are not without sound philosophical and scientific basis. The propagation of the joint family system ensured social security. The festivals are scientifically related to weather cycles. The traditional religious restrictions on diets are related to nutritional requirements of the body are various stages of life and the environment. In fact a whole re-learning movement has started from a scientific study of traditions.

Realising this, the University introduced a very innovative STUDY ABROAD PROGRAM. This program has two parts. One is offering special incentives to foreign students to obtain degrees from India. In this a special collaboration has been established with EDCIL and Ministry of Human Resource Development. Through these agencies students from other developing countries like Bhutan and Afghanistan etc. are enrolled for degree and post graduate courses. THE INNOVATION HERE INVOLVES THE MARKETING OF THE SERVICES ABROAD THROUGH THE EMBASSIES.

The second part of this program is more innovative. In this part nearly 40 different courses covering Indian heritage are offered to 'foreign students. They are both credit and non-credit courses. The credit courses are designed in such a way that the students taking these courses are awarded credits in their courses by the foreign universities in which they are studying. The courses cover a very wide range beginning with Gandhian Philosophy to rural development to ecology and design to Indian Film and Music, Mehndi and Indian cookery etc. Areas like Opportunities and strategies for doing Business in India, Contexts of Indian Business Practices, Journalism and Public Relations, Tradition and design process in India are also covered in these courses. During the initial year itself three students from U.S.A. availed of this program and were amazed at the service offered by the University. This shows that with proper identification, attractive marketing and wise collaborations Indian Universities have no dearth of services which they can sell abroad.

Catering to Domestic Needs

It would be foolish to ignore the threat imposed by foreign entrants in the Indian education system. But, at the same time one should realistically look at their clientele. The foreign universities still have prohibitive charges for most of the Indian population: In India the percentage of urban and middle income population still does not cross 35 percent of the total population. It is only this and other higher groups which can afford and aspire for foreign education (even though in many cases their quality and employment potential remains dubious). Have we given sufficient thought to the rest of the 65% - the most needy and the "generally invisible to the policy makers" part of the rural population? Gujarat University decided to introduce innovative job oriented courses for them. Even when many of these courses were offered on self financed, the fee was generally within the paying capacity of the lower middle class. Some of the land mark courses being offered under this vision are related to forensic science, port management, financial and investment analysis, taxation (value added tax), financial Management, Performing Arts to name a few. The placement record of the first batches of these courses has been excellent. Thus the university has managed three objectives with this innovative exercise. One is to cater to the needs of the needy section of the society in a better manner, the second is to increase the employability of the students and the third is to generate funds for the expansion and development of the University.

CONCLUSION

This illustrative example is just the initial step in the long path of progress of the University. This case is being presented to emphasize that every University in India has the strength to withstand international competition by first of all taking care of the neediest sections of the society. Then they can start offering their unique knowledge system and base by modulating the supply through innovative courses and judicial marketing strategies abroad. One can recall that when the industrial sector was opened up, the Indian businessmen were even more apprehensive about the foreign invasion. But the phenomenal growth experienced in the industrial sector of India during the last decade would have been a pipe dream in a regulated atmosphere. Like the industries, Indian Universities have also been caged tigers and upon release from the cages of restrictions, they are afraid to venture out into the jungle. The tiger, however, never loses its bravery and nor will the Indian Universities. They will again conquer the jungle of free trade in service to bring back the glory of Nalanda and Taxila.

11

Knowledge Management—Emerging Perspectives

P.N. Singh

INTRODUCTION

Knowledge management is the hottest subject of the day. The rising tide of data can be viewed as abundant, vital and necessary resources. With enough preparation we should be able to tape into the reservoir and ride the wave by utilizing new ways to channel raw data into meaningful use. That information, in turn, then becomes the knowledge that leads to wisdom which means skill to put the knowledge to the meaningful use. When we encounter a piece of data, our first action is usually to attempt to find a way to attribute a meaning to it. We do it by associating with other things. When a pattern relation exists amidst the data and information; the pattern has the potential to represent knowledge.

Till, recently, knowledge was considered inferior to capital. However, today, knowledge is considered as value creator and knowledge management as a competitive tool. It is accepted that knowledge works as a recipe, a defined procedure to deal with a concrete and routine situation. Knowledge provides confidence in the work and it further improves capability and understanding that enables to envision us of handling different situations and anticipate implications and judge their effects. Data, information, knowledge and wisdom are interrelated Davenport & Pustak, (1998) observed. "Knowledge is a fluid mix of framed experiences, values, contextual, informations and expert insight that provides a framework and expert insight for evaluating and incorporating new experiences and information. It originates and applied in the minds of knowers. In organizations it often becomes embedded not only in documents or repositories but also in organizational routines, processes, practices and norms". Knowledge is an emerging set of organizational design and operational principles, processes and structure and application of technologies that help knowledge workers enhance their capability.

The interesting aspect of knowledge is that unlike other depreciating assets, knowledge actually appreciates and multiplies in value as more sharing occurs. Thus, it becomes the true resource of sustainable competitive advantage. According to Ducker (1970) "the basic economic source is no longer capital or natural resources. It is and will be knowledge". Knowledge creation and knowledge renewal both are very significant. Knowledge has always been an essential component of all human progress. Knowledge capital is the way an organization derives wealth from its information resources on a regular basis.

HISTORICAL

According to Malhotra (1997), knowledge that is contained in the minds of organizational members is the greatest organizational resource. Malhotra posits, therefore, that knowledge management is not only about managing knowledge assets, but also managing the interpersonal and organizational processes that act upon these assets. In a 1998 study, Malhotra further defines knowledge management as a synergistic combination of data and information processing capacity of information technologies, and the creative and innovative capacity of human beings.

Collaborative knowledge management is necessary for a company to : (i) remain competitive; (ii) adapt to a rapidly changing environment; (iii) innovative; (iv) responsive to the demand of e-business; (v) fully capitalize and develop its people; (vi) support effective relationships with suppliers, partners and customers.

De David (1997) suggests that organizational culture relevant to firm creates, shares and uses knowledge. He also suggests four ways in which organizational culture influences behaviors central to knowledge creation, sharing, and use. (i) culture and particularly subcultures shape our assumptions about what knowledge are, and, hence, what knowledge is worth managing. (ii) culture mediates the relationships between individual and organization-level knowledge. (iii) culture creates the context for social interaction that ultimately determines the value an organization derives from knowledge. (iv) culture shapes the processes by which new organizational knowledge with its accompanying uncertainties is captured, legitimated, and distributed.

Douglas Weidner (2002) states that knowledge manager integrates, connect and collect for effective knowledge process, i.e. (i) reinforce natural instincts to build trust and a culture of knowledge sharing; (ii) provide appropriate technology-enhanced collaboration tools; (iii) provide intuitive repositories for accumulating critical knowledge (iv) enrich the technology with managerial practice and business process.

Therefore, this paper gives an insight that knowledge management implementation will require collaboration and creativity leading to organizational learning, knowledge culture building, organization development and employee satisfaction.

Knowledge Management

The content of knowledge is the point of focus. Knowledge management is content management. It is also a goal driven activity as utility is apparent in a direct relationship between knowledge management and an objective or mission. It is directed to formalizing and codifying knowledge. The information technology plays here a great role. Professionals with relevant knowledge and the knowledge suppliers are asked to explicate and codify it. Knowledge management is focused on articulating and exploring knowledge. Information technology had a facilitating role in the communication among the knowledge carriers. "Knowledge is good when it is new, innovative and fertile; knowledge processes are good when they are highly interactive and dynamic and knowledge management is good when it achieves open interaction between professionals."(Batra, 2007)

Theoretically, knowledge management is seen to have the potential to influence many spheres of an organization. It refers to a systematic and explicit building renewal and application of knowledge to maximize an organization's effectiveness and return from its knowledge assets, where knowledge assets, the knowledge regarding the market, products, technologies and the human capital that an organization owns would enable its business process to generate profits. The sources of knowledge assets can be internal (e.g.; employees, documents, processes, tools etc.) or external (customers, market analysis etc.)

Organizational knowledge is a combination of tacit and explicit knowledge. Explicit knowledge includes assets such as the organization's trade mark, patents, customer profile, market intelligence etc. Tacit knowledge is deeply embedded in the minds of individual employees and the ways in which they handle a task, solve a problem and conduct management themselves. "The broad objectives of knowledge management are to be : know the knowledge assets and to leverage the internal and external expertise to develop and exploit intangible assets including technology, know how etc". (Tandon,2007). Knowledge management is to provide right knowledge, at the right time to the right person. This would enable individuals to make appropriate and informed choice based on relevant information pieced together in intelligent systems.

In today's information driven economy, organizations uncover the most opportunities and derive value from intellectual rather than physical assets. To get the most value from an organization's intellectual assets, knowledge management practioners maintain that knowledge must be shared and must serve as the foundation for collaboration. The knowledge management programme can lead to one or more of the following:

- Foster innovation by encouraging the free flow of ideas.
- Improve customer services by streamlining response time.
- Boost revenue by getting products and services to market faster.
- Better market intelligence.
- Streamline operations and reduce costs by eliminating redundant or unnecessary processes.

- Enhance employee retention rate by recognizing the value of employees knowledge and rewarding them for it thereby preventing knowledge walk outs.

Knowledge management caters to the critical issues of organizational adaptation, survival and excellence in competitive environment .Essentially, it embodies organizational process to seek synergetic effect by combining information technology, capital and innovative capacity of human beings. Knowledge management is an emerging set of processes, organizational structures, applications and technologies that air to leverage the ability of capability of capable, responsible and autonomous individuals to act quickly and effectively.

In knowledge management processes three stages are involved, viz.

(i) Knowledge Generation: It includes all activities like knowledge creation, knowledge acquisition, synthesis, transmission of knowledge and knowledge adaptation. It brings to light knowledge that is new to individuals and organizations.

(ii) Knowledge Codification: It means representation of knowledge so that it can be reused either by individuals or by an organization with the help of rules.

(iii) Knowledge Transfer: This entails movement of knowledge from one location to another. It can be transferred from one person to another or from one job to another through communication channels by accessing the site of the different experts.

Knowledge management is affected both by external and internal factors. External factors affecting knowledge management are globalization, international competition, suppliers, external factors, sophisticated customers etc. which are beyond the control of the management. Internal factors include fast changing production process, technological capability and human behavior.The biggest challenge that knowledge management vendors face is explaining what knowledge management is and how it can benefit a corporate environment.

To get their foot into the door, vendors must integrate knowledge management in corporate culture. After, the organizational culture is modified; the next challenge is to evaluate the firm's core knowledge. A third challenge is learning, how knowledge can be captured, processed and acted on. A fourth challenge is addressing the still neglected area of collaboration. A sound collaboration capability means helping company, helping company employees share documents and needed informations for all kinds of projects. The real benefit of collaboration is innovation.

The rapid advancement of knowledge exchange tools like internet, intranet and ware is setting the stage for knowledge management. The great potential of this emerging concept lies in how well we share the know-how to augment the decision making quality and capacity of the organization. To promote a knowledge management environment, companies must consider cultural, social and organizational changes as well as technological support. They must also add systems and applications in their I.T infrastructure in the interest of integration and knowledge sharing. One area that a company must address is how to manage its intellectual capital, the sum of knowledge of the human resources of the organization. Knowledge is not a technology, but an activity enabled by information technology, produced by people.

The knowledge Workers

We are living in a continuously changing world fraught with uncertainty, market fluctuations and aggressive competition Today's emerging age of knowledge economy has created a new breed of employees whose intellectual capital is the accumulated experience, commitment and potential for developing and maintaining the learning organizations. Such a breed is referred as the knowledge workers. According to one source, a knowledge worker already made up one third of U.S workforce. It is the fastest growing employment sector of wealthy countries. The driver of success in knowledge economy is knowledge. It is impressive that people can earn a living by working with some thing as intangible as knowledge. "Any one who makes a living out of creating manipulating, or disseminating knowledge is knowledge worker (Bennet, 2001)". They are the people who use their heads more than their hands to produce value. Thus, a knowledge worker is the product of experience, value, process, education and the ability to creative, innovative ideas in tune with the culture of the corporation. Managers, lawyers, system analysts, teachers, doctors, etc. are all knowledge workers. A knowledge worker must be a man of thinking skills, committed to continuous learning, innovative, creative, risk taking, decisive and action taking. They must consistently support their leaders, their peers and the organization as a whole. Related to their core competency is a sub culture of referrals and knowledge exchange.

An organization of people with ingrained commitment to improve their capacity to credit and produce and to introduce a change is called a learning organization. It is a group of people continually enhancing their capacity to create to what they want to create. The role of leader in learning organizations is more of a facilitator than a supervisor, a teacher than an order giver and designer. Learning and teaching are two faces of same coin. In teaching the focus is on knowledge transfer from the instructor to the learner. Learning should promote a new way of thinking, not just facts. Learning organizations are the breeding ground of knowledge workers.

Based on research by Natrajan & Ganesh, (2007) it has been recognized that at the heart of an organization strategy and process, is a force, which is termed as knowledge force, which is powered by the knowledge of the workers and employees. "It is this fire power that determines the growth strategy of the organization. The focus should be on creating the knowledge force and once the organization learns how to generate, and sustain this knowledge force, it starts experiencing impact". When the organization grows focus shifts from the fire power' to the processes and parameters which need to be managed, hence the subject of knowledge management becomes more relevant.

Knowledge force is to be understood as that force witch enables the organization to move forward on the strength of certain knowledge of the firm drawn from experiences, intellect, education and interactions with the market place, supported and nurtured by the entrepreneur in such a manner that the organization is conscious of industry and technology dynamics. Knowledge force refers to the force created by knowledge. The four building blocks of knowledge can be summarized as follows:

- Entrepreneurial energy
- Employee capability
- Industry orientation
- Customer orientation

It should be noted that the relevance of the above four key dimensions are with respect to IT entrepreneurships which come together to create a dynamic thrust that unleashes knowledge force. Developing versatile employees and leveraging their different capabilities in order to cope with different situational needs is a matter of pivotal importance for knowledge based organizations.

Information Sharing Systems: Defining the Future of Learning

Information system is an organized way of sharing data/ informations /ideas. In most industries like manufacturing, it is easy to observe and measure the quality of the product or the end result based on indicators, tests and observations. It is easy to control the quality of processes because every attribute of the finished product has a corresponding manufacturing process. However, in case of educational institutes it is difficult to map the attributes of the finished product to manufacturing processes. That is because the end result is the value addition to students in the form of skill, understanding, attitudes etc.

With the help of information sharing systems the quality of education may be enhanced saving a lot of time for every body. It is now easy to imagine, what kind of network applications would be required to build an information sharing system for educational institutes. Application like discussion forum blogs, on the repositories and base content management applications are a must. Information systems have been implemented in past using traditional web development/web-programming methods by resourceful universities and institutes. What is now required is a dedicated team of web-programmers, editors etc. to create web-pages and upload data in electronic format based on inputs from teachers The modern way of implementing an information system in colleges is to use a portal framework which can also provide content management facilities.

The development in information technology especially in the field of collaborative applications is going to define the way of life in educational institutes. Looking at the bigger picture, we can say that these advancements have resulted from the latest requirements of students, teachers and administrators globally. Information system can therefore, reinforce the prominence of "centers of learning" in the emerging knowledge economy.

Doz Yues & Wilson Keely (2008) observed "Building knowledge network is the call of the globalised era. The need to access skills, knowledge and capabilities means organizations must learn to draw value from research and development sites across the world. Innovation is global the way forward. The need to access the skill and capabilities is the falling number of scientific and technical students in tertiary education in the west. It means there are not the brains to meet the requirement of many industries. No where the skill gap is starker than in the aerospace industry, from which 40 percent of the current engineering staff will retire within the next five years according to the "Economist." Secondly, technology convergence has opened up new possibilities for collaboration. It is not easy task to co-ordinate and manages such diverse net works that traverse cultural as well as geographical boundaries. A key challenge is to build an integrated innovation network in which all of the constituent parts work well together with each making a valuable contribution to global product development. In an integrated network, knowledge should be shared and reused. Different communication channels are appropriate for different types of knowledge.

Managing Knowledge for Growth

In dynamically changing environment, organizations have to develop flexible strategies based on knowledge. Constant up-gradation and utilization of knowledge have become a key factor for the survival of firms in the market. In recent years organizations based on knowledge have grown like anything in the country. The organizations which successfully utilized knowledge have not only added value for their customers but their credibility has also become visible through the reduction in their cost of production. For the growth of business it becomes imperative for the government to provide enough sources of quality knowledge.

Liberalization of trade has developed an immense need for the development of knowledge for both goods and service sector for domestic and international trade purposes. The growing awareness and easy availability of services by international players can make things quite difficult for domestic service producers who may not be ready to domestic market. Knowledge may also help us in attaining high level outsourcing business from developed countries of the world.

The outsourcing business we receive from other countries at present is mainly low cost business process outsourcing and there is a tremendous scope for India entering into the area of project and management consultancy, repair and maintenance work on ships, power installations, medical equipments, pre-publishing services, research and development in various disciplines. In goods sector corporates have to find a solution for the following questions like; (a) how to respond to the technological changes taking place in the market? (b) how to attain flexibility in the product design to meet the ever growing aspirations of the customers? (c) how to improve the customer's perception of the product? (d) how to utilize the information for product improvement and organizational efficiency? These questions can be easily tackled by organization where tacit knowledge flow is smooth and updated regularly.

It is no doubt that service sector has grown a lot in recent years and it contributes 54% to the G.D.P of country. The growth of India's export of services has been the fastest in the world growing at the rate of 9% per annum since mid 1990. This growth has been mainly due to I.T. enabled services and transport which account for 50% and 30% respectively. This structural shift in the economy needs to be sustained.

Although India boasts of a big pool of educated people yet the skill crunch at home is making business organizations to look outwards. This has exposed the hollowness of the system According to Mc. Kinsey and NASSCOM within five years India will find a shortage of 1,50, 000 I.T. workers and 3,50,000 business process staff. It is mainly because most of the existing institutions in the country fail to impart industry useable knowledge to students. The suggestion of the knowledge Commission to increase the number of universities may only help us to have more quantity while as there is an immense need for developing quality. The quality needs to be developed at all levels. It looks an irony to talk of making higher education industry oriented and neglecting the primary levels.

Imparting higher education is in no way different. While government institutions in the field of higher education have little interest in improvement, private ones have started to use it for their profit motives. The dearth of good teachers, absenteeism of teachers and irrelevance of the course curriculums is the haul mark of higher education. There is no recognition of skill of a worker rather degrees are preferred for all type of jobs. This has strained the existing infrastructure and has started a mad rush for merit. There are very less chances for India to reap to much of knowledge process outsourcing with the existing nomenclature.

India could have attained more success in the knowledge market had it promoted knowledge in an organized manner. We have failed to find out new markets for our services. Currently the over concentration in a few markets has limited our scope to earn more. At present U.K. and U.S.A. are the major trading partners in our sale of services. Their combined share accounts for more than 50% of India's export of service. We have yet to get acceptance in non English speaking countries. India can achieve a remarkable position in the international sale of service only if it gets success in improving and diversifying the existing pool of knowledge in new areas of trade,. The institutions of higher learning may have to be industry friendly, need to restructure themselves with the changing times. There is an immense need for industry academia interaction.

There are currently 79,736 Indian students enrolled in colleges and universities of U.S.A. Education generated $13.4billion in export revenue for U.S.A. in 2003. The success of foreign universities can be ascribed to the failure of domestic Universities to maintain a higher standard. The need of the hour is accountability in the education sector.

CONCLUSIONS

India can not maintain a competitive edge due to low wages in the sale of its services abroad for too long, as, in the recent years nearly 25 countries have entered in the fray of BPO business and some countries bear a cheaper labor cost than we do. We may have to go for value addition in the sale of services from B.P.O. to K.P.O. We shall synergize on specialized knowledge to tap the untapped service market.

The success in service sector will develop linkage effect on the other sectors of the economy. We shall allow private participation in knowledge development under proper regulatory set up.

Foreign investment should be allowed in education sector so as to reap future benefits. It may make education sector competitive and industry oriented. The voccationalisation of education needs to be carried out at different levels to reduce the pressure on the existing institutions of higher learning.

To think of India achieving more from international trade without improving its knowledge pool at domestic level seems a distant dream.

12

Higher Education and Globalization

Panjab Singh

INTRODUCTION

Higher education in India has expanded many folds since independence. The number of universities has increased from 20 in 1947 to more than 400, colleges from 500 to 18064, teaching staff from a meagre 15,000 to about 5 lakh and student population in higher education from 1 lakh to over 112 lakh today. Many fold expansion in institutional capacity of higher education has enhanced enrolment ratio from less than 1% in 1950 to about 10% in 2007. These developments notwithstanding, it is strongly felt that there are a number of challenges that need to be addressed urgently. The foremost priority, at this juncture, appears to be enhancing access to higher education. At the same time, the enhancement in enrolment ratio has to come with equal opportunity and inclusiveness and quality education. Therefore, access, inclusiveness and quality are the key issues confronting higher education.

"Education is simply the soul of a society as it passes from one generation to another" (Chesterton, G.K.)

The problems of the Indian higher education system relate to its huge and mammoth size, providing access and equity to all, especially marginalised sections of the Indian society, with relevant and quality education and tackling resource constraints. Coupled with these are the problems of unplanned growth of institution and student enrolment.

Historically, India had very strong and internationally acclaimed system of education including higher education. In ancient India, there was strong *'Guru-Shishya' parampara* (Tradition). We also had reputed universities in ancient India like Takshashila in North, Nalanda and Vikramashila in East, Vallabhi in Kathiawad, Kanchi in South and Nadia in Bengal. The newer era of higher education started with the British initiative in the 19th century. In July 1854, Woods Despatch had proposed establishment of universities in India. Accordingly, Calcutta, Bombay and Madras Universities were established in the year 1857, which have celebrated their 150th anniversary a year ago. In 1882, the first Indian Education Commission under the Chairmanship of W.W. Hunter was established. The report dealt with indigenous education, primary education, secondary education and university education. In 1913, the Education Policy led to establishment of new universities within each province. Accordingly, the Central Hindu College was converted to Banaras Hindu University in 1916 and Mohammedan Anglo Oriental College into Aligarh Muslim University in 1920. Universities were also started at Mysore, Hyderabad and Patna. The Sergent report of 1944 was an effort to develop a national system of education in India, which suggested formation of University Grants Commission.

During the post independent period, the First Education Commission was constituted in 1948 on university education. The Commission was chaired by Dr. S. Radhakrishnan and also known as the Radhakrishnan Commission. This Commission stressed on "autonomous status of universities". In July 1964, the second Education Commission known as the Kothari Commission was appointed to establish well designed, balanced, integrated and adequate system of national education capable of making the powerful contribution to national life. The Commission emphasized on "expansion of higher education, enhancing quality of higher education and research; and use of dynamic techniques for management and organization". In 1968, the National Policy on Education was adopted based on the recommendations of the Kothari Commission, which led to the considerable expansion of education facilities all over the country. The National Policy on Education was adopted again in 1986, which was in response to the non-implementation of 1968 educational policy. This policy emphasized on "elimination of disparities, equal access to every Indian of requisite merit, enhancement in support to research and inter-disciplinary research promotion". In 1990, the Ramamurthy Committee was appointed to review the National Policy on Education 1986, which laid emphasis on quality of higher and technical education, its relevance to the needs of society and industry.

Since independence, we have progressed on many fronts, e.g., science & technology, space research, atomic energy, health care, education; but at the same time there are areas where we need to address urgently as national need, as large mass is out of the arena of development. We are the third largest higher education system in the world but only 7% of our youth are enrolled in higher education (age group of 17-24). We say that we are country of intellectuals supplying manpower to the world but 35% of the population is illiterate. We have a target of 20% enrolment in higher education by 2020, but the school dropout rate (1st to 10th) is 62.69% (some states and communities up to 90%). The economy of the country is booming, but one-fourth of the population is still below poverty line. We are ambitious to be a nuclear super power, but our human development index is 0.595, we are on 127th position in the list of 177 countries. We have got 73% population residing in rural areas, but 90% (approximately) of educational institutes are in urban areas (particularly in higher education). India's national policy says "education is social good", but many governments are withdrawing from the responsibility. Our tradition says "*Acharya Devo Bhava*", i.e., "Teacher is like God", but look to the ground reality? Our tradition says "*Maatru Devo Bhava*", i.e., "Mother is like God", but women illiteracy rate in the country is 45% (Bihar 66%).

"When you educate a man you educate an individual; when you educate a woman you educate a whole family" (Mciver, Charles D.)

With spectacular growth in higher education, India is becoming a genuine knowledge society, knowledge economy and aiming to be a global super power. This has all happened because of the growth of education in the public sector and recent initiative or participation of private sector, but there is a big question mark; who are the beneficiaries of the current education system? When we go into detailed analysis of these reports, there are serious gaps between different classes or groups of the society, different regions of the country, which is quite alarming. The issues which need attention are illiteracy rate, dropout rate in the schools (up to 10 std.), gender inequality, urban-rural divide, regional imbalance, poor-rich divide and social divide. We have to unfold each one of these factors, identify their probable reasons and their possible remedies. The number is very limited that is contributing to the national economy and internationalisation of higher and technical education or professional manpower.

It is always debated, as to whose responsibility it is to maintain the quality of education whether policy makers, administrators, universities, teachers, society or students. Needless to say, it is a joint responsibility of all the stakeholders, which needs coordinated efforts and definite commitment to improve the system. I feel that the university system should take lead as they have got pool of intellectuals with infrastructure to do research and training. We desire to be a developed country, we have to make special efforts to promote education for disadvantaged sections of the society for a balanced growth, otherwise large section of the society will be left out of social and economic growth, which will have negative impact on democratic and economic growth.

GLOBALIZATION AND EDUCATION

Globalization at the macro level is about frictionless flow of capital, services, goods and lobor across the globe. It is also about global sharing of ideas, knowledge and culture. It is about creating a shared concern and plan for global issues like poverty, AIDS and environment. Tom Friedman calls such a world a 'Flat World' while Mr. Narayan Murthy, IT giant, calls it a 'Globalized World'. At the microeconomic or firm level, it is about sourcing talent from where it is best available, producing where it is most efficient and selling where the markets are, without being constrained by national boundaries.

The primary objective of every nation is to ensure prosperity, harmony, peace, and joy comes only if abject poverty is eradicated and prosperity is ensured. Only way we can eradicate poverty in India is by creating jobs with disposable income. This is a massive task. Several estimates put the number of unemployed in India around 250 to 300 million. Every year, we are adding about 35 to 40 million new job seekers to this massive figure. This problem is exacerbated when we realize that abut 70% of these youngsters – aged between 18 and 25 – are illiterate or barely literate. As against this, the country has been able to generate hardly two to three million jobs a year. It means we are moving towards a grave situation that may become explosive. Let me add another dimension to this problem. About 92% of the jobs are in the unorganized sectors where the salaries are low and benefits are non-existent. There is a third dimension. About 65% of the population or 650 million Indians are in rural areas and their primary livelihood is from agriculture and related services that just add 26% to the GDP. Thus, we have two gigantic problems – generating employment for 35 to 40 million new entrants to the job market every year, and enhancing the per-capita income for the vast majority of 650 million Indians employed in agriculture and related sectors.

It is evident that the latter problem can only be solved by one or more of three initiatives – increasing the prices of agricultural commodities, improving the yield in agriculture and moving people from agriculture to some other sector. Increasing the prices of agricultural commodities massively is not feasible in view of low global prices of food items and the impact of such increase on the large number of poor people in the country.

The growth rate in the agriculture has gone down from 3.2% pre-1985 to about 1.9% during the current decade, making life worse for the rural folks. The production of rice and wheat, the two staple food items for Indians, has declined or remained constant between 1999 to 2005 at around 85 and 75 million tonnes, respectively. If the population grows at 2.5% per annum, the per-capita GDP in agriculture will remain the same even ten years from now. If our economy continues to grow at the current rate of 8.0% over the next ten years, and the agriculture sector grows at 2.5%

during the same period, then, in 2017, agriculture will contribute to just 16% of our GDP as against the current 26%. To get to the same per-capita GDP in agriculture as the national per-capita GDP, at the current 8% growth rate, by 2017, we have to move a whopping 100 to 120 million people from agriculture to other sectors (assuming 4 to 5 family members per earning member). Hence, we have to move at least 10 million to 12 million people a year from agriculture to other sectors for the next ten years. Add to this, the problem of 35 to 40 million people to be employed in either new jobs or better earning jobs. To achieve required growth, besides many initiatives, we have to improve the quality of education in both primary and higher education. The Indian universities and educational institutions rarely figure in global rankings. China has done a remarkable job in this area. We must liberalize the education sector like we liberalized the industrial sector in 1991. All institutions of higher learning have to become completely autonomous. There should be greater interaction with well-known universities abroad. Syllabi will have to be revised rapidly to keep pace with changes in the world. Role learning, the bane of the Indian higher education system, has to give in to problem-solving orientation. Also involve the private sector and create Public-Private Partnership (PPP) to enhance efficiency of the government. The government brings focus on public good while the private sector brings focus on efficiency, effectiveness and accountability.

"Today we enjoy a social structure which offers equal opportunity in education. It is indeed regrettably true that there is no equal opportunity to take advantage of the equal opportunity" (Stocks, Mary, Baroness).

Literacy has emerged as an important factor in growth as it influences adoption of technology, use of modern inputs like machines, IT Network, etc. Literacy will play a far more important role in a globalized world than it did in the past. If we talk of agriculture which in the future will be increasingly science-led and will require modern economic management, high return to investment on education is expected. It hardly needs to be emphasized that education would be an extremely important input for agriculture, which in view of tough competition just cannot be sustained by a target group of unskilled rural workers, however massive. Indian agriculture, as a part of the world agriculture system, has to keep pace with the fast and vastly changing technologies, new products and product varieties, expanding and complicated information systems, new market strategies, new services and so on. Tomorrow's Indian farmer will have to wear global outfit; he has to be different from himself. The role of knowledge and skill is paramount; education holds the key to all these emerging pre-requisites. The case for rural education in India could never be as strongly visualized, and pleaded for, as it is now.

These facts advocate for a system of education, which should aim at producing entrepreneurs, who would go out proudly into the world and create a multiplying economic impact, rather than look at the system to absorb them as employees. The system should aim to increase 'job creators' and not 'job seekers'. The education system should be such that it is easily accessible to masses especially in marginalized region and to the marginalized sector of the society. It should be affordable to masses, and meet the quality standards while being relevant to the society's needs besides maintaining its flexible and innovative character.

TASKS AHEAD

Today, through education, we have access not only to the knowledge of our own direct ancestors but also the accumulated experience and wisdom of people the world over. With the development of modern media, education offers both unprecedented richness of content and the capacity to deliver it. If moded delivery systems, we could utilize the opportunity to close the education gap that separates the world's most prosperous communities from their poorer cousins. The pace of India's future progress will depend to a large extent on its ability to make available the latest and most useful knowledge to vast sections of the population.

Our educational system has remained outside the expanding social and economic systems. On the contrary, it should have become a driver for creating the new social and economic system and thereafter develop a close linkage with this system. This further means that we must build a new social contract between the universities and the society. This will require an innovative approach, which is not a mere derivative of the past.

Distance education through invoking IT should eventually lead to the establishment of cyber universities imparting anytime, anywhere and anyone education. For quality education, quality teachers and faculty is a must. The teaching job may be made more attractive to encourage inflow of good faculty. Higher education, general and technical, must have links with and have relevance to all industrial and societal endeavours. A large number of centres of excellence in areas having such relevance need to be established in several of our educational institutions to meet quality manpower demands arising out of technological changes, user's needs and globalisation of economy. Demand – driven non – formal institutions in diverse areas must be encouraged. The programmes of these institutions must be linked with those of the formal educational system through credit transfers, vertical mobility, bridge courses and other mechanisms.

Institutions are the foundations of required social change and advancement of any society. Most of our research institutions have become 40-50 years old, the infrastructure, the equipments have become old and obsolete. They need immediate renovation and replacements. The process of mushrooming of institutions and entire-building needs to be curbed. Rather than horizontal expansion, we now need to consolidate and revamp the existing institutions and bring in inter-institutional partnership in order to maximize the returns from our investments in education and research. The need for organization and management (O & M) reforms in areas of human resource development, incentives and rewards for the performers, impact assessment and evaluation with inbuilt transparency, project-based budgeting, and decentralization linked with accountability are some of the critical elements associated with the future growth of the system. Hence, the enforcement of required change in the O & M system is fully justified now than ever before. Public-private sector linkages are also to be built and institutionalized faster. Similarly, institutional collaboration with the advanced research institution will have to be strengthened for required excellence in science as well as for human resource development. The Information Communication

Technology (ICT) networking at the global level will provide access to value-added information and knowledge, so critical for the advancement of science. This would demand a massive change in the existing IT culture in the system.

Excellence in science will have to be recognized through needed change in our incentive and reward system. In future, centres of excellence will have to be built around scientists and not around institutions. These centres of excellence will have to take added responsibilities for human resource development in their field of expertise. Also institutions will have to undertake an ambitious programme for HRD through careful planning and separate allocation of resources.

Change is a sign of growth. No organization that shows resistance to change can grow. Change is also a difficult process and requires commitment of not only the leader, but of the entire organization and the system. Often the process of 'change of mindset' meets with stiff internal resistance. Yet the dynamic institutions have grown through needed periodic reforms in order to meet the new challenges over time.

In 2005, CHEPS, a Dutch think-tank on higher education, proposed a range of development scenarios outlining possible alternative routes for higher education. The main themes were three: system diversity; governance; funding and quality. Three scenarios emerged from the process, named *Centralia, Octavia* and *Vitis Vinifera;* they indicate how very different could be the development paths followed in higher education. The question is not only which movement will prevail but also who will decide the course of action.

Centralia, the city of the sun, is characterised by a top-down organised system diversity; a higher education sector well controlled and funded by the public; and organisational rigidity. Control over the institution should remain in academic hands but with strong professional support in terms of management. As to the quality of education, it would be based on graduate employability and guaranteed by a central accreditation system.

Octavia, the spider-web city, is characterised by much greater organisational diversity; it shows flexibility and higher education is in constant flux – in terms of programmes and students. Emphasis is on leadership and considerable effort is being made to coordinate the relationships among the different actors involved, largely because of the importance of private-public partnerships. Quality is ensured by a web of accreditation agencies.

Vitis Vinifera, the city of traders and micro-climates, shows extreme organisational diversity, which even makes higher education difficult to characterise or classify. Private markets are allowed to have considerable influence and higher education is considered to be a private good. The education provision itself is largely web-based. Assessment of quality is mainly in the hands of the market.

CONCLUSION

At the threshold of 21st century, global changes in demography and economy have had their impact on India as well. Employment opportunity patterns are changing with the challenge of providing skilled human power, which is confident, flexible and equipped with knowledge and technical skills needed to effectively face the socio-economic realities of the new country. In nearly two decades from now, 45% of Indians would be in their twenties. This would lead to a need for trained persons who can compete at the national and global level. While outlining the concerns, it is a matter of great pride that Indian youth potential in the IT, electronics, biotechnology and financial fields has made a mark world over.

SECTION : V – RE-ENGINEERING AND REFORMS FOR GENERATION OF KNOWLEDGE CAPITAL

13

A Proposed Paradigm for Re-engineering Higher Education in India

S.M. Paul Khurana

INTRODUCTION

Entering the Portals

"Tiny feet trudging by the dusty roadside;
With bags on their backs, walking many a mile;
With school in their hearts, and stars in their eyes;
Innocent young faces, eager, dreaming, all smiles."

This touching poem captures the essence of a great revolution that has been sweeping the Indian country side: a revolution very profound ushering in an era of hope and emancipation from centuries of poverty and backwardness. The scenario is equally poignant in the moffusil towns and small cities across the length and breadth of the country with enrolment soaring in colleges and universities. These changes have very subtly been transforming the loci of socio-political power centres and redefining the economic base of the country.

The winds of global change have at the same time been transforming the form and content of our educational system. Contemporary education has become much less a function of natural endowments and more a function of technology and skills. Mother Nature and history have been relegated to a predicate status whilst technologies have come to occupy centre-stage.

The current scenario in education can perhaps best be described by paraphrasing the words of Charles Dickens, who at another place and another time said: "It is the best of times and the worst of times." In the contemporary situation it is the best of times because education has priority attention of the government, industry and public at large as never before. And it is the worst of times because the infrastructure prepared in the Nehruvian era has predictably deteriorated with poor maintenance, leaving it in the hands of unqualified politicians and unscrupulous private players. Another cause of worry is the fact that our educational system is attuning itself more with the requirements and ethos of the Western world and is developing a fundamental disconnect with the Indian countryside. However, before launching into a rigorous analysis of the contemporary educational scenario and emerging dysfunctionalism it would be pertinent to make an overview of its backdrop.

Backdrop to the Contemporary Scenario

The recorded history of education in India starts in the first millennium B.C. with Taxila and subsequently Nalanda (the first ever formal universities) that used to attract scholars from even distant lands. In ancient India the hub of the educational system were "gurukuls", a variant of the residential schools of the modern era, wherein a striking feature of both oral and written instructions was the religious base. This is in contrast to the secular underpinnings of the present day system.

The modern system of education in India has its moorings in the British era, with its pronounced emphasis on imbibing European knowledge and culture. But the Britishers never really encouraged a spirit of critical enquiry or independent thinking in our students, which is actually so vital to the advancement of knowledge.

In independent India the aspirations for education have been high since independence. Education was chosen to be the principal instrument for the country's transformation from a poor, dependent, and economically backward imperial colony into an advanced developed nation. In the longer design for this transformation that calls for economic development as well as extensive social and political change, education was charged with two major responsibilities.

First, education was to provide the manpower required for economic growth and for the efficient delivery of services such as healthcare, transportation, communication and community welfare considered basic to a developed society and to contribute to the advancement of knowledge in the manner required to place India at par with the developed world.

Second, education was to function as an instrument of equality. But it was soon recognized that these objectives were the very opposite of those in British India. So appropriate policies and facilities were instituted to gear education to the new objectives. To enable them to advance knowledge and to produce the manpower required, universities in independent India have been equipped with adequate facilities for undergraduate as well as postgraduate education, in the full range of disciplines available at universities in developed countries.

Our policy formulators have also stressed easy access to education overcoming barriers of age, caste, social, economic and geographical conditions. This is exactly where the open universities offering distance education prove their worth. There are open (and some 'closed' ones too!) universities in the country with setting up of Dr. B.R. Ambedkar Open University Hyderabad in 1982, IGNOU in 1985, etc. Apart from these, there are about 64 Universities and education institutes which are also offering correspondence courses.

Other than Universities, Institutions of National Importance like the seven IITs, six IIMs, All India Institute of Medical Science, New Delhi, Post Graduate Institute of Medical Education and Research, Chandigarh, Indian Agricultural Research Institute, New Delhi, Indian Institute of Advanced Studies, Shimla, Indian Statistical Institute, Kolkata, National Institute of Pharmaceutical Education and Research, Mohali, South Indian Languages Prachar Sabha, Chennai, and Sri Chithra Thirunala Institute of Medical Sciences and Technology, Thiruvanantapuram, have been established by acts of parliament.

Universities and many others centres of science and scholarship are, in principle, autonomous institutions. But those that were designed to be autonomous have had their autonomy progressively whittled down.

There is growing concern in our country over the erosion of autonomy in such institutions. Many people feel that there is now less autonomy in these institutions than there was in Nehru's India. The single most important impediment to the maintenance of autonomy is the flourishing of patronage that has become even mere deeply entrenched with the creation of new public institutions. The roots of patronage lie deep in Indian society and culture, but the compulsions to it should be examined and dealt with. The system has acquired so many ramifications that everyone, including the Education Secretary, complains about it, but nobody is able to do much about it except to continue their dependence for funds on the Govt. (i.e., the bureaucratic system). Hence their freedom to make rules for 'autonomous' Universities/ Institutions for internal governance has become restricted, and they have been made to fall in line with rules made by external (i.e., Govt. regulatory) agencies. When they find it hard to comply with rules in whose making they had no part, financial and other sanctions are applied by the Govt. The Government generally does not interfere directly with the constitution and functioning of autonomous institutions, but it does so indirectly through committees of distinguished academics over whose composition it keeps a close watch. This was pointed out by Prof. Andr´e Beteille while speaking on the Autonomy of Universities recently.

Further, the setting up of Private Universities by Acts of the State Vidhan Sabha has been indeed a thought provoking and educative experience. Madhya Pradesh happens to be the first State to allow the establishment of private universities in the country, with the Maharshi Mahesh Yogi Vedic Vishwavidyalaya to be followed by several others. This mushrooming was later controlled following the PIL filed by Prof. Yashpal, former Chairman, UGC. The judgment of this PIL ultimately set the standards, foundation and guidelines of the setting up of private universities in the country.

Statistically, in India, today there are 273 university-level institutions, including 52 Deemed Universities, 40 Agricultural Universities, 162 traditional universities, 33 technical, 18 medical, 3 Information Technology, 1 Journalism, 6 Law and 12 open universities, while many others are on the anvil and in the pipeline.

With so much investment both in financial muscle and intellectual prowess today, India should no longer depend on developed countries for higher education or for qualified manpower. It has the world's third largest pool of scientifically and technically trained personnel. The products of Indian higher education are accepted for employment worldwide. Students from many countries come to India for higher education. Research, which was rare in British India, is now quite well established and being recognised globally, although, no doubt, much has to be achieved on the technology frontiers and in making use of truly indigenous technology.

Contentious Issues

Until about two decades ago, there was euphoria over all this, which was perhaps justified. After all it was this very system that had produced the likes of President Abdul Kalam and the Infosys founder-Chairman Narayana Murty. They are but a few stellar examples of the thousands of bright products of our education system. The system has served both the purposes, that of providing expertise for economic development as well as of transforming the lives of those who have suffered centuries of deprivation and marginalization. It has done so by equipping them with skills and enhancing their capability for negotiating more social and political space for themselves and their progeny in independent India.

The system has of late, either on to account of design, defect, or poor maintenance, been stretched to the limit, opening fissures here and there. In order to meet the radical new aspirations of modern India as well as incorporate the continuing requirement of social change education needs intensive rethinking – or possibly a revamp.

A serious problem is that of underemployment and unemployment of graduates. This lack of educational engineering is often explained away with the statement that the economy has not grown at the desired pace and on the scale required to absorb all the manpower that the institutions of higher education produce. Yet, many positions in industry, in government administration and even, surprisingly, in educational institution lie vacant for want of suitably trained persons. This can be partly because qualifications for employment are narrow and rigidly defined. But it is mainly due to a measure of mismatch between what higher education produces and what the country needs.

Although having increased phenomenally, facilities still fall very short of demand. For some professional programs, there are more than 500 applicants per seat. The unrest this generates is so intense that in some States, the Government has to administer student admissions. To meet the demand, facilities are constantly stretched beyond capacity. As a result, the quality suffers. For instance, when classes were small teachers were able to encourage questions and stimulate interaction, in spite of teaching by the lecture method, extensively used in the country. But now as they lecture to a large number it is no longer possible. Quality is also affected by the fact that only a few students are academically motivated. Most pursue a degree not for the status it carries but because it is a required qualification for employment. Students in the professional stream take courses that are relevant to their future growth and job, and, regardless of their initial attitude, many do get deeply interested in those courses as they move on. But more than 70 percent of the students are enrolled in the basic disciplines of arts, science and commerce, in courses that have little relevance to the occupations they will eventually take up. Students are aware of this, and hence remain indifferent to their studies, i.e., they are only there to pass the time for getting a certificate/degree, and as examination- driven as their teachers.

While the quality and relevance of education thus suffers, equality does not fare any better. In fact new inequalities have emerged. Professional education has steadily grown in prestige. Among professional institutions the new apex ('star') institutions are considered to be a class apart. It is significant that the students who succeed in the competition for admission to professional courses in general, and to these institutions in particular, largely come from well-to-do educated families and superior schools. The privileges of wealth are visible in the fact that both private colleges that charge hefty fees and European, North American and Australian universities that peddle expensive courses have no dearth of students.

Another sign is that the parents who can afford to do so send their children abroad for higher education. Until recently, this happened after completion of the first degree. Now as quality declines and admission to better institutions has become highly competitive, many students are sent abroad even for the undergraduate degree .

The effort to provide equal opportunities for education is also defeated by the fact that facilities for schooling are highly uneven and unequal. Most significant is the finding that hardly 65 percent of children in the relevant age group complete primary school and that less than 30 percent complete high school.

Certainly the reservation policy has enabled the disadvantaged castes and tribes to advance significantly, in education as well as in employment. But the process has become highly politicized. For instance, the performance level of candidates admitted to reserved seats at institution such as the Indian Institute of Technology is significantly lower than the cutoff point for open admission, but attempts to bridge this gap with remedial courses are rejected as discriminatory. In the Indian Parliament, these institutions have been accused of trying to maintain international standards at the cost of national realities. And most institutions of higher education are neck-deep in litigation over reserved admission, as well as reservations in appointment to faculty and administrative positions. In the present scenario, higher education in India can hardly claim to have functioned successfully as an instrument of quality. Yet, there is visible, as well as statistical, evidence of a complete transformation of the structure of opportunities in the country for the traditionally disadvantaged castes and tribes, for women and for the classes that not very long ago had little or no access to higher education and to empowerment through education.

A thought-provoking question that arises is, should India concentrate on quality or on quantity of Education? Should we just focus on literacy rates or on having better self-confident graduates, whose knowledge is deep and practically implementable? Under the impact of Information technology, the skills needed in different occupation sectors are converging, as more and more jobs demand fundamental (generic and abstract), rather than sector-specific, skills. This widening of perspective is only possible if the Universities take cognizance of the fact and the respective Boards of Studies make remedial provisions in their curricula.

No system operates in a vacuum and our education system is no exception. Today, Indian society needs changes to its structure and it's exhaustive values to make education meet its real needs and not to ponder to what it sees is good business. Also, students in India have become mercenaries looking to cash in on educational degrees rather than learn/ do what they enjoy doing. Many take courses that lead abroad. So until society values and/ or rewards practical skills, there is not much hope for a drastic change in the Education scenario in India. What India needs in addition to the conventional pattern of education, is apprenticeships and vocational training for many skills that are needed to get its economy going and those with required skills rewarded.

It must also be realised that higher education does not operate independently but depends on the inputs of primary (now even pre-primary), middle and secondary education. Any roadmap should cover the entire range, starting from the period of childhood to that of an employed adulthood.

The Panacea

Some of the solutions are pretty obvious. We need to invest heavily not only to make our universities world-class, but also to have more accessible primary and secondary education. We also have to strike the right balance between educational democracy and an elitist view of education. Admissions to the university especially in basic sciences and highly professional courses, should be only for the most deserving and competent young persons capable of achieving something to make the country confident, and self-sufficient in newer technologies without borrowing them from the West.

It is difficult to remove the manufacturing defect. In higher education, manufacturing defects persist since its inception. Volumes have been written and discussed but without any action.

The nation needs an integrated approach to get talented and motivated teachers. The process to mold a future teacher, practices must be started after 12th, like medical, engineering, MBA profession.

We should think of two phases :

1st phase will start with young students after the 12th class.

2nd phase : All India Academic Services, which shall entail direct/lateral entries after post graduation. This will stop unqualified and scrupulous entry as teaching faculty and stop political interference.

It was a lack of vision that education planners have not so far seen the scenario of future. How did it happen that when medical, engineering, and agriculture education was being planned, higher education was left out? A common perception about higher education is that nobody gets job in the above-mentioned fields anywhere he pokes his nose in the academic field. Political pressure makes it worse. Once a person is indicted on the basis of recommendation he will 'oblige' the same source at least thirty years: this could go up to thirty generations! The Examination system becomes an instrument to award marks, positions, gold medals. The quality of Ph.D.s, the basis of entering higher education, is in question. The UGC effort of NET was waived.

To prevent malpractices in Higher Education recruitment must be sacred. For this an All-India Academic service AIAS may be introduced by the same examination body-UPSC. It should have a data bank of vacant posts. An strict audit on academic achievement should be made compulsory.

SUGGESTIONS

1. Create an All India Academic Services (AIAS).
2. Also have State Academic Services (SAS).
3. Inter University Transfer System may be implemented.
4. Like Life Award (Promotions) there should also be a Punishment System for Demotions.

Apart from the above, a general policy of education is recommended below:

I. BASIC RECOMMENDATIONS

1. Compulsory education for all up to 10th standard.
2. Free education for girls in public schools up to 10th standard.
3. Free education for those who are below poverty line up to the highest standard.
4. English needs to be introduced from Class I.
5. Reservation of seats :

(a) 50% seats should be "reserved seats" which should be offered to students considered eligible for educational upliftment by an act of parliament. These students should form a single group without any sub-division on any account. The other 50% seats should be "unreserved seats" which should be offered to students who are not eligible for any reservation.

(b) Any seat remaining vacant in any category should be allotted to student belonging to the corresponding other category.

(c) Seats should be reserved only upto the graduate courses and in polytechnics.

(d) In graduate courses 50% of "Reserved seats" and 50% of 'Un-reserved seats' should be reserved for girls.

(e) There should be no reservation of seats in

- Post graduate courses.
- Doctoral Courses.
- Professional and technical courses.
- In private schools and colleges not receiving government's grant or aid.

(f) Reservation of seats should end automatically at the end of 10 academic years, without any provision for extension or replacement by any new reservation policy.

(g) No educational institution should be permitted to be established by, or named after, or its admission restricted to any particular caste, community or religion.

II. LEVEL OF EDUCATION

1. Pre primary education : For two years
   (a) For children from 3 to 5 years of age.
   (b) Emphasis should be on 'Montessori' line of teaching.
2. Primary school education : For five years.
   (a) 1st to 5th standard.
   (b) Children should have completed 5 years of age at the time of admission in 1st standard.
   (c) Emphasis should be on teaching, reading, writing and elementary arithmetic. Basically three languages should be taught-English, Hindi and one of the other regional languages.
3. Secondary school education : For five years.
   (a) 6th to 10th standards.
   (b) Children should have passed 5th standard examination at the time of admission in 6th standard.
   (c) Emphasis should be to make students basically 'literate' and to acquire civic, moral and ethical values.
4. Intermediate College Education : For two years.
   (a) 11th and 12th standard.
   (b) Students should have passed 10th standard examination with atleast 50% marks in each subject for admission in 11th standard.
   (c) Emphasis should be to lay foundation for the future course students adopt.
5. Graduate college education : For three years.
   (a) Students should have passed 12th standard examination with atleast 50% marks for admission in 1st year graduate courses.
   (b) Emphasis should be to make students proficient in the subjects chosen by them and make them suitable and acceptable for non-professional, non-technical un-skilled jobs or careers.

6. Post graduate college education : For two (or more*) years.
   (a) 'Previous' and 'final' years.
   (b) Students should have passed final year graduate examination with atleast 60% marks for admission in the 'previous' post graduate class.
   (c) Emphasis should be to make students acquire highest and specialized knowledge in the chosen subject.
7. Doctoral courses : Minimum of three years.
   (a) Students should have passed 'Final' postgraduate examination with at least 75% marks. Admit only through a state level competition by the University.
   (b) Emphasis should be on research work, publish atleast two papers and then only submit thesis.

Poly-technic Education : For two to four years

1. Students should have got atleast 50% marks in the 10th standard examination to join any one of these courses.
2. Emphasis should be on practical training so that students acquire sound working skill and knowledge about the job they select.

Professional, Technical and Agricultural education.

1. Students should have passed intermediate examination with atleast 50% marks to join any one of these courses.
2. Length of the courses, teaching and training should be governed and supervised by the respective national councils.

III. TEACHING INSTITUTIONS

1. Montessori schools:
   (a) In the cities and towns these schools should be privately run, and situated at short distances.
   (b) In the villages there should run by the government .
2. High Schools :
   (c) These schools should be either privately run or government aided

*(as essential in certain technical subjects).

(d) Teaching should be for primary and secondary standards.

3. Intermediate colleges :

(e) These should be private or government aided in the cities.

(f) Government should open these colleges in towns only if no private or government aided college is present there.

4. Degree Colleges :

(g) These should be private, government aided, government or university colleges located in cities and towns.

(h) Teaching should be for graduate and post graduate courses.

5. Universities :-

(i) These may be private or government institutions having effective autonomy and located in cities.

(j) Teaching should be for graduate, postgraduate and doctoral courses.

6. Polytechnics :

(k) These may be private, government aided or government run institutions,

(l) These institutions may run uni-disciplinary or multi-disciplinary courses.

(m) Teaching and training should be for various types of manual jobs.

7. Professional, Technical and Agricultural Institutions :

(n) They may be private or government institutions run autonomously and recognized by the respective National council.

(o) Teaching should be for graduate, post graduate and doctoral courses.

IV. ADMISSIONS

1. In Montessori school admission should be optional, but no student should be refused admission.
2. In high schools no student should be refused admission. Each class may be divided into sections of not more than 20 to 30 students.

3. In intermediate colleges, degree colleges and universities, seats in every class should be fixed, Fresh students should be admitted with priority. Repeaters may be admitted if seats remain vacant, on the basis of higher total marks.

4. In polytechnics no student should be refused admission in any chosen course.

5. In professional, technical and agricultural institutions admission should be as per rules laid down by respective National Council.

V. EXAMINATION AND QUALIFICATION

1. Montessori education :

   (a) Teachers should regularly assess the performance of children and, if necessary, advise the parents accordingly.

   (b) A certificate may be issued to the students at the end, mentioning their over all performance as – 'Average' or 'Above average'.

2. High School education :

   (a) Promotion from 1st standard to 5th standard and from 6th to 10th standard should be given to all students. They should be asked to repeat in the same class if their attendance is less than 90%.

   (b) Final examination of 5th standard and 10th standard should be conducted by a "Board of primary and secondary education" at the state level. Students getting less than 45% marks should be asked to repeat in the same class. Students whose attendance is less than 90% should not be permitted to appear in the final exam.

   (c) A certificate should be issued to successful students at the 10th standard examination by the 'Board of Primary and secondary education' mentioning only total marks obtained by them.

3. Intermediate education :

   (a) Promotion from 11th standard to 12th standard should be based on an examination conducted at the college level with 50% pass marks in each subject.

(b) Final intermediate examination should be conducted by a "National Board of Intermediate Education" with 50% pass marks in each subject.

(c) Students who fail to obtain 50% marks in any subject should be asked to repeat both in 11th and 12th Standard.

(d) A certificate should be issued to successful students at the 12th Standard examination by the 'National Board of Intermediate Examination', mentioning the subjects they appeared in, and only total marks obtained by them. No 'division' should be allotted.

4. Graduate and post Graduate courses :

(a) Examination should be conducted by the university both for 'Previous' and 'Final' years with 50% pass marks in the graduate courses and 60% pass marks in post graduate courses.

(b) Students who fail to obtain pass marks should be asked to repeat.

(c) A 'Degree' should be awarded by the university to successful students in the final examinations, mentioning the subjects they appeared in, without giving marks obtained or any division..

5. Doctoral courses :

(a) Students should be asked to defend their thesis before three external examiners, separately, appointed by the university. Each examiner individually and confidentially should inform the university about the students as 'Satisfactorily defended the thesis' or 'could not defend the thesis satisfactorily'.

(b) A 'Degree' should be awarded to the students who defended his thesis satisfactorily in the opinion of majority of examiners.

(c) Honorary doctoral degree may be awarded by the university to a person for outstanding achievements or contributions in any field, whose name is recommended by academic council and approved by the Executive Committee. This should not be a routine but a rare event.

6. Polytechnics education :
   - (a) Promotion to higher class should be based on day to day assessment by the teachers.
   - (b) If necessary period of training may be extended.
   - (c) A 'Diploma' should be issued by the institution to the students on completion of course satisfactorily.
7. Professional, technical and agricultural education :

Examination and award of qualifications should be according to the rules laid down by respective National Councils.

VI. AWARD OF MERIT IN THE FINAL EXAMINATIONS

1. In graduate and postgraduate courses :
   - (a) Students getting more than 90% marks in any subject should be given 'Distinction' in that subject.
   - (b) Students getting more than 90% total marks should be given 'Honours'.
2. In doctoral courses :
   - (a) Examiners should be asked to give their opinion about the thesis before the students defend it. They should write confidentially whether in their opinion the thesis is 'Average' or 'Out-standing.'
   - (b) If the thesis is considered 'Out-standing' by all the three examiners, successful students should be declared as 'Passed with honours'. This should be mentioned in the degree awarded.

VII. REPEATERS

1. Repeaters in more than one subject.
   - (a) They should be asked to get registered as 'Private candidates' in their own institutions, on payment of regular fees.
   - (b) They should appear in the next regular examination in all the subjects.
2. Repeaters in one subject only.
   - (a) Repeaters in the 5th standard should be permitted to join 6th standard as regular students. They should appear

next year, and subsequently every year if necessary, only in the subject to be repeated in the 5th standard examination till they obtain atleast 45% marks in the subject. They should not be permitted to appear in 10th standard examination until they do so.

(b) From 10th standard examination to the 'Final' post graduate examination students may be given 5 grace marks if the total marks obtained are more then pass marks, failing which they should be asked to get registered as 'Private candidate' and asked to appear next year only in that subject. They should pay reasonable part of the regular fees.

3. Registered Private candidates :

   (a) Separate coaching classes and practicals should be arranged for 'Registered Private Candidates' only.

   (b) Teachers who take these coaching classes and practicals should be given reasonable extra allowance.

VIII. SCHOLARSHIPS AND GRANTS

1. State Government should award Rs. 500/- per month for one year, as merit scholarship to encourage continued studies, to the top three students passing the final examination in different graduate courses, if they join post-graduate course.
2. Each university should award Rs. 500/- per month for one year as a token of merit scholarship to the top three students passing the previous postgraduate examination, if they continue their study in final year.
3. Refundable grants should be made available by the State Government and Universities through banks, charitable public trust and such other organizations to the students in professional and technical courses.
4. Private scholarships, grants and awards should be accepted by every teaching institutions, on the terms and conditions expressed by the donors.

IX. EXTRA- CURRICULAR MATTERS

1. Primary and Secondary Schools.

   (a) Schools should arrange games and other extra-curricular activities for the all students.

   (b) The students should not be permitted to join rallies organized by social, religious or political organizations.

   (c) Mid-day meals should be provided to all students in primary standards, and to those students of secondary standard who opt for them. They should be given 'mid-day meal coupon' daily at the time of attendance. School Canteen run by a recognized social organization on 'no profit no loss' basis, should provide quality lunch packets to the students against the 'mid-day meal coupons'. To ensure lunch quality, nation/state-wide standard should be fixed and adhered to.

2. Regular students of intermediate, graduate and post graduate classes should be encouraged to form their groups to plan and execute only creative extra-curricular activities under the guidance of a senior professor.

3. Hostel accommodation should be provided only to the regular students on the basis of merit.

CONCLUSION

Education and especially higher education is a vision. A vision not just a decade or a hundred years hence but perhaps even a millennium ahead. Contemporaneity and relevance although of extreme importance in educational engineering are by themselves inadequate instruments for such a vision. These need to be supplemented with what may be called knowledge for the sake of knowledge-an effort to build mountain of theory germinating from pure subjects. The fond hope is that these dizzy heights shall be scaled at some later point in the life of our civilization, perhaps then meeting the rigours of contemporaneity and relevance. But what we need right now is visionaries who have foresight and commitment.

Acknowledgment: The author wishes to acknowledge the extra ordinary of suggestions made by Dr. M. P. Mishra which have been incorporated in the roadmap. And the help of Dr. R.K. Anand as well as Profs Ram Shankar & Uma Tripathi for editorial assistance, compilation, etc.

RELEVANT SOURCES

1. NKC Report to the Nation. 2006. (National Knowledge Commission Report, 2006. University News (Spl., issue : 45: Nov. 26-Dec. 02, 200).
2. Census of India. 2001. Govt. of India, New Delhi.

Websites:

1. www.kfa.org.
2. www.ugc.ac.in.

14

Shaping the Indian Higher Education System for Knowledge Capital

S.M. Paul Khurana and P.K. Singhal

"The object of education is to prepare the young to educate themselves throughout their lives." – **Robert Matnard Hutchins**

ABSTRACT

India has made rapid strides in the knowledge economy mainly through its Business Process Outsourcing (BPO) industry since the economic liberalization that commenced since nineties. Based on patent filing alone, Indian research and development efforts have been prolific in some key areas including Information Technology and Electronics, Pharmaceuticals and Biotechnology, and Engineering and Design. At present, nearly all the major multinational companies of the world have their research and development centers in India based on the cheap availability of skilled human resource here. India's share as a service provider to the world is over 25% of the offshore service markets. India's ambition to emerge as a hub for research and development and maintain its leadership in BPO will depend upon the adequate availability of highly skilled man power and its faster transition from business process outsourcing to knowledge process outsourcing. This requires new paradigm shifts in management strategies of our education system as well as massive investment in infrastructure and faculty requirements. There is a need for a clear focus of specialized institutions at tertiary level of education to develop and provide domain expertise in global practices and services.

INTRODUCTION

India has developed one of largest education system in the world with over 400 universities, 20,500 colleges and 0.5 million teachers providing enrollment to nearly 12 million students (Thorat, 2008). Despite a rapid growth in the Indian higher education system during the recent times, we still cover only 10% of the relevant age-group population (18 to 23 year age group) against an average of 40 to 50% in the developed societies. As high as 80% of youths graduating from our institutions is not employable (Dhaka, 2007). None of our institutions figures among the top 100 institutions of the world according to a recent survey (Times Higher Education – QS World University Ranking Survey, 2008). Most of our institutions suffer from serious significant shortfalls of the qualified and skilled faculty (Chadha et al., 2008). The ongoing mission of the Indian Government to enhance enrollment to 15% by 2015 may be severely limited on account of short availability of skilled faculty alone. Most of our institutions of higher education including the professional ones have developed a great disconnect with the market and social requirements of the community. The gap between our universities and those in the outside world is also widening at a brisk pace. There is a pervading perception that our institutions are producing the graduates which the market hardly requires and what the market requires for its expansion the universities hardly produce. Such a scenario, if not corrected in time, may force us to lose the competitive edge in becoming the global economic power vis-à-vis other developing countries.

The present Indian higher education system tailored mainly by Lord Macaulay over a century back is afflicted with serious malaises in addition to being increasingly irrelevant to the needs of the emerging global knowledge society. The major mode of imparting of higher education in most of our colleges and universities including the professional ones is still based on rote (repetitive) learning and memorization rather than development of critical skills through problem solving and conflict resolution. Most of our graduates lack confidence and soft professional skills that further aggravate the problem of unemployment. Such practices hardly encourage creativity and innovation among the target group who over the time has become adapted to pass the examination based solely on memorization to obtain their degrees. As a result, the certification system of our universities has lost its credibility in the sense that bulks of our graduates are hardly competent and qualified for the job profiles relevant to their degrees. This has led to plethora of tests certifying the knowledge and skills of the youth in order to find suitable persons for a job. This has significantly dented the credibility of university degrees and made them increasingly irrelevant for the employers, who in turn are required to make massive investments in making our graduates competent to handle a diverse array of jobs. Further, the Indian Universities have been suffering mainly on account of severe resource crunch due to larger allocation of public money for primary education, wider expectations of the society for highly subsidized higher education, and deteriorating quality standards due to exodus of excellent human resource to the industry. The rigid control of Indian institutions of higher education by statutory legislations and its widespread centralization are only deepening the rot. There is an urgent need to reform this crumbling higher education system to regain the credibility among the market and society and to emerge as a hub of global knowledge capital.

The Designing of Curricula

"I never teach my pupil, I only attempt to provide the conditions in which they can learn." **– Albert Einstein**

Under the current regime of global society, a student would like to pursue a learning environment that provides him knowledge and skills relevant for a rewarding career. This may mean that the courses and programmes must keep pace with the developments in their respective fields in a facilitative learning environment well supported with facilities. The student should be allowed to pursue a discipline of his interest together with the flexibility of changing his preferences from one programme of study to another with relative ease. A domain based credit system can be designed based on the core and elective courses. The core courses should be confined to a particular discipline whereas the electives can be selected from an array of related diverse disciplines of the domain. Such a system can be made modular with multiple credits and exits. The student should be provided a complete independence in selection of elective courses. The student should be thoroughly exposed to practical and theoretical concepts. The personality and skill development components should be integrated with such a degree system. The student must be empowered with such capacities as analysis with vigor, critical thinking and problem solving, and planning things on the global scale. In addition, the student should be imparted with necessary job (soft) skills such as articulation and communication, leadership and team work, and branding that should promote entrepreneurship and innovativeness in him. The award of the degree should be based on earning of the minimum credits by the students in a stipulated period of time. A higher credit score or exceptional performance should entail award of honours degree to the student. For example, a domain of biotechnology would comprise core courses of biology, chemical technology and informatics, and the electives from related disciplines of law, management, mathematics, political science and sociology.

The designing of curricula needs to be assigned solely to the stakeholders, i.e., academia in synergy with prospective job providers. The curriculum should be designed based on the conceptual framework, application oriented skills and domain exigencies, facilitating an integration of our degrees with the global ones. Such a curriculum should be able to cater to the needs of the market as well as society and satisfy job aspirations of the student. The instruction programme should facilitate generation of enquiry, new ideas, development of innovative minds and excellence in manning of private and public services. The teacher should have autonomy to decide the best mode(s) of instructions and assessment in order to achieve the above-mentioned objectives. This system envisages a unique degree programme for a university or college, doing away with the necessary evils of centralization and uniformity. This may require diverse faculty, some of which are expert in the hard skills of the course while the others are expert in the soft skills.

The Faculty Development

There are significant gaps between Indian universities and

those outside the world in terms of quality global standards, as is evident from the recent Quality Standards Survey of the World universities released in 2008. A major shortfall in this direction is the inability of our institutions to attract and retain the qualified and trained faculty. A sizeable portion of highly educated and professionally qualified manpower is increasingly becoming a part of the corporate sector both in highly lucrative segments of the domestic and international markets. It is this population of the educated youth which is best qualified to be faculty in our universities and colleges. But the packages offered by the corporate sector are extremely attractive vis-à-vis those offered by our institutions of higher learning, discouraging the brilliant and talented youth to opt for teaching as a viable career. This is true for institutions in central, state as well as private sectors. This has led to a dearth of qualified faculty in higher education. According to a recent survey by the Pay Review Committee based on a sample of 47 universities and 1401 colleges, representing respectively 11% of the universities and 7% of the colleges in the country, conducted during April to July 2008 (Chadha et al., 2008), 58% of the sanctioned positions of faculty at the state University level and 41% of those at the college level are lying unfilled in the country. In our 400 odd universities, on average, there are 50-100 vacancies, making a shortfall of 20,000 teachers. Further in order to enhance enrollment during the XI plan period, the central government is starting nearly 100 institutions, which may require at least 10,000 teachers. If we include colleges in these estimates, the shortage of teachers may stagger to a whopping figure of 50,000. The institution of part-time, ad hoc, guest or contractual teachers has started proliferating to compensate for this shortfall, which is further damaging the quality of teaching in both basic and professional institutions.

The shortage of qualified and skilled teachers can itself become a major impediment in realization of our dream of making India a major hub of research and development and knowledge super power by 2020. This may also cripple the Indian endeavor of its transition from *business process outsourcing* to *knowledge process outsourcing*, which is so vital in making it a *knowledge super power*. We have to devise an effective strategy to plug this hole through major improvements in pay structure and service conditions of faculty.

1. We must attract and retain qualified and trained faculty of high order to impart creativity, entrepreneurship and innovativeness among the pupil.
2. The faculty must be granted autonomy in designing the curricula and modes of students' assessment to maintain their creativity, enterprise and motivation.
3. The governments should retreat from syllabus design and instead focus on monitorial role.
4. We must invest substantially in quality research at our higher education institutions to make a mark worldwide and to satiate professional hunger of the qualified faculty.
5. The institutions can liaise with the industry in creation of novel ideas, products and processes wherein faculty and students are active partners.
6. An active participation of teachers in research and outreach programmes should enable them to be continuously updated with the latest developments in their disciplines. This will remove to some extent the need of teacher training programmes as is being practiced today by AICTE and UGC through faculty development programmes: e.g., orientation/ refresher courses, etc.

This strategy can make the teaching career a rewarding and satisfying option for our brilliantly educated youth in direct competition with the corporate sector. This can also rapidly restore credibility of the universities for a renewed engagement with the community, improve employability of the trained youth, and make the institutions self-sustainable through additional generation of revenues. Such a synergy among the administrators, students, teachers and industry can vastly promote generation of knowledge capital catalyzing the regional and national development.

The Coverage Expansion

India, despite being one of the largest higher education systems in the World, is able to provide enrollment only to 12 million youths, which covers hardly 10% of the relevant age-group population in contrast to 36.5%, 54.6%, 11.3% and 23.2% coverage in the countries of transition, developed, developing states and the world, respectively. Most of our colleges and universities, and other institutions of advanced research, are located in the urban areas as against two-third of our population located in the villages where hardly one-third of educational institutes are situated. Further, most of the rural institutions are even devoid of proper infrastructure and enough teachers and other necessities for basic teaching. The human resource, including those from rural background, trained in the higher education predominantly under urban ambience, is not willing to use its expertise in imparting the education and training to the rural youth. There are widespread disparities between genders, among inter-social groups and across geographical locations throughout the country. A country of billion people requires approximately fifty million seats in the University system. We need to at least triple the students' enrollment in our universities and substantially improve quality of higher education in the next 10 or 15 years. We need a cohesive futuristic plan to achieve this goal by the state and central governments. This may imply that India should have a minimum of 1200 universities and 50,000 colleges including the existing ones by 2020. At present, there is a clear North-South demographic divide that has political consequences against the dream of making India a developed nation by the year 2020. India, thus, has an arduous task of investing huge capital for upgradation of infrastructure in the existing institutions. It is also required to create new colleges and universities to fulfill the aspirations of bulk of our youths. This can hardly be afforded by the nation today in view of an acute shortage of public resources. Moreover, the widespread illiteracy in the country itself demands a much higher allocation of the public resources to the primary and secondary education sectors. Need not to emphasize that they depend greatly on higher education for teachers. In fact, both higher and school educations are complimentary and supplementary to each other.

The formal system of higher education is highly capital intensive because it is class-based and can handle only a limited number of students per teacher at a time. The increasing number of students in conjunction with declining number of teachers is making it rather difficult to provide personalized education to students in our formal system. The non-formal system of open and distance education, introduced to supplement the formal system of class-room teaching, is less expensive than the formal system since it removes the requirement of an optimal student : teacher ratio and the handicap of limited geographical reach. But it also fails to deliver personalized education to the pupil. These two modes of education have introduced new methods and practices of common syllabi, uniform examinations and common achievement levels for earning degrees with a defined grade. These follow the factory model of mass education and are hardly amenable in promotion of competency and soft skill levels of the degree holders that are sole requirements of the emerging knowledge economy. New strategies are required to increase the coverage, offer ready access to a large number of aspiring learners, reduce the costs and time of the higher coverage, and to provide an *Anybody – Anytime – Anywhere* education model. We need a paradigm shift in higher education from traditional modes of classroom and open and distance education to revolutionary modes such as electronic education or teaching (e-education) and e-learning. The latter can facilitate a comprehensive coverage and mass personalization of quality education in short time and at cheap costs by employing the convergent tools of Information and Communication Technologies (ICT). This can also obviate the geographical limitations of the traditional modes.

The e-learning is an on-line interactive learning programme employing latest web or satellite tools capable of multicasting through data, video and voice delivery of contents to the learners. The major trend setting ICT tools that can facilitate personalized interaction between teachers and learners are broadband and mobile internet, grid network architecture, software and convergence of various modes. The framework and infrastructure required for e-learning are listed below:

1. **Network with latest hardware and technologies** providing network access to anyone, anytime and anywhere,

2. **Software tools and techniques** enabling creation of databases and information flows,
3. **Digital contents on a knowledge grid** facilitating curricula of high quality, relevance and utility to both teachers and learners,
4. **Education delivery system** ensuring developmental and quality relevance for individuals, institutions and community, and
5. **Quality assurance and certification mechanisms** incorporating the prescribed quality standards of e-learning.

The strategy should hinge on creation of national and regional e-education networks with the defined framework and infrastructure by developing suitable models to address problems of disadvantages and disparities. India has recently started experimenting with such networks through 'EDUSAT' and limited transmission of web-casts and web-conferences by IITs and IIMs. The teachers, experts, community leaders and industry captains should be promoted to use these networks in evolution of various developmental models. This can also establish close linkages between higher education, society and economy, which may be directly connected to economic, employment and sustainable development agendas of the nation.

We may think of establishing "**cyber**" or "**virtual**" universities as virtual organizations vis-à-vis standalone traditional institutions forming consortia of member institutions on local, regional or national levels with a focus on delivery of quality education of global standards. Such universities should optimally integrate cutting-edge ICT applications in their day-to-day functions to create content databases for real time availability and updating the learners, partners and teachers. These should also empower the member institutions to survive the competition from the mega international players in this era of global societies. The concept of virtual university is, therefore, a bold and engaging vision statement to enable the consortia members to be leaders of quality tertiary education within a short span of time at much cheaper cost. The relevance and success of such a concept will be governed by the abilities of consortium members to:

1. Plan the innovative programmes,
2. Develop the required quality contents,
3. Ensure efficient delivery of such contents through reliable ICT platforms,
4. Satisfy various needs of the diverse group of students,
5. Provide support services to learners, and
6. Synergize with conventional on-campus and off-campus learning programmes.

The Management Strategies

Most institutions of higher education in India are being controlled in one form or other through government legislations that have remained largely unchanged for the past century and hardly support creativity and innovation not only among the students but in teachers too. Only 10% of India's 18 to 23 year age group avails higher education mainly because of capacity constraints. Most of our graduates (as high as 80%) remain unemployed simply because they lack required knowledge and effective marketing of their capacities and skills. The Indian stride in maintaining leadership in areas of *business process outsourcing* and *knowledge process outsourcing* would be severely limited in future due to lack of quality skilled manpower. In order to retrieve this dismal situation, the Indian higher education system needs to be deregulated together with optimization of the installed capacity. The institutions of higher learning, therefore, need to be reengineered and reformed to regain its credibility and restore its signaling system. This requires a paradigm shift in our education system that can promote competitiveness, creativity and globalization of our human resource. The Indian higher education system should provide a platform for gradual integration of its degrees with the best available in the world. Massive investments are required in creation of new institutions equipped with world-class learning environment, which can hardly be afforded by the nation today. Therefore, private initiatives in providing higher education need to be encouraged in a big way without the evils of licensing and 'bureaucratic' regulation. Autonomous accreditation institutions without government control can take effective care of quality standards in private and public institutions.

In the current regime of ICT revolution characterized by exponential expansion of information and knowledge, identification and utilization of creativity is of paramount importance in effective management of institutions of higher education. This regime also requires the institutions to cultivate students and teachers with ability, competence, confidence and vision for being successful in their life. It is the creativity that facilitates generation of new ideas and innovative products in any institution. Creativity encourages the pupil and faculty to think beyond the existing boundaries, to rely upon imagination, to break away from conventional ideas, and to formulate alternative strategies and solutions. Creativity in individual is promoted when there is an efficient transfer of knowledge that in turn fosters creativity in an institution. Innovation is the process of translating new creative ideas into tangible results with social impact. In achieving higher levels of development, the knowledge strategies hinge critically on entrepreneurship and innovation towards creation of high value-added products and processes. Innovative approaches can substantially reduce costs of manufacturing the novel products and processes, raising revenue and profitability for better sustenance of institutions of higher learning. Thus, the universities and colleges involved in knowledge generation through creative and innovative minds can synergize with the industry in formulation of novel products and processes and providing their easy access to the society. Such a synergy will not only help in improving the job prospects of our graduates and finances of our institutions but will also improve the economy and living standards of our society by reaping the fruits of the knowledge economy. If India has to achieve global leadership, it has to create an environment of innovation and ensure speedy transfer of products from laboratory to the market (Chandrashekhar, 2008).

The effective management of our institutions of tertiary education including the professional ones should incorporate basic tenets of knowledge such as *know what, know why, know how, know who* and *know when. Know-what* refers to knowledge of facts, i.e., it refers to basic structure or working of an organization, ingredient of a product, etc. Access to this type of knowledge is always with those who are connected with organization or process and very little of this knowledge is perfectly public. Therefore, the user has to invest in building absorptive capacity for effective utilization of this knowledge. *Know-why* refers to knowledge about principles and laws, i.e., it refers to principles of a process like working of nature or human brain. Scientific work aims at theoretical model of know-why type of knowledge and some of this work is placed in the public domain. Still it does not provide an easy public access and therefore enormous investment in learning is required for obtaining such information. *Know-how* refers to skills, i.e., the ability to do something. It refers to skills of a scientist or an artisan for performing a specialized task. These are rooted in experience-based learning that leads to use of skills in problem solving. This knowledge can provide an effective medium for obtaining pertinent facts. *Know-who* refers to those persons who know what and what to do, i.e., it refers to communication with people with proven expertise. Such experts are the most important for building a composite knowledge base in development of multi-tasking products and processes. Such people can help in translation of incomprehensible. *Know-when* refers to one's ability to time an action and to foresee the incomprehensible ahead of time. This knowledge is gained through in-depth and intimate knowledge about a process or a system. This knowledge facilitates thinking out of the box based on gut feeling or intuition. The people bestowed with such knowledge may be responsible for a high degree of entrepreneurship and innovation in any institution.

The Quality Assurance

"We generate our own environment, we get exactly what we deserve. How can we resent a life we have created ourselves?"

–Richard Bach

The massive expansion has made Indian higher education a complex phenomenon since a diverse array of institutions and providers with different missions and visions are involved in widely different locations. The institutions include traditional universities, technical institutes, polytechnics, open and distance education universities and community colleges. The education providers are also a diverse lot such as central and state governments, private amateurs and entrepreneurs, non-profit organizations, and minority as well as religious bodies. The quality and relevance of many of these institutions has recently come under greater public scrutiny in terms of their outcome, especially the employability of its graduates and quantum of their contribution to creativity and innovations. There is a growing skepticism in the society about the credibility of degrees being awarded by our institutions of higher education and especially for their greater disconnect with the market and social expectations. Since India is an active partner in globalization of higher education as a signatory to GATT and WTO agreements, the international rankings and internationally acceptable accreditation standards are also becoming major issues engaging the attention of the planners and policy makers. Quality of higher education has thus become a major concern for one and all the stake holders.

India has developed formal mechanisms of assessing the quality of higher education in the last two decades mainly through establishment of such autonomous accreditation agencies as National Assessment and Accreditation Council under the control of University Grants Commission for basic education and National Board of Accreditation under the control of All India Council for Technical Education for professional education. The emphasis of quality management in Indian higher education by these mechanisms is still based on the processes, ensuring that the institutions must meet their stated goals. However, the rapid globalization of our society and economy demands that the emphasis should shift from the processes to the outcomes, which may require the institution to deliver what is expected from it in terms of quality standards of its outputs including competencies and skills of its trained youths. This may also require measurement of outputs and standards across the national system of higher education. Quality measurements must encompass the two major goals of higher education in the present context, which are the supply of knowledge workers enabling the country to participate in the global knowledge economy and the provisioning of the ways and means for sustainable development of the society at local, regional and national levels preserving its culture and values.

CONCLUSION

The changing landscape of higher education requires greater initiatives and openness, innovation, and experimentation. The management of higher education should incorporate concepts of ***Know What, Know Who, Know Why, Know-how*** and ***Know When.*** It is only with the restoration of the first rate teaching and learning experiences linked to skills required by the market and the society that our graduates will acquire decent jobs and the university itself will regain new dignity and relevance in the community. A dynamic and vibrant academic environment can easily foster generation of novel ideas by challenging the orthodoxy, thinking out of the box and exploitation of the hidden territories. We have to understand that diversity of thought, freedom of expression and crossing the forbidden boundaries are the major drivers of the knowledge economy in the world. This is now a well established axiom that centralization and uniformity both are arch enemies of creativity and excellence. Autonomy, therefore, can not be a privilege that we grant to academics, it is rather the very basis of a vibrant university life. We have to learn fast that teamwork and multitasking are the new determinants of value addition in products and processes. We must strive to hinge on the knowledge strategies that promote generation of new and high value-added products and processes, entailing huge revenues with high profitability, rather than on our traditional approach of adapting to foreign technologies in enhancement of our domestic productivity. A determined and cohesive plan of action with a holistic vision and integration of all the stakeholders can facilitate our transformation from a *knowledge society* to *knowledge economy*. There are many recent success stories of such a transformation happening in India that can provide enough confidence and trust for such an initiative. India is bestowed with 550 million odd people below the age of 25 years waiting to be manicured and molded to generate the knowledge capital. We only need to take them ahead with a defined and revolutionary vision in making our nation a super knowledge power in the next 20 years by believing in Fritjof Capra's Phrase – ***"Think globally, act locally"***

REFERENCES

1. Chadha, G.K., S. Bhushan and V. Murlidhar. 2008. Teachers in universities and colleges – current status regarding availability and service conditions. In Higher Education in India: issues related to Expansion, Inclusiveness, Quality and Finance. UGC Report, University Grants Commission, New Delhi. pp. 202-213.
2. Chandrashekar, T.K. 2008. Brain drain and innovation – Convocation Address. University news 46(10): 14-16.
3. Dhaka, M.S. 2007. Beyond the prescribed curriculum. University News 45(51): 4-9.
4. Thorat, S. 2008. Emerging issues in higher education – approach and strategy of 11th plan. In Higher Education in India: issues related to Expansion, Inclusiveness, Quality and Finance. UGC Report, University Grants Commission, New Delhi. pp. 1-26.
5. Times Higher Education – QS-World University Rankings 2008. QS Quacquarelli Symonds Ltd., 9 October 2008.

SECTION : VI – STRATEGIC ALLIANCE BETWEEN ACADEMIA AND INDUSTRY

15

Strategic Alliance between Academia and Industry-A Review of Current Thinking

Anjana Daiboo, Brij Kishore Baguant and I. Fagoonee

INTRODUCTION

Strategic Alliances are becoming more and more prominent in the global economy. A Strategic Alliance is "an agreement between firms to do business together in ways that go beyond normal company-to-company dealings, but fall short of a merger or a full partnership". The greatest change in corporate culture, and the way business is conducted, may be the accelerating growth of relationships based not on ownership, but on partnership. The potential of strategic alliances is enormous. If implemented correctly, some authors claim that they can dramatically improve an organisation's operations and competitiveness. Companies are forming alliances to obtain technology, to gain access to specific markets, to reduce financial and political risk, and achieve or ensure competitive advantage.

Strategic alliances have been formed more recently between business corporations and universities with the intent of mainly funding joint research programs in exchange for options on the results of the research that might solve their practical business problems strategic alliances between corporations and academic institutions are worth studying for four key reasons; first, these alliances are growing in significance in terms of producing various patents, prototypes, and licenses through their research projects.

They are also important from the standpoint of global competitiveness and increasing demand for innovation in products and processes. The other reason is their increasing vitality in serving as a stepping-stone for a more complex collaboration that involves multiple firms, universities and other research centres. These alliances are also playing an important role in the national R&D policy, and affect the distribution of resources considerably.

The perspective of the University as a key contributor to wealth generation and economic development has increased in recent decades. Academic research has become "endogenised and integrated into the economic cycle of innovation and growth". Within the current knowledge based economy, the University acts as both "a human capital provider and a seed-bed for new firms" and innovation. As a consequence, governments are encouraging the development of the "entrepreneurial university" through policies designed to promote and sustain university-industry-government interaction in order to produce graduates with skills that would increase employability and productivity the soonest possible upon joining their workplace. Skills development, employability, development of an entrepreneurial culture and social enterprise are becoming the key driving factors in nurturing such partnerships and in promoting a win-win situation.

The extent and nature of industry-academia collaborations have increased in size and complexity. As scientific questions become more complex, securing government funds to carry out large-scale collaborative and interdisciplinary research needed to answer them is difficult. The commonest and most important academic/industry relationships are :

(i) research relationships, in which industries support university-based research through grants or contracts;

(ii) consulting relationships, in which industries compensate universities or members of their community in exchange for advice or information

(iii) patenting or licensing relationships, in which industries obtain the rights to commercialise intellectual property owned by Universities, by either purchasing or licensing university patents;

(iv) equity relationships, in which members of the University community or academic institutions themselves own substantial equity positions in new companies;

(v) training relationships, in which industries support the research or educational expenses of doctoral or postdoctoral trainees, or contract with universities to provide training to industry employees.

However, terms like 'Partnership', 'Collaboration' and 'Network' have multiple meanings, developed in complex environments, at various levels –individual, group, department, institution, sector and country. The form of partnership depends on the institution's historical legacy, research capacity, institutional capacity as well as its financial base. For example, traditional forms of partnerships are still prevailing in South African institutions (Kruss, 2005) and they include:

- Donation, one of the oldest forms of partnership, typically in the form of the endowment of a chair or building;
- Sponsorship, with postgraduate student research funding as a core focus, given the imperative for industry to respond to socio-economic development needs in the 'new South Africa' and to strengthen its corporate social responsibility portfolios.

In these forms of partnership, the relationship between Higher Education and Industry is primarily limited to a financial one, and higher education is left free to continue with its intellectual projects, with few conditions imposed.

According to Dooley and Kirk (2007), in order for University and Industry to establish and sustain collaboration, they must gain mutual benefit from the interactions. The benefits from a University perspective of collaborative research with the industrial partners include the following:

- Access to sources of research funding in addition to their traditional public sources. This allows the managers of research centres to deepen their competencies and increase the capacity of research undertaken. It also provides increased stability for retaining research staff by "bridging" gaps between public funding calls.
- Increased access to proprietary technology held by industry that facilitates the discovery process. This technology can take the form of process equipment that increases capacity or speeds up the discovery time or materials such as chemicals and compound libraries developed by industry.
- Enhanced status when competing for publicly funded research due to ability to demonstrate channels by which research output can be disseminated effectively to the public and contribute to the economic development of the country. The importance of the ability for University to be able to demonstrate lies in the fact since public funding in the UK has become dependent on the perception of whether it will make a direct contribution to the economy.
- Faster feedback loops relating to the output of the University's discovery science.

When examining the industry benefit derived through University-Industry collaboration, the key drivers include:

- Access to base scientific competence built up within the University through public research funding. This University competence is often world-class in standard and within a niche area of science where the industry partner may be weak. This is particularly true in relation to the biotechnology sector, where the complexity of the innovation process makes it increasingly difficult for any organization to possess all the necessary competencies.
- Access to knowledge that has been developed within the research centre through decades of publicly funded research.
- Access to world-class academics who are both scientifically and industrially aware of the state of the art.

- Acquire competitive advantage by gaining access to better leads through faster channels than their competitors, thereby enhancing the product development process.
- Access to rich sources of highly skilled researchers. Often collaborative research with university can be more cost-effective since universities may already have the infrastructure in place from research activities.

While there are clear benefits for both parties to interact, there are also significant challenges that must be overcome. Although there is evidence to indicate the power of university-industry collaborations, "the intensity of these relationships and the tangible outcomes generally lags behind". These challenges include:

- The differing cultures of the organisations can impede success. The two sectors operate on different timescales, have different objectives to fulfil and often have different value systems (Abebe *et al.*, 2005). Finding the appropriate balance that satisfies both stakeholders is the biggest challenge to be faced.
- Another challenge is the conflicting desire of academia to publish and industry to maintain secrecy to secure intellectual property rights and maintain competitive advantage.
- The issues relating to ownership of IP and the division of revenue amongst the parties are often an area of strong debate among collaborators. Disagreements are common in this area, with industry claiming that IP from universities is often over-priced and ignores the risks industry is exposed to while commercialising it. Universities fear that Industry may steal their discoveries and generate revenue streams that rightly belong to the University. Only through defined processes and trust can this challenge be overcome.
- Organisations must adapt their strategies in response to their external environment. These changes can result in the level of interaction between University and Industry either increasing or decreasing in importance. Since much of the

academic research is long-term in nature instability in industry support can result in difficulties for the University in planning for the future.

Moreover, as stated by Kruss (2005), a single institution is likely to have a range of partnership forms co-existing in different Faculties and departments, or even in a research centre, to meet distinct purposes. For instance, a research unit may have a core funding from a Science Council supplemented by sponsorship to fund postgraduate students and a range of consultancies to meet specific financial requirements. However, each form of partnership has specific implications. So, for instance, consultancies are favoured as a means of staff incentive and retention, as well as a means of initially drawing in potential industry partners. On the downside, consultancies have a potentially negative impact on the research and teaching functions of academic centres and departments in that they draw away the focus and energies of academic staff into projects for their own private gain. Similar tensions are inherent in the contract forms of partnership which have become critical to institutional income. The potential restrictions on intellectual property imposed by industry partners, particularly with respect to peer-reviewed journal publication and postgraduate theses, can impact negatively on an institution's research productivity and reputation.

The basic collaboration process between academia and industry usually starts with each party identifying what can possibly be acquired from the alliance and the potential needs of the other party. It then proceeds to form a joint working group that basically develops the mission and organisation of the strategic alliance. The critical step then will be to implement the collaboration proposal and evaluating the major activities and outputs. According to Dooley and Kirk (2007), companies whose competitive advantage depends on exploiting advanced technologies must establish efficient flows of science discoveries into their R&D pipelines and these are pursued by University research centres. The rate of new knowledge creation by research centres depends on a number of factors (Dooley and Kirk, 2007) which include:

- The focus of the funded research must be of sufficient intellectual challenge and scope. This engages academics since it offers the potential for breakthrough discoveries which may lead to publication material.
- The correlation between the area of research and the competencies of the research centre undertaking the research. The presence of a large body of informing knowledge will provide a platform for the research trajectory. The presence of leading experts and infrastructure also affects the scale of the research facilitating new knowledge development.
- The research has to be of sufficient priority for all stakeholders to ensure that necessary resources are available. Similarly, it is important that the collaborative research undertaken between university and industry is viewed as worthwhile by public funding agencies, otherwise there is a risk that public funding of the research centre will decrease, thus damaging its research capacity.

The second element influencing the capability of the innovation process is how to enhance the speed of knowledge transfer and exploitation. The first factor affecting the rate of knowledge transfer will relate to the relationship that exists between the two parties. Where close relations have been established over a long period of time, there is a greater level of trust and openness between researchers relative to sharing research outputs. Key individuals need to exist within the University to champion University-Industry partnership and reduce institutional barriers that impede effective knowledge exchange. This is because some within the University will view knowledge exchange as a threat. This has lead to researchers engaged in collaborative research often being forced "to establish new institutional formats" outside of the traditional university structure in order to facilitate their way of working. This means that organisational design, or more specifically intra-organisational design must be structured and coordinated to support knowledge exchange between University and Industry. Another factor influencing the innovation process relates to the appropriateness of the channels utilized by University for interfacing with industry.

Increased focus on licensing and patenting can act as a constraint on the speed at which knowledge can flow between the parties. Focus by the University on other channels such as collaborative research does not prevent the use of these channels at a later stage (Dooley and Kirk, 2007).

According to Abebe *et al.* (2005), the commitment of senior management of all parties involved in the strategic alliance is often a critical success factor. Senior management's commitment to an alliance is important not only to ensure that the alliance receives the necessary resources, but also to convince others throughout the organisation of the importance of the alliance. The focus on a close working relationship creates value for both partners. By dedicating people, time, and attention to the differences within the partnership, the project management tries to balance their values in order to avoid conflicts. First, the research in each field must be truly leading edge and must be relevant to the company's competitive advantage. Secondly, the individual matches between university researchers and their corporate counterparts are needed to transfer and apply the research findings into the corporation (Elmuti *et al.*, 2005).

Academia-industry relationships represent a union of wisdom and wealth. Universities exist to do research that benefits mankind while the goal of industry is to make profits. There is thus concern that the integrity of science is at risk by this different value system. To restore a balance between these contradictory values systems to overcome the issue of conflicts of interest and promoting progress while maintaining public trust in research is not an easy task. The challenge is to be open and guide these relationships to get the best and overcome the weakness of bias. Effective collaboration occurs where partner organisation possess synergistic goals and the complementary assets to facilitate achievement of these goals. It is also nurtured where the consortium develops structures and relationship based control systems that encourage knowledge exchange. In this way, both University and Industry can benefit from the collaboration and both enhance their long term sustainability and innovative outputs (Dooley and Kirk, 2007).

One will never be able to gauge the full benefits of academic/industry partnerships. For this reason, very often, a token-form of recognition and motivation is given to the participating staff, for example, by 'affiliating' industry staff through adjunct academic positions at the University or counterpart positions for academic staff in Industry, as introduced during recent years at the University of Mauritius.

REFERENCES

1. Abebe M., Elmuti, D. and Nicolosi M. 2005. "An Overview of Strategic Alliances between Universities and Corporations", *The Journal of Workplace Learning*, Vol. 17, No. 1/2, pp.115-129.
2. Dooley, L., Kirk, D. 2007, "Grafting the entrepreneurial paradigm onto academic structures", *European Journal of Innovation Management*, Vol. 10, No. 3, pp. 316-332.

SUGGESTED READING

1. Gershom, E. S. 2007. "Academia- Industry- Alliance at what cost?", *The Science Creative Quarterly*, Issue 3. http://www.scq.ubc.ca/academia-industry-at-what-cost/
2. Guthrie, B. M. 2006. "Business-University Research: Improving Interactions between individuals". http:/ www.innovationcanada.ca/en/articles/business-university-research
3. Kruss, G. 2005. "Harnessing Innovation Potential?", *Industry and Higher Education*, pp. 131-142.

SECTION : VII – CORPORATE GOVERNANCE AND SOCIAL RESPONSIBILITY

16

Professional Development of Educational Administrators : An Urgent Need

Pankaj Mittal

INTRODUCTION

Efficient administration of the universities and institutions of higher education has assumed paramount importance in the wake of emerging challenges before the tertiary education. The problems of Indian higher education system are of access, equity, relevance, quality, and resource crunch. Globalization is having its immediate impact on higher education because of shrinking space, shrinking time and disappearing borders as a result of the information and communication revolution. While dealing with the question of administration and governance of universities, we concern ourselves primarily with the organizational set-up of the universities, the different categories and classes of their officers, and the composition, functions and powers of the various statutory bodies, which constitute the traditional components of the university set up. It seems essential in this connection to enumerate the objectives or goals of university education. These are relevant since the vision and competence level of the educational administrators must conform to the ideals, which these institutions are supposed to adhere.

1.1. What then is the object, purpose and goal of university education? In 1947, Pandit Jawaharlal Nehru the first Prime Minister of India-a great statesman, while addressing the graduates of the Allahabad University said, "A university stands for humanism, for tolerance, for reason, for the adventure of ideas and for the search for truth. It stands for the onward march of the human race towards even higher objectives. If the universities discharge their duties adequately, then, it is well with the nation and the people". This statement very eloquently describes the essential purpose or goal of university education.

2. ROLE OF UNIVERSITIES

2.1. University education has manifold functions to discharge. Pursuit of excellence in knowledge and advancement of knowledge have so far been the main functions of university education. This approach, however, is no longer adequate in the context of rapid national development, social change and globalization. The function of a university today is not only to enable the students to attain excellence in knowledge, but also to contribute directly to national development and to furnish intellectual and moral leadership to the community at large. Today when the nations across the globe are struggling to march towards the establishment of an egalitarian society, based on political and economic justice and social equality, university education can no longer remain a passive spectator. Thus the goal of university education has a dual character; firstly the pursuit of knowledge and the attainment of excellence in different disciplines and secondly the development of a sense of ethos which makes the university community conscious of its obligations to the community at large of which it is an important segment. Educational administrators thus have an onus to play a key role in continuously marching ahead to achieve the following goals:

(i) Internal transformation to relate the university education to the life, needs and aspirations of the nation. The existing system of education is largely unrelated to life, and there is a wide gap between its content and purposes and the concerns of national development. There is a growing feeling that the universities must come out of the "ivory tower", not only because the intellectuals should have a commitment to social problems and the cause of humanism and justice, but also because knowledge should be related to social purposes, and research should contribute materially to the transformation of society. It involves a continuous review of the educational system and a more careful planning of the content of education. The university organization has to be responsive to these changing social needs. At the same time, in view of the rapid advances in various fields of knowledge, it is imperative that the prevailing system of education and methods of instruction should be critically reviewed from time to time. There has to be a continuing emphasis on experimentation and innovation, particularly in the field of postgraduate education and research, to enable the educational system to retain its dynamism.

(ii) **Qualitative improvement** to ensure that the standards achieved are adequate, keeps continually rising, and become inter-nationally comparable. In order to improve the quality of instruction as well as to impart to it a social relevance, there should be a greater contact between higher education and the problems of life and society. No longer can we afford isolation between universities on the one hand, and industry, agriculture, rural development, public administration etc., on the other. The organization of the university should, on the one hand, prevent the growth of an exclusive caste system of academics and administrators, and on the other, encourage mobility between the universities and the various sectors of national life and economy.

(iii) Expansion of educational facilities broadly on the basis of manpower needs with an emphasis on equalization of educational opportunities. Also, it is becoming increasingly necessary for different universities to cooperate for specialized or general purposes, to set up and maintain common laboratory/ library, services, to pool effort and resources for deve-loping specialties, and to undertake joint programmes of research, seminars, etc. The specialized knowledge developed in one university should be available to other universities. There have been rapid changes in methods and techniques, and the specializations within each discipline have been growing quickly in depth, sophistication and diversity. On the other hand, the distinction between disciplines is becoming more and more blurred, and no fruitful contribution can be made to knowledge, if attention remains confined within the narrow sphere of individual disciplines. This also emphasizes the importance and need for co-operative research by teams of scholars, who may belong to several disciplines.

2.2. Various ongoing and emerging challenges in higher education sector call for appropriate skills and competencies on the part of educational administrators to prepare the institutions to take on these challenges. An administrative machinery, which is not equipped with the necessary skills, knowledge and attitude and which is not in harmony with the needs of progress, can retard the pace of development. A flexible pattern of organization, which is responsive to the changing needs of society, global trends and knowledge, can be a powerful factor in accelerating progress. In an era of collaborative education, globalization and competition, the higher educational institutes will have to be managed more professionally. The traditional university administration being run with 19th century tools will have to give way to modern management techniques with qualified, professionally trained and proactive administrators.

3. EDUCATIONAL ADMINISTRATORS: ROLE, RESPONSIBILITIES AND CHALLENGES

3.1. Education administrators provide instructional leadership as well as manage the day-to-day activities in the colleges and universities. Education administrators set educational standards and goals and establish the policies and procedures to carry them out. They also supervise managers, support staff, teachers, counselors, librarians, coaches, and others. They develop academic programs; monitor students' educational progress; train and motivate teachers and other staff; manage guidance and other student services; administer record keeping; prepare budgets; handle relations with parents, prospective and current students, employers, and the community; and perform many other duties. In universities, responsibilities are divided among many administrators, each with a specific function.

3.2. The pressures associated with the jobs of educational administrators have multiplied in recent years, as workers in these positions are increasingly being held accountable for ensuring that their institutions provide quality education while meeting all necessary regulations and guidelines prescribed by the statutory bodies and coping up with the additional challenges presented by current budget shortfalls.

3.3. Educational administrators must possess the essential qualities of leadership, determination, confidence, innovativeness, and motivation. The ability to make sound decisions and to organize and coordinate work efficiently is essential. Because much of an administrator's job involves interacting with others, such as students, parents, teachers, and the community, a person in such a position must have strong interpersonal skills and shall be an effective communicator and motivator. Knowledge of leadership principles and practices, gained through work experience and formal education, is important. They must possess an ability to assess the emerging requirements for quality academic attainments and take necessary steps to fulfill them. A familiarity with computer technology is a necessity for education administrators, who are required to gather information and coordinate technical resources for their students, teachers, and classrooms.

4. TRAINING AS A TOOL FOR PROFESSIONAL DEVELOPMENT

4.1. The most effective way to achieve the goal of professional development of educational administrators is to impart them training in accordance with their roles, responsibilities and needs. The National Policy of Education, 1986 and Programme of Action, 1992 have also identified training of Educational Administrators as one of the thrust area.

4.2. The training for educational administrators needs to be developed taking into account the system changes and the interface between administrators, academicians and the students. The goal of training of managers should be the management of change. The development of a holistic vision of education is necessary for academic managers. It requires the persons with capacity for flexibility, innovativeness, creativity and a vision. He has to work as a facilitator while ensuring team work and networking rather than bureaucratic hierarchical management styles.

4.3. The training at different levels has to be of different type corresponding with the nature of responsibility and duties to be performed by the concerned employee and past experience. Training at higher level has to be more conceptual and strategic in content while, at lower levels, it has to be more specific. A matrix of functional responsibilities should be developed to identify the training needs.

4.4. Inbreeding in the university system is causing problems with little fresh blood entering it. The training for in-service people is therefore, a major requirement. Also, after training, when a person returns, he/she faces difficulties in change because the system is the same and people are not ready to accept the changes. Therefore, *it is necessary to train the whole unit rather than the person through decentralization with small training units at each university, which would be more effective.* The training should be mandatory for promotion and each institution should formulate its own training policy.

4.5. Three components of training should be emphasized, *i.e., knowledge, skills and attitude development.* The administrators at the top level have numerous functions *i.e.,* they are multi-functionaries whereas at the lower level the functions designated are very specific in which they are expected to be efficient. Emphasis in training should be on shared values of the organization and this should be taught at all levels.

4.6. The training structure should be flexible rather than bureaucratic approach to training. It should impart training based on the functional responsibility of the person. ***We should produce effective administrators (to do right jobs) rather than only efficient administrators (do jobs rightly).***

4.7. Considerable emphasis should be given to value addition, effective resource allocation on a priority basis and team work. The training should not be only for now but also preparation for future decades. Hence, a futurological exercise would be relevant, say till 2020.

5. SUGGESTED STRUCTURE OF TRAINING

5.1. Training programmes for educational administrators may be made at three levels:

*- **Level I comprising Vice Chancellors, Pro-Vice Chancellors, Directors and Registrars.***

The Vice Chancellor and senior officers have to take strategic decision about the vision and the future growth of the concerned institution(s). Therefore, wide ranging training inputs to facilitate these officers to develop both short-term as well as long-term vision is considered necessary. Besides, the participants should be imparted necessary training to acquire skills on various aspects of administration, e.g., admission, teaching, examination, appointment to academic bodies, handling students, teachers and employees association, extension activities as well as the outreach programme, convocations, conferences, conflict and crisis management, interaction with authorities outside the institution, research, publication relations, etc. In addition to the administrative skills, the other important skills to which these participants shall be exposed to are financial and legal skills.

The training shall be imparted using the multiple strategy including seminars / workshops, across the table discussions, briefing session, audio visual demonstration, handbook and manual for self-learning, papers for ready consultation, national / international exposures by way of visits and interaction. Since this training is being imparted to highest echelons of universities, it may be named as **"Round Table Conference"** which can be organized at a national level as a five days intensive programme by an institution specifically established for the purpose or through a network of already available training institutions.

Level II comprising Finance Officers, Controller of Examinations, Deans and equivalents.

The training for this category must emphasize on the need for these personnel to orient them to be service providers (facilitators) rather than merely assuming restricted role of controllers. Appropriate training must be imparted to help them in discharging the functions related to dealing with the students, effective management of the areas of teaching, research, examination and extension work, ability to function as motivators, team players and leaders – inter-departmental and intra-departmental interaction skills including curriculum development, computer literacy, behavioral and organizational structure, education policy, finance etc. the topics like budget, tenure and promotions, incentive schemes shall also be included. In addition, interactive tele conference inputs are suggested in the last two days of training.

A product mix of training methodologies including lecturers group discussions, didactic simulation, and computer simulation on administration system, case studies, road building, self development exercise, use of training tools such as video, multi media and virtual realities, projectors etc. can be used. The training may be named as **"Orientation Programme"** to be organized a regional level by identified institutions for a period of two weeks.

- Level III comprising Section Officers, Assistants, and Upper Division Clerks and equivalents.

Initially a broad based basic programme should be offered to cover subjects like organization analysis, office management noting and drafting, forms and procedure of communication editing of files, elements of book keeping and accountancy, file system, writing skills, management system and computer training etc. The participants should be exposed to the over all functions of the university and changing environment. The course should also emphasize the behavioral aspects of administration and focus on the need to bring about change in the attitude of the personnel to improve the image of the university through better and more efficient services to its different clientele groups.

The second higher-level course may focus more on practical aspects concerning the specialized functions of the university such as examination, finance or accounting in much greater depth. In addition, the participants could be exposed to problems of higher education, computer applications in university administration procedures, rules, ordinances and the functioning of the Executive Council, Academic Council, Court and other statutory bodies Further, case studies should be used to highlight the need to develop skills required to attend to the more specific problems faced by the organization.

At the third level the emphasis may be on human relations and conceptual skills needed for efficient university administration. Subjects like organizational change and development, communication skills, inter personal skills, simplification of techniques of office supervision and management, group behavior and team building and an advanced course on application of computer in the examination and financial branches could be highlighted.

Participatory learning method should be emphasized. Involvement of the participant in the learning process is essential. Specific case studies, group exercises, individual project requirements and class sessions on specific problems faced by the individual organization should be given priority. Audio visual aids and computer etc. shall be widely used. The participants shall also have a choice to learn either by attending the regular sessions or through distance mode for which special packages need to be developed, since it becomes difficult to release the participants for a longer period of time from their work place.

Programme should be offered in a modular form and the participants may be awarded a Certificate or Diploma on the completion of requisite credits. The training may be named as **"Staff Development Programme"** which shall be an intensive programme of 3-4 weeks duration. These types of programmes shall be organized either at the individual organization level or at the regional level. Networking among the institutions who are already engaged in offering similar programmes may be beneficiary.

5.2. Evaluation of The Training Programmes:

In case of officers at Level I the written and oral feed back from the participants shall be made use of to evaluate the impact analysis of the training programe. In case of officers at level II the impact of training shall be evaluated through written feed back from the participants by using multiple choice questionnaires *before and after the programme* for the benefit of the instructors. Efforts should be made to get feed back from the concerned institutions, 3-6 months after the programme regarding applicability to their work situation. For level III at the end of the programme the impact of the training should be evaluated through questionnaires suitably devised for the purpose and by making the participants undergo a simple test, which evaluates their learning capabilities during the training programme. The score obtained in the test may be indicated on their certificates, which would encourage them to learn and perform better.

5.3. Impact Analysis of Training:

Impact analysis should be done to measure the impact of the training on the participants. Effective tools shall be used to evaluate the behavioral changes inculcated during the training. The impact analysis shall be done on regular intervals to continuously update and improve the contents and methodology of the training programmes. Moreover, the training shall not be taken up as a one-time activity, and shall be treated as a life long exercise to continuously update the staff.

6. TRAINING : MANDATORY OR OPTIONAL

Till now in India the training of educational administrators has not been given due importance it deserves. It depends upon the individual person whether or not he wants to join a training programme to improve his efficiency and skills. Rather in Indian conditions not many opportunities are available to the employees for such training. Making the training mandatory, may introduce a type of dullness and rigidity on the part of employees, which in turn will affect the quality of training. On the other hand making it optional will not encourage the individuals to participate in training who visualize training as a gain for the organization in which they are working rather than a personal gain. It would, therefore, be best to adopt a strategy whereby although the training is not made mandatory yet the individuals are encouraged to take up the training programmes on their own. One offshoot of training could be rewards. This is a matter, which each institution could decide within the boundary of its facilities and limitations. The activity itself shall act as a reward to the participants. A few decades ago there was nothing called 'Training of Administrative Staff'. Today, it is being thought of, conceptualized and implemented in educational institutions to some extent. Is it not a reward, even if it sounds narrow? Moreover, appreciation or reward or certificate must be a part of the programme; and most of the institutions organizing such training programmes must do so. One of the possible ways could be to link training with the career advancement. To accomplish this, although the training shall not be one of the essential requirements for promotion, it should enable the individuals in getting accelerated promotions, if they undergo training programmes. This is particularly applicable to Level III training indicated above which comprises of about 95% of the staff in Indian conditions. As far as, motivating the participants at Level I are concerned, it has to be the case of self-motivation which should be propagated by the central agencies like University Grants Commission through effective marketing strategies. For level II, the training shall be made a pre-requisite for taking charge of the new assignment. This will ensure that a trained person is handling the job efficiently and has adequate leadership, qualities to accomplish the job effectively.

7. EXISTING TRAINING FACILITIES IN INDIA

Unfortunately, the academic administration, unlike other services, does not belong to any organized cadre or service in India. Thus, they are deprived of any cadre support for their professional growth and career advancement. Some orientation programmes for senior educational administrators are organized at institutions like National University of Educational Planning and Administration (NUEPA), Administrative Staff Colleges, Association of Indian Universities and some individual universities but these are highly inadequate considering the very large number of academic administrators in the country to be trained, especially those at the junior and middle levels. Unlike the teaching faculty, they get only a few opportunities for attending seminars, conferences, workshops, etc., so essential for their continuous professional growth.

A Committee setup by the Government of India to suggest measures to augment training facilities for university and college administrators has recommended the establishment of a National Institute for professional development of educational administrators.

8. PROPOSED MODEL

8.1. The suggested nodal training institution at the national level may be named as "National Institute for Training of

Educational Administrators". This institute may have its sub-units at regional level (existing training institutions may be used for this purpose) to impart training. However, to ensure the uniformity and quality of training, core programmes shall be designed by this institution with a scope of regional variation based on the local needs. The major objectives and functions of this institution shall be to formulate training policy, provide facilities, promote research and management of higher education institutions, identify training needs, design training programmes and also act as a national resource centre for sharing of information and expertise in a flexible manner and shall be capable of responding effectively to change needs. The main functions of the institute may include the following :-

(a) To facilitate and promote training of university and college administrators;

(b) To identify training needs, design training programmes and assess the impact of training at the university and college level;

(c) To assist the development and delivery of high quality training materials, to produce generic training literature and facilitate access to them;

(d) To undertake and support advanced training of trainers;

(e) To assist in the setting up of Centres for Human Resource Development (CHRD) in universities for training of secretarial staff.

(f) To establish and recognize Regional Resource Centres for training of middle-level functionaries of universities and colleges and to coordinate their activities;

(g) To undertake training of policy level administrators of university and colleges;

(h) To promote the use of distance education for in-service training of university and colleges administrators;

(i) To assist in the development of local support services for training;

(j) To provide a forum for sharing of information, expertise, ideas and experience in the field of educational administration at the tertiary level.

(k) To conduct and promote research on various aspects of higher education in India and abroad;

(l) To provide information and consultancy services for training of university and college administrators, including selection of appropriate technology;

(m) To facilitate inter-institutional linkages and cooperation in the area of staff training and

(n) To explore feasibility of involving the corporate sector in human resource development in higher education institutions.

8.2. The proposed institute is conceived as a compact nodal institute with a small institutional set up to undertake staff development activities for educational administrators in the country. The nation wide staff development activities will also necessitate the development of training materials (print, audio visual, etc.) and self-instructional multi-media packages. While the staff at the headquarters shall engage themselves in the development and conduct of programmes and also carry out related research activities to further strengthen them, the implementation activities shall be decentralized. The decentralization process will ensure the involvement and participation of the regional training institutes for the implementation of such programmes. The institute may conduct number of orientation and in-service courses to cover all levels of the administrative staff in the universities.

8.3. However, it would be difficult to train the lower staff at the national centre and it would be desirable that the universities conduct training courses for Clerks, Assistants, Superintendents and Assistant Registrars at their own levels. However, for Assistant Registrar and equivalent level administrative staff, a training course may be organized at zonal or national level. For Vice Chancellors, Pro-Vice Chancellor and Directors the national centre shall organize Round Table Conference every three months to train newly inducted personnel in the system. Each university shall have a training budget and 1-2% of salary budget of the administrative staff should be earmarked for training. The training shall be imparted in a modular fashion with various modules, each module of one-week (25 hours) duration. 12 modules of 12-week duration could lead to a Certificate course. 24 modules of 24 weeks could lead to a Diploma course and 42 modules of 42 weeks could lead to an Advanced Diploma. Each week can be devoted to a different module covering various aspects and subjects for training. The transfer of credits should be possible after required standardization of modules.

8.4. In addition to training the administrative staff, emphasis shall also be laid on **training of trainers**, which can effectively be imparted through the national level institute to maintain quality of training.

CONCLUSIONS

The comparative study of the contents, methodologies and inputs of the training imparted by the existing institutes gives us a positive feeling that there is a general awareness among the top echelon of university administration about the need and importance of the staff development activities for the administration/national academic staff. This augurs well, but steps are needed to make this awareness more effective in terms of encouraging the staff towards organization of the participation in such programmes on a regular basis. Although, the idea about the usefulness of this important area is catching up, given the type of organizational culture as exists in the institutions of higher learning, thinking on such measures essentially remains boardroom oriented and does not percolate downwards.

The need of the hour is to make all senior officers / managers aware of its need, importance and relevance, and get them involved in the same. The result will be undoubtedly rewarding. Mere sending nomination of officers for a particular programme is not sufficient. One has to do lot more. Pre-training briefing, post-training debriefing, providing encouragement to participate keeping the room open for discussions with them on specific ideas allowing them to bring innovative ideas and implementing them to the extent possible within the parameters of organizational policies and principles are some of the factors which could make training very attractive and effective.

We have great faith in the ultimate effectiveness of training for development of Educational Administrators. We have no way to side track this area; we can only encourage and pursue it more vigorously for the betterment of the participants, target groups and the organization as a whole.

17

Management of Higher Education Among Scheduled Tribes of India: Science and Technology for Future Strategy

A.K. Kapoor

ABSTRACT

India harbors 84.3 millions of tribal population, constituting 8.2% of its total population and about 15% of total geographical area. Being essentially ecosystem people, they live in complete harmony with nature and natural resources under diverse ecological and geo-climatic conditions ranging from plains, forest, hills to inaccessible areas. They generally inhabit remote and underdeveloped areas of the country with low human density and inadequate access to even basic amenities, education, employment opportunities and affordable health care services. The objective of higher education for the tribal population may range from primary objectives, such as employability, enhancing the earning potential, seeking and advancing knowledge and wisdom, research and experimentation, to more serious secondary objectives like attaining mental and spiritual growth, engaging in quest for the unknown, facilitating better life style and developing scientific outlook. During the last few years, the governmental efforts have focused on improvement in economic conditions of the tribes through introduction of various developmental programs and schemes, mostly related to agriculture, horticulture and peasantry. Their literacy rates have also increased due to higher participation in schooling. A critical analysis of development programs and their effect on tribal households, however, shows that developmental programs can come into conflict with educational programs until and unless the tribal households reach a threshold level of income and land size.

INTRODUCTION

The term 'tribe' has originated around the time of the Greek city and the early formation of the Roman Empire. The original Latin term, '*tribus*', has since been transformed to mean 'a group of persons forming a community and claiming descent from a common ancestor' (Gregory, 2003). According to Morris (1980), a tribe is a 'group of persons with a common occupation, interest, or habit, and a large family'. The layman's understanding of the word 'tribe' is invariably synonymous with primitiveness, savagery and wildness. The tribes or aborigines were ascribed the lowest position in the human civilization, of which the highest level was said to have been achieved by the white men in the west. In other words, the tribes became the conceptual opposite of the westerners.

In modern India, the term 'tribe' came in vogue first when the British penetrated interior areas of the country at the beginning of their rule. The early military campaigners, administrators and Christian missionaries were stuck by the quaintness of the certain people in terms of their social behavior and practices and at times also their physical features. They were taken as 'cultural enclaves' (Bara, 2002). Convinced by these broad features, the early British aptly found in these unusual humans the Indian 'tribe' as counterparts of these indigenous people as encountered in Africa, America and Australia.

DISTRIBUTION OF TRIBES IN INDIA

The tribal communities live in about 15% of the country's areas in various ecological and geo-climatic conditions ranging from plains, forest, hills to inaccessible areas. The life style of tribal people is primarily conditioned by the ecosystems bringing them is in tune with nature and natural resources. The country's wide ranging diversity in nature and natural resources present a varied tribal population throughout India's length and breadth. In general, most tribal populations inhabit under developed areas of the country that are remote having low density of population and lacking in adequate access to basic amenities, education, employment opportunities and affordable health care services. It is because of these reasons that creation of critical infrastructure like communication, drinking water, education, health, roads, etc. has always been left out by development agencies on one pretext or the other like economic non-viability, high cost, etc. in the tribal areas. As a result, the physical infrastructure in the tribal areas is inadequate and at a much lower footing then the rest of the areas keeping them as Primitive Tribes still today.

The word ' Primitive Tribe' in Indian setting was first of all conceived in 1931 by J.J. Hutton. Later, he was joined by W.V. Grigson (1938) in the framing of the guidelines for the welfare of the tribes. The word 'tribe' has not been defined anywhere in the constitution of India. It is a matter of great debate among the academicians, administrators, and development planners throughout the country regarding the concept of 'tribe' and 'primitive tribe'. But the Article 342 of Indian Constitution states that the scheduled tribes are "tribes or the tribal communities or parts of or groups within tribes or tribal communities", which the President of India may specify from time to time by public notification. As these communities are presumed to constitute the oldest ethnological segment of the Indian society, the term 'Adivasi' ('Adi' mean 'oldest' and 'Vasi' means 'inhabitant) is commonly used to designate them. The International Labor Organization Convention 107 held at Geneva on 5th June 1957 classified these people as indigenous. There are 75 Primitive Tribal Groups (PTGs) in India who are characterized by

1. a pre-agriculture level of technology,
2. a stagnant or declining population,
3. extremely low literacy, and
4. a subsistence level of economy.

SCHEDULED TRIBES

The term 'scheduled tribes' first appeared in the Constitution of India. The Article 366 (25) defines Scheduled tribes as "such tribes or tribal communities or parts of or groups within such tribes or tribal communities as are deemed under Article 342 to be scheduled tribes for the purpose of this Constitution" (Ghurye, 1959). This Article says that only those communities who have been declared as such by the President through an initial public notification will be considered as Scheduled Tribes. Any further amendment in the list is through an Act of Parliament. The list of Scheduled tribes is State- specific, and a community declared as Scheduled Tribe in a state need not be so in another state. The essential characteristics were first laid down by the Lokur Committee. The criteria followed for specification of a community as a Scheduled Tribe is not spelt out in the constitution but has become well established. It takes into account the definitions in the 1931 Census; the reports of the First Backward Classes Commission (Kalelkar Committee), 1955; the Advisory Committee Report on Revision of SC / ST Lists (Lokur Committee), 1965; the Backward Classes Commission Report (Mandal Committee), 1980; the Backward Classes Commission Report (Rao Committee), 1982.

There are 573 / 613 scheduled tribes as notified under Article 342 of the Constitution of India (Kshatriya and Kapoor, 2003; Kapoor, 2008), spread over different States and Union Territories of the country with the largest number being in the state of Orissa. The main concentration of tribal population is in Central India and in the Northeastern States. However, they have their presence in all the States and Union Territories except Haryana, Punjab, Delhi, Pondicherry and Chandigarh. The Indian states predominantly populated by the tribal people (tribal population more than 50 percent of the total population) are Arunachal Pradesh, Meghalaya, Mizoram and Nagaland, and the Union Territories of Dadra and Nagar Haveli and Lakshdweep. (Annual Report, Ministry of Tribal Affairs, 2004-05). The population of scheduled tribes has been on the increase since 1961. With the growth rate of the population of Scheduled tribes at 24.45 percent during the period 1991-2001, more than half the scheduled tribes population is concentrated in the states of Madhya Pradesh, Chhattisgarh, Maharashtra, Orissa, Jharkhand and Gujarat. The Schedule Tribe population has witnessed highest growth rate of 80.8% in the state of Karnataka, followed by Nagaland (67.2%).

The lowest growth rate was recorded in Andaman and Nicobar Islands (10.1%), followed by Himachal Pradesh (12.0%).

MAJOR STUDIES CONDUCTED ON TRIBES

As early as in 1901, Census Organization of India under the stewardship of Sir Herbert Risley has done some pioneering work on the tribal communities. In 1931, Hutton, the then Census Commissioner of India, resolved to continue and extend the anthropological investigations which were initiated by Risley. He was the first one, who made serious attempt to list the primitive tribes in the census of 1931 (Gupta, 2005). Tribal research in India started as early as in 1784 when the Asiatic Society of Bengal was established by Sir William Jones to study 'nature and man' (Kapoor, 1996). Their cosmology, religious practices, belief system, rites and rituals, marriage pattern, language, dress pattern, festivals, village set up, etc had always been different from the main stream of life, thus attracting more and more anthropologists. (Dalton, 1872; Crooke, 1896; Seligmann, 1911; Elwin, 1939; Furer-Haimendorf, 1943; Roy, 1961; Vidyarthi, 1963; Bhowmick, 1963; Tiwari, 1984; Chakraborty, 1990; Hodson, 1989; Sharma, 1994; Sahu, 1995; Sharma, 1996 and Sahu, 1998, Kapoor, 2006) All these authors have focused on ethnographic phases of the lives of the tribes.

The writings of Rivers (1906) and Radcliffe-Brown (1922) began the tradition of writing full length monographs on the tribes. Roy (1921) reviewed such studies by these scholars in the first issue of 'Man in India'. First Indian anthropologists, S.C. Roy, wrote the full length monograph on Munda in 1912, which was followed by a series of five monographs (1915, 1925, 1928, 1935 and 1937) on different tribes of Chotanagpur. With the entry of Verrier Elwin (1939) and Furer- Haimdendorf (1945, 1962 and 1969), the tribal studies in India received a fresh impetus and several monographs on the tribes of Madhya Pradesh, Andhra Pradesh and later north east India were written by them.

Soon the trend of the literature produced by scholars changed from pure ethnographic accounts to the study of demographic accounts, process of social change, transformation development, relation between environment and economic structure, literacy, poverty psycho-social perspective, genetics, gender, tourism, non-government organization and tribes, management of health, disaster, resources, intellectual property rights, economic policy and impact on tribals and human rights etc (Chandra, 1969; Mohan, 1975; Prasad & Kapoor 1982; Kapoor, 1990-1996; Sastry, 1993; Fernandes and Raj, 1996; Patra et al, 1997; Soni, 1998; Kapoor, 1998; Sharma & Sharma, 1999; Kapoor, 2000 a,b,c; Baraik & Lakra, 2003; Biswas and Kapoor, 2003; Kshatriya & Kapoor, 2003; Gupta, 2005; Gupta and Kapoor, 2005; 2006; 2007; Gupta and Gupta, 2005; Shukla, 2005; Dixit, 2006.) but there are hardly any studies on education pattern among Scheduled Tribes (Sujatha, 1994).

TRIBES AND HIGHER EDUCATION

Higher education can be broadly surmised as education beyond the school level. The objective of higher education may range from primary objectives, such as employability, enhancing the earning potential, seeking and advancing knowledge and wisdom, research and experimentation to more serious secondary objectives like attaining mental and spiritual growth, engaging in quest for the unknown, facilitating better life style, and developing scientific outlook. According to Seth and Parida (2006), there has been rapid expansion of higher education in the country in terms of enrolment, number of institutions, number of disciplines and courses, number of teaching faculty, etc. since independence. The system has undergone a unique transformation from an elitist to an egalitarian one. Therefore, all sections of the population have gained enlarging the system. However, the disparities between the disadvantaged group, viz., women, scheduled castes (SC), scheduled tribe (ST), other backward classes (OBC) and minorities and non-disadvantaged groups have continued till date. There is a need to provide special care and opportunities to the traditional disadvantaged population in a democratic society such as scheduled castes, scheduled tribe, which stresses egalitarianism, social justice and economic development for all sections of society. It is with this in view that the Indian constitution provides an ideal of equality of opportunities. Specific provisions have been made in several articles of the constitution for the realization of the promise made in the Directive Principle so as to improve the social and economic status of various groups. Under article 17 of the Constitution, untouchability has been abolished and its practice in any form has been forbidden. Land reforms have also been enacted to revert back land to the tribal and to allot land to the scheduled caste population. Stipends, scholarships, free tuition, monetary aid for books, stationery and free accommodation in hostels are provided in an attempt to increase literacy and education among the SC and ST students from various groups. Certain percentage of seats is also reserved in educational institutions, as are jobs in government and public sector. Members of various groups also enjoy relaxation of qualification and age norms while seeking government or public sector employment. In the pursuance of these privileges, appropriate funds have been provided in the various Five Year Plans for welfare programs of these populations (Govt. of India, 1996). Different efforts have been made by Education Commission (Kothari Commission, 1964-65), National Policy of Education (1986 updated 1992) and National Assessment and Accreditation Council to ensure greater access to the disadvantaged groups. Despite these provisions and safeguards, their representation in higher educational institutes and in the workforce remains largely minimal as per our Census Report 2001 (Seth & Parida, 2006)

A Central Tribal University has also been set up for the first time in Madhya Pradesh to retrieve the situation. It has been observed that the gross enrolment ratio (GER) among the scheduled tribes is 6.33% as compared to 16.6% in the general population and 8.5% in OBC. According to Thorat (2008), the SC, the ST and the OBC populations from all religions suffer from lower access to higher education. However, the scheduled castes within the Hindu and the Sikh suffer more acutely than the scheduled casts belonging to other religions. Similarly, the scheduled tribes within the Hindu fold suffer more than their Christian counterparts (Thorat, 2008). Between 1991 and 2001, literacy rates have increased for girls as well as for overall numbers of scheduled caste and scheduled tribe groups due to higher school participation (Government of India, 2006). The total literacy rate for scheduled caste groups during this time increased by 17.28% among the scheduled caste and by 17.5% among scheduled tribe population.

At state level according to Government of India (2006), the literacy rate among scheduled tribes was the highest in Mizoram (89.34%), followed by Lakshadweep (86.14%), Sikkim (67.14%), Uttarakhand (63.23%) and Himachal Pradaesh (65.50%). In contrast, the other states show less than 50 percent literacy like Bihar (28.17%), Andhra Pradesh (37.04%), Orissa (37.37%), Rajasthan (44.66%), Madhya Pradesh (41.16%), etc.

It is pertinent to point out here that some of the scheduled tribes have achieved good education and produced a number of medical doctors, scientists, university teachers and civil servants, for example, Dhodia, Dhanka and Bhil of Gujarat, Meena of Rajasthan, Bhotias of Uttara Khand, Lohaoulis and Kinnaurse of Himachal Pradesh, Khasi of Meghalaya; Munda and Santhal of West Bengal. It has also been observed that many scheduled tribes do not opt for higher education. An all India survey has to be carried out for the same that can throw some light and the various reasons thereof. In spite of constitutional guarantees and persistent efforts, tribal communities continue to lag behind the general population in education, what to talk of higher education. The reasons can be many such as problems and difficulties at levels of policy planning, implementation and administration of the policies, admission in colleges, medium of instruction, curriculum, social, economic and cultural backgrounds of tribals and finally the psychological problems and awareness levels of 1st and 2nd generation of tribals.

Enhancing Higher Education Access to Tribals.

In last few years, the efforts of the government have been directed towards improving economic conditions of tribes by introducing various developmental programs and schemes, mostly related to agriculture, horticulture, and peasantry. A critical analysis of development programs and their effect on tribal households shows that till tribal households reach a threshold level of income and land size, the economic development programs generally come into conflict with other activities like education. In a way, it can be said that these development programs seem to be adversely affecting the education of various tribal groups (Sujatha, 1994). Although over the last decade international aid has rightly stressed upon the importance of concentrating on the poor, it has neglected tribal areas and thereby the majority of disadvantaged people, a phenomenon which is particularly true for education (IFAD, 2001). Basic education is a fundamental human right in itself and essential for reducing poverty and improving the living conditions of tribal and rural populations. Yet children's access to education in tribal areas is still much lower than in urban areas, where adult literacy and the quality of education are much higher. Moreover, curricula and textbooks in primary and secondary schools often have an urban bias, are irrelevant to the needs of tribal people, and seldom focus on the skills needed for life in tribal areas. There is also a general lack of awareness among ministries of education, agriculture, health, finance and others as well as universities and research institutions concerning the importance of targeting the basic learning needs of tribal people.

Although past investments in tribal areas have been scarce with slow progress, a new awareness and consensus about the importance of focusing on tribal poverty has been growing, facilitated also by the Millennium Development Goals (MDGs) set by the United Nations for the year 2015. The fact is that investments need to be reallocated to the rural and tribal poor in order to achieve the MDGs by 2015 including the eradication of extreme poverty and hunger and assurance of complete primary education to all the boys and girls of the target population. This requires a multi-sector and multi-disciplinary partnership by the involved agencies. The success of such an innovation will be regulated by the following variables:

- Incorporation of education of tribal people at the core of National Plans of Education together with strengthening of the institutional capacities. The efforts aimed at reducing poverty and hunger should, therefore, be accompanied by sound education policies for the tribal people. This can be achieved if the educational needs of tribal communities are given due consideration at every level of governance, including planning and finance.
- Expansion of access to schools in tribal areas, by promoting or supporting initiatives aimed at improving children's

nutrition and capacity to learn by providing school canteens and gardens, focusing on education of tribal girls and women, designing flexible academic calendars by accommodating the local agricultural production cycles, etc.

- Provision for lifelong education through open and distance modes including the information and communication tools.
- Improvement in the relevance of education for meeting the needs and interests of tribal people. This can be achieved by supporting participatory curriculum development, teachers training, life skills for a rural or tribal environment, nutrition education, and awareness about mitigation and prevention of prevalent diseases like diarrhea, Malaria, HIV/AIDS, etc.
- Better understanding about the ethnographical background and respect for each other's cultures (Gasperini, 2002).

Science, Technology, Education and Sustainable Development.

There is an all-time high threat perception to the very existence of tribal societies throughout the world due to rapid loss of biodiversity and natural resources from their natural habitats as a result of their high consumption by the modern societies. In order to maintain these tribal populations and improve their economic and social status, it is imperative to adopt practices of sustainable development. The latter requires more active engagement and participation by everyone in how science agendas are set and how its findings are used in welfare of the human society. Besides, enabling the policy makers to make informed decisions requires timely access to reliable knowledge that is generated by science and technology and rests on the three pillars of sustainable development. Education in science and technology is vital to develop knowledge-action linkages. Education in science and technology is needed to develop intellectual capital if it has to contribute to sustainable development. This requires local and regional inputs to define priorities and approaches that incorporate traditional knowledge into the science and technology processes through the concepts of co-production of knowledge. There is also a need to develop understanding of local complex interdependent aspects of sustainable development. Scientists and technologists must be able to adapt existing technologies to meet local requirements and improve efficiency of production processes. Education in science and technology is also necessary not only to deal with problems but also to take advantage of the local natural endowments, especially bio-diversity, cultural diversity, language and indigenous knowledge, particularly the knowledge possessed by women in areas of health, sanitation, food preservation and agriculture. This is also needed to develop critical thinking capabilities to help people consider evidence, arguments for and against the issues, goals and the ways to reach them. Much of the knowledge and wisdom required for sustainability resides in people and in their landscapes and cultural artifacts. Wisdom comes from experience, traditional practices and formal experimentation, comparison and analysis. Memory and innovations in technology and institutions drive the choices regarding as how to use environment and resources. Education is a key to the prospects of sustainability becoming an important principle or criterion for decisions (Corell and Eckley, 2002).

Education is an important tool for changing behavior. One of the important requirements to achieve sustainable development is to change the consumption behavior of the rich and powerful both in developed and developing countries. The data indicate that the richest 20% people of the world account for 80% of consumption of global resources, whereas the poorest 20% people account for only 1% of the consumption. Reduction in consumption is resisted and often seen to threaten lifestyles, competitiveness and profitability. If we want to ensure that the models of consumption of affluent societies do not become the norm, and that affluent societies reduce consumption without viewing this as a threat to their lifestyle and competitiveness, science and technology education can play an important role.

Science and Technology Curriculum for Sustainable Development.

A proper designing of the curriculum is required to ensure contribution of science and technology to achieve sustainable development. Such a curriculum should:

- focus on hard facts of science in applying right technologies in harmony with local human values, cultural settings and knowledge of market and politics,

- recognize and demonstrate scientific knowledge as an iterative process, i.e., it cannot have answers to all the problems and there are inherent uncertainties in the use of scientific knowledge.
- integrate indigenous knowledge with modern knowledge. For sustainable development, knowledge and application of new and existing local, culturally appropriate and low cost traditional technologies are vital, as is the merging of new technologies with traditional technologies.
- address new ways of balancing equity, economics and ecology.
- address the impact that poverty and excessive consumption are having on the natural resource base.
- promote gender equity, e.g. greater prominence is required for the work of women scientists and mathematicians in the curriculum to keep girls motivated.
- include progress on health, hygiene and sanitation, particularly in the fields of infectious diseases, health of mother and child and access to clean water.
- include development in the field of agriculture such as land-use and land-cover change, improved irrigation practices, more sustainable use of agricultural chemicals, production and use of genetically modified plants and use of traditional knowledge and technologies.
- provide an understanding of how some areas of science and technology such as water, energy, disposal of waste, land use and consumption of resources by the rich and powerful on one hand could lead to possible conflicts, while on the other, could contribute to conflict reduction and prevention, if dealth with properly.
- enhance the understanding of ethical issues being raised, by challenging society's values, as recognised by the 1999 World Conference on Science (cf Goel, 2002).

Tools for Change and Improvement

1. Many articles on higher education have been written and will be written in future also. These articles are not taken seriously by the concerned planners or Ministry of Higher Education or the Concerned bodies of Higher Education.
2. It can be stated that there should be linkage of schools with universities, which can give a continuity in Education.
3. We should have 'Indian Education System.
4. Priority should be given to these who wants to open colleges in Tribal areas.
5. Regional Tribal Education Centres under Panchayat or Block should be opened for various types of education training to be given by tribals themselves.
6. Distance education/ correspondence courses centres should be opened in tribal areas where the concentration is more than 60%.
7. Govt. has made provision for ST students abroad with fellowship but the rate and progress is very slow.
8. ST students should be given preference for researches in Universities and research Institutes.

CONCLUSION

This vision is practical-it can be put into practice in villages and towns, in homes and universities, in the North and the South. It can be implemented because it is an approach, not a recipe. Quality improvement is an incremental process. There is no single starting or ending point because there is no one 'right' ways to do it. What is important is to share the vision, to understand what it means in terms of a particular learning situation, and then to find places where quality can be improved in light of the existing context.

This is not an impossible dream. Every learning environment can be improved with small changes on a regular basis. When maintained, these changes can build into major reforms that have a broad support base and, as a result, improved quality becomes the responsibility of everybody.

REFERENCES

- Annual Report. 2004-05. 'Ministry of Tribal Affairs', Government of India.
- Bara, J. 2002. 'Tribe- Beast or Man: Case for a New Concept of Tribe', *Social Action*, April- June, 51:121-221.
- Baraik, V.K. and B.M.R. Lakra 2003. 'Literacy of Scheduled Tribes in Jharkhand- Patterns and Disparities', 1991-2001, *Indian Journal of Adult Education*, 64 (3-4): 19-34.
- Bhowmick, P.K. 1963. 'The Lodhas of West Bengal- A Socio-Economic Study', Punthi Pustak, Calcutta.
- Biswas , R.K. and A.K. Kapoor 2003. 'Educational Profile of Kamar Tribe', *Indian Journal of Adult Education*, 64 (3-4): 35-41.
- Boas, Franz 1911. 'The Mind of Primitive Man', The Macmillan Company, USA.
- Chakraborty, D.K. 1990. 'The Great Andamanese: Struggle for Survival', Seagull Books, Calcutta.
- Chandra, M. 1969. 'Socio-Economic Change in the Tribes of Andhra', pp 199-221 In: *Trends of Socio- Economic Change in India*, M.K. Chaudhari (Ed.), Indian Institute of Advanced Studies, Shimla.
- Corell, R.W.and N. Eckley (Eds.). Initiative on Science and Technology sustainability: Insight and perspective from the Regional ISTS workshops 2002, London.
- Crooke, W. 1896. 'The Tribes and Castes of the North –Western India', Government Printing Press, Calcutta.
- Dalton, E.T. 1872. 'Descriptive Ethnology of Bengal' (Reprinted 1960), Government of Bengal, Calcutta.
- Dixit, N.K. 2006. 'Racial Identity and Rights of Tribes and Tribals', Vista International, Delhi.
- Elwin,V. 1939. 'The Baiga', John Murray & Co., London.
- Fernandes, W. and S. Anthony Raj 1996. 'The New Economic Policy and GATT- Their Impact on the Tribals', pp. 295-323, In: *Tribes in India*, R.S. Mann (Ed.), MD Publication, New Delhi.
- Furer- Haimdendorf, C.V. 1945. 'The Tribal Population of Hyderabad', Hyderabad Revenue Department, Census.
- Furer- Haimdendorf, C.V. 1962. 'The Apa-Tanis, Their Neighbours- A Primitive Civilization of the Eastern Himalaya', Routlodge and Kegan Paul, New York.

- Furer- Haimdendorf, C.V. 1969. 'The Konyak Nagas', Oxford University Press, Oxford.
- Furer-Haimendorf, C.V. 1943. 'The Chenchus – Jungle Folk of Deccan', Macmillan and Co., London.
- Gasperini, L. 2002. Education for Rural people: addressing a neglected majority. pp. 139-142. Commonwealth Education Partnership. London.
- Ghurye, G. S. 1959. 'The Scheduled Tribes', Popular Press, Bombay.
- Goel, V. 2002. Science & Technology Education for Sustainable Development. pp.142-147. Commonwealth Education Partnership, 2003, U.K.
- Gregory, R. J. 2003. 'Tribes and Tribal Origin, Use and Future of the Concept', *Study of Tribes and Tribals*, 1 (1): 1-5.
- Grigson, W.V. 1938. 'The Maria Gonds of Bastar', Oxford University Publishers, London.
- Gupta, S. and Shilpy Gupta 2005. 'Development Fallacy or Reality: A Case of Birhor Tribes of Chotanagpur', pp. 562-583, In: *Primitive Tribes of India*, P. Dash Sharma (Ed.), Serial Publications, New Delhi.
- Gupta, Shilpy 2005. 'Human Rights and Primitive Tribes – An Anthropological Perspective', pp. 17-34, In : *Primitive Tribes in Contemporary India*, S.K. Chaudhuri & S.S. Chaudhuri (Eds.), Mittal Publications, New Delhi.
- Gupta, Shilpy and A.K. Kapoor 2005. 'Human Rights, Development and Tribe- A Study Among the Lahoulis of Himachal Pradesh', In: *Human Genetics, Health and Ethics in Research – Anthropological Perspective*, Krishan Sharma (Eds.), Panjab University, Chandigarh.
- Gupta, Shilpy and A.K. Kapoor 2006. 'Reported Crime and Actual Crime- A Mis Match – A Study Among the Lahoulis of Himachal Pradesh', *The Indian Police Journal*, 52(3).
- Gupta, Shilpy and Kapoor, A.K. 2007. Ethnicity and Social Variability among Lahoulis. Man and Life, 32 (1&2): 15-24.
- Hodson, T.C. 1989. 'The Naga Tribe of Manipur', Low Price Publication, Delhi.
- Hutton, J. H. 1931. With Complete Survey of Tribal Life and System', In: *Census of India*, Vol. I, Gyan Publishing House, Delhi.

- IFAD, Rural poverty report 2001. The challenge of ending poverty. IFAD, Rome, 2001.
- Kalekar, K. 1955. 'Report of the Backward Classes Commission', Vol. I, Government of India.
- Kapoor, A.K. 1990. 'Genetics and Tribals- An Anthropological Perspective', *South Asian Anthropologist*, 11:55-62.
- Kapoor, A. K. 1999. 'Law and Scheduled Tribes- A Socio- Legal Perspective', pp. 175-82, In: *Backward Communities*, V.K. Pant and B.S. Bisht (Eds.), Gyan Publishing House, Delhi.
- Kapoor, A.K. 1996. 'A Plea for Socio-Economic Development of the Tribals of Central Himalayas' , pp 163-172, In : *Man and Development in the Himalayas*, A.K. Kapoor and D. Singh (Eds.), Academic Foundation, Delhi.
- Kapoor, A.K. 1998. 'Role of NGOs in Human Development-A Domain of Anthropology', *Journal of Indian Anthropological Society*, 33: 283-300.
- Kapoor, A.K. 2000 a. 'Environment, Man, Technology and Development in Western Himalayas: Role of Anthropologist Vs. NGOs', *Man and Life*, 34:1-7.
- Kapoor, A.K. 2000 b. 'Environment , Health and Development in Sahariyas-A Primitive Tribe of Rajasthan', pp. 105-134, In: *Environment, Health and Development-An Anthropological Perspective*, P. Dash Sharma (Ed.), S.C. Roy Institute of Anthropological Studies, Ranchi.
- Kapoor, A.K. 2000 c. 'Ecology and Religions Practices Among the Bhotias in Himalayas', pp. 221-235, In: *Tribal Religion: Change and Continuity*, M.C. Behra (Ed.), Common Wealth Publishers, New Delhi.
- Kapoor, A.K. 2006. Ecology, Disease Pattern and Indigeneious Healing Aspects in Himalayan Communities. pp. 1-12. In: Indigenous Health Care & Ethno-medicine. A.N. Sharma, R.K. Gautam & A.K. Gharami (Eds.). Sarup & Sons, New Delhi.
- Kapoor, A.K. 2008. Environment, Ethnicity and Elderly: A Study in various Environmental Zones of India (under Publication).
- Kshatriya, G.K. and A.K. Kapoor 2003. 'Population Characteristics of the Bhils of Rajasthan', *Indian Anthropologist*, 33(1): 1-5.
- Lokur, B.N. 1965. 'The Report of the Advisory Committee on the Revision of the Lists of Scheduled Caste and Scheduled Tribes', Department of Social Security, Government of India.

- Mandal, B.P. 1980. 'Report of the Backward Classes Commission', Vol. I & II, Government of India, New Delhi.
- Mohan, H. 1975. 'The Parhaiya – A Study in Culture Change', Bihar Tribal Welfare Research Institute, Ranchi.
- Morris, W. 1980. 'The American Heritage Dictionary of the English Language', Houghton Miffin Company, Boston.
- Patra, P.K.; C. Dash and A.K. Kapoor 1997. 'Role of Mass Media in Tribal Development' , *Vanyajati*, 46 (2) : 11-16.
- Prasad, R.R. and A.K. Kapoor 1982. 'Obstetrical Practices Among the Bhotia Tribals', *Tribal Research Bulletin*, 4(2): 7-8.
- Radcliffe- Brown, A.R. 1922. 'The Andaman Islanders- A Study in Social Anthropology', Cambridge University Press, Glencce.
- Rao, M. N. K. 1982. 'Report of the Backward Classes Commission', Secretariat, Hyderabad.
- Rivers, W.H.R. 1906. 'The Todas', Mac Millan and Co., London.
- Roy, B. 1961. 'Ethnographic Study of Soligas', In: *Census of India*, Part V-B, No. 6, Monograph Series, Karnataka.
- Roy, S.C. 1912. 'Mundas and their Country', City Book Society, Calcutta.
- Roy, S.C. 1915. 'The Oraons of Chotanagpur', Author's Bar Library, Ranchi.
- Roy, S.C. 1921. 'Anthropological Researches in India', *Man in India*, 1: 11-56.
- Roy, S.C. 1928. 'Oraon Religion and Customs', Man in India Office, Ranchi.
- Roy, S.C. 1935. 'The Hill Bhuinyas of Orissa', Man in India Office, Ranchi.
- Roy, S.C. 1937. 'The Kharia', Vol. I and II (with R.C. Roy), Man in India Office, Ranchi.
- Roy. S.C. 1925. 'The Birhor- A Little Known Jungle Tribe of Chotanagpur', Man in India Office, Ranchi.
- Sahu, C. 1995. 'Birhor Tribe', Sarup and Sons Publications, New Delhi.
- Sahu,C. 1998. 'The Birjia- A Primitive Tribe of Bihar', pp. 42-53, In; *Tribal Culture and Identity*, Chaturbhuj Sahu (Ed.), Sarup and Sons Publications, New Delhi.

- Sastry, V.N.K.V. 1993. 'Chenchu Food Gatherers and Hunters of Nallamala Forests- Problems of Transition', *Man and Life*, 19(1&2): 83-96.
- Seligmann, G.G. 1911. 'The Veddas of Ceylon', Cambridge University Press, Cambridge.
- Seth, M.K. and B. Parida. 2006. Educational Assessment of Scheduled Caste & Scheduled Tribe Communities: A Study from Orissa. Man and Life, 32: 87-98.
- Sharma, A.N. 1994. 'The Bharias of Patalkot', M.K. Offset Printers, Bhopal.
- Sharma, P. D. 1996. 'The Parhaiyas of Palamau- An Ethnographic Study', Bihar Tribal Welfare Research Institute, Ranchi.
- Sharma, S.P. and J.B. Sharma 1999. 'Tribal Demography', Radha Publications, Delhi.
- Shukla, A. 2005. 'Indian Tribes- A Psycho-Social Perspective', Kanishka Publications, Delhi.
- Soni, L.N. 1998. 'The Bhil', In: *Tribal Culture and Identity*, Chaturbhuj Sahu (Ed.), Sarup and Sons Publications, New Delhi.
- Sujatha, K. 1994. Educational Development Among Tribes: A study of Sub-Plan Areas in Andhra Pradesh. South Asian Publishers, New Delhi.
- Thorat, S. 2008. Emerging Issues in Higher Education: Approach & Strategy in the 11th Plan. Paper presented in conference on Hihger Education & 11th Plan. 11 Nov, 2008. Vigyan Bhawan, New Delhi. Published by UGC, New Delhi.
- Tiwari, D.N. 1984. 'Primitive Tribes of Madhya Pradesh', Tribal Development Division, Ministry of Home Affairs, Government of India, New Delhi.
- Vidyarthi, L.P. 1963. 'The Maler –A Study in Nature –Man Spirit Complex in a Hill Tribe of Bihar', Book Land Pvt. Ltd., Calcutta.

18

Higher Education Governance in the Changing Context

K. Sudha Rao and Mithilesh K. Singh

ABSTRACT

Higher education has attained a crucial position in the recent past all over the world in general and Asian countries in particular due to unbelievable transformations in the World's geo-political order, globalization of the society and economy, technological revolution, especially the information technology, etc. The latter changes have also resulted in loss of monopoly of the institutions and countries, demanding for increased accountability, quality, relevance and transparency. It is obvious that decision making processes and the practices of any particular country is geared towards achieving the goals slated by its national policy, which in turn directly influences the systemic governance and management practices. Keeping in view the "State of the Art" conditions of higher education in India in general and the institutions in particular, an attempt has been made to present an overview of the concepts, structure, system and techniques of governance and management of higher education, followed by procedures that are in practice in India. Further, its implications on the present system of higher education and its impact on the society have also been described. At the end, the behavioral aspect of governance and management

have been explored to understand the existing differences in terms of quality of institutions irrespective of the fact that the policies, rules, regulations, norms and standards are nearly uniform in the central and state universities.

INTRODUCTION

The term 'governance' refers to the 'processes of decision-making within an institution [which] . . . enable an institution to set its policies and objectives, to achieve them, and to monitor its progress towards achievement'. Governance of public universities is significantly influenced by government policies with particular emphasis on efficiency. The Dearing Committee Report[2]. made valuable recommendations on the 'effectiveness of management and governance arrangements' in the universities. It also recognized three guiding principles for the success of any university:

- Institutional autonomy should be respected to *improve their management practices, develop their innovative capacity, and strengthen their capacity for modernization of their curricula in meeting the market and learner needs more effectively,*
- Academic freedom within the law should be protected, and
- Governance arrangements should be open/transparent and responsive.

"Without real autonomy and accountability, universities can be neither really responsive nor innovative. In return for being freed from dysfunctional over-regulation and micro-management, universities need to recognize the importance of accountability and professional management" (Communication of the EC, 10th May 2006).

Most of the Higher Education Institutions faced crises of confidence in governance at some stage or the other in their evolution. Some problems are distinctly structural, but many are financial stemming generally from the pressing financial exigencies owing to government cutbacks or declining local or international enrolments. Some were related to the governance of dysfunctional units within otherwise well-governed Institutions. Many problems arose simply because public universities are constantly in a state of flux and metamorphosis in tune with the nature of academic life. Frequently, perceived governance crises prompted the governing bodies to make exaggerated changes in governance models in order to produce radical and different results. Such overreaction may invariably result in bad governance practices, especially when glitches in personnel and financial systems lead to micromanaged financial systems in which every transaction is scrutinized for irregularities.

MANAGEMENT CONCEPTS AND TECHNIQUES

The nature of educational institutions and its changing functions, emerging form challenges, complexities, etc. in academic administration, had led the public to apply modern management concepts (corporate sector/entrepreneurial concepts) to the higher education sector as well. The advocacy of applications of corporate management methods to higher education sector is an accepted reality today. Some believed that the break with traditional concepts of academic administration is sufficient to warrant the label of a managerial revolution. Whereas the others believed that management concepts coupled with evolving notions of planned changes and technological innovation con-stitute a majestic design for bringing educational revolution at all levels. The governments of many countries are providing generous funding for the development, design, and dissemination of management techniques that surpass the futuristic dreams of many. The advent of the managerial revolution has not been without criticism. Numerous critics have cast doubts upon the effectiveness of system's analysis, operation research and engineering design as applicable to the complexities of higher education has been questioned. The applicability of systems approaches to education had been questioned. It is believed that scientific-economic-technological approaches do have limitations and do narrow the perspective in which education must be viewed. Yet, the educationists have been adopting new technologies to fulfill the various requirements of the learners. Knowledge management (KM) is one of the new concepts expected to improve continuous teaching-learning practices in educational institutions, and thereby to retain excellent teachers in the Higher Education Institutions for production of employable students.

Creation of learning environment is the key to the success of higher education no matter which country it is. Education is closely associated with KM to identify, create and share updated information and existing knowledge with every one. Recent developments in information and communication Technology (ICT) help faculty to create and share high-quality multimedia contents through web-based knowledge sharing system, supporting collaborative learning among teachers and students. Exchange of ideas and opinions between professors and students is expected to facilitate the success. Further, taking initiatives for sharing knowledge and experiences among teaching faculties and students has become essential as these are the key resource material for higher education institutions. Such an environment is expected to streamline the availability and dissemination of necessary information to the students about curriculum, assignments, tests, lecture notes, references, URL links, latest technology information, white papers, discussion forums, Desktop Video Conferencing and so on. However in most of the higher education institutions, teaching faculties don't get access to effective ICT tools for creation and sharing their knowledge base among themselves and student communities. The awareness about the use of ICT tools for developing knowledge, improving effective Teaching – Learning processes is, therefore, limited in developing and under-developed countries. Even in a country like India, rural India is totally different from urban India and within the latter metro cities are far different from other big cities.

There has been a great concern over the past decade regarding the establishment of the linkages between higher education institutions and potential employers. The institutions are under continuous pressure from the industries and regulatory bodies to gear their courses in such a way that the students are equipped with skills suiting to that of the workplace and that of the subject-specific knowledge. In general, the higher education that was giving priority for creation and dissemination of knowledge and focusing on developing the critical minds is now gearing itself towards providing skill and knowledge inputs to match the requirements by the employers.

GOVERNANCE: THE CONCEPT

Governance as a concept and its role in functioning of higher education system is well established and in practice since British Rule in India. The interpretation and application of its principles for actual system's management have been varying depending on the structural and functional relations that are operating in the country. Yet, the common understanding remains as: it is the way in which private and public players are seeking to solve university/organizational problems, it pertains to the decision making power in the organization, and above all it is related to the capacity of the institution to change, adapt and adopt to cater to the institutional needs and that too in time. The scope of governance constitutes state regulations, stakeholders' guidance, academic self governance, managerial self governance, accountability and competition. Some of the major decision making bodies that are directly or indirectly involved within the ambit of governance are regulatory bodies at the central and state levels, and Senate/Court, Syndicate/Executive Council, Board of Management, Academic Council, Finance Committee, etc. at the institution level.

Governance under the new paradigms of fast emerging knowledge economies and societies throughout the world including India, expecting the universities to be engines of the change, demands a flexible approach to enable itself to respond to the changing needs of the system at the center, the state and the institutional levels. At the same time, an increase in flexibility demands less of state regulation, which in turn raises issues concerning accountability, state supervision, intermediate organizations like research councils and quality agencies, performance-based funding from the governments, quality assurance procedures, handling of external and market influences, effective co-operation with society, efficient internal governance, dynamic role of leadership, and creation of innovative new bodies as supervisory boards or 'boards of trustees' with 'lay members', etc. Such changes in the governance, both in terms of content and context, may enable institutions of higher education to attain key positions in terms of Economic (knowledge economy) and Social value (massive participation). At the same time, it can make the system much more complex and challenging for the managers of the system.

GOVERNANCE: STRUCTURE MODELS

A 'one-size-fits-all' model of governance does not exemplify good practice. Conversely, governance problems may be comparable in different institutions of higher education. There is a need to avoid replication of bad practices, incorporation of good practices and benchmarking the same for replications. Modeling after any new governance structure at the university level requires a sustained commitment to understand what an institution was, what it is and what it wishes to be, and what it might become. Such modeling should be done within the framework of a strategic planning exercise, preparing stakeholders including the political class for prospective changes. Every model of governance has political ramifications that need to be considered without becoming captive to them. In effect, governing bodies should serve as the agents of change. More often than not, resistance to change stems from a lack of willingness to change, fear of unknown or fear of its consequences. The test of a governing body's capacity for change ultimately lies in its willingness and ability not only to recognize deficiencies in governance models but also in arriving at viable means of its remedy (Carnegie Commission on Higher Education, 1973). Some of the models are illustrated below for better understanding of the governance structure:

1. *Governance by the academic staff:* The most traditional model assumes that universities should principally be governed by its academic staff by entrusting unrestrained governance powers to the university senate or by having greater faculty representation on boards of governors, or both. A strong rationale for this model is that academic staffs are generally best equipped to understand the academic goals and aspirations of a university and the ways of achieving them.

2. *Corporate governance:* This is based on a business-enterprise model that is grounded in the captivating rationale of corporate efficiency. It mainly concentrates on the fiscal and managerial responsibility of those who are designated for governance of the university. This is an outcome based on the belief that public universities are poorly managed and fiscally deficient. The institutions of higher education are adopting this model in the recent past under the belief that corporate governance may redress these deficiencies.

3. *Trustee governance:* This model has acquired some cogency in universities over the period, though it started originally with charitable vision but has acquired the goal of profit as well. This model is articulated structurally through the mechanism of trust duties. In effect, trustee boards have a fiduciary duty to discharge their trust 'with the utmost good faith' towards the beneficiaries of that trust.

4. *Stakeholders Governance:* This model operates through representation of a wide array of stakeholders including students, academic staff, alumni, corporate partners, government and the public at large in the board. The stakeholder model exemplifies shared governance, which is different from faculty governance. It vests governance in multiple representatives not limited to academic staff alone. It is different from corporate governance in the sense that business and profit is not the sole motto. The governance authorities as representatives are distinct from professional and business focused boards; and the stakeholders' mandate extends beyond the efficient management and fiscal responsibility. As it is most inclusive, stakeholders' governance provides for wide participation of internal and external stakeholders in decision making.

5. *Amalgam Model of Governance:* This is a combination of academic staff, corporate, trustee and stakeholder governance models. This model usually involves readiness to experiment with innovation in university governance and is reliable to incorporate the strengths of different governance models to suit the specific needs of the university. The Amalgam model of governance's responsibilities are: building the knowledge base of the whole

society; profit in the for-profit activities; prudent, appropriate and complete expenditure of funds provided by government for specific purposes; producing innovations that underpin economic development; ensuring freedom for academic staff to provide public comment and give advice on issues in their areas of expertise; building critical mass in those discipline or professional areas in which the university seeks to excel; and providing an environment where students have the opportunity, what-ever their background, to achieve all that is possible for them.

Indian Context.

Historically, India has been the land of teachers and learners. "Guru-Shishya" parampara is age old tradition that was never quantified in terms of monetary gains either to guru or shishya. It was always treated with highest value and as something above quantification. Knowledge has always been regarded as the highest virtue in Indian society. The concept of a university is believed to be as old as ashrams of the ancient Hindu tradition that existed for adult learning. As far back as 1500 BC, teachers would retire to clearings in the forests, far from the noise of settlements, and attract a group of young men willing to join them in living a life of contemplation and philosophical discussion (Fletcher, 1968). The well-known universities at Takshashila and Nalanda existed centuries before modern ones came into existence in Europe and other parts of the world. The establishment of first set of modern universities in India was recommended by the British colonial administration in 1854, which were set up at Bombay, Calcutta and Madras in 1857. During the next 90 years, development of higher education was slow with only 20 universities and 500 colleges at the time of Independence in 1947, which enrolled around 230,000 students.

The post-independence era has witnessed a tremendous expansion of higher education making it today the third largest in the world next to US and China. Currently, India is proud of its 421 universities and nearly 20, 918 affiliated colleges having an estimated enrollment of over 11.2 million students (MHRD, 2008). A large majority of students, about 82 percent, account for enrollment in general education courses in the faculties of arts, science and commerce. The open and distance learning (ODL) institutions have also made significant impact on the higher education system. The Indira Gandhi National Open University (IGNOU), established in 1985 at New Delhi, and 13 State-level Open Universities and private universities share for about 25 percent of the total enrollment in higher education. Despite its large size, it has been able to cater to only about 11.3 percent of the relevant age group (18–24 years), while corresponding figures are more than 50 percent for the developed countries and 20 to 30 percent for developing countries. This scenario illustrates the need for a massive expansion of higher education facilities in the near future and demands better governance and management of the system.

The XI Five Year Plan challenges for India are different and unique from the earlier ones. Each of these issues though appears to be singular at the surface level, they have several in built and complicated sub issues that are more difficult and most sensitive. For example, quality is a challenge and access is an issue. All those who are aware of returns and benefits of higher education system are also in know of what knowledge to get, where to get it, how to get and how to use it for their benefit and can easily access it. This group has already exploited the system to their advantage and they need no guidance. But it is a greater challenge to provide quality access to those who are unaware of all these (as they are not exposed to institution, leave alone quality institution). Like wise, expansion of higher education with equity, inclusiveness, quality with excellence, funding including from the private players, academic and administrative reforms, and globalization all have provided benefits to people at urban and higher socio-economic levels. The challenge lies in reaching the deeper layers of the society and benefiting those, who were hitherto neglected and have remained as silent spectators of exploitation. Any discrimination further in access will only promote division among the educated products.

The present system of higher education still continues to be highly bureaucratized with multiple controls by Central and State Governments, statutory bodies like UGC, AICTE and others. Added to this is the politicization of the system and interferences from all quarters. Though the vocabularies used in Acts and

Statues, Policies and Programs provide for all that is required for a good management of a university, in actualities the vested interests have contributed towards differences in quality.

No doubt system is heavily subsidized by the Government. Up to 90 percent of the operating costs are paid for by the state government. But the lack of expertise of the leaders in financial management and managerial skills is facilitating the vested interest to grab power in the system and use it for their own advantage.

The efficiency of fund utilization in universities seems to be the weakest link.

Salary and compensation for teaching staff though improved after the Sixth pay commission, the question remains "is there a change in features, attitudes and sensitivity towards students that is proportionate to the hike in salary". Lack of professional ethics is the menace of the universities. A small percentage of committed and devoted teachers are bearing the total work loads of the institutions. The common statement such as higher education institutions are unable to attract and retain qualified and trained teachers may change over the period. But that may not guarantee the performance system if the governance system of the university is improved. Vested interest and influences in selection and recruitment have made the system to compromise on quality. Teachers are the brain of the Higher Education Institutions and it is they who need to create that atmosphere and provide supportive environment for learning and academic quality in universities. Selection of right individuals is very crucial and of course is at stake now.

Infrastructural facilities range from the best to inadequate. Laboratories need upgradation for better teaching. Even today thousands of colleges have no computer labs and, teachers, leave alone students, have even touched the computers.

Steady electric power supply is not available in the rural areas. Computerization is still a dream for the rural colleges leave alone its acquaintance and use by the rural students. In fact, it has created a great gap between the classes within the class. With such inputs given to the students (mere paper, syllabus, curriculum, no. of years, examination, certification, etc.) can it be called a degree?

India has a few very good institutions comparable to any other in the developed country and is producing the best who are employed in the world market even before their education is complete on the one hand and large number of mediocre degree churning mills – the destiny of the product of such mill is left to the god's grace and individuals luck.

Expansion with Equity.

It's true that India has experienced appreciable growth in terms of number of institutions during last six decades and particularly since 1990. More of state universities, some central universities and selected few good deemed to be universities(like IISC) and large number of the recent origin deemed to be universities of varied quality, few institution of national importance and many open universities in addition to private universities, and host of universities that are affiliating in nature are existing today. All the more interesting is the fact that at times an affiliating college is bigger in size (in terms of enrollment and physical infrastructure) than the university main campus. With all these, still India is not able to accommodate 89% of relevant age group population in the higher education system.

Above all, the bright spot of today's Indian Higher Education is that there is a commitment at all levels to support the system. In this support even the politicians, private partners, public including rural remote uneducated mass is interested. Providing finances for the system, expansion, Access, Equity and Relevance has become the major goal of one and all. India has accepted the facilitating policies such as globalization, privatization and Internationalization. Private participation and is encouraged. People are active participants in the process of development.

Present scenario reflects rural – urban disparities, inter-state variation, disparities in enrolment across income, caste, gender etc. According to the figures available (2003) the gross enrolment ratio ranges between rural and urban; female and male; Muslims and Hindus: rural poor and non-poor; urban poor and non-poor has been 7.76 to 27.20; 11.02 to 15.25; 8.19 to 12.00; 1.30 to 7.12 and 5.51 to 27.15 respectively. And even amongst these enrolled there is disparity in access to quality, education, nature and number of courses available, quality teaching library, laboratory & technology, facilities available. Disparities created due to theses facilities within the high range group is responsible for creating educated but dissatisfied, disturbed and frustrated youth who are disillusioned and are left with inferiority complex. The need for expansion is unquestionable priority. But with a caution-expansion not in mere numbers but with quality and relevance is the need. XI plan has proposed for focused expansion and with proper identification of hitherto unattended areas to address these issues of disparities. Again all good intentions until and unless carried to the field level without commitment and sincerity results in unintended outcome

While talking of accessibility, it needs to be emphasized that accessibility only for the sake of accessibility would not only add to the nation's financial burden but also would result in production of human resources that are neither helpful to themselves nor to the nation in any way. Lack of employment opportunities due to irrelevant courses (either helps for skill development or personality development) pushes the people to lose faith in the system

Quality and Excellence.

While referring to quality, it may be necessary to realize, that, it is a concept which is intangible in nature but is felt by one and all. Ensuring quality education demands structural and functional reforms in addition to commitment of enhanced financial resources, better infrastructure; greater use of ICT; teaching and learning in smaller groups; granting and exercising autonomy to the faculty and departments. Above all *'quality faculty and their development from time to time'- 'faculty recharge programmes' to arrest faculty stale that enable them to retain their vibrancy and dynamism in research, in their learning, unlearning and relearning, innovation in devising new methods of teaching etc. Keeping in view the student competencies* quality demands transparency in Administration and management, commitment of academic and non academic staff.

Surprisingly from amongst the 128 universities that are accredited by NAAC the grades obtained are: 32% at A and above,

52% at B and B+, and 16% at C levels. Similarly 68% of colleges at B, 23% at B grade which proves the quality differences between the existing universities and colleges.

XI plan has proposed four fold strategy to overcome the deficiency in the existing system- (i) bringing non 12(B) institutions under the orbit of UGC's grant, (ii) reducing the quality gap by helping B and C grade institutions, (iii) setting up of new universities / colleges / institutions with quality infrastructure, quality faculty and efficient academic and administrative governance and (iv) focus on providing quality teachers. For this purpose the, plan outlay is 19.8% of the total budget allotted for education. Major portion of this amount would go to setting up of 30 central universities. 8 IITs, 6 IIMs, 10 NITs, 2 school of Architecture and to meet the financial requirement public-private partnership is accepted as a way out though it is mentioned that private partnership should be inspired by a strong commitment to philanthropy (like TIFR, TISS, IISc. etc.) rather than mere profiteering and commercialization of higher education.

Recommendations of the Knowledge Commission (NKC).

The NKC, an advisory panel constituted by the central authority, recommended for an Independent Regulatory Authority to avoid multiplicity of regulatory bodies with overlapping mandates, that has resulted in overregulation and under governed system, to the extent, of their own mistake regulation for governance. Instead of single, national-level regulatory authority, NKC has recommended for an agency with separate councils for ensuring standards and quality with full autonomy & accountability for engineering, medicine, management, pharmacy, architecture, nursing and other individual professional programs. Each council would be responsible for laying down parameters on the growth and development of their fields by deciding on setting up of new institutions, designing and updating curriculum, faculty improvement, carrying out research, and other key issues. Though it is a good move, as is expected about all innovations, most of the existing regulatory bodies are opposing this recommendation as it would take away their powers.

The Regulatory bodies that were suitable at earlier context were established with great hopes at different points of time, no doubt proved its worth as a suitable structure and function that were designed to suit the then requirement. But the context today is totally different. Hence the need for changes in the very governance and regulatory structure, and the needed changes within these structures- be it UGC. AICTE, NCTE, EC, Syndicate, BOM for that matter

Synergies: Reflective Assessment.

The earlier discussion in forgoing paragraph has revealed how changes in the higher education institutions have become unavoidable against the backdrop of changes that have taken place already in the society and hence the very survival of the system is dependent on the systemic changes suitable to the present time.

The developments could be viewed as nationally distinct outcome of the struggle to define the true nature of knowledge between the actors such as states and politicians, institutional leaders and students, researchers and intellectuals and representatives of businesses and others in the society. The main question remains how different actors, with different interests, struggle for their own interests in a broad sense, how they form coalitions or alliances, devise strategies and form regimes, characterized by preference for certain forms of government regulation, internal organization and leadership and resist any change and innovation.

Although universities are still predominantly public in most countries, the way in which public authorities administer them are driven by university–state alliances, political-administrative interests and a semi-competitive logic based on incentive policies where public support depends partly on teaching and/or research performance.

Improvement in the quality of education is another aspect requiring urgent attention. Unconditional cooperation in curriculum development, preparation of instructional material, interactive teaching, implementation of innovative practices, use of new technologies, optimum utilization of existing resources, exchange of experts, and promotion of collaborative research are the need of the hour. Transparent systems of recruitment and selection of teachers, promotion keeping in view the quality as the main agenda without political interferences is the only solution.

Privatization of education though not new to Indian system is unavoidable due to social pressure and financial compulsion. To ensure exploitation that is not promoted and to guard against excessive profiteering, governments must monitor such institutions so that privatization and commercialization does not lower the quality

As private professional higher education gains strength, market-oriented value system may seep into society and are likely to dominate future policy-planning strategies as well. The business like and profit-oriented education is likely to inculcate and perpetuate competitiveness, self-centeredness, and related materialistic values among youth in India which is detrimental to Indian values inherited with rich culture and tradition which is valued all over the world. In the long run, such a system may vitiate the society at large in which values of the market place dominate social behavior. Governance and regulation are important to understand its role in terms of 'Why' 'what' and 'what not' 'Where' 'Where not' 'How' and 'How not' 'When' and 'When not'. Without understanding these mere pushing the file in a routine fashion may not deserve the purpose.

It is clear that the input each university gets from governances varies depending on the quality of governance system- UGC, AICTE, NCTE, State Secretariat /BOM/EC/AC, Syndicate etc. Though at the national level uniform policies, programs, schemes guidelines etc. are made, it's reach in and its totality including understanding and intentions behind such a policy depends on the intelligence, commitment and sincerity of the members at different levels and their acceptance absorption, interpretation and implementation. It is the quality of Governance of members who are at this level responsible for making policy for respective institution and contribute for all the differences in quality at the institution level. It is time for introduction of *Indian Education Service* for ensuring quality of members for the governance of Higher Education Systems.

Gestalt has identified several laws that guide human perceptions and consequent behaviour in different situations. Individuals are influenced by certain factors that surround them which influences their thinking and decision making. To name a few are Law of Frequency, Law of Regency, Law of Size, Law of Brightness, Law of Proximity, Law of Intensity etc.

It appears Gestalt theory of perception (1890) is applicable to governance and decision making bodies equally effectively as it is with others. More so, in University Syndicates, Senates, EC, BOMs where members are nominated with several considerations and each one brings along with the heavy bag pack which are settled into these decision making bodies more than the university agenda.

Though in principal systems, quality is the major agenda, members' bahaviour in these meetings could be analysed in the context of above states laws.

Law of Frequency and repetition: Invariably the attention of the members in these bodies gets drawn towards an issue which comes up as agenda frequently again and again and hence draws attention of the members faster than other important issues. For example if an agenda has backing of members in the board, support of power corners and members intervenes in the system frequently, the tendency of these bodies is to settle the issue first even if it is not for any other reason at least to avoid nuance value be it at national, state, university or college level. The statement that the *crying child gets its feed first* works.

Law of Recency: Any issue which is most recent in the memory of members, surfaces at the top level and gets attention of one and all, instead of a much more serious issue that requires attention of the VC or the Board Members. It may be necessary at this juncture to draw the attention of the readers that any Board/Syndicate/ EC meeting may last for a maximum of 6 to 8 hrs. which again is rare. Most of the times the meeting last for hardly 4 to 5 hrs. It may not be an exaggeration to reveal that there are universities that are habituated to finish the agenda in 3 to 4 hrs. It is not to underestimate the quality of time gone into decision making, yet, keeping in view the size of the institution, the attention and commitment needed by the governance to guide the system, the time that is actually devoted to understand the issue and then decide matters more effectively.

Law of size: Thanks to Gnanam committee report (1990) which suggested that the size of the university court should be of 100 members. The Court (Senate) may review the broad policies and programmes of the university and may make suggestions for the improvement and development of the university. It should not be the supreme governing authority and should have no powers to make statutes or approve the budget.

The executive council (Syndicate) should be the principal executive body of the university to coordinate and monitor the functioning of various sub-systems in the university structure. It should be the executive, administrative and financial authority with statute and Ordinance making powers about university authorities/bodies/committees/officers as also administrative and financial matters.

Which made an important recommendation regarding the need for arriving at an optimum size of Governing Bodies-be it Academic Council or Board of Management/Syndicate/Executive Council, to ensure quality of Decision making. Large numbers facilitate groups formation which in turn forces the decisions on the basis of numbers rather than the nature and the quality. Much of the decisions based on the majority may not be suitable for the academic institution yet the size influences the leadership to compromise on the issue at times even sacrificing the institutional interest. Similar thing can be noted in case of state and national levels for decisions taken at the regulatory bodies, for example in Delhi university colleges.

Law of Brightness: it is seen time and again in the decision making process that certain members with their tactical presentation with good vocabulary and communication skills are able to sweep over the whole process in comparison to the others who may be genuine, concerned, committed and having better ideas but lacking in vocabulary and communication skills may not draw the attention – it should call for lack of brightness.

Law of Intensity: The volume with which the issue is presented seem to take upper hand like the loud voice and high pitch in the meetings, than others, who present with slow voice and low pitch even an important issue. Majority of the issues pertaining to quality hardly draws the attention of all the board members where as appointments, promotions and financial matters draw the attention of all members. Political nominees invariably use this as a strategy. The university strikes, involvement of different groups of people in the campuses, be it student, academic or non academic staff are able to influence the decision makers through this process. The big sound, the media presentations, the noise and disturbances that it creates in the campuses etc. keeping all these in view the kind of compromises that takes place in the Decision making process is of great concern and a major challenge to all the members no matter at which level of governance the members are located.

Law of proximity is another factor which brings in familiarity into the context for influencing the decision making process and the beneficiaries invariably use this trick and make use of such opportunities for their own benefit. Many times, agenda of the people who are in the proximity of leadership and the members of the governance get settled faster (at times in their favours) than the issues concerning others. Similarly the issues pertaining to main university campus (be it infrastructure or personnel) get priority attention in comparison to those in the affiliated colleges.

It is revealing to know that irrespective of the fact that such important meetings are loaded with agendas and many other important inputs, still human factor does intervene in the process of decision making. Keeping this in view it is essential to introduce a pre-induction/in-service training for all the personnel who are employed in the Governance structure at all levels and be made compulsory for all those who are not from the education sector and even for those from, the education sector who have not held the decision making position.

RELEVANT SOURCES/SUGGESTED READING

Altbach , P.G. and Chitnis, S. 1993. Higher Education Reform in India: Experience and Perspectives, Sage Publications, London.

Basu, Aparna. 1972. Essays in the History of Indian Education. Delhi, India: Concept.

Bleiklie I. 2005. 'Academic Leadership and Emerging Knowledge Regimes', in I. Bleiklie and M. Henkel (Eds.) Governing Knowledge: A Study of Continuity and Change in Higher Education, Dordrecht: Springer.

Bleiklie I. 2007. 'Systemic Integration and Macro Steering', Higher Education Policy 20(4): 391–412.

Bleiklie, I. and Byrkjeflot, H. 2002. 'Changing knowledge regimes — universities in a new research environment', Higher Education 44(2–3): 1–14.

Braun, D., & Fran‡ois-Xavier, M. (Eds.). 1999.Towards a New Model of Governance for Universities? A Comparative View, Jessica Kingsley Publishers, London.

C.A.B.E Committee Recommendations, June 2005. Govt. of India.

Chauhan, C. P. S. 2004. Privatization of higher education: A socioeconomic perspective. *University News*, 44 (7), pp. 35 - 39.

Clark, B.R. 1998. Creating Entrepreneurial Universities: Organizational Pathways to Transformation, Oxford, New York, Tokyo: IAU Press/Pergamon.

Damrosch, D. 1995. We Scholars. Changing the Culture of the Universities, Cambridge and London: Harvard University Press.

Dharmpal. 1983. The Beautiful Tree: Indigenous Indian Education in the Eighteenth Century. Delhi, India: Biblia Implex.

Drèze, Jean, and Amartya Sen, Eds. 1997. Indian Development: Selected Regional Perspectives. Delhi, India: Oxford University Press.

Education Commission. 1964–1966. *Education and national development: A report*. New Delhi: Government of India, Ministry of Education.

Fletcher, B. 1968. *Universities in the modern world*. London: Pergamon, p. 11.

Frank, D.J. and Meyer, J.W. 2007. 'Worldwide Expansion and Change in the University', in G.A. Krücken, A. Kosmützky and M. Torka (Eds.) Towards a Multiversity? Universities between Global Trends and National Traditions, Bielefeld: Transcript Verlag.

Gibbons, M., Limoges, C., Nowotny, H., Schwartzman, S., Scott, P. and Trow, M. 1994. The New Production of Knowledge. The Dynamics of Science and Research in Contemporary Society, London, Thousand Oaks, New Dehli: Sage.

Gnanam Committee on University Management. 1990. Constituted by Govt. of India.

Gornitzka, Å., Kogan, M. and Amaral, A. (Eds.). 2005. Reform and Change in Higher Education. Analysing Policy Implementation, Dordrecht: Springer.

Gupta, A. 2007. India: The new private sector. *International Higher Education, CIHE, Boston College*, no. 46, Winter, pp. 17 – 18.

Huq, Muhammad Shamsul. 1965. Education and Development Strategy in South and Southeast Asia. Honolulu, HI: East-West Center.

Krücken, G.A., Kosmützky, A. and Torka, M. (Eds.). 2007. Towards a Multiversity? Universities between Global Trends and National Traditions, Bielefeld: Transcript Verlag.

Meyer, J.W. and Ramírez, F. 2000. 'The World Institutionalization of Education', in Schriver, J. (Ed.) Discourse Formation in Comparative Education, New York: Peter Lang Publishers, pp. 111–132.

National Knowledge Commission Recommendation (NKC) on Higher Education, 2006. http://www.knowledgecommission.gov.in/recommendations/higher1.asp

Readings, B. 1996. The University in Ruins, Cambridge, MA and London: Harvard University Press.

Schultz, Theodore W. 1961. "Investment in Human Capital." American Economic Review 51 (1): 1–17.

Selected Educational Statistics. 2005-06. MHRD, Govt. of India.

Singh, Mithilesh Kumar. 2006. Challenges of Globalization on Indian Higher Education, University News, Vol.44, No. 19, May 08 - 14, 2006.

Singh, Mithilesh Kumar. 2006. Autonomy in Higher Education: Regulatory and Legal Issues, Background Paper for EPSI. 2006.

Sudha Rao. K, & Singh, Mithilesh Kumar. 2007. University Education in India: Challenges Ahead, University News, Vol. 45, No. 02, Jan. 08 - 14, 2007.

Sudha Rao. K, & Singh, Mithilesh Kumar. 2005. Appointment of Vice Chancellors: Rules, Procedures and Intentions, University News, Vol. 43, No. 37, Sept. 12 - 18.

Sudha Rao. K, & Singh, Mithilesh Kumar. 2002. Self Financed Courses un the Universities and Colleges, University News, Vol. 40, No. 43, Oct. 28 - Nov. 3, 2002.

Taskforce on Higher Education and Society. 2000. Higher Education in Developing Countries: Peril and Promise, The World Bank, Washington.

Teichler, U. 1988. Changing Patterns of the Higher Education System. The Experience of Three Decades, London: Jessica Kingsley.

Teixeira, P., Jongbloed, B., Dill, D. and Amaral, A. (Eds.) 2004. Markets in Higher Education. Rhetoric or Reality?, Dordrecht: Kluwer.

Thorat, S. 2007. A circular to all Indian universities regarding XI Five Year Plan for higher education. New Delhi: University Grants Commission.

Tilak, Jandhyala B. G. 1988. Educational Finances in South Asia. Nagoya, Japan: United Nations Centre for Regional Development.

Turk-Bicacki, L. and Brint, S. 2005. 'University-industry collaboration. Patterns of growth for low and middle-level performers', Higher Education 49(1–2): 61–89.

UNDP. 2001. Human Development Report. New York: Oxford University Press.

UNESCO. 1999. Estimates of literacy rates for 2000. UNESCO Statistical Yearbook.

UNESCO. 1992. Improving Effectiveness of Higher Education Institutions: Studies of the Management of Change, International Institute for Educational Planning (IIEP), Paris.

World Bank. 2000. Higher education in Developing Countries: Peril and promise. World Bank-UNESCO, Washington D C.

19

Creating Excellence

V.K. Arora

INTRODUCTION

The role of a teacher has never been as challenging as it is today. It is challenging because a teacher can no longer act as a model knowledge bank when new ideas, concepts and strategies change the world almost daily and when 'facts' of yesterday become 'misinformation' of today. It is challenging, because the new clientele of education in schools and colleges is a more diverse group of students than at any time during the history of education in India. Dealing with such a lot with the object of helping them to develop their talents and personality to the point of excellence is not an easy task. The National Policy on Education (1986) stipulates, "The principal role of a teacher is, and will always be, teaching and guidance of their pupils, not only through classroom instruction and tutorials, but by personal contact and numerous other ways teachers have always employed for building the character of their pupils".

It means that in addition to competency in the subject matter, a teacher is required to sharpen his individual skills to learn and teach better, to handle different types of students, and to conceptualize different reactions. Subject-matter competency is easy to be acquired by developing skills of data-collection, data-analysis, research, making use of library and experimenting with best known methods of teaching and learning to update knowledge of self and students. Problem-oriented seminars, symposia, summer institutes, workshops and conferences are organized on a regular basis, all over the country, to enable teachers to discuss their research findings, interpret recent trends in their respective fields of study, and widen their intellectual horizon. In addition to subject-competency, certain skills in communication and social integration are also absolutely necessary for teachers of today. If a teacher leads a duteous life and can inspire his students, he is sure to create a positive difference in institutional output and environment. He does not need to undergo any formal personality development training or resort to any complicated philosophical study for this. By simply focusing on his attitude, action and aspirations, he can create excellence in his personal and professional life and may bring qualitative improvement all around.

COMMUNICATION

The intrinsic strength of a teacher lies not in anything he says or does outwardly but in the vibrations he sends out. *A teacher must send positive vibrations to make a strong impression on the pupils.* In making speeches, solving problems and counseling students, a teacher should use simple and positive words and phrases. Words have tremendous power. Words create our thoughts that in turn create our feelings. When someone thinks 'I am worthless', he or she feels worthless; one doesn't even have to be aware of words, they can exist sub-consciously with the same effect. Words create mental images, arouse emotions and affect decisions. A teacher can learn from salespersons. The feeling of being happy, successful and contented among them develops their own vocabulary. They express *agreement* not the contract; *investment* not the price, *valued* at but not the costs, *involved* but not the sold, *presentation* but not the pitch. When one makes it a point to color his words with positive phrases, he will notice a great uptake in his ability to hold attention. *Some positive key words and phrases have to be made a part of our vocabulary.* These may be control, commitment, choice, concentrate, firm, flexible, friendly, influence, improvement, enjoy, mentally tough, learner, persistence, problem-solver, smooth, service, silence and the like.

Also, try to eliminate profanity from your vocabulary and use simple and pleasant words and phrases. Teachers who use difficult and high-sounding words are inclined to be over-bearing and stuffed-shirts. And stuffed-shirts are usually negative people. The only thing that counts about one's vocabulary is the effect on others' mind. Words are the raw-material of thoughts. They determine how you and others react. Excellent teachers are specialists in creating positive, forward-looking, optimistic pictures in their own minds and in the minds of others.

A sure and fine way to quickly improve your all-round communication is to immediately eliminate 'should' and 'have to' words from your language. Notice the effect and reaction of those words on the people you are talking to. Do they not seem to shut down, get defensive and become angry? What happens to you when you find yourself being 'should' and 'have to'. Make sure the words you choose are building bridges not the walls. Build castles while speaking, don't build graves. Your talking has to be positive right from the time you get up in the morning, as morning–thoughts set the pattern for the whole day. If you do not use the early morning hours to sort out your thoughts, what other time will you have to do so?

ATTITUDE

The quality of life depends not on 'where we are' or 'what we have' or 'what we are', but solely upon our mental attitude. If we want our system to change, we will have to change ourselves first. The external world is a reflection of the inner. Outward conditions have very little to do with that. We tend to blame others for our sufferings and failures, but forget that others are like that because we are like this. The moment we see the other side suffers like we do and empathize with their sufferings, things begin to change. We are linked to each other, and all that exists, through our interconnected vibrations. The unseen hand that shapes our world is our very self. What we see and achieve is the direct result of what we perceive. John Milton was conscious of it, when he wrote in **"On His Blindness"**:

> **"*The mind* is its own place, and in itself can make a heaven of hell, a hell of heaven".**

Most of us are generally unconscious of this duality in ourselves. We mistake ourselves to be the ideal and are usually blind to our own imperfections. If we carefully watch ourselves, we may discover that almost all of us have a sense of morally strong, physically loving and socially disciplined human being that 'we should be'; but in the mental zones of our emotions we are tantalized by our petty feelings and attachments and behave like 'Curs fed by the wayside gutters'. Our attachments distort the ideal and create sensuous selfishness in us that needs to be brought into unison with our pure intellect. No teacher, preceptor, book or guide can help us in this mental-rehabilitation. It has to be done solely by ourselves. Most of our attitude is shaped during the formative years by our environment, education and experiences. Environment creates culture, experience sets patterns, and education elucidates values. It can also be the result of childhood conditioning. If we were criticized a lot as a child, we may well look for the same faults in our children and students and go on wasting tears on 'might have been'. The need is to turn tears into sweat as we go after 'what can be'.

The world has always been imperfect in the 'throes of agony', 'erosion of values' and 'tottering on the brink'. The pages of history shriek with the tragic tales of man's inhumanity to man. But after reading the story of progress of science and technology, one may realize that conditions today are infinitely better than what they used to be in earlier times. The world as a whole is constantly changing and growing better. Teaching too has changed its way. The student-teacher chemistry has evolved from **Guru** (teacher) as God and **Guru** as all knowing to **Guru** as a 'friend, philosopher and guide' and **Guru** as someone 'who does not always know the best'. He is regarded today as one of the many sources of learning. At best, he can only inspire or motivate students to learn from him, and from each other to become responsible citizens of society. His responsibility is to develop his students, guide them in a meaningful way, give them space to grow and encourage them to realize their full potential.

Resist the temptation to argue on frivolous issues. Ask yourself two questions before arguing on any topic: (a) is it really important enough to talk about? and (b) have I ever gained anything substantial from arguing on a subject like this earlier? Remind yourself that it is better to lose an argument than to lose a friend, when the debate heats up. For cultivating excellence, it is imperative to have the attitude that cements social cohesiveness. If you bear a grudge against someone, you put yourself in a prison house of your making. You waste your energies in harboring the thoughts of revenge. 'An eye for an eye' is a wrong approach. "It would make the whole world blind", said Gandhi. Had Duryodhan forgotten the loud comment and derisive giggle of her sister-in-law, Dropadi, on mistakenly falling into a pool of water in the Mayasabha, had Dropadi forgiven her brother-in-law, Dushasan, for disrobing her in the court of Kauravas, and had Dronacharya been not smarting from vexation caused by insult he suffered at King Drupad's court, the war of Mahabharata could have been averted. It is not what others do hurt us most, but our response to these acts. Chasing after the poisonous snake that has bitten us will only drive the poison through our veins into the total system. Is it not desirable to take immediate measures to get the poison out? Carnegie (1950) has a very interesting story to guide us in this respect:

George Rona, an attorney of Vienna, fled to Sweden during the World War II. He had no money and needed a job to survive. Since he knew several languages, he wrote to every importing and exporting firm for a position as correspondent. Most of them declined his services, but the proprietor of a firm wrote the nasty letter hurting Rona's sentiments "What you imagine about my business is not true. You are both wrong and foolish. I do not need any correspondent. Even if I did need one, I would not hire you because you can't even write good Swedish. Your letter is full of mistakes".

George Rona felt insulted "What did this Swede mean by telling him that he could not write the language! Why, the letter this Swede himself has written was full of mistakes". So George Rona wrote a letter that was calculated to burn this man up. Then he paused and said to himself "Wait a minute now. How do I know this man is not right? I have studied Swedish but it is not my native language, so may be I do make mistakes. I do not know anything about. If I do, then I certainly have to study harder if I ever hope to get a job. This man has possibly done me a favor even though he did not mean to. The mere fact that he expressed himself in disagreeable terms does not alter my debt to him. Therefore, I am going to write him and thank him for what he has done."

So George Rona tore up the scorching letter he had already written and wrote another that said, "It was kind of you to go to the trouble of writing to me especially when you do not need a correspondent. I am sorry; I was mistaken about your firm. The reason that I wrote you was that I made enquiry and your name was given me as a leader in your field. I didn't know I had made grammatical errors in my letter. I am sorry and ashamed of myself. I will now apply myself more diligently to the study of Swedish language and try to correct my mistakes. I want to thank you for helping me get started on the road to self-improvement."

Within a few days, Rona got a letter from this man asking Rona to come to see him. Rona went and got a job.

Forgive those who have done wrong to you in the past. We may not be saintly like Jesus Christ and Mahatma Gandhi to love our enemies, but for our own moral and intellectual growth and better interpersonal relations we need to forgive and check the tendency to get even with our enemies. *Forgiveness is a sort of creativity. It sets you free from the self-inflicted torture.* It brings peace and new possibilities in life. It is the best way to elevate the quality of our lives.

ACTION

With this kind of attitude, if teachers come forward to act in a spirit of cooperation and commitment, they will find the world around them changing. *Our society has become critical of teachers because many of them reflect crash opportunism, drift towards passion, political partisanship and greed of pelf and power in their day-to-day conduct.* Instead of pursuing the higher values of life, they copy the conduct of third rate politicians. Instead of guiding students to righteous path of living, they seem to be guided by their mannerism, either to gain cheap popularity or to overcome the sense of inferiority arising from their lack of competence or devotion to studies. Provision of facilities in the institutions for quality teaching, improved training, inducing research and frank discussions on academic issues are usually neglected by them. Only a few ambitious ones strive to update their subject-knowledge. Others do not even feel the necessity of doing it and are hardly aware of the latest developments in their disciplines.

Criticism and apprehensions are necessary virtues of a developing system. If taken in the right spirit as hints for self-improvement, they may sound rational. It is true that many of our difficulties are the result of the process of change and development, but it is also true that most of the teachers in our schools and colleges are performing their duties only perfunctorily. They are not at all concerned with qualitative improvement of the output. Teaching is a very honorable profession. Hindu scriptures regard it as a "Yajna" – a self-sacrificing work undertaken in a spirit of self-dedication for God's favor to all, because it creates and moulds the social and cultural life of a nation. It awakens the sleeping spirit. But if we accept our profession half-heartedly, we cannot put our best into it. We begin to blow up limitations, develop pessimistic disposition and gradually lose interest in teaching. Since there is a greater multiplier effect in this profession, our lack of interest boomerangs on our wit making us dullards bit by bit. The life-enriching profession, thus, takes away the vigor of life for one simple reason: the non-acceptance of profession. The problem, therefore, is more with us than with the system and so also is the remedy.

Be enthusiastic. Wake up your life. Begin to accept your profession totally. "When you do the things you ought to do when you ought to do them, the day will come when you will do the things you want to do when you want to do them. Hard work is the accumulation of the easy things you didn't do when you should have" (Maxwell, 1993). Therefore, lose yourself in action. It is also the best anesthetic ever known for sick nerves and the surest way to be successful and remain happy in life. Remember Louis Pastuer's words that "peace is found in libraries and laboratories". Because the men and women in libraries and laboratories are too absorbed in their work to worry about themselves, researchers rarely suffer nervous breakdowns. They don't have the time for such luxuries. If you give your best shot to what you are doing, things will happen to change. Teaching inspires and motivates the people to do their best. Be willing to give your one hundred percent to your students and institutions.

Manipulation won't work. People possess the knack to discriminate between sincerity and pretension. If you are conscious, committed and generous and act virtuously, it is fine even if you are not doing well financially. There are two currents of consciousness and energy in this world. One is expansive and the other is contractive. An expansive attitude generates self-awareness, while contradiction brings with it a sense of guilt, fear or pain. Look to nature. It is expansive. The sunlight, air, water, rain showers are its bounteous gifts given to us absolutely fee. But the ignorant man runs after his own profit and pleasure all the time, ignoring the interests of others. He tries to get more and more money for less and less work. He seems to have forgotten the age-old Indian saying that "By taking, and not paying for that, you become a **Thug** (Swindler), but by giving you become a **Thakur** (Lord)".

People talk highly of Buddha, Mahavira, Jesus, Guru Nanak, Gandhi, Mother Theresa, and Nelson Mandela because each one of them believed in giving more than in receiving. What we sow is what we reap. Anything that has value in life if given to others is returned to us in a like manner. Give love, you get love in return, give respect you get respect; give knowledge and you become knowledgeable. You always feel happy by making others happy. Even if you want material comforts, wealth and affluence, help others to become materially affluent and wealthy. This Universal law of nature exhorts us to abolish every vestige of selfishness and separateness in our hearts and do our best to contribute to the progress of humanity. The man who only thinks of himself will not get much out of life. Victor Hugo in his novel 'Les Miserables' has a message for him.

A convict had escaped from prison. He sought shelter for the night. The priest obliged him by giving food and a bed to sleep. In the middle of the night, he decamped with the silver plates from the priest's house. The next morning, the police, who had caught him, brought him to the Church. The holy priest feigned surprise and asked the policeman "Why did you harass him? I gifted the plates to him last night". The policeman apologized and went away. The convict was wonder struck. To crown it all, the priest took up two silver candle-stick stands from his desk and gave them to the thief with the words, "Remember life is to give, not to take". The convict took them and left. He was transformed thereafter, living a life of service and sacrifice.

In a sense, giving is synonymous for receiving. So is sacrifice for service. The way to gain anything is to lose it first. The English word 'currency' is taken from the Latin word '*currere*' meaning to 'run' or 'flow'. Money should be kept flowing. The more one runs for it, the more it recedes. You crave for it, and it eludes you. And even if you happen to amass wealth by taking advantage of your position and cunning, you turn impure and demonic. "Where wealth accumulates, men decay", said Oliver Goldsmith. Hence, giving is the only way of receiving. "We shall have to work for giving up altogether all desire for results. People will call us both good and bad. But we shall have to work like lions, keeping the ideal before us, without caring whether the wise ones praise or blame us.", said Swami Vivekananda (Advaita Ashram, 1986).

ASPIRATIONS

Excellence comes from quality of choices and decisions. Wise amongst us do not hanker after the **Preyas** – pleasant and immediately attractive – and get stuck in a round of pleasures. They have the propensity to listen to their inner voice (pure consciousness) and do only what conduces genuine welfare – the **Shreyas**. The path of pleasure and profit, though exciting and capable of yielding sensate satisfaction, is transient and incapable of giving the sense of fulfillment to man. It is tautological, not creative. It tends to increase tension, sorrow and frustration in life. All holy scriptures, therefore, condemn the path of **Preyas** as unrighteous and unworthy to follow. On the other hand, the path of **Shreyas** is regarded productive and valuable as it offers opportunity for fulfillment and self-development. And like other paths, the path of **Shreyas** too runs through the course of life itself not outside of it. It runs through a series of pleasure and pain, wisdom and ignorance, joy and sorrow, victory and defeat, ups and downs and all such dual concourse.

The journey on the path of **Shreyas** begins with a clear understanding of one's aspirations. "Some things are within our control and some things are not", writes the Stoic philosopher, Epictitus (Lebell, 2003). "Within our control are our opinions, aspirations, desires and the things that repel us outside our control, however, are such things as what kind of body we have, whether we're born into wealth or strike it rich, how we are regarded by others, and our status in society. We must remember that those things are externals and are therefore not our concern. Trying to control or to change what we can't only results in torment" (Lebell, 2003). "Circumstances do not rise to meet our expectations. Events happen as they do. People behave as they are. Embrace actually what you get" (Lebell, 2003). It is unwise to be possessive and excessively concerned with other people's impressions. People who subordinate their reason to be immediately attractive and pleasant are slaves to their senses. They foolishly run after externals. When teachers are seen making needless obeisance to petty politicians, undue craving for coercive power positions and excessive greed for money and comforts, the society-symbols are distorted. People rush to have false symbolic things, disturbing the system. Teacher himself is responsible for his denigration and lowering the image of teachers as a class. Those desirous to achieve excellence should stop chasing (false) success symbols and try to form the habit of asking themselves on every occasion, 'what is the right thing to do now', and making it their business to draw out the best in others and becoming the role models for society.

CONCLUSION

In short, the quality, competence and character of the teacher are important factors in influencing the quality of education and its contribution to personal and social development. Teachers basically are of three types: (a) complaining type, (b) compromising type, and (c) inspiring type. If one belongs to the third type, he can do much in directing the students to human excellence. The end is to make use of knowledge to enrich the lives of others. Mere transferring knowledge from books to students is like transferring bones from one grave to another. For qualitative output, besides teaching the subject, a teacher has to transfer the disciple's awareness into a new dimension of creating excellence. Such a teacher can open up a new horizon of knowledge in which science, philosophy and ethics will be synthesized in one integrated understanding. We cannot hope to build a better world without improving the individual-psyche. Both teachers and students should work to achieve this objective.

REFERENCES

Advaita Ashram. 1986. Swami Vivekananda, Complete Works. Vol. VII. Advaita Ashram, Calcutta, 1986, pp. 231-232.

Carnegie, D. 1950. How to stop worrying and start living. Kingsword Survey, Fourth Impression, the World' Work Ltd., pp. 115-116.

Lebell, S. 2003. The Art of Living: A new Interpretation by Sharon Lebell. Harper Collins Publishers, a Joint venture with India Today Group, New Delhi, VIII Impression.

Maxwell, J.C. 1993. Developing the Leader within You. Thomas Nelson Publishers, Nashville, 164 p.

SECTION : VIII – ENVIRONMENT AND ETHICS

20

Value Education Model from St. Joseph's College, Trichy

R. Rajarathinam

INTRODUCTION

Education is a methodical effort towards learning basic facts about humanity. And the core idea behind value education is to cultivate essential values in the students so that the civilization that teaches us to manage complexities can be sustained and further developed. It begins at home and it is continued in schools. Everyone accepts certain things in his/her life through various mediums like society or government.

Value education is important to help everyone in improving the value system that he/she holds and put them to use. Once, everyone has understood their values in life they can examine and control the various choices they make in their life. One has to frequently uphold the various types of values in his life such as cultural values, universal values, personal values and social values.

Thus, value education is always essential to shape one's life and to give him an opportunity of performing himself on the global stage. The need for value education among the parents, children, teachers etc. is constantly increasing as we continue to witness increasing violent activities, behavioral disorder, lack of unity in the society etc.

The family system in India has a long tradition of imparting value education. But with the progress of modernity and fast changing role of the parents it has not been very easy for the parents to impart relevant values in their wards. Therefore many institutes today conduct various value education programs that are addressed to rising problems of the modern society. These programs concentrate on the development of the children, young adults etc. focusing on areas like happiness, humility, cooperation, honesty, simplicity, love, unity, peace etc.

History of the Course

St. Joseph's College (Autonomous), Tiruchirappalli, Tamil Nadu was established in 1844 by the French Jesuit Fathers of the Toulouse Province of France. As a premier religious institution run by the Jesuit Fathers, the importance of imparting spiritual values along with secular education was the visionary mission of the founding Fathers of the college. As per the Constitution of the Society of Jesus the tertiary education imparted should comprise of the following:" Since the aim of the Society and of the teaching it provides, is to help towards the knowledge and love of God and their growth in grace..." So the Department of Catechism /Religious Courses was established with objective of teaching religious doctrine and values ever since the inception of the college.

It was then called Religious Instruction and was meant to train the Undergraduate students in the tenets of the Catholic Religion and enable them live life righteously, believing and following the sacred values, commandments and the sacraments that they were trained in.

The course was so designed that the values imparted helped the students to discriminate between good and evil and to cherish those eternal universal values at any cost in life. It also enabled them to acquire true knowledge and dispel ignorance, error and misconceptions. The course was given such importance that it had a direct bearing on the life of the students influencing their conduct and character. The Constitution also declares, "Great care must be taken that those who come to Jesuit colleges to acquire knowledge, also learn to behave as befits a Christian.... The teachers for their part should see, each of his pupils that they comply."

From the earliest days, the Catholic students had to take a course on Religious Instruction, the other Christian students, a course on the Bible and the non-Christian students on Ethics.

In the year 1978, St. Joseph's was one of the earliest colleges to be conferred with the autonomous status. There was a change of perspective in imparting the course. It was considered Part IV in the UG curriculum. The three streams of the earlier period were maintained with one of instruction per week. Every Semester terminated with a summative exam well ahead of the Semester Examinations. The written test carried 60 marks, attendance 10 marks and assignment 30 marks summing up to an aggregate of 100 marks for the Continuous Internal Assessment. Since the Course was administered for four semesters the total marks was calculated with the average taken in the four semesters. If a student did not get an aggregate of 40 marks (passing minimum), he was not given the degree. This system which was an advancement of the earlier pattern instilled an amount of seriousness among the students.

However the course pattern was widely felt to be given peripheral importance as there was no separate Board of Studies and matters pertaining to the course were not discussed in the Academic Council of the college.

In 1998, the following important changes were effected in the curriculum of this course:

- The label "Foundation Course" was introduced.
- The chief objective of the course reflects the visionary statement of Rev. Fr. Pedro Aruppe, S.J., the former Superior General of the Society of Jesus, that the education imparted should train students to be men and women for others.
- A separate Board of Studies was constituted for Foundation Courses offered.
- Deliberations were passed in the Academic Council.
- The course was given 2 credits with 2 classes per week for four semesters.
- The complete syllabus was placed before the Academic Council for approval after the discussion held in the Board of Studies.
- New components like Social Analysis were introduced in the course.

The Renewed Objective

The objective of the course was spelt out as to impart high quality value oriented realistic knowledge that provides love and acceptance of self and real knowledge of the world in which we live that encourages life long openness to growth. The course was linked to the Extension Department, SHEPHERD (Science and Humanities for People's Development).

Under this unique programme of the college, 70 villages in the immediate neighbourhood of the college, spanning over three districts are adopted by the college and various projects are planned and executed by the students of the college. Each class adopts a particular village for this purpose.

To initiate the students very effectively into this programme in a meaningful manner special orientation is given in the foundation course for all the UG students in the first year under the nomenclature "Social Analysis".

The input gets the students trained theoretically to take up the SHEPHERD programme in the second and third year of their UG programme seriously. The same training also helps the students, if they continue their post graduation studies in the college.

COURSE CONTENTS OF THE CURRICULUM

Special Features

The course contents are designed to bridge the gap between men and men, men and society, men and life changes and life challenges.

In order to help students get exposed to problems and their remedial measures, the department organizes seminars, workshops, group discussions etc. to make them agents of social changes in whatever capacity they work as individuals or groups or institution after their studies. The course thus envisions providing a firm grounding in the following avenues:

1. It provides excellence in its work of formation and witnesses to that excellence.
2. It also provides adequate personal care and concern for others. It prepares students for active participation for the liberation and service of others.

3. The course also gives a clear picture about the contemporary society where social inequalities, social injustices, dehumanizing poverty etc. have become very common and helps the students to be agents for social change.
4. The Annual Conference for staff of these courses provide a strong background to teach the contents of social ethics in an impressive way.
5. This programmed course is designed to be a feeder course for making students social service agents, value oriented leaders, counselors, listeners, organizers of liberation movements, promoters of physically challenged people.

Revitalizing the Teaching of Ethics

Counselors are available in the campus in the form of mentors in each class, besides a professional counselor to attend to the counseling needs of the students on the campus. In the class of ethics every attempt is made to discover and develop the kingdom values which are opposed to the excessive materialistic and consumerist tendencies of the modern world.

It provides a spiritual vision of the world in the face of materialism. It provides a genuine concern for others in the face of egoism; simplicity in the face of consumerism and the willingness to work for the cause of the poor in the face of social injustice. The students are given training to relate the values picked up in the classroom and apply them in their daily life. Hence the teaching methods are experience-based and participatory.

Soon after admission, a one day orientation programme is arranged for freshers to explain the need and importance of the Foundation Course programme and thereby the students are motivated to take up this programme seriously and with the right frame of mind.

Highlights of the Course

- The components of the Foundation comprise Value Education, Personality Development, Social Education, religion and ethics, communication skills etc.

- To supplement the theoretical knowledge given in the classroom, necessary exposure programmes for the students are arranged. The course provides the necessary theoretical input for the SHEPHERD programme.
- The textbooks are prepared by the faculty of the Foundation Course.
- The Faculty members are drawn from various departments and are given training in handling the components of the course.
- Seminars and orientation programmes are conducted periodically for the staff members to update the teaching of ethics and religion.
- Monthly department meetings are held to discuss the problems of students and the staff.
- Social problems in the form of case study cum group discussion involving students are arranged and assessed.
- Teaching of ethics and religion is considered as the Foundation Course and due weightage is given to it for the award of the University Degree.

Evaluation

The evaluation of this course consists of Continuous Internal Assessment (CIA) and the summative semester examination with equal weightage in the ratio of 50:50

The CIA consists of three components:

- Two centralized written tests for 30+30 marks
- The second component is left on the or initiative of the individual teacher in charge of the course who conducts any four forms of evaluation like Open Book Test, Case Analysis, Group Discussion, Panel Discussion, Seminar, Assignment, Snap Test, Quiz etc. for 35 marks.
- The third component is attendance for 5 marks.

The Semester Question Paper consists of the following pattern:

PART A – Concepts, Defininitions Recall type of Objective questions 20 × 1=20

PART B – Critical assessment and comment on questions to be answered in 150 words each 5×6 =30

PART C – Analysis or Synthesis type of questions either/or type to be answered in 500 words 2×15=30

PART D – Two Case Studies Application Oriented to be analyzed and answered 2×10 = 20

CONCLUSION

On many an occasion, several alumni of our college like the former President of India, Dr. APJ Abdul Kalam, Dr. Rangarajan, Mr. Gopalaswamy, Mr. Sujatha (Tamil novelist) and several others of high acclaim have never failed to mention the impact of the Foundation Courses on their life, spiced with real-life incidents and case- stories of how they had stood by values inspite of all the bureaucratic pressures and materialistic concerns, and how they have tided over many problems and taken up challenges to emerge out victoriously as true Josephites in mind and spirit.

There can be no greater testimony than the lived experience of these great men who shine as illustrious examples of how life should be led meaningfully during one's sojourn on this planet. They comprise the stars that shine in the firmament of the Josephite sky.

21

The Miracle of Motivation in Higher Education

Davis George

INTRODUCTION

1. Discover the Power in Your Wings.

"The higher education so much needed today is not given in the school, is not to be bought in the market place, but it has to be wrought out in each one of us for himself; it is the silent influence of character on character," said William Osler.

India has one of the largest 'Higher Education System' in the world. Education in India is seen as one of the ways to upward social mobility. Good education is seen as a stepping stone to a successful career and life. Education System in India currently represents a great paradox. On the one hand we have IIMs & IITs that rank among the best institutes in the world and on the other hand there are number of schools in the country that don't even have the basic infrastructure. Even after more than 60 years of independence we are far away from the goal of universal literacy. But on a positive note, Indian professionals are considered among the best in the world and are in great demand. This signifies the inherent strength of Indian education system. To improve upon the quality of Higher Education we have to ensure that all the stake holders of Higher Education are highly motivated.

Among all the stake holders, the quality of education has much to do with the quality of teachers. "The quality of a nation depends upon the quality of its citizens. The quality of its citizens depends- not exclusively but in critical measure-upon the quality of their education. The quality of their education depends, more than upon any other single factor, upon the quality of their teacher." These words of the American Commission on Teacher Education cannot be over-emphasized. To ensure such high standards, teachers have to be self driven and highly motivated. How true, "A teacher affects eternity; he can never tell where his influence stops," said Henry Brooks Adams.

There is a story of a mother eagle, which gently coaxed her offspring toward the edge of the nest. Her heart quivered with conflicting emotions as she felt their resistance to her persistent nudging. "Why does the thrill of soaring have to begin with the fear of failing?" As in the tradition of the species, her nest was located high on the shelf of a sheer rock face. Despite her fears, the eagle knew it was time. Her parental mission was all but complete. There remained one final task- the push. The eagle drew courage from an innate wisdom. Until her children discovered their wings, there was no purpose for their lives. Until they learned how to soar, they would fail to understand the privilege it was to have been born an eagle. The push was the greatest gift she had to offer. And the decisive moment dawned and the eaglet was gently pushed from the cozy and comfortable nest into the unknown horizon. It was her supreme act of love. And so one by one she pushed them, and they flew. Even the eagles need a push!

The difference between achievers and non-achievers is that the first group is motivated and the second group is not. Most people are good and qualified. Most of them can perform much better than what they are. But they desist and resist change as it would dislodge their comfort zone and they would prefer to remain where they are and as they are. Fewer expectations, less demands and less work. And they think it works. They have to be shown that the same things can be done in a better way. **The missing link is the spark of motivation. Achievers do not do different things but they do things differently.**

Motivation is everybody's problem. You are Principal of a college and you want to motivate your staff. You are a teacher and you want to motivate your students. The parents want to motivate their children. From the time when we get up in the morning to the time we go to bed at night, we run into dozens of situations where we need to motivate others. If we're frustrated in our efforts (and, who isn't?), we may give up.

Without motivation there is no change. No learning. No actions. And, the most important fact of all is that without motivation, there are no results. Life can only be understood backwards; but it must be lived forwards. Pablo Casuals, the great cellist, was asked why, at eighty-five years of age, he continued to practice five hours a day. He replied, "Because I think I'm getting better." Life is about growing; it is about change. As it is said, those who are not busy being born are busy dying. As said by Henri Bergson in, Creative Evolution, **"To exist is to change; to change is to mature and to mature is to go on creating oneself endlessly."** How true it is that we cannot become what we need to be by remaining what we are. Motivation accelerates this process of becoming. The path we shall follow in this article is not one laden with positive platitudes, but rather it is a quest for insight, wholeness, integrity and better performance. We shall embark upon a journey of discovery, to reflect upon and clarify what is truly important and meaningful in our pursuit for academic excellence.

2. Motivation—Defined and Explained.

Motivation is that invisible force that ignites the mind and sets your heart with feelings of zeal and zest and propels you into action. It can persuade, convince, inspire, encourage and lead you into action, changing your vision and life. It is the driving force in our lives. It comes from a drive to succeed and have fulfillment in life. One has to cultivate the right attitude and positive self-talks. To be inspired and motivated means to move forward with purpose and enthusiasm. Purpose denotes clarity of intension while enthusiasm is derived form the Greek *entheos*, a god or sprit within. The motivated and inspired person comes to life with the purpose and passion, with the daily desire to grow and contribute. Only managers who can deal with uncertainty, with ambiguity, and with battles that are never won but only fought well can hope to succeed. Motivation knows your purpose in life, growing to reach your maximum potential, and sowing seeds that benefit others, enabling you make your life a success. Success is a journey rather than a destination. You will never exhaust your capacity to grow towards your potential or run out of opportunities to help others. You will never have the problem of trying to "arrive" at an elusive final destination. The very moment that you make the shift to finding your purpose, growing to your potential, and helping others, you are on the path of success. The only true measure of success is the ratio between what we might have been and what we have become. In other words, success comes as the result of growing to our potential. It's been said that our potential is God's gift to us, and what we do with it is our gift to Him. Our potential is probably our greatest untapped resource. Henry Ford observed, "There is no man living who isn't capable of doing more than he thinks he can do." Find out what you are searching that will set your soul on fire and pursue it. And then, as President Theodore Roosevelt said, "Do what you can, with what you have, where you are." Never wait for inspiration or permission or an invitation to get started. That is motivation.

3. How do we motivate others?

A new employee is to be molded to the culture and expectations of the organization. Training and Orientation Programmes will be of immense help and inservice training will do wonders. Often the new recruits are not properly introduced to the demands of the work and the expectations of the organizations and the students. Professional organizations take special care at the time of recruitment and induction. They explain to them the terms and conditions, conventions and traditions, expectations and demands, vision, mission, objectives and means. SWOT analysis of the teacher and college will be of immense help to take stock of the ground reality and make strategic planning. This will have direct bearing on the performance. Performance appraisal from the beginning itself will create competitive and healthy attitudes. How true, a motivated professional learns the trade and brings in the required changes and lasting result, but a de-motivated employee starts sabotaging the company and spreads the negativity all around. Performance is the parameter of motivation. A self-motivated person's performance appraisal will show qualitative results. De-motivated and ineffective staff should be identified and set aside, ignored or taken to task. Self-driven and self-motivated people will not look for reason outside themselves. They have their own inner resource to translate their dream into reality. It is about driving people and friends towards higher levels of achievement. Staff members, teaching and non-teaching, is the only sustainable resource center of the institution. If they are well motivated they will do much better and faster. Motivation is the willingness of an individual to do something better than otherwise done.

3.1. Translate your dream into reality:

Before you think about mobilizing the staff to achieve results, you have to be clear about the results your college* aims to achieve—its vision and mission. You also have to be clear about how you plan to achieve that mission—your college's strategy. The mission states in broad terms the college's purpose. The strategy lays out a plan for fulfilling that purpose—a set of more specific goals to be achieved, an array of approaches to be used, a mechanism for evaluating progress and improving continuously.

The mission should capture the very reason the college exists; the strategy should be the blueprint by which the college leader acts to achieve that mission. Your mission and strategy are critical building blocks for all the activities that fall under the term "human resources". When you recruit and select new teachers, you look for individuals that have the qualities needed to implement the strategy and achieve the mission. When you help individual staff members or teams set goals, you align those goals with the college's broader aims. When you provide coaching or design professional development opportunities, you seek to build the specific capacities that allow the college to live up to its purposes.

A dream gives us direction and increases our potential. A person who has a dream knows what he is willing to give up in order to go up. If you move in any direction other than toward your dream, you'll miss out on the opportunities necessary to be successful. Without a dream, we may struggle to see potential in ourselves because we don't look beyond our current circumstances. But with a dream, we begin to see ourselves in a new light, as having greater potential and being capable of stretching and

---

*College here stands for your institution/Department/organization.

growing to reach it. Every opportunity we meet, every resource we discover, every talent we develop, becomes a part of our potential to grow toward that dream. **The greater the dream, the greater the potential. E. Paul Hovey said, "A blind man's world is bounded by the limits of his touch; an ignorant man's world by the limits of his knowledge; a great man's world by the limits of his vision." If your vision – your dream – is great, so is your potential for success.**

3.2. Setting goals: prerequisite for motivation:

According to a study of American employee attitudes, only about half of the employees say they understand how their organizations will assess their job performance. Supporting performance needs to start with making expectations clear. Without clear expectations, it's difficult for staff to know where to focus their energies, how to improve, or whether they're doing a good job.

When thinking about setting goals and expectations, keep in mind these points:

Align individual and team goals with college goals. Ensure that teachers and other staff are applying their energies in ways that help the college achieve its mission; work hard to align expectations for individuals and teams with the broad goals of the college.

As familiar as you are with your college's mission and goals and with your expectations of staff, each staff person comes to your charter college with a lifetime of experiences that shape how he or she sees the world. To keep staff on the same path as your college, you must communicate your goals and expectations repeatedly. That means repeating the same things, in new and inspiring ways, and it means encouraging the staff to find new ways of making the mission and goals more real in daily college life. Write it, say it, draw it, talk about it, and improve it. Here are some concrete ideas:

- Focus on a particular college goal at each faculty meeting. You might do this by reviewing the benchmarks for the goal, outlining progress or highlighting particular efforts towards the goal, and/or asking teachers to speak about his/her ideas for and/or

- Perceptions of the goal.
- Post the mission and college goals around the college and on college paraphernalia (t-shirts, mugs, letterhead, etc.).
- Provide professional development (e.g., training, coaching) around college goals and expectations. Base teacher evaluations (e.g., self, peer, and college head) in part on how the teacher is contributing to college mission and goals.
- Celebrate the reaching of benchmarks.
- Communicate mission and goals to parents so that they may also keep teachers focused on the college's vision. Model the behaviors you demand of your staff. Set goals at all relevant levels of the college. Every college is organized differently. Some have departments; others have teams, and so on. Whatever your college's organization, create a goal-setting framework that matches the college's structure. If your teachers are organized into different departments, for example, set goals for each Department, and then for each individual within the department. As you move "down" the structure, goals become more specific and tailored. For example, all teams in the college may share broad goals having to do with improving student achievement in the core subjects. But different grade levels may have different emphases or additional goals, depending upon unique challenges faced by the team. And within teams, different teachers may have different goals based on the challenges they face and the particular developmental needs they bring to college. Consider multiple goals and measures. It would be unusual to find a college where the expectations for a teacher's performance could be boiled down into a single goal or indicator. Performance for professionals is likely to involve a range of attributes, and your systems of goals should reflect the complex nature of the professional's job.

3.3. Make Goals "SMART":

There are lots of catchy frameworks for thinking about what makes a goal or expectation a good one. Here's one such framework that may help you evaluate the expectations you currently have for staff, and set new ones. A goal is "SMART" if it is Specific, Measurable, Ambitious but Attainable, Relevant, and Time-based:

3.3.1. Specific. Goals like "the teacher will contribute effectively to curriculum planning process of the college" aren't very helpful in guiding a teacher's decisions and activities. To be effective, expectations need to contain very specific ideas about what kinds of behavior and performance are valued.

3.3.2. Measurable. Leaders and staff need ways of measuring whether a team or individual staff member is attaining each goal. "Measurable" does not necessarily mean "quantitative." But even qualitative attributes can be measured - not with simple scores on tests, but using rubrics that define different levels of performance. Creating such rubrics is hard work, but without them, it is impossible for everyone to understand what constitutes high performance.

3.3.3. Ambitious but Attainable. Setting goals requires striking a tough balance. On one hand, to spur improvement, goals must be ambitious, pressing staff toward higher performance. On the other, they must be attainable or staff will soon come to disregard them as "pie-in-the-sky."

3.3.4. Relevant. Think of relevance in two ways. One, noted above, is relevant to the college's broader goals. The other is relevance to each staff member's own professional development. Most people work hard to attain goals they find intrinsically valuable, and decades of research on educators makes clear that this generalization applies particularly to people working in colleges.

3.3.5. Time-based. Goals should have a timeframe attached to them - a statement about when the goal should be achieved. This month? This semester? This year? Over the term of the charter? There is a place for all kinds of timeframes, but each goal should have one that makes sense.

3.4. Performance appraisal:

Evaluating, improving and rewarding your college and its staff are critical devices of creating a motivating, high-performance climate. Good performers in organizations of all kinds find it motivating both to hear what they are doing is appreciated and to learn how they can improve their own performance. A well-designed performance appraisal process and appropriate reward system can help you feed the natural desire of committed staff to succeed.

Your evaluation process should begin with your college mission and goals and individual staff role expectations. You then must seek ways of measuring how your college, teams and individual staff members have contributed to meeting goals and expectations. The best evaluation processes address both measures of achievement (to what extent the goals have been met?) and the underlying causes if they have not been.

3.5. Rewards, recognition to reinforce motivation:

A natural outcome of rewards, recognition and non-cash awards is to reinforce and guide behavior. For example, not using rewards to discriminate between high and low performance (at a college, team or individual level) reinforces the message that performance does not matter. Not surprisingly, research has shown that high-performing organizations are more likely to use rewards that discriminate between high and low performance than are average performing organizations. Rewards must be designed carefully to reinforce the behavior that achieves college's mission and goals. Monetary rewards are temporary and short-lived; they are not gratifying in the long run. In contrast, seeing an idea being implemented can be emotionally gratifying by itself. People feel that they are not being treated like objects. They feel part of a worthwhile team.

Re-engineering Performance Management: Breakthroughs in Achieving Strategy Through People, offers a simple list of such motivating actions:

- Defining staff performance expectations
- Communicating expectations with staff
- Creating a "motivating environment" (using influence strategies and visionary leadership)

- Coaching employees (both before and after assessment; to improve both strong and weak performance)
- Assessing performance (both achievement of goals and behaviors used to get there)
- Confronting poor performance
- Reinforcing good performance
- Modeling the behavior you want your staff to emulate

4. Build a "college climate" that encourages performance.

4.1. Write out and make inspirational speeches. Let the staff and the public know who you are and what you stand for, what the organization's purpose and mission are, what your expectations are and what others can do together to make the mission happen.

4.2. Articulate the mission statement often and passionately. When ever you speak to the staff, write memos, or issue bulletins, reiterate the mission statement.

4.3. Develop a yearly theme that is consistent and connected to the college's mission. This is necessary to break the mission into workable, understandable segments.

4.4. Be visible to the staff, students, to the parents, to all constituencies. Walk around. Be in the classrooms. Observe work in progress. Everyone needs to see the leader and know who he or she is and what his or her expectations are.

4.5. Publicize successes and celebrate progress of individuals, groups, or a class. Recognize small wins as well as large ones.

4.6. Departmental meetings, Academic Council meetings, and Staff Council meetings will keep everyone informed and abreast. Programmes like Art of living, Vipassana and Yoga will infuse new life into the staff.

4.7. We have developed a new motivational programme for the staff called "Onward Inward Journey", wherein each Head of the Department gives an input session on topics of academic interest and the discussion is concluded by the Principal with his comments, observations and concluding remarks. This has been found very interesting, enriching and participatory.

5. The key to motivation: respond to human needs.

In an article in the Harvard Business Review, Frederick Herzberg outlines both types of factors based on a number of studies conducted in a cross-section of organizations and with a broad range of employees. These studies suggest that factors responsible for job satisfaction include: achievement, recognition for achievement, the work itself, responsibility, and growth or advancement. Factors responsible for job dissatisfaction include: company policy and administration, supervision, interpersonal relationships, working conditions, salary, status and security.

Motivation is all about finding out the need inside a person, which if satisfied, will make him work more efficiently and produce better results about which he takes pride. The process of motivation begins with an unsatisfied need, anything that he desires about is deprived of. This creates tension, and when it is positively dealt with, results in increased efforts and better performance. When it is negatively dealt with it results in poor performance, frustration and aggression. When needs, legitimate or otherwise, are not met it results in employees' indifference and inefficiency.

Needs can also be classified into two categories: organizational and individual. Individual needs will have to be structured, regularized and channeled into organizational need fulfillment. Individual willingness to make extra efforts and walk the extra mile must be enlisted for optimum performance and productivity. This should also cater to satisfy the individual, personal needs of the persons concerned. The failure to perceive what people really need is the biggest motivational problem. The more you understand about the needs that motivate people, the more effective a motivator you become. The core of motivation is meeting needs. If a person's needs are all being met, he's totally satisfied with his situation and isn't open to any kind of change. The satisfied person is generally self-motivated – but if he isn't, he's pretty hard to motivate. One should be aware that trying to fit everyone into the same mold yields people who don't fit in at all. Different strokes are needed for different folks. "The only person who behaves sensibly is my tailor," said George Bernard Shaw. "He makes new measurements every time he sees me. All the rest go on with their old measurements."

Abraham Maslow was the father of the human potential movement. He spent years researching the healthy personality and learned that all of us have the same basic needs. These needs always come in the same order, for everyone on earth. The second level need won't even be considered until the first level need is met. The third level need will become an important priority when the first and second levels are taken care of. And so on. Maslow's hierarchy shows that you can't motivate a person through his higher needs until his more basic needs are met. In his theory on the hierarchy of human needs it is said that an individual progresses through five need levels- physiological (relating to his need for food, sex and other basic requirements), safety (relating to his need for shelter, security), social (the need for friends, family), esteem (relating to his need for recognition and respect), and finally his self-actualization, reflecting the need for achieving greater things. A successful manager will have to discern the changing profile of individual needs and reasonably respond to it.

5.1. Communication is at the heart of motivation.

One of the biggest impediments of good motivation is bad communication. The problem runs all the way from our most stately boardrooms to our most humble homes: workers and children alike are unable to please their motivators because they frankly don't know what's wanted. Motivation will improve when communication improves. When you want someone to do something, make sure you communicate very plainly what's wanted, specifying how big, how soon, what for, how expensive etc. That means, you yourself need to know what you want. Sometimes management is the blind leading the blind out to shoot – and the casualties are people. When the staff knows precisely what's wanted he or she will be able to provide it.

Some suggestions on communicating effectively:

- Define why you need to communicate. Decide how you want the teacher to respond – what do you want him to think, feel, and do? Set clear objectives.

- Carefully choose the setting of the communication. People respond differently to communications in different settings: in an office or out in the hall, over the phone or in a memo, from a podium or sitting around a table. Select the setting that will best help you accomplish your objectives.
- Select the right time for the communication. Mondays are different from Fridays for anyone. Don't try to have a heart-to-heart talk with your staff at the very moment when he's ready to leave for home.
- Use a variety of effective ways of communicating ideas: charts, pictures, stories, metaphors, analogies, a perception, and feelings.
- Get the audience involved in the message. The more they personally do during the communication, the more they'll remember.
- Make use of verbal and nonverbal communication.
- Learn to communicate your feelings and thoughts; your new vision and mission in life, in such a way that they understand the benefit of it.
- Communicate positive strokes, timely correction and guidance. Rather than fear, motivate by caring, persuasion, a challenging assignment, a little praise or with a pat on the back. Encouragement and clear indication of the advantages and disadvantages of the given assignment will spur them on to greater accomplishment.
- Communication is not only speaking but also listening. One must learn to listen not only with his ears but also with his/her heart to the ideas, suggestions and other comments. Academic Leaders who establish a climate that's conducive to suggestions end up being more effective. They feel more motivated and assume responsibility for what they're doing, and they respond accordingly. Leaders make all the difference in how they respond to suggestions. The leader doesn't have to follow all the suggestions he or she receives, but each suggestion should be treated with respect.

5.2. Minimax: Minimize Weakness and Maximize Strengths.

The more you're able to minimize weaknesses, the stronger your group becomes. If, in addition, you're able to maximize strengths, your staff will be incredibly motivated. Minimax is a valuable motivational tool. The person who uses it is able to get the most out of those he works with.

Step 1: Avoid Emphasis on Weakness: If you waste time trying to correct a lot of weaknesses, you'll just end up with frustration and dejection. And if you look for weaknesses to avoid when you're hiring, you'll probably end up with mediocrity. Emphasis on weakness destroys morale. It can destroy your entire operation.

Step 2: Build on Strength: It's not enough to avoid emphasis on weakness. That first step will make the employee glad you're off his back – but it won't help him grow. So you build on his strengths. Learn what he does best, and then help him do it better.

When you recruited your staff you have seen something outstanding about him, something that made you say to yourself, "This one can really do the job!" Always keep that initial enthusiasm in mind. What job was it you knew he could do? Answer that question and you've got a good lead on his main strength. Now build on it. Help teachers to enjoy their work. Healthy habits and healthy practices would enhance the process of motivation.

5.3. Faculty Development Programme.

For motivating the staff our focus and thrust should be on human resource development programming for the staff. Much of the college development would depend on the inner disposition of the staff. On going in-service training programme, refresher courses, attending national and international seminars and conferences will enable and empower them to explore the unexplored frontiers of knowledge. Often stagnation in profession is the result of lack of academic exposure. Encourage the staff to invest their time in research and publication. A good teacher is the one who is willing to learn till the very end. Reading motivational books and the latest books and journals in the subject concerned will give the necessary insights and fresh ideas to become better and more effective capacity builders. Our students are entering into a highly competitive world and they should have the benefit of a really learned professor. He should be able to inspire and motivate the students to have a scientific temper and the required skills and attitude to apply his knowledge to build up a better world. He should be aware of the national and international challenges and should have the ability to respond positively and proactively. A teacher who is a role model in academic excellence and excellence in character formation will be able to bring the required transformation in the lives of our youth.

Education is not just filling the empty minds with information but formation and transformation of the mind, heart and soul. Education is a process of exploring possibilities and blossoming our own innate and God-given talents, so that students can make a difference in the lives of others. Going beyond the concept of giving analytical intelligence (IQ) alone, one should be able to give emotional intelligence (EQ) and spiritual intelligence (SQ). Who else can do this better than a well-informed, committed and motivated teacher? As it is said, a teacher affects eternity, and no one can say when his influence stops.

CONCLUSIONS

Yes, we can

The American President Barack Obama captured the imagination of American people with his much acclimated caption, "Yes, We Can." Most of the time capabilities and potentials remain underutilized because of our own doubts and negative thinking. We need to constantly change "Can't into Can." As Barack Obama said, "Yes, we can. Yes, we can change. Yes, we can. Yes, we can heal this nation. Yes, we can seize our future. And as we leave this great state with a new wind at our backs and we take this journey across this great country, a country we love, with the message we carry from the plains of Iowa to the hills of New Hampshire, from the Nevada desert to the South Carolina coast, the same message we had when we were up and when we were down, that out of many, we are one; that while we breathe, we will hope. And where we are met with cynicism and doubt and fear and those who tell us that we can't, we will respond with that timeless creed that sums up the spirit of the American people in three simple words - yes, we can." (Transcript of Sen. Barack Obama's remarks after he won the Democratic Presidential primary in South Carolina).

The miracle of Motivation consists in helping others to discover the power in their wings and strength in their roots. Mobilizing and motivating people to achieve results is one of the principal imperatives of the college Principal. But effective colleges also face a compelling opportunity to do things differently when it comes to mobilizing and motivating the staff, just as they do when it comes to teaching and learning. But the hard work of helping people achieve their best ultimately happens not on the pages of a guidebook, but in the colleges themselves. This hard work starts with the building blocks of mission, strategy and governance. It moves from there to creating the major systems of people and resource-management discussed in this publication—recruitment and selection, setting goals, coaching and development, evaluation, and rewards. It comes together in the culture the college creates; the ways of working together that make the college a unique place to be employed, and to be educated. And—if it's successful—hard work pays off resulting in improved learning for children. President Theodore Roosevelt said, "Do what you can, with what you have, where you are." Yet never act on it. They are waiting for inspiration or an invitation to get started. The only true measure of success is the ratio between what we might have been and what we have. In other words, success comes as the result of growing to our full potential. Our potential is probably our greatest untapped resource. Henry Ford observed, "There is no man living who isn't capable of doing more than he thinks he can do."

Helping the people carry out the college's strategy and achieve its mission is the job of the college's leadership. The Principal plays a pivotal and crucial role in building the college community. When we study the powers and functions of the Prime Minister of Britain, we see that he is the first among the equals and he is the sun around which the planets revolve. He is the cornerstone of the cabinet arch and he represents the people and government.

Similarly, the Principal of a college has the most significant function to fulfill in providing academic and visionary leadership and sustained progress of the college. The miracle of motivation will significantly change the way governance is structured in the college and can have a great influence on how Heads of various departments carry out their work and produce results; how students become self driven to achieve their goals. The institutional ethos will dramatically change when all the stake holders are motivated and self driven. In our relentless pursuit for excellence in Higher Education, only academic leaders can make the miracle of motivation happen.

RELEVANT SOURCES/SUGGESTED READING

1. Bennis, Warren. 1989. On Becoming a Leader. Reading, MA: Addison Wesley Publishing, 1989.
2. Heifetz, Ronald A. 1994. Leadership Without Easy Answers. Bellknap Press, 1994.
3. Herzberg, Frederick. 1987. "One More Time: How Do You Motivate Employees?" Harvard Business Review. September-October 1987: 109-120.
4. Kane, Pearl Rock and Alfonso J. Orsini. 1999. "Attracting and Retaining Teachers of Color, "National Association of Independent Colleges Magazine, Fall 1999.
5. Katzenbach, Jon R. and Douglas K. Smith. 1992. The Wisdom of Teams: Creating the High Performance Organization. Harvard Business College Press, 1992.
6. Monroe, Lorraine. 1997. Nothing's Impossible. Random House.
7. Palmer, Parker. 1993. To Know As We Are Known: Education As a Spiritual Journey. San Francisco: Harper, 1993.
8. Senge, Peter. 1990. "The Leader's New Work" in The Fifth Discipline: The Practice and Art of the Learning Organization. New York: Currency Doubleday, 1990.
9. Sergiovanni, Thomas J. 1996. Leadership for the Collegehouse. San Francisco: Jossey-Bass Publishers, 1996.
10. Showers, Beverly, Carlene Murphy, and Bruce Joyce. 1996. "The River City Program: Staff Development Becomes College Improvement". In Learning Experiences in College Renewal: An Exploration of Five Successful Programs, edited by Bruce Joyce

and Emily Calhoun. 13-51. Eugene, OR: ERIC Clearinghouse on Educational Management, 1996.

11. Weiss, Tracey and Franklin Hartle. 1997. Reengineering Performance Management: Breakthroughs in Achieving Strategy Through People. St. Lucie Press, 1997.
12. Khera Shiv. 1998. You Can Win, Macmillan India Limited 1998.
13. Shinn George. 1985. The Miracle of Motivation. Better Yourself Books,: Bombay.
14. Hanks Kurt. 1997. Motivating People. Argus Communication: Allen.
15. Maxwell John C. 1997. The Success Journey. Thomas Nelson Publishers: Nashville.
16. McNally David. 1994. Even Eagles Need A Push. Dell Trade Paperback: New York.
17. Chaudhuri Arindam. 2001. Count Your Chickens Before they Hatch. Vikas Publishing House Pvt. Ltd.: New Delhi, 2001.
18. Covey Stephen R. 1990. The Habits of Highly Effective People. Simon & Schuster: New York, 1990.
19. Covey Stenphen R. 1992. Principle Centered Leadership. Simon & Schuster: New York, 1992.
20. Covey Stenphen R. 1995. First Things First. Simon & Schuster: New York, 1995.
21. D'Souza Anthony A. 2001. Leaders for Today Hope for Tomorrow. The Pauline Sisters Bombay Society: Mumbai, 2001.
22. Kalam APJ Abdul. 2002. Ignited Minds. Penguin Books India Ltd.: New Delhi, 2002.
23. Scott Gini Graham. 1987. Mind Power. Prentice Hall International: London, 1987.

22

Existing Environment in Higher Education and Ethics

Usha Rao

INTRODUCTION

The very fact that teaching is a profession entails that teaching is a specialized activity for which specialized knowledge or training is required through specialized institutions. A good institution will produce individuals who will be devoted to the profession and make their mark in the activities organised by them while going to the field. If examples with respect to engineering and medical institutions in India and abroad are considered, one will agree that the onus of getting good teachers lies on the institution that prepares the professionals. Further, the institutions alone do not matter much; it is the teachers in the institutions who produce desired individuals. Teacher educators are responsible for producing quality teachers. But regret to mention that the teacher educators have never taken the aspect of professionalism very seriously. They have been criticising the process of teacher education rather than providing answer to problem faced by them.

An Alarming Issue.

Observation of process norms ensures quantum and quality yield. Surprisingly, though, the teaching faculty and students are present on campus, but, some of them do not attend class. What to label this phenomenon ? Present Absent. On the contrary in some of the faculties, there is very little presence. There are off campus classes by the private sector. The question is, when 80-85% attendance is compulsory, then, without completion of attendance, how these students are permitted to appear at end for examination ? How about their continuous, comprehensive internal evaluation ? Still serious issue is professional ethics. More serious are the problems with distance education and open education programmes.

Higher Education Maintenance and Expansion.

There is a problem of maintenance and expansion of higher education. A large number of institutes of higher education have constituted of variety of committees, such as, Admission Committee. Work Load Committee, Fee Committee, Selection Committee, and Salary Committee. In spite of all efforts by the institutes of higher education, there are problems, such as :

- A large number of State Universities are under staffed.
- The teaching staff positions are sanctioned by the Central Government, but very often there is no State-concurrence.
- There is abrupt cut on the teaching and non-teaching staff positions by the States.
- Staff salary on paper is different and in actuality is different; more so, in case of sizeable institutions run by a large number of private trusts.
- There is degeneration of a sizeable number of higher education institutions in terms of various parameters - input, process, throughput, and output.
- There are demand and supply in-equations.

There are problems of all types of viz. maintenance, preventive, corrective, adaptive and perfective. We have significantly lesser number of higher education institutions than what we need to establish six more IITs. open more IIMs, establish 1000 more universities. These are excellent recommendations by the Committees and Commissions. But, how to ? Professors cannot be produced over overnight. Merely pumping money, bestowing grants and laying foundation stones do not ensure suitable infrastructure. Expansion of Higher Education is beyond the limited data bases and faculties of Committees and Commission; it demands a countrywide debate and discussion.

Increasing Demand and Dilution.

The increase in the demand for higher education, be it liberal or technical, has been unmanageably large, rapid and pressing. Particularly, Law, Commerce, Engineering and Education Faculties are over loaded. Higher Education is at the cost of the innocent public, which is investing with high hopes, but, little returns. There are problems of transition from +2 stages to Higher Education institutions. We have blind floods in Higher Education, neither knowing their origin nor destination. There are gaps between the academic attitude and academic aptitude of sizeable students enrolled in higher education. There are gaps between the teaching attitude and teaching aptitude of sizeable teachers employed for higher education. There are imbalances in student and teacher strength in various streams and programs. We have market oriented higher education be it admission, instruction or placement. There is competition, fair or foul.

It must be said with regret there is a lot left to be discovered/constructed in the areas of laser technology enhancement, transportation and space research. Rather than abstract and empty, mathematics needs to be more real meaningful Languages should be to register specific and functional. Commerce should be more with service motive. Technology is sweeping the globe. But, there is more of media crowd than culture.

Invalid Evaluation in Higher Education.

Evaluation in higher education is largely invalid right from input through process to output to placement. Our admission criteria in most of the faculties are faulty, because we do not have the research base with respect to the predictors of performance in various programmes. Still, the classical Norm Reference Testing continues in most of the institutes of high education, promoting competition. Rarely, we go by Criterion Referenced Testing and Item Response Theory. In the interview boards, rather than trying to know what the candidates know, we try to make them feel stupid by making them conscious of what they do not know. A large number of interview board fail to discriminate finely between candidates. The problem becomes still severe, when we need to discriminate between 98th and 99th percentiles. Internal evaluation, revaluation, double valuation, centralized evaluation, all have question marks. A person with B+ passes the life situations, whereas, A+ fails. What do the degrees of a degree represent, if not the helplessness of the Higher Education system ? Rather than grading our product on an n point scale, could we have pass and not pass in higher education realizing mastery learning ?

A sizeable number of educational institutions do not observe healthy constellation and ethical climate. Many academic administrators are not in a position to observe the laid down acts, rules resolutions and ordinances. The true test of administration is when the rules and acts are silent. At times, the conditions demands administrators to be over and above the system at the same time not against the system.

Let us now poke our nose towards value-system. Value-education really sheds an important light on the entire education system. The teacher must follow the rules and show respect for all students, "Do as I say, not as I do definitely does not work. It is said that model teachers earn respect by being fair genuine, hard-working, caring and good listeners. Students believe that what a teacher does is more important that what a teacher says. To them actions clearly speak louder than words.

The following strategies are recommended for teachers for teaching value education :

1. Educating the whole person by focusing on student knowledge, behavior and feeling.
2. Choosing content that honors and rewards virtue in examples, and encouraging reflection on values content.
3. Using quotes, pledges, sincerely, with high expectation for all students codes, and guidelines.
4. Communicating clearly, consistently.
5. Developing student skills in resisting peer pressure, maintaining self-respect, and resolving conflicts in non-violent ways.
6. Being a good role model through positive personal example.
7. Using and requiring respectful language.

8. Using the creation of and even-handed enforcement of just classroom rules to teach core values.
9. Reinforcing the deligent work and virtuous behavior of students with praise and appreciation.
10. Correcting unethical, immoral an disrespectful behaviour or become an enabler'.
11. Having students work together co-operatively in heterogeneous groups.
12. Involving peers, parents and community.
13. Encouraging student involvement in community service, and
14. Teaching not preaching.

The value education is targeted at elementary level because it is widely recognized that values are learned at a very young age and the basic personality of the child is formed at the age of 3 to 4 years. Some children come to school with these values well established but the environment around them helps to modify these values as they mature. These values, which are modified throughout life, become more resistant to change.

Most of the value education programs are concentrated at the elementary, level though most irresponsible acts are committed by adolescents and by adults. Psychiatrist William Glasser (1965) author of "Reality Therapy" insists that it is never too late to teach values which strengthen character. He concludes, "the teaching of responsibility is the most important task of all higher animals .... That it can be taught only to the young is not true ... Responsibility can be learned at any age.

Prof. Kedar, former Vice-Chancellor, Nagpur University speaking at the Asian Educationalists' Conference on Human Rights and Education held at Brahma Kumaris Academy for a better world, warned that "There is no direct connection between technological progress and values, because if there is, then with the rise of technological and scientific knowledge, the values must also be at their peak. But this is not the situation today. Egotism, anger, violence, downfall of knowledge, wisdom, etc. are prevalent everywhere. Today's education simply increases the competitive spirit."

Value education is an important, yet sometimes neglected subject area in today's classrooms and curriculum. Despite explicit statements demonstrating schools and colleges' positions on value development among students, the precarious nature of the topic makes value education difficult to implement. However, value education can be adequately addressed in both the classroom and college curriculum. Particularly with an increasingly diverse composition of students and faculty, recognizing, developing and communicating personal values, ethics and morals cannot be ignored. In sum, understanding both classic and contemporary approaches are essential in creating a community that both acknowledges and appreciates diverse values and beliefs.

Today's younger generation, through ethical standards, must be told that women can play an important role in reshaping the social, economic and political life of our country. Napoleon once said, "Give me good mothers and I will give you a good nation."

Thus, a country where women are suppressed, can never prosper and perhaps because of this, the future of India today is gloomy and uncertain !! The feeling of " its never too late" should be inculcated in blooming buds, through value education.

Impart of ICT on Education.

In our day-to-day life we all require some or the other information for which we depend on different types of resources like television, radio, newspaper, environment, etc. These resources provide us with data which when grouped together in some relevant manner and processed in our mind, results in some meaningful thoughts, known as information. Information is used for decision-making. Information remains useful for a particular timespan or we can say that information is useful only for the time period in which, we reach an appropriate decision.

Now what is the need for INFORMATION ? In today's world knowledge is the basis of all development and organized activity. **Information when interpreted precisely and accurately gets converted into knowledge.**

The impact of information and communication technology (ICT) on education is only just beginning to be felt. The technology forces that affect the future of education are of two kinds. First and foremost there is a strong demand for information and communication technology to become a part of general education : to be learned, in appropriate dosages, by practically anybody, at all stages of educational life, from elementary school to life long learning. Second, there is the use of this technology as a delivery tool to present information anytime, anywhere via portable interactive multi-media devise, and to enhance the learning process. Thanks to a quality of interaction unequalled by any previous educational technology.

The learning process can be enriched in many subjects because of the volume and range of information which computer data bank can provide. Learning process can be further facilitated because of the flexible mode (multimedia etc.) and speed of presentation of learning material. Computers can be used as a resource in teaching and learning at all levels of education.

We can get education from schools, televisions, radios, newspapers, environment and computers etc. Science has changed the face of the earth in the past one fifty yeas more rapidly than in the previous 100 years. This could be possible only with the rapid development of science and technology in areas like Agriculture, Industries, Medicine, Mass Media, Computers, Surgeries etc. the list is endless. Modern man (as we call him) cannot think of many things, where science can be left behind. It has already entered or as we say, infiltrated our daily life.

Information and communication technology has shrunk the world. Taking an example of computers. Computers are one of the biggest wonders created by science. Because of the ability of computers to store, analyze and retrieve large amounts of information, they have had a strong influence on the way we do things. From the development of ATM machines, electronic cash registers, multimedia games, computers are becoming more and more part of every day life. However, computers can only do what they are instructed to do.

CONCLUSIONS

The main aim of these educational programme is to break the literacy gridlock.

"The entire object of true education is to make people not merely do the right things, but enjoy them; to make them not merely industrious, but to love industry; not merely learned, but to love knowledge; not merely pure, but to love purity; not merely just, but to hunger and thirst after justice."

As an unfortunate result the twentieth century finds few recent guides to avoid, or to follow. American literature offers scarcely one working model for higher education. The student must go back, beyond Jean Jacques, to Benjamin Franklin, to find a model even of self-teaching. Except in the abandoned sphere of the dead languages, no one has discussed what part of education has, in his personal experience, turned out to be useful, and what not.

A potter or a sculptor possesses the skills of pottery or sculpting but when we wish to acquire the art of sculpting or pottery we do not have any particular institute that treats it as a separate discipline and provides the art of pottery or sculpting as a means of education; but the son or a daughter of a potter or sculptor may acquire the skill and utilize it to earn their livelihood and simultaneously get educated.

Here we should understand that low income group people can afford this kind of educational courses and if such courses get some importance in the industry then it might offer a new outlook for young aspirers in the generation to come.

It is through the skills a person possesses in life that he/she aspires for.

It is also said therefore, that, education plays an important role in the economic development of a nation.

RELEVANT SOURCES

Acharya, R. 1990. (Chairman) *Report of the Committee for Review of National Policy on Education 1986*. Govt. of India, New Delhi.

Bok, D. 1982. Beyond the University : Social Responsibilities of the Modern University, Cambridge, Harvard University Press.

Ben-Peretz, M. 1995. Curriculum of teacher education programmes. In L.W. Anderson (Ed.) *The international encyclopedia of teaching and teacher education*. New York Elsevier Science.

Bristor, V.J. Kiner, S., Lapp, S., and Ridener, B. 2002. The teacer education alliance (TEA): A model teacher preparation program for the twenty-first century. *Education, 122* (4), 688-699.

Cobb, V.L. 1999. *An International comparison of teacher education.* Washington, DC : ERIC Clearinghouse on Hedge, B.M. (2001), Examinations are no health tonic. The Hindu, New Delhi.

Jha Pavankumar. 2006. 'Communication Technology in Higher Education'. Rajat Publications, New Delhi.

Joshi Rajiv. 23rd April, 2008. 'Importance of E-Learning at School Level'. Loksatta Career Counsellor, The Express Group, Mumbai.

Krishna Sagar. 2006. 'ICT and Teacher Training' Author Press, New Delhi.

Yash Pal (Chairman). 1993. *Learning without burden,* Govt. of India, New Delhi.

23

Teaching Ethics of Environment

G. S. Mishra

INTRODUCTION

Our planet-earth- is just like our loving mother who not only nurses us but showers her blessings on us without any selfish motive. For example our mother-earth gives us food and fruit to eat, cotton and wool to clad our body, water and milk to drink, fresh air to breathe in and keep healthy, wood and steel to construct our houses and medicinal herbs to cure our diseases. She entertains us with so many beautiful and amusing things like flowers and rainbows, gardens and landscapes, rivers and streams, sun, moon and stars, birds and animals etc. Again she holds us in her lap when we are born or when we depart from this world. In short from our birth to death she helps and supports us with love so that we may live happily and enjoy this world.

But have we ever thought of what we are giving her in return? Instead of expressing our gratitude to her we are cutting trees ruthlessly to devoid her of her green clothing. We are killing her birds and animals to make her lifeless. We are polluting her rivers, streams and fresh air to make her unhealthy, we are throwing racklessly the waste material on the face of the earth and destroying her beauty and cleanliness. We are converting her beautiful and fertile land into an ugly barren land. In short we have been very ungrateful to her. So the question arises why we are so ungrateful to our mother-earth. The reason is very clear. We have not learnt or have not bean taught the ethics of environment.

In the absence of this we are engrossed in the following irrational and harmful activities :

Water Pollution: Though three fourth part of our earth is covered with water yet we have only 0.3 percent water which is useful for drinking. According to a survey by our national environment engineering research institute India's 70% of this drinking water is polluted and so it is not safe for drinking. Because out of our 14 big, 44 medium and many small rivers almost all are in the grip of pollution. The reason is that our drainage pipe lines drain the waste water with garbage into these rivers. Our industries also drain their waste water with harmful chemicals into our rivers. Chemical fertilisers with pesticides and waste material lying on land also drain into our rivers through rain water during the rainy season. Moreover ignorant persons wash their dirty clothes, buffaloes, bycycles, motorbikes, cars, trucks, buses etc in these rivers, Again many people immerse the remains of dead bodies, flowers, garlands and religious sacrifice in these rivers. All these things taken together highly pollute our rivers and other sources of drinking water like wells, tanks, reservoirs etc. with the result that they become the cause of so many diseases.

To remedy this situation we must follow the ethics of environment. For this we will have to change our traditional views, religious customs, rites and superstitions. Municipalities, corporations and district panchayats must not be allowed to drain the polluted water and garbage of towns and cities into our rivers. They must make alternative arrangements. Similarly our industries should be compelled to install a water treatment plant so that polluted water is cleaned and reused for their industrial purpose with the result that their polluted water will not be drained into our rivers. To some extent the waste water of industries can be utilised for agricultural purposes also. All the above activities or arrangements are important ethics of environment. Unfortunately we have not invented any good way to teach the ethics of environment to our citizens. This can be done best through print and electronic media. Governments of various states and the centre in India must come forward to make it possible. Still important for these governments is that they should introduce enviromental education from primary school to university level. The easiest way to implement this without increasing the load of curriculum is to introduce at least one lesson on environmental education in the compulsory language book of every class with proper gradation. All the above mentioned suggestions must be translated into deeds at war footing.

Air Pollution: Due to air pollution the nature's prescribed proprotion of different gases has been disturbed. Population explosion, industrialisation, urbanization pleasure-loving attitude have played major role in increasing air pollution. Increase in the number of industries, factories, vehicles, dirty polluted gutters, aeroplanes, atomic explosions, nuclear furnaces have not only increased air pollution but have given birth to so many incurable diseases like asthma, cancer etc. and are also responsible for global warming.

In order to check air pollution first of all we should follow the golden rule of environmental ethics - *cleanliness is godliness.* If we keep our houses, roads, drains, gutters clean. we can check air pollution to a great extent. Plantation of trees is a valuable remedy for checking air pollution. The tradition of planting one tree on one's birthday should be encouraged. Installation of treatment plant for waste material of industries and factories should be enforced. We should limit the number of vehicles. Also we can switch over to CNG system of fuel. Vehicles running with the help of batteries should be preferred. Industries and factories producing air pollution should be shifted to remote areas. Cottage industries should be protected and encouraged. As the English poet William Wordsworth said that the world is too much with us so we should switch over to simple living and natural life. Smoking should be strictly prohibited in public places. In short it is the collective effort which can help us in checking air pollution. Here again we need the help of environmental ethics or environmental education from primary school to university level.

Sound Pollution: Disco-Music, Orchestra music, pressure horns, loundspeakers used during religious festivals and various functions, sirens of factories, crackers, fireworks and bombs used during marriages and Deepawali festival and other ocasions produce sound polution. Sound pollution is increasing day by day due to the process of industrialisation and urbanisation. Commonly 50 decibel sound does not do any harm because it is not teasing to the ears. But common traffic and loudspekers produce 90 decibel sound, heavy traffic creates 95 decibal sound, horns of motor cars produce 110 decibel sound, disco music 120 decibel sound and cracker or bomb explosion 170 decibel sound. All these cause sound pollution. Which affects us badly. It can create sleeplessness, headache, tension, fretfullness, peevishness, deafness, dumbness high blood pressure, indigestion, fatigue etc.

To control sound pollution we will have to follow the golden rule of self control. In other words we should control ourselves and avoid using or enjoying disco music, explosion of crackers and bombs, pressure horns, loudspekers etc. The use of silencers to control the noisy sounds of various vehicles and many machines is a must.

Land or soil pollution: Anything which by mixing in the soil makes it polluted and harmful creates land pollution. Though soil itself contains calcium, phosphate, iron, sulphur, nitrate, copper, potassium, salt etc. which help in growing vegetation, when household waste material, pesticides and chemical fertilizers get mixed with the natural soil it becomes polluted. Similarly when waste material of different industries and factories mixes with the soil it adds sulphurdioxide, fluoride, nitric oxide, mercury, cadmium etc. in it and pollutes the soil. Again radioactive particles produced by nuclear explosions and polluted matter of atmosphere also, getting mixed with soil, make it highly polluted, that badly affects the vegetation, birds, animals and human beings on the earth. They become deformed and sickly. Similarly thoughtless and improper use of chemical fertilizers and pesticides badly affects our foodgrains, fruits, vegetables and make them poisonous. By eating these things we intake the slow poison in our body. Even the child in the womb gets affected by the remains of these pesticides and chemical fertilizers in mother's body. According to a research the remains of pesticides DDT, BHC in ample proportions were found in the milk of 15 women of Punjab. Similary the affect of these pesticides and chemical fertillizers is seen in the milk of cows, buffaloes and other animals. Indian

Agriculture Research Institute found that out of 17 samples of milk 0.02 ppm DDT was found in 13 samples. Even the eggs of hens were found having pesticides. A study of AIMS shows that fat tissues of citizens of Delhi contain the remains of DDT. The remains of pesticides and chemical furtilizers mainly affect the heart, mind, eyes and kidneys. Despite all this, 80 thousand tons of pesticides are used in India every year. The reason is that we have not caught and we have not been taught the ethics of environment. This ethics alone can check this horrible situation. We need to switch over to green manure, compost, cowdung and minimise the use of pesticides and chemical fertilizers. Similarly we should switch over to natural pesticide prepared out of margosa tree (Neem). Very restricted use of pesticides should be allowed by the governments of states and center. Most improtant is that environmental educaion from primary to university classes should become the compulsory part of our curricula.

Nuclear Pollution: Due to materialistic desire and outlook man wants to get more and more worldly pleasures. For this purpose he hoards money which not only gives him power to purchase pleasures but honour in the society. The more moeny he gets the more he wants. To protect his hoarded money and pleasure, arms race has become the identification of modern age, which has not stopped even after getting nuclear weapons. The testing of nuclear weapons, the radio active waste material produced by isotopes of nuclear institutes have polluted the earth a lot. It creates barrenness, disabilty, skin diseases, and even cancer. Moreover its pollution destroys vegetation and the fertility of land. The production of so disastrous nuclear weapons clearly shows the lack of ethics regarding environment. The big powers themselves are afraid of one another as they know that any nuclear warfare will destory the whole world. Thus world peace is in danger. It can only be upheld when all nuclear powers take a vow for disarmament and destory all the nuclear weapons gradually under the observation of United Nations. New testing of any nuclear weapon should be totally banned. *Live and let live* should be our motto and world peace should be our aim.

Social Pollution: Social pollution though not to be included have yet needs a brief mention. It means the mental pollution pervading the human society side of our life but also the economic, political and religious fields of our society. And such weaknesses and vices have created so much social pollution that rule of law has gone to winds and rule of might has prevailed. So might is right in our society at present, whether it is a man or nation. The result is that ethics- science of morals, rules or principles of behaviour - has no place in the present modern society. Personal gain has become the guiding factor of human life. This has turned man into an animal. All the morals or human values have lost their effect. We are modern but not cultured. Human values like social security, love, brotherhood, pity, sympathy, sacrifice, social service above self, benevolence, non violence have lost their meaning. In order to overcome these deficiencies and defects of our society we will have to inculcate moral values in our students of schools and colleges. We should keep in mind that moral values can easily be inculcated in the students of primary and middle schools, as they are like wet soil which can be given any shape you like. But it is difficult to inculcate moral values in the students of higher secondary schools and colleges. Their bad habits, weaknesses and vices should be dealt with iron hand and sympathy whichever is necessary in a particular case.

Cultural Pollution: Western culture and civilization which developed in India due to British rule and westernised educational system through English medium instruction has greatly affected Indian culture and civilization. Indians who are totally engrossed in English language, western culture and civilization think this change as good and praiseworthy. Only those who know the greatness and importance of indian culture think that this change is nothing but a cultural pollution which has changed Indian's life style - their mode of eating, drinking, clothing, way of thinking, behaving and living - with the result that they have become materialistic, money-minded, discontented, urbanised, self centered, sensual and are mad for wordly pleasures. In short they prefer money to morality and want to remain busy in enjoying four D. parties which give them the chance of rejoicing in drink, dance, dinner and damsel. Whereas Indian culture and civilzation aims at simple living and high thinking. This gives more importance to morality in comparison to money. Here spirituality and religion get priority over science and technology, and human values like sacrifice, selfless service, benevolence, public wefare, love, non-violence are part of the life. This leads to natural and simple life without much ornamentation.

To check this cultural pollution first of all we will have to change our educational system which at present is following the footsteps of western culture and civilization giving much importance to science education ignoring sprituality completely. In fact niether science can prevail an ideal life style nor sprituality alone can do this. It is the wise combination of the two that will lead us to ideal life style. Only is why Swami Vivekanand advised us to counstruct the place of science on the foundation of sprituality. The great scientist Albert Einstein supported this view saying that science is blind without sprituality and sprituality is lame without science. Thus by coordinating between science and sprituality we can develop an ideal life style in which the dream of world brotherhood, world-peace and world family - *Vasudhaiva Kutumbakam*- can be realised.

Speech Pollution : In the modern age we claim to be domocratic but our ego is so strong that we can not tolerate any objection or opposition in our life *i.e.*, we have neither caught nor have been taught the human value of tolerance. The result is that from the road up to the parliament we see the examples of speach pollution every now and then. Even our legislative assemblies of various states and the parliament of India occasionally put up examples of speech pollution. The reason of speech pollution is that we speak first and think afterwards. But in fact it is the lack of ethics in our life that we easily fall prey to speech pollution. Our great poet Tulsidas has advised us that sweet words create happiness around us. But in fact this advice or ethics should be taught to each student in our schools particularly because human values can be inculcated in the students when they are young. It is generally said that human values are not taught but caught. Human values are caught easily when they are taught through moral education.

In the end it would not be irrelevant to discuss here the relationship between environment and ethics. In my opinion our environment, whether it be physical, social, cultural, mental or emotional, can be kept clean, amicable and peaceful with the help of ethics - the science of morals or rules of behaviour. In fact ethics in its totality has five parts - 1. Habits, 2. manners, 3. human qualities, 4. human values and 5. Sanskars. All these five parts play an important role in keeping our environment clean, amicable and peaceful. So ethics should be the compulsory part of our school education. It would be proper to discuss here about the above mentioned five parts of ethics one by one.

Habits : Habits can be good as well as bad. Good habits prevent the environment from pollution. So good habits should be adopted and bad habits should be discarded. For example good habits like putting the waste material or rubbish in the dustbin, closing the gate of any residence after entering or coming out, maintaining a garden, planting trees and protecting them are helping in keeping the environment clean, green and healthy. Whereas bad habits like not cleaning one's nails, body and residence, throwing waste material here and there, not closing the gate of residence after entering in and coming out, smoking, taking liquor and drugs, stealing things, scolding, quarrelling, speaking lies etc. pollute our physical and social environment.

Manners : Manners are always good. They are not only profitable to those who show them but also to those towards whom they are shown. But lack of manners pollute our social environment. Whereas presence of manners make our social environment amicable and pleasing. There are 10 manners - 1. obediance, 2. obligation, 3. gentlemanliness, 4. good behaviour, 5. respect for elders, 6. humbleness, 7. gentility, 8. love for younger ones, 9. attitude of service towards elders, 10. decorum. These manners are shown towards elders, juniors and persons of equal status. These manners have their roots in the culture of the society. That is why the manners of different societies and cultures have different forms. But expression of respecting our elders giving affection to younger ones and love to persons who are equal to us is the same everywere. Acording to Indian culture parents and gurus are highly respected. In this the role of manners is very positive.

Human Qualities : Human qualities make a person good and even great to some extent. They are different from human values in the sense that human qualities mainly profit the person who possesses them. Whereas human values profit mainly persons other than the person who possesses them. In short the area affectted by a human quality is limited. Whereas the affect of human value is wide spread or extensive. There are 30 human qualities. These thirty human qualities are: 1. Celibacy, 2. Cleanliness, 3. Courage, 4. curiosity, 5. Discipline, 6. Tolerance, 7. Plainness, 8. Honesty, 9. Healthiness, 10. Initiation, 11. self allegiance, 12. Proper use of time, 13. Punctuality, 14. Purity, 15. Curiosity, Regularity, 16. Sincerity, 18. Simplicity, 19. Self Discipline, 20. Self Reliance, 21. Self Respect, 22. Confidence, 23. Self Supoport, 24. Self Study, 25. Self Sufficiency, 26. Self Control, 27. Abstemiousness, 28. Wisdom, 29. Investigating Attitude and 30. Forbearance.

Out of these thirty human qualities cleanliness, healthiness, initiation, regularity, sincerity, self reliance, self sufficieney, wisdom, investigating attitude, etc are very helpful in keeping the physical environment clean, green, healthy and beautiful, Similarly celibacy, courage, discipline, tolerance, honesty, punctuality, purity, sincerity, simplicity, self support, self sufficiency, self control, forbearance are helpful in making social environment peaceful enjoyable and friendly. Again the human qualities like celibacy, courage, tolerance plainness, honesty, self allegiance, proper use of time, punctuality, curiosity, regularity, sincerity, simplicity, self respect, confidence, self study, abstemiousness etc are helpful in maintaining cultural environment harmonious and intact, without any pollution.

Human Values: There are thirty nine human values which need to be inculcated in the students of schools and colleges. These are as follows –

1. Acceptance of cultural values of others. 2. Liberality, discard of untouchabiliting. 3. Citizenship, 4. Sympathy towards others, 5. Concern for others, 6. Respect person's prestige. 7. Cooperation, 8. Taking democratic decisions, 9. Respect the prestige of physical labour, 10. Dutyfulness, 11. Equality, 12. Friendship,

13. Reliability, 14. Liberty, 15. Helpfulness, 16. Human view point, 17. Justice, 18. Kindness, 19. Pitifulness towards animals, 20. Sincerity towards duty, 21. Leadership, 22. National Unity, 23. National Awareness, 24. National concurrence, 25. Patriotism, 26. Resourcefulness, 27. Respect for others. 28. Social Justice, 29. Oneness of humanity, 30. Social responsibility, 31. Socialism, 32. Compassion, 33. Secularism or equality of all religions, 34. Sincerity in collective work. 35. Group attitude, 36. Protection of public property. These are mentioned by B. R. Goel in his booklet. But in my opinion three more human values should be added to this list. These are (1) Not to steal (2) Not to hoard money and (3) Concentration.

Perpetual Human Values - There are 11 perpetual human values, (Love), (charity), (welfare of all) (devotion) (non violence) (peace) (socialservice) (truthfulness) (universaltruth) (worldbrotherhood) (brotherhood).

Against six coomon manners the extra four are (1) humbleness (2) Love for younger ones (3) attitude of service towards elders and (4) decorum. Thus we have 10 manners, 30 human qualities, 39 general human values and 11 perpetual human values. So the total comes to 90 and not 83 as proposed by Shri B. R. Goel. Similarly Shri B. R. Goel mentioned only 36 human values wereas in my opinion they are 39. The extra 3 have all ready been mentioned above.

On the basis of above metioned justification we come to the conclusion that in order to control social, cultural and speech pollution we will have to inculcate almost all the manners, human qualities and human values among the students of colleges in general and among the students of schools in particular. Let us not forget that when human values become the part of one's character then they become sanskars or in other words human values realised in life.

Now the question is how to inculcate human values in the students. There are following four methods of inculcating human values :

1. Teaching human values through plug points in each subject. - While adopting this method we will have to depend upon corelation technique. For example we can corelate human value of equality while teaching poverty under economics. We can also talk there about human values of sympathy, concern for others, cooperation etc.

2. Direct method of teaching human values through books of moral education.- In this method first we will have to prepare books suitable for teaching human values. A sperate period will have to be provided to teach human values through the book of moral education.

3. Indirect method of teaching human values by maintaing a suitable atmosphere and tone in the edcational institution. - In this method the educationl institution frames rules which every student is required to follow. For example the rule that *waste material should always be put in the dustbin.* The students by following this rule catch the human value of cleanliness, discipline, sincerity, self reliance etc. Similarly the observance of silence, prayer, chorus also inculcate in the students the human values of self control, regularity, peace, secularism etc.

4. Teaching human values through co curricular activities. - While playing and participating in cultural activities students learn the human values like cooperation, respect for others, friendship, helpfulness, sincerity, oneness of humanity, group attitude etc.

CONCLUSION

The above discussion proves that if we want to realise clean and green India, physically and mentally healthy India we must educate our people for reducing or removing all types of environmental pollution through ethics - science of morals or value education.

SECTION : IX – EMERGING MODELS

24

Emerging Issues in Higher Education—Approach and Strategy

Sukhadeo Thorat

INTRODUCTION

The higher education in India has witnessed many fold increase since independence. During 1950 and 2008, the number of universities has increased from 20 to about 430, colleges from 500 to 20,677 and the teachers from 15,000 to nearly 5.05 lakhs. Consequently, the enrolment of students has increased from a mere 1.00 lakh in 1950 to over 116.12 lakhs including 47.09 lakhs women students. As a result, the access to higher education measured in terms of gross enrolment ratio has increased from less than 1 percent in the early 1950 to 10 percent in 2006. If we include certificate and short term diplomas the ratio will be around 14%.

Emerging Issues.

Despite this progress, we are faced with number of challenges which include (a) lower access to higher education, (b) inter-group disparities in access to higher education, (c) problem of quality education, (d) Need of Relevant education, and (d) Use of appropriate academic and administrative governance structure and practices.

I must mention that Prime Minister, Dr. Manmohan Singh Ji has taken special interest in giving lead to new thrust on higher education. In his Independence Day address this year, he called the 11th Five Year Plan as India's "National Education Plan". This is being formulized by Shri Arjun Singh Ji with deep interest. The Planning Commission and UGC have supported these efforts in giving a practical shape.

Therefore the central thrust of the 11th Plan is centered around four main goals, namely **expansion with inclusiveness, quality, relevant education, and academic and governance reform**.

The 11th Plan placed main focus on "Inclusive Education". The emphasis on Inclusive education, is based on the understanding that, expansion of higher education is necessary both for promoting economic growth and poverty reduction. Higher education can be made a source of inclusive growth.

Strategy for Higher Education.

We recognize that the access to higher education has increased from 1% 1950 to 10% in 2006, with ten fold increase, but also painfully aware that, the 10% level compares poorly with the world average of 23%, about 35% for middle income countries and 40% to 85% in developed countries. International experience shows that in developed countries the gross enrolment ratio varies between 20% to 90%. Thus 20% enrolment ratio in higher education seems to be critical threshold for our country to become economically advanced.

Therefore 11th Plan set the target from present level of 10% to 15 percent GER to be achieved by 2012, which is equivalent to an increase in enrolment from 14 million to 21 million (a net increase of 7 millions) by 2012. It needs to be recognized that 5% net target is quite ambitious. We have been able to increase the enrolment ratio by 10 percentage points in fifty five years (that is from 1% in 1950 to 10% in 2006/7), and now under 11th Plan we plan to increase half of that increment, within only five years.

The 11th plan proposed bold steps and it is matched by an equally bold increase in the central allocation to higher education. The 11th Plan intends to achieve this target through joint strategy of increasing the number of universities, colleges and vocational and technical institutions and enhancing the "Intake Capacity" of existing institutions.

Under the expansion strategy, 30 new central universities and 374 colleges under the initiative of Prime Minister, Dr. Manmohan

Singh, 8 new IITs, 20 NITs, 20 IIITs, 3 IISERs, 7 IIMs, SPAs, new Polytechnics in un-served districts, 500 new community Polytechnics and new 210 community colleges constitute the major program of expansion of educational capacity.

The expansion in access to higher education has to come with inclusiveness. We recognize that, inclusiveness will be realized only by focusing on groups which, at present have lower access to higher education. The groups with lower access to higher education are STs, SCs, OBCs, girls, Muslims, physically challenged and poor in general. Among the women, the ST, SC and Muslim have suffered the most and particularly from the rural areas.

The strategy of Inclusive education includes support to universities and colleges located in 374 educationally backward districts, opening of new colleges in these 374 districts, and special support to universities and colleges located in rural, hilly, remote, tribal and border area. Of the 90 Muslim concentration districts, a sizable number comes under these 374 districts identified for central support.

There are schemes which will support programmes for colleges/universities with high concentration of SCs, STs, OBCs, girls and Muslim students. It will strengthen schemes to improve language and competency through remedial coaching, women's hostel and fellowship programmess for girls, Muslim students and Rajiv Gandhi Fellowship for SC/ST students. Further, an implementation of Oversight Committee and Sachar Committee recommendations will help enhance the access to OBCs and Muslims, respectively.

The 11th Plan also emphasizes on expansion of higher education with quality and excellence. It recognizes that quality in higher education will come through good physical infrastructure, quantity and quality of teachers and proper academic and administrative governance structure and practices in universities and colleges.

The new initiative for quality improvement includes measures such as (a) improvement in infrastructure (b) faculty improvement,

(c) fellowship programs to increase the supply of good quality teachers.

It has also developed schemes for "bridging the quality gap between A and C state universities and colleges" and schemes to support the universities and colleges which at present do not receive UGC grants (approximately 71 state universities and about 6000 colleges). Under both schemes one time grant will be given to state universities and colleges with a matching contribution from the states and colleges. This is an important initiative which has been taken for the first time.

The UGC will set up an Inter-University Centre for Research, Policy and Monitoring of Higher Education, whose main function will be to build up data base on all aspects of higher education, develop policies and evaluate the monitoring of the schemes.

In the 11th Plan there is a major initiative for developing relevant education, through promotion of vocational and technical education. With creation of 8 new IITs, 20 NITs, 20 IIITs, 3 IISERs, 7 IIMs, 2 SPAs, new Polytechnics in un-served districts, 500 new community Polytechnics, 210 new community colleges and expansion of the intake capacity of existing vocational and technical institutions in public sectors, the supply of technical and skilled human resource will expand quite substantially.

Another important initiative for improvement of quality is introduction of academic and administrative reforms. Academic Reforms will include changes in admission, examination methods with focus on internal assessment, switch over to semester system, acceptance of grade and credit system, teachers assessment and others.

The other important initiative includes reform of Affiliating system, preparing framework for Public-Private partnerships, rationalization of fee structure, regulation of Deemed Universities, including the rationalization of Admission and fee structure, regulatory framework for collaboration by universities and colleges with universities and institutions in other countries with respect to dual degree arrangement, sharing of courses, credit transfer, sharing of teaching, etc.

Financial Allocation.

The proposed expansion in the higher education in the 11th Plan is amply testified by the sheer size of the 11th plan which is of the order of Rs. 84943 crore at the current prices as against Rs. 9500 crores of allocation and actual expenditure of around Rs 8000 crores during 10th Plan. It is almost 9 times increase against the allocation for and 10 times against the actual expenditure of higher and technical education during 10th Plan.

During the 10th Plan the central plan allocation increased by 66 %. During 11th Plan, it has increased by 968%. Government's commitment to raise public expenditure on higher education at least to 1% of GDP from the exiting 0.33% of GDP has been in the background of 11th Plan proposal.

The priority to higher education is also reflected in 2008/9 budget, which has increased by 133% over the last year in nominal term. The increase being relatively higher for technical education, - 194% and about 90% on university and higher education. The allocation on various heads indicates the priority in terms of expansion, inclusion, quality and relevant education, including the allocation for new universities, colleges, vocational and technical institutions.

This bold initiative, however, will require leadership at the level of universities and colleges, which are spread across the country.

25

Refurbishing the Affiliation System in India: Some Practical Thoughts

M.M. Salunkhe

INTRODUCTION

With the emphasis on the 'Quality', 'Access', 'Equity' and 'Inclusion' in the XI plan, the University Grants Commission has all set for new agenda of 'Reforms in University Administration'. The fist issue on the agenda is recasting the long lived system of affiliation of colleges to universities. At present India has nearly 388 universities. The National Knowledge Commission suggests it needs 1,500 to become a knowledge society. To increase the enrolment rate in higher education, a UGC committee has suggested starting an additional 735 universities in the country during the 11th Plan ending 2012 to increase the gross enrolment rate to 15% from the 10% at present. The committee, set up to suggest reforms on the affiliation system and monitoring of education in 11th plan, has worked out a formula of 20,000 students per university to achieve the target. As per these criteria, the requirement would be 735 universities in the country by 2012. While on one hand the UGC is emphasizing the 'autonomy', on the other hand a strategy is also been devised to rationalize the affiliation system. The present article brainstorms issues pertinent with the existing affiliation system and suggests useful reforms to strengthen the same.

2. Affiliation System: A world wide Scenario.

In Europe the system of autonomy was heavily put in the action in the year 2003, which resulted in some good results such as improvement in transparency, rationalization of university courses marching towards entrepreneurial paradigm. Interestingly it also resulted in merger of the colleges, closure of poor quality programmes, and improvement of results, quality control and making the institutes more accountable [1]. In Ireland, the University Act 1997, Section 14, mentions emphatically about the institution autonomy, wit the premise that the institutes will satisfy the legitimate demands of stakeholders [2]. However, the model seems to be successful with the model of only 5 Colleges per university. In US, the autonomy was brought in a phased manner. Initially in the year 2005 a legislation was passed outlining three levels of autonomy while it was amended to level 3 i.e. more autonomy in 2006. The Level 2 autonomy was only restricted to certain areas such as Information technology, Procurement and Capital outlay the purview of which was increased only to the institutes performing well administratively, financially and operationally capable of handling the increased responsibilities [3]. However, the system is successful as there is continuous evolution in the benchmarking parameters for the colleges such as cost of education, merit components, shift from inputs to outcomes, expanded academic programs etc. In yet another interesting implementation of academic course autonomy to colleges in Canada, the new teaching requirement allows each college to have more autonomy in choosing its appropriate standard as its own syllabus among the three of the previously established standards (fundamental, intermediate and advanced) in College English Teaching instead of the past unique standard. Opposite to the traditional teaching model (teacher + book + blackboard style), the new model CAT (Computer-aided Teaching) was adopted, for the first time, as an official requirement. This resulted into some positive changes such as solving the problem of teacher shortage, more concern of teachers about the students', comprehensive competence and students' awareness of autonomous learning; a more flexible learning surrounding and students can decide what, how and when to learn by themselves etc. [5]

There are some positive stories in favour of affiliation system and transforming from independent to University affiliates colleges. The pharmacy schools in China are experiencing the dramatic changes, together with the booming economics and continuous education reform. In the last ten years, one major structural change in the higher educational system was the merger of several medical and pharmacy schools with several major universities. The environment for these pharmacy schools have been changing dramatically from independent or medical university settings into being affiliated to comprehensive and multidisciplinary Universities. They are really experiencing positive growth in all the aspects [6].

The model of affiliation used by the University of Botswana by Adeyemi et al. [6] also reveals affirmative results. In the above mentioned communication, the role of external examining is assessed, the term moderation is defined in the context of affiliation, and the procedures used to moderate teaching practice are scrutinized. Using the moderation reports and data relating to the period 1991–96, the principal issues that have arisen are reviewed and analyzed, and their significance is assessed. An evaluation of some of the main outcomes, in terms of the impact made on the affiliated institutions, is then undertaken, in tandem with the way in which experience has brought about modifications made to the moderation procedures. As presented in this paper the universities could use the affiliation system for teaching, practice moderation to raise standards and improve institutional practices in teacher training colleges.

3. Autonomy IN, Affiliation OUT: Indian Scenario.

In India the induction of the autonomy and partial discontinuation of the affiliation evoked a mixed success.

The affiliation model followed in London was derived from the University of London that was founded about 600 years after the second British university, viz. Cambridge was started. The difference between London on the one hand, and Oxford and Cambridge on the other, was that at London, the university did not do any teaching. All the teaching was done by the colleges; however, the syllabi were prescribed by the university and examinations were held and evaluation done centrally, as at Oxford and Cambridge. It was the model of London that was adopted for Bombay, Calcutta and Madras, the first Indian universities.

The system suited the Indian context at that time, as there were already many colleges in different parts of the country started by different voluntary agencies. The universities gave recognition for the work that the colleges were doing and helped to standardise it. The universities could not take any direct part in the teaching as most of the colleges were far away from university headquarters.

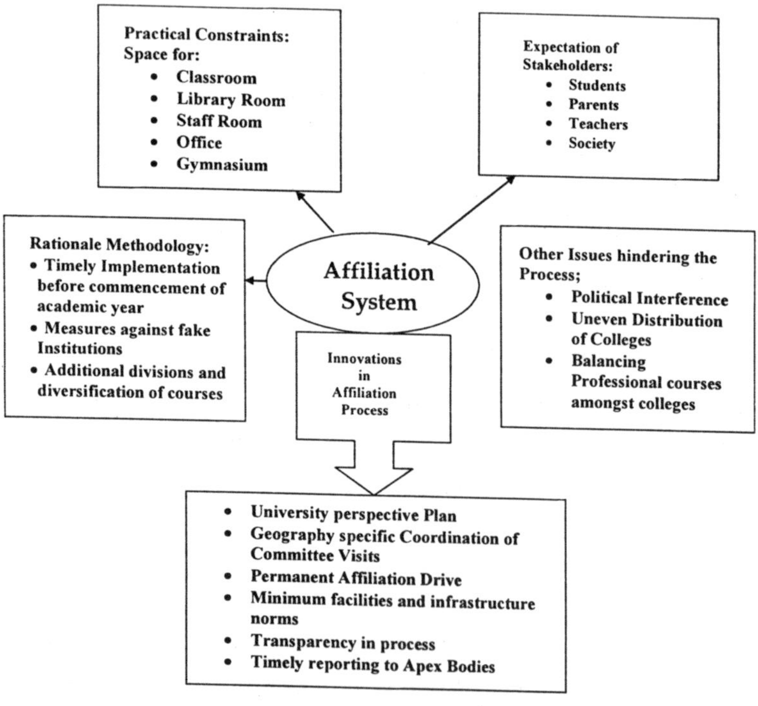

Fig. 1. Diarchy of the Affiliation system.

Kothari Education Commission way back in 1966 recorded its concerns over the autonomy as "In international comparison it would be wrong to compare our first degree in Arts, Commerce and Science with the corresponding first degrees of educationally advanced countries." The Commission suggested that radical changes in the structure of higher education particularly in the control of the Universities over the colleges, would improve the quality of education in the colleges.

Recently there was a de-affiliation threat, in many colleges affiliated to Sambalpur University due to non-fulfillment of basic university norms, especially those pertaining to the number of teaching staff, their recruitment, availability and basic infrastructure. However, the autonomous colleges remain unmoved even with large number of contractual teachers. A survey by the Sambalpur regional director for higher education office in March 2007 revealed that of the 31 government colleges out of 886 teachers' post only 609 were functional [4]. Some paradoxical issues also emerged with University granting affiliation while the other apex bodies denying permission to the courses. In the year November 2002, the Madras High Court imitated sup-motu petition against ten engineering and pharmacy colleges, pulling the university for granting the affiliation. These colleges failed to get the AICTE, PCI approvals for years together and were functioning only on the basis of University affiliation. The Madhya Pradesh is leading in granting complete financial and administrative autonomy to all government engineering and polytechnic colleges. Even in Karanataka, even UGC granting the autonomy to 31 colleges in the State, the State Government approved only to six of them in view of protecting teachers rights.

4. Managing Affiliation system: Working in the in Diarchy.

Model of the present affiliation system and the possible innovations is conceptualized in figure 1. The present affiliation system works in diarchy with certain assumptions which are difficult to fulfil by the constituent colleges in the given constraints of funding. Practical thinking by the administrators at the intersection of the constraints might lead to a more practical approach as showcased by the present paper.

The nested model of the state-of-art affiliation system implicit back and forth reiterative approach which is not only time consuming and laborious but also leads to procedural delays. The late affiliation poses delay in commencement of the courses and academic year on one hand while the expectation from the apex bodies to fulfil the attendance of the students on the other hand, which even leads to the dilemma in the academic administration. The best practise of affiliation posed by the challenges of the 21st century is the increased demands by the stakeholders of the institutes of higher learning viz. students, parents, teachers and society. However, in many instances the affiliation norms are ill-defined to access these indicators. The stakeholders expect performance from the institute taken as a whole and not from the isolated constituents such as teachers or infrastructure. The shared belief in the value of the institute should be incorporated in the norms of the affiliation. Some of the notable norms required to be incorporated are as follows:

- Employee Empowerment: The level of authority and freedom given to the employees
- Out of box activities: Weightage should be given to the out of box activities such as 'Extra Mural Studies and Extension Work'
- All the staff as Educators: Even the non-teaching staff should be inculcated to act as an educator rather than service provider.
- Encouragement for Integrated Services: The institutes should be encouraged to bring about reforms to offer Integrated Services such as 'one stop system' which will save valuable time of the students. The internal coordination amongst the various administrative units of the colleges would realize the above rather than sending students to various units.
- Encouragement be given for Technology Enhanced Administrative Model' which will encourage the students to be online and not inline.
- High-quality learning environment: By exclusive use of OHPs, LCDs and modern audio video means
- Mobility of the students to Higher Education
- Creating a Safety-Sensitive Culture by implementing student insurance schemes

5. New Complex Steering Paradigm for the Colleges.

There are two contradicting trends emerging in the Higher Education Scenario posing the challenges for the colleges in India. One trend in completely pessimistic, with a view that the colleges are under threat especially the traditional courses. The other ray of hope is optimistic, with a motto of 'entrepreneurial colleges', which could be the engines for the buzzing 'knowledge economy'. Harping on the later approach would require scrupulous norms for starting the new colleges under the framework of the affiliation system. Strengthening the existing affiliation system would facilitate forging links between the University, College and Society as shown in figure 2 wherein the colleges can act as the change agents to ensure their sustainability for a long time.

6. Need of Common Benchmarks.

The affiliation system in every university has its own regulatory norms. A common benchmarking throughout the nation would facilitate a systematic and periodic evaluation for measuring the performance against the Best Practice in order to identify improvement potential. In order to attain this there is need to restructure the very formulation of the visiting affiliation team that would ideally comprised of:

- Process Specialists (Experts in Educational Policy).
- Stakeholders (A student representative or Parents, a social worker etc.).
- Customer Representatives (Industry representative, Would be Employers for the students).
- Data Collection and analysis (A Statistician for impact analysis).

This is high time for amendment of the state wise University acts to incorporate the above to bring about harmony for the sake of comparison amongst the colleges.

The benchmarks should be further divided into the essential and desirable. The essential being the Land, Built up Area, Computers requirement, Library, Full time faculty, Laboratories etc. The desirable attributes such as Operational fund, Approach road, Potable water supply, electrical generator, canteen, hostels for boys and girls, guest house, accommodation for faculty, digital library, students' common room would further form the basis for the autonomy and granting permanent affiliation status. Many colleges are also not aware regarding the security issues in the laboratories. The affiliation visiting team should ensure that the security norms are followed in the laboratories to avoid any fatal incidents.

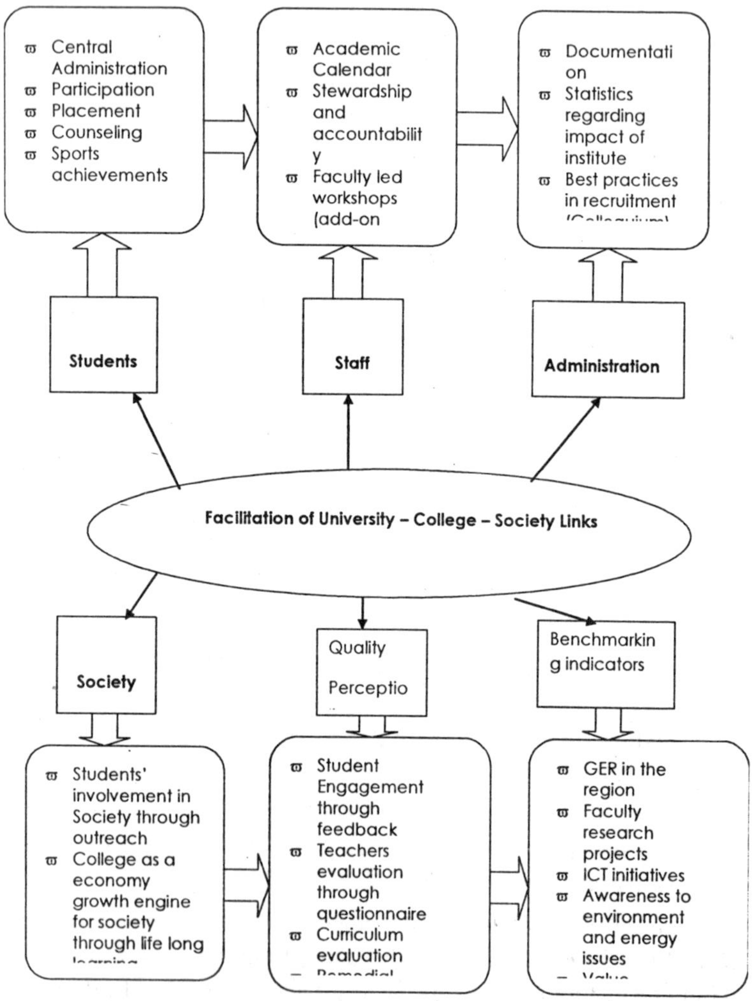

Fig. 2. Forging the Links with stakeholders through affiliation system.

7. Timeliness and Surprise Visits.

With the high number of colleges affiliated to an University, the time frame for completion of the entire process poses several challenges for the Universities. In view of this the colleges should be encouraged to form the liaison groups for the affiliation purpose on a permanent basis. This group should be entrusted to maintain the entire documentation required for the process and communicating the same to the University. As far as possible soft copies should be encouraged and communication through email/ web be followed. This will be consistent with the UGC's welcome initiative to connect most of the colleges with the broadband internet connectivity. The colleges should also be directed to launch their websites to enhance their visibility and the same should be one of the indicator in the affiliation granting mechanism. Many a times an individual college may prepare and showcase the readiness only for the sake of affiliation. This would hinder the very purpose of the process as throughout the year there might be several lacuna. This can be addressed by 'surprise visits' in few sample institutions to ensure that the same framework is being followed as was shown at the time of affiliation visiting team. On the University side the technology can help to prompt reporting to the apex bodies to complete this entire process in a timely manner before commencement of the academic year.

8. Encouraging the Best Practices.

The affiliation system can serve as appropriate agency to motive the colleges to go for the best practices. The indicators for the best practices should be circulated well in advance to all the colleges so that they can prepare well in advance and this will stimulate a growth culture for the excellence in education. Some possible best practices are mentioned below:

- Establishing the connection between the stake holders' feedback and revision in the governance.
- Class quiz and awareness to national and global scenario.
- Implementing collaborative group learning to inculcate team spirit.

- Incorporating the personal and contextual influencing the teaching-learning process.
- Live case studies with the help of ambient industries and corporations.
- Early planning of lectures and displaying the same on the notice board for the students' benefit.
- Out of class interaction with the students on their academic and other issues.
- Harping on orals, group discussions and questionnaire to improve soft skills.
- Formation of alumni and periodic meetings for feedback.
- Motivating the students for the Healthy, safe and drug free lifestyles.
- Delivering the programs to match community needs, norms and differing cultural requirements.
- Periodic teacher training on good classroom management practices.

CONCLUSIONS

Affiliation system ensures a "buffer" protecting the institutions from political interference with their internal management and members of their staff from limitations on their lines of enquiry or expressions of opinion. On a national scene, while the differences seem to be creeping in between the National Knowledge Commission and UGC as regards to the extent of autonomy and the "needs-blind admission" with respect to the cost of higher education, the Universities can forge ahead with innovative reforms strategy in the affiliation system to protect the rights of the stakeholders. These reforms and innovations will have a positive impact in the sense that they will make the procedure transparent and less time consuming and help the University in maintaining high educational standards. On a national scale joint approach and strategy for bringing the reforms in the affiliation section is the need of an hour as it can serve the purpose of capacity building and a step further in granting the 'autonomous' status in phase wise manner to avoid the academic chaos.

An opinion flow for mere outcasting of the "Affiliation Process" needs to be reviewed cautiously. Rather a recasting should be thought of to link affiliation / autonomy linked to accountability. However, the quality monitoring mechanism for the autonomous institutes will again require a periodical "Quality Monitoring" body which can be facilitated by strengthening the state of art affiliating sections in the Universities. Framing entirely new system for 'autonomy' is not free from the threats to the academic sovereignty and quality as well as for protecting the rights of the stakeholders.

There is good scope for strengthening the existing affiliation system by incorporating the methodic approaches of relevant data collection, streamlining the time consuming processes, encouraging an open and transparent governance free from personal bias and eliminating the narrow to critical few recommendations. The reforms suggested in the paper would definitely bring about transforming the colleges from a mere supply demand chain perception to value added academic change agents. Thus the affiliation section is envisioned to have a bright future to bridge the gaps between colleges, students, parents, employers and society.

REFERENCES

1. The changing relationship between government and universities in three European countries, J.C. Verhoeven, Centre for Sociology of Education, KU Leuven, Belgium 2003.
2. University Autonomy – Safeguarded by Appropriate Accountability, Retrieved from http://www.nuigalway.ie/celt/webcasts/JimBrowne/jim_browne_CELT%20Symposium%205-6th%20June%202008%20Presentation.ppt.
3. Higher Education SubcommitteeDelegate Harvey B. Morgan, ChairmanJanuary 15, 2007, Retrieved from http://hac.state.va.us/subcommittee/2007_subcommittee/higher_education/files/01-15-07/HigherEducationIssues—01-15-07 pdf.
4. De-affiliation threat over colleges, Pramod Kumar Patnaik, August 25, 2008.
5. Changes and Efforts of College English Teaching, Li Jin and Suzhen Ren, www.linguist.org.cn/doc/uc200605/uc20060518.pdf.

5. Zhu, Y., Zhou, F., Lu, W., Ye, D. and Zheng, H. 2006, Jul, "A Comparison Study between Independent and University-affiliated Pharmacy Schools in China — Does "University Setting" Benefit Pharmacy Education?" Paper presented at the annual meeting of the American Association of Colleges of Pharmacy, Sheraton San Diego Hotel & Marina, San Diego, California, USA <Not Available>. 2008-09-05 from http://www.allacademic.com/meta/p119277_index.html.
6. University Affiliation and the Role of the University in the Moderation of Teaching Practice in Botswana, M. B. Adeyemi and A. G. Hopkin, Higher Education, Vol. 33, No. 4 (Jun., 1997), pp. 415-431, Published by: Springer.

26

Challenging Times for Indian Education

P.N. Srivastava

ABSTRACT

Indian higher education system has not kept pace with its economic development. There is much to be desired with respect to the existing state of faculty, infrastructure and quality in institutes of higher education. Though there are few internationally reputed institutions in the country such as Indian Institute of Science, Indian institute of Technology, Indian Institute of Management, Jawaharlal Nehru University, Delhi University, Poona University, etc., a score of other institutions face lot many challenges to meet even the national minimal academic standards what to talk of International standards. The Government of India has recently launched a massive expansion plan in area of primary and higher education with a massive investment of Rs. 1.3 trillion. There is a great need to upgrade the existing facilities, consolidate the existing smaller institutions into a bigger one based on domain or theme, and to attract world-class faculty for improving the academic quality according to the world standards. A better trained human resource is vital in making India as one of leading economy of the World.

INTRODUCTION

"No subject is of greater importance than that of education. It is the men and women in a country that make and build a

nation and it is education that is supposed to build those men and women" **– Jawaharlal Nehru**

The rise of Indian economy has been noticed and acknowledged by the whole world. It has now been accepted that India could be one of the top five economies of the world within a few years. In order to cope up with this and continue to compete, India will have to integrate with the world in its development of proper human resources, which is poor at the moment. The education system will have to be radically upgraded to cope with a world of intensifying competition. Availability of skilled and intellectually proper human resource in vital sectors of economy and technology would be extremely necessary. It is the time to develop and create a time bound strategy of training our young people to maintain the frontiers of growing industrial technology. At present, about 10% of students between 17 to 23 years of age are going for higher education and it is planned to increase it to 15% by the year 2015. While it is very much needed, one will have to look into their quality as well. Just the number would not do since unemployable graduates (like the ones that we are producing today) would some day, sooner than later, create social chaos. One has only to look into the survey report of a NGO, Pratham, released more than a year back, that 50% of the children of government schools between the ages of 8 to 14 cannot read a simple paragraph while 65% of them cannot do a simple two-digit multiplication or division.

Our higher education system is not geared to produce accountability or attract talent. The U.G.C. survey rates 68 per cent of institutions to be of medium to poor quality. The National Assessment and Accreditation Council's (NAAC) report notes that two-third of our universities and 90 % of our colleges are functioning below even the most minimal acceptable level of academic quality. It is shocking to hear the Chairman of the University Grants Commission (UGC) saying, "Of the total of 14,000 colleges and 224 universities under University Grants Commission purview, only about 600 colleges and 167 universities are eligible to receive developmental grants. The rest don't even meet minimum academic quality requirement". It would also be worthwhile for the UGC to look into how the self-financing programmes are running in the universities under the purview of the UGC without creating proper facilities for years.

Deemed University

One has only to look into how 'Deemed University' status is being given to new institutions without proper infrastructure and faculty. A fair percentage of them are being run for money and not for education. The philosophy behind starting deemed universities was that there were a number of large, multi-disciplinary institutions/colleges with established reputation of being good institutions of long standing, which therefore should be given selectively the status of deemed universities to have the freedom to initiate their own courses and syllabi, conduct their own examinations and award degrees. Some years back, the whole philosophy was discarded and hordes of even new institutions and even a number of old institutions without any reputation have been granted this status, more because of political considerations rather than their academic excellence.

"De-Nouveau" deemed university status, along with others, has also been given to many private technical institutions that have no proper facilities. In a recent survey on technical education, it has been said "Our technical institutes are churning out students by the thousands every year, but are they all employable? Far too often, they're not." With the situation that is prevailing today, it should not be surprising that the Chairman of the National Association of Software and Services Companies (NASSCOM), Kiran Karnik, observed "only 20% of the technical graduates are employable? I do not know how the UGC and the Government of India confer Deemed University status to the institutions. I wonder why one of our best medical institutions in the country, Armed Forces Medical College at Pune was not granted the deemed university status while the Army Institute of Technology at Pune was rightly given the status of a Deemed University". In a personal communication to me, Prof. M.S. Swaminathan, a noted agricultural scientist remarked "When the first two Deemed Universities under the UGC Act 1956 – The Indian Agricultural Research Institute, New Delhi and the Indian Institute of Science, Bangalore – were conferred with the status of University in 1958,

the then Chairman of UGC, Dr. C.D. Deshmukh, pronounced that these two universities should serve as benchmarks while granting this status to other institutions in the future. What a fall from this goal." I wonder if the eyes of UGC and the HRD Ministry would open to the realities of degradation that they are bringing in Indian higher education.

World Class Universities

For the first time in our history of over 60 years of independence, we are thinking about universities and world-class universities besides, of course, primary and secondary education. Before thinking of creating world-class universities or National or Central universities, whatever we may call, we must know that world-class universities are not built. They develop into world-class universities by their own doing. Let us consider the top 15 universities in the world, whether by the standards of World Times Report or the Shanghai Report that did not consider universities with less than ten thousand students in their listing. These institutions were created as good institutions centuries back and gradually grew into world-class universities by their own work and continue to be so till today. They were not created as such. Even Nalanda had achieved its world-class status by their work and had not been created as such. What have we done to our best institutions in the country such as Calcutta, Bombay, Madras, Allahabad universities, etc. after we got our independence? We only saw them being ruined doing nothing to save them. In fact, we were responsible to ruin them. We should only try to establish good universities with good faculty, proper facilities, total autonomy and full support without any governmental control. While developing new universities we must also discuss ways and means as to how and from where are we going to get faculty. And if we appoint sub-standard faculty today, let us not forget that they will be there for the next forty years. We have to take recourse, no doubt, to the technological developments that are taking place today that may come to our help to some extent.

Before thinking of starting world class universities, should we not think of helping some 20 to 25 best Indian universities to become world-class? We may give extensive financial support, change their acts and statutes asking them to impart under-graduate studies as well. I have devoted my life in universities for about 60 years starting from the University of Allahabad that was then one of the premier universities of the country, University of Rajasthan, Jaipur that was made a very good university since the Vice-Chancellor, Mohan Singh Mehta invited very good academics from all over the country, and Jawaharlal Nehru University, New Delhi where I was invited in 1974. What has happened to the University of Rajasthan, Jaipur, good people have started deserting the university because of political interference? I have written a lot about the attention being given to the universities. My Presidential Address given in The Indian Science Congress session at Jaipur, 1994 had even invited the attention of the editorials of the national dailies writing that my warning had come not a day too soon. Professor Sir John Kendrew, one of the Nobel Laureates who had attended the Congress, had in his letter addressed to me said "Your Congress was a great success and I particularly appreciated your own forthright remarks about the contemporary problems of Indian science. I only hope that they have met with some response from your government authorities." Nothing of the kind happened. I had, of course, emphasized that whatever was true for science was, perhaps, worse for social sciences and humanities. I feel very happy that things are changing now and hope that we would make good use of the opportunity that has come our way.

We should Develop Faith in Our Universities

In India, even today, there are a few good universities that may not be world-Class but are still recognized internationally. Have we given them the recognition that they deserved? Some years back we decided to start Indian Institutes for Science Education and Research in different parts of the country on the recommendations of expert committees. They all are deemed universities. Do they fulfill the meaning of a university, which should be multi-disciplinary and multi dimensional? Why is it that the good universities of the country such as Jawaharlal Nehru University (JNU), University of Delhi (DU), University of Hyderabad (HU), Poona University (PU) or Jadavpur University (JU) were not considered for this purpose? They could have done a better job with much less financial input?

Another one is being created for Nanotechnology at Mohali. Why has one of Indian Institute of Technology (IITs), Indian Institute of Science, Bangalore or JU, etc were not entrusted with this responsibility? In Mohali besides an Indian Institute of Science Education and Research, the Department of Biotechnology is establishing an Agro-Food cluster comprising National Agro-food Biotechnology Institute and a Food Bioprocessing Unit. Why should the Ministry of Human Resource Development, the Department of Science and Technology and the Department of Biotechnology not come together and establish a world-class University making all these institutes a part of a bigger institution? The HRD Ministry would have to open only the faculties of Arts, Humanities, Social Sciences and Commerce for this. Why should the Prime Minister not intervene so that the various departments come together for this and not play their own tunes? What better use of finances could take place?

Numerous small institutions have been established in Bangalore. Why is it that they were not made a part of Indian Institute of Science? Why was the National Brain Research Institute, a small institute established in Manesar, Gurgaon and not in All India Institute of Medical Sciences, New Delhi where there would have been greater interaction among larger disciplines of brain research? Efforts, no doubt, had been made to establish the institute of Plant Genome Research in JNU only for the purpose of land but not for interactions with other related disciplines. Why was it not made a part of JNU or DU where a team of good researchers in Plant Genome Research already existed and where interaction with a larger number of scientists would have been easier? I would not like to go into the reasons that were purely individual based and given political support. Let us look into the real world-class universities, Yale, Harvard, Princeton, California, Chicago, Oxford, Cambridge, Tokyo, etc. They are huge institutions with multidisciplinary and multi-dimensional character where interaction among various disciplines is possible, rather than being stand-alone small institutions where it is not possible. In all these universities, undergraduate studies form an important and integral part of studies. In India, a good number of universities were established in the seventies including JNU and HU that had nothing to do with undergraduate studies. My own efforts to do this for Life Sciences failed since it was not allowed by the UGC on the pretext that JNU was a postgraduate institution where undergraduate studies were allowed only in Foreign Languages since such programmes did not exist in other universities. In the University of Allahabad, one of the Indian premier universities in the past, where I was a student, the undergraduate course was the most important one. In post-graduate classes, stress on formal lectures was reduced while more time was devoted for guidance and training to stand on our own feet.

Availability of Proper Faculty

Another factor that must concern us is the availability of proper faculty. We may have infrastructure, we may have library, we may have instruments but from where are we going to have instant number of faculty. It is a common knowledge that 15-20 per cent faculty positions are vacant in all the IITs, IIMs and major universities because of the non-availability of proper faculty. And once you appoint a sub-standard faculty, they are going to be there for at least 30 to 35 years. We will have to develop a balanced mechanism to attract talented people that are really willing to return home from abroad and contribute to our education and research. We may also consider employing people from abroad on contract who may be willing to work in India. A national register of interested persons can be created and made available upon request to any institution that may consider them for suitable appointment.

Modern educational and information technologies will have to be used at all levels. Eminent teachers through nationwide conferencing facility can deliver series of online lectures. Lectures can be delivered for 45 minutes leaving 15 minutes fur question-answer session. Reliance Web World is currently providing such a video-conferencing facility at a cost of Rs. 14,000 per hour. It is going to be competitive and cheaper in course of time. It is being used by Pakistan soliciting services of Indian teachers by paying $ 200 for a lecture. A lecture can be used to deliver to about 15-20 colleges/universities at a time. Advantage of the Internet

Laboratories, facilities being developed by the IITs along the lines of Massachusetts Institute of Technology Labs should also be taken for teaching and training.

Can we Change Our Way of Working?

I have said that we are in a golden period as far as education is concerned. Are we ready to change our way of working so that the Plan stipulations are implemented in the right spirit? Probably not! Many ambitious projects have been stipulated. For the implementation of any new scheme, there is a long and elaborate process. For the project clearance, a Detailed Project Report (DPR) has to be prepared that has to be cleared by the Planning Commission. Thereafter, an Eligible Financial Contract (EFC) has to be prepared and cleared by the Finance Ministry. Finally, the DPR and the EFC are to be cleared by the Cabinet of the Indian Gevernment. These steps are necessary, but why is it that they cannot be simplified so that they take less time to complete. And why is it that majority of projects that have gone through all these steps have not been completed within the stipulated time and budget? Consider this example. Some years back, the Government of Karnataka State had put up a large green board next to a bridge that was under construction in Bangalore with a date marking the beginning of the project and the planned completion date. Initially, the second figure said 2002. As 2002 came and went, a sticker appeared over it that said 2004. Another sticker finally appeared over the earlier faded one, this time also specifying the month June 2006. The bridge eventually was completed and opened in 2007.

The present scenario for the implementation of the educational plans for the XI Plan also looks unsatisfactory. Of the amount of Rs. 84,943 crores approved for some new projects and up-gradation of institutions, only a small amount has been allocated in the central budget of the first two years of the Plan, i.e., 2007-2008 and 2008-2009, and that is paltry sum of Rs. 3,263 and Rs. 7,600 crores, respectively, accounting for hardly 8% of the total approval. It is not certain that even this small amount would be spent in time for the stated purpose. Should we then not find ways and means to change the way of our working? The good thing that the government has come about is that the funding of the XI Plan can be spent till 2014.

Before closing let me quote a few extracts from what I read in Indian Express (16 November, 2008) from the forthcoming book* "Imagining India" by Nandan Nilekani of Infosys, that I have been writing about for a long time. This has given me a lot of satisfaction.

1. "India's policy makers and politicians have agendas and blueprints, and our plans have been nothing if not exhaustive. Our big weakness has been in execution."
2. "A fast-growing economy such as India's has a very short window implementing reforms that broaden access for a large group of people" and if I am allowed to add I will ask as to how shall we do it with the educated people that we are producing?
3. "When it came to the goal of attaining universal education, the country has revised its target time and again, all the way from 1959 to 2010. We will miss it this time as well". I have already dealt with this in my article.

CONCLUSION

It is heartening that the present government has increased the funding of education to 6 % of the gross domestic product (GDP) for the first time since the Kothari Commission recommendation about 40 years back to retrieve the situation, although it had been promised by all the Prime Ministers since then. The present Prime Minister deserves full credit for announcing this. Further, the Government of India has levied a surcharge of 2.0% of the direct taxes for supporting the primary education and another 1% for the higher education in the country. The funding of education till recently has reached to only 3.79% (paltry 0.7% for higher education) of the GDP, but it is forecast to reach 6% by the year 2012. The Government of India has announced to add scores of new institutions during the XI plan period, that include 6000 Government Schools, one at least in each block, 370 Government Colleges, 30 Central Universities (based on JNU as a role model), 7 Indian Institute of Management (IIMs), 8 Indian Institute of Technology (IITs), and 20 Indian Institute of Information Technology (IIITs) with an investment of Rs. 1.3 trillion (US $ 26 billion). The size of the education sector with this huge investment is expected to grow from 7.0% in the X Plan to 19.6% in the XI Plan.

*Already in market.

27

Transforming Stones into Milestones: New Roles of Vice Chancellor in the 21st Century

Kamelsh Joshipura

In the beginning, I must mention that at a point Dr. B.R. Ambedkar has called teachers as the charioteers of the nation. It means that the nation is a chariot and education its wheels. The chariot is worth its name if it moves in the right direction for which it is necessary for the wheels to move i.e. change and reform in accordance with the needs of time. In this context I must state that the realization of the dream of development in India basically rests on the total change in our education system. Indian education system is operative through its Universities and colleges as the third largest in the world after America and China. Along with its expansion and development, several fundamental issues and challenges have also come in front of us in the form of policy framing, administrative reforms and restructuring, quality enhancement and broadening of the base of the higher education. When we talk of providing access to higher education to more number of students, then the most important challenge, of quality improvement in higher education *per se,* comes in front of us. In the XI Five Year Plan, a target is set to take the enrollment ratio to 15 per cent and thus reach out to seven million students more. **But we have to ensure not only rise in gross enrolment ratio but also qualitative education.**

In India, before the establishment of Madras, Calcutta and Mumbai as affiliating Universities in 1857, the colleges were autonomous. This affiliating system was framed then keeping the limited number of colleges in view. In comparison to that, at present, there are **more than 20,000** affiliated colleges and **410** grant-in-aid Universities in the country. **The number of new Universities might go up every day.** If we count the number of the deemed Universities and the private Universities, the base and field of operation of the Universities have remarkably gone up. In addition, private and foreign Universities are offering a variety of programmes to the students. The demand for professional programmes is going up and the demand for programmes in the pure sciences and humanities/social sciences are lagging behind. It further appears that the governments are gradually withdrawing their helping hands from higher education. Under such circumstances, particularly in India, there is an urgent expectation from the Universities that they come forward to fulfill the social aspirations and market requirements and cater to the global needs. One must not forget the fact that in this age of privatization, liberalization and globalization, even if there is privatization and commercialization of education and many more foreign universities come to India, how can the State conventional Universities ignore around 70% of the students who, in India, happen to come from the lower middle and middle class as well as the rural areas? The State conventional Universities must ponder over this in the light of this perspective. Apart from this, in this changed and changing scenario, the Vice-Chancellors are supposed to play a very versatile and dynamic role to sit the circumstances. This change is inevitable and no Vice-Chancellors can remain aloof from it. **The Vice Chancellor in the contemporary society is not only a CEO, but also a manager of knowledge and knowledge providers, receivers and users, i.e. teachers and students are managers of knowledge.**

Let's not think about the role, status and expectations from the Vice-Chancellors during the British rule. But if we glance at the 40 years after our Independence i.e. from 1950 to 1990, then we would feel that the place of the Vice-Chancellor was held so high that no one dared to influence him in any way. The status or the role of the Vice-Chancellor is, in principle, the same even today. In those days, the role of the Vice-Chancellor was restricted to very significant, decision and policy matters with regard to administration and management. Nevertheless this does not imply that the Vice-Chancellors did not play any role in the development of education during those four decades. They have played a very important role in it.

In the last ten years, the role of the Vice-Chancellor at that time and now has changed a lot, particularly in the matters like (1) Decision–making, (2) its implementation, (3) his direct involvement, (4) his vigilant leadership and pro-active approach, (5) his activist-like role, (6) his direct involvement in managerial affairs, (7) his significant and keen involvement in all the matters of the university and his result-oriented actions, (8) the expectations from the Vice-Chancellor, (9) expectations from them in the matters of development, and (10) in the matters of interaction and maintenance of the relationships between University and other social sectors i.e. mechanism for interaction between the University on the one hand and other social sectors on the other.

Before the year 2000, there had been specific criteria for appointing a Vice-Chancellor out of the highly educated, senior adept and respected people, however the concept is maintained even today. It was believed that highly experienced and aged scholar would be preferred as the Vice-Chancellor, today there has been a revolutionary change in this matter in many states including Gujarat. In the past, the involvement in national and international matter was as important as the coo and over their own subject of the Vice-Chancellor. At local ground, only serious or worthy matter would bother them but today the workload has become heavier to tackle. Earlier it was easier for any Vice-Chancellor to move out of country often for week or weeks, today the Vice-Chancellor fights many battles at many fronts investing more time at local grounds in decision making and guidance, which has become inalienable part.

1. Sound financial status and resource mobilization.
2. To attain a global height.
3. Fulfilling the local needs.
4. Direct guidance in teaching, learning, research and other curricular aspects.
5. To attain and establish quality in education.

The Vice-Chancellors today have to be involved in each and every aspect with determined leadership and supreme management, maintaining the status-dignity of the designation. How to get desired and result-oriented work from the employees beginning from the registrar to the lowest of the teaching and non-teaching staff in the best possible way is a new challenge to the Vice-Chancellor, as the present age requires keen attention, and pro-active approach in all the fields concerning the university.

In the established management of any state conventional universities of India, the Vice-Chancellors shoulder as many responsibilities as required for governing the state. On one hand, is the run for development and on the other, these are a huge number of university departments of various subjects, affiliated colleges of various streams and their employees. The university has to uphold the diplomatic relation with the state, the U.G.C. and councils adhering to their rules and regulations within the three years of his term, the Vice-Chancellor can know only tip of the ice-berg in the ocean. One more challenge today is to face the print and electronic media.

The serenity, nobility, principles, ethics **and erudition** of any scholar at this particular designation is put to the acidic test on the ground reality of the university. **Hence, the following points need to be considered:**

1. The contribution of an elderly, senior scholars as the Vice-Chancellors of the past is unforgettable, but with all due respect, the present scenario requires a young and industrious person as a Vice-Chancellor.
2. One should not attain such a height as makes him blind to what happens at the foothill / ground. One should come out of a notion of how or way to become interested in the petty matters or the subordinates would manage them. One must be vigilant enough to prevent any injustice.
3. Discipline is inevitable for any institution and one must maintain the dignity of the designation also till it does not prove to his weakness.
4. The commercialization of the state university is not at all required. The government has stopped providing building grants which is now available from the U G.C. only. The

university should be made financially strong by offering self-dependent syllabi, vocational courses, the development fees from the students and affiliation fees from the self financed institutes.

5. The Vice-Chancellor may have sound background of any subject; one more demand of the post is the judicial activism for which one must have the knowledge of law and direct involvement in it.

It will not be incongruous for me to mention a few initiatives taken by the Government of Gujarat in education in keen consultation with Vice Chancellors of the Universities. In Gujarat, the government has appointed young, yet experienced, academically strong and result-oriented teachers as the Vice Chancellors. Moreover, it has ensured non-interfering attitude in the University affairs. It has further strengthened the Vice Chancellors by funding the Universities with adequate financial support for vocational and professional courses and also for new courses like Marine Sciences and nanotechnology among others. The government has initiated various new schemes e.g. SCOPE, Digital English Language Laboratories, NAAC Accreditation, Digital English Language Laboratory Project, Gujarat Knowledge Society, Gujarat Knowledge Consortium with full cooperation of the Vice Chancellors.

In brief, the Vice Chancellor in the new role has to multitask as a manager of knowledge, a manager of the managers of knowledge i.e. teachers, learners and researchers, manager of financial resources, a creator and disseminator of knowledge and above all lead the entire community of knowledge providers and seekers through his or her example. He or she has to plan and implement new strategies for making the University locally relevant and globally competitive by accepting the challenges of globalization and converting them into opportunities. There would certainly be the stones in the path but the successful Vice Chancellor will be the one who would transform stones into milestones.

28

Education for Empowerment through Community Colleges

Xavier Alphonse

The Concept of a Community College is based on the following :

1. Community College is a College with a difference.
2. Community College aims at the Empowerment of the Poor, Marginalized and Disadvantaged sections of the Society
3. Community College promotes skills development, for

   Knowledge (Information)-Theory 30%

   Attitude 40%

   Skills 30%
4. Community College makes people fit for life and fit for a job.
5. Community College matches education with employment and self-employment opportunities.
6. Community College is a community effort, collaborates with Industry, Employers and Community Leaders.
7. Community College responds to Industrial, Employment and Social Needs.
8. Community College teaches – Life-Skills, Communication Skills, English, Computing Skills, Work-Skills, Hands on Experience, Preparation for Employment.
9. Community College is education for Livelihood and capacity building.

10. The key words of the Community Colleges are Access, Flexibility in Teaching and Learning, Cost Effectiveness (minimum fees), equal opportunity and Quality in Training.
11. Community College responds to the Un-employability problem.
12. Community College is Local Specific.
13. Community College is an opportunity College. It gives hope and opportunity to those who otherwise will not have an opportunity.
14. Community College Motto is "Including the Excluded and Giving the Best to the Least".
15. Community College helps the individual to discover his / her own talents and capacity – Discovery Channel.
16. Community College is transformative education – Social change, alleviation of poverty through employment and income generation.
17. Community College is a college by the people, for the people and of the people.
18. Community Colleges are present in 18 States of India, 207 Community Colleges and served 55,000 people, 75% have got employment, 15% of them have gone for higher education. It is also present in East & South Africa and PNG.
19. Community College gives hope. The students are "Miracles of Hope" who create a change in Society.
20. Community College gives horizontal mobility – providing employment at the middle level, a salary of Rs. 2,000 to 9,000. Vertical mobility going forward for Undergraduate Degree education is being contemplated.

The need for the Community College system is based on :

- **Exclusion and Elimination**
- **Mismatch between Education and Employment**
- **Capability Poverty**
- **School dropouts**

The curriculum of a Community College is given in the table below :

TOTAL NUMBER OF CREDITS

Category	*Programme*	*Weeks*	*Hours*	*Credits*
PART I	Life Skills	21 Weeks	630 Hours	21 Credits
PART II	Work Skills	21 Weeks	630 Hours	21 Credits
PART III	Internship and Hands on Experience	8 Weeks	390 Hours	13 Credits
PART IV	Preparation for Employment and Evaluation	2 Weeks	60 Hours	2 Credits
	TOTAL	52 Weeks	1710 Hours	57 Credits

F One Credit = 30 Hours of work.

LEVELS

Level I

Below 10th Std – 6 months (School dropouts) certificate programme with 16 credits.

- **Bridge course to complete equivalent to 10 standard. Eligibility into One year diploma programme - Community College.**

Level II

10th std passed – One year diploma programme - 32 credits. Bridge course to Complete equivalent to 12th standard.

- **Entry into 1st year UG course in the Conventional Universities, Open Universities and Institutions of correspondence courses.**

Level III

12th Passed diploma programme – 32 credits.

- **Entry into the second year Undergraduate Programme – IInd year into Conventional Universities, Open Universities and Distance Education.**

Level IV

The Community College can also offer associate degree programme of two years.

(64 Credits) which will lead to entry into third year programme.

Suggested – Equivalent Courses

- Diploma in Health Assistant (32 Credits) à **B.Sc. Nursing II Year.**
- Diploma in DTP Operator (32 Credits) à **BCA (or) B.Sc. Computer Science II Year**
- Diploma in Catering Assistant (32 Credits) à **B.Sc. Hotel Management II Year**
- Diploma in Sales and Marketing (32 Credits) à **B.B.A. or B.A. Corporate Secretaryship**

II Year

- Diploma in Office Management (32 Credits) à **B.Com (or) B.A. Corporate Secretaryship**

II Year

- Diploma in Electrical and Electronics (32 Credits) à **B.Sc Electronics II Year**
- Diploma in Early Childhood Care Education (32 Credits) à **B.A. Education II Year**
- Diploma in Eco Farming Enterprises (32 Credits) à **B.Sc Agriculture II Year**

HISTORY OF THE COMMUNITY COLLEGE MOVEMENT (1995-2008)

- **1995 -** Pondicherry University Community College - 1
- **1996 -** Madras Community College - 2
- **1997 -** Madurai Community College - 3
- **1998 -** M. S. University Community Colleges and Community Colleges started by NGOs - 08
- **1999 -** Chennai Corporation Community College, Tenali and Nallapadu JMJ Community Colleges, Andhra Pradesh - 25
- **2000 -** RUHSA Community College, Vellore - 33

- **2001** - Vivekananda Pratishthan Community College, Maharashtra,

  SDA Roorkee Community College, Uttaranchal AID Community College, Garhwa,

  Auxilium Community College, Kottayam, and Udhayam Rural Community College for Women, Trichy - 43

- **2002** - Chrompet Community College, Ertram, Rural Community College, Adaikala

  Annai Rural Community College, Tabitha Community College, Dr. Chandra Devansan rural Community College, Sahaya Annai Community College, YWCA Community College, Church Park Community College, Auxilium Community Colleges, Pullurthy and Kattappana, - 57

- **2003** – St. Teresa's Community College, Eluru and Tarbes Community College, Bangalore, Teresian Community College, Villupuram, Tamil Nadu, St. Teresa's Community College, Nagoonhalli, Karnataka, Auxilium

  Community College, Trivandrum, Kerala,

  St. Xavier's Community College, Mapusa, Goa - 75

- **2004** - Pravaham Community College, Tamil Nadu,

  Ursuline Community College, Gumla

  St. Aloysius Community Colleges,

  Jabalpur, Bhopal Community College, Madhya Pradesh - 88

- **2005** – Upaya Science and Technology, Rajgangpur, Orissa, M.S. Panwar Community College, Solan, Himachal Pradesh,

  University Community College, Hyderabad,

  St. Joseph's Community College, Visakhapatnam,

  St. Ann's Community College, Srikakulam and Arilova,

  Kovalam Community College

  (Tamilnadu), Deepanjali Community College, Gumla (Jharkand) - 125

- **2006** – KRUPA Community College, Paddapai, Gangasaras Community College, Pattukottai, SMSH Community College, Kodayanallur, BWDA Community College, Villupuram, Maria Nivas Community College, Nandigama, Mysore Mines Community College, KGF, Vijayamari Community College, Mangalore, Mount Carmel Community College, Kottayam, SVD Community College, Mumbai, Bethany Community College, Noida, Bethany Community college, Ludhiana - 160
- **2007** - Ceyrac Community College, Kancheepuram Dt., Vivekananda Community College, Ramanathapuram, New Hopes Community College, Porur, Cluny Community College Karaikal, Government Polytechnic Community College, Manesar - 188
- **2008** - Prasannakumari CWC Community College, Kilpauk, Chennai, Bethel Community College, Coimbatore Shishu Mandir Community College, Bangalore, Christu Raj Community College, Pala, Kerala, Don Bosco Community College, Keela Eral, - 207

COMMUNITY AND INDUSTRIAL PARTNERSHIP

- **Success of Community College - Active dynamic ongoing Industrial, Rural, Agricultural, Commercial and Service organisations of the locality.**
- **Ways of Assistance**
- **Designing the Curriculum for various job oriented courses**
- Serving as members of the Advisory Board
- Being part time instructors for teaching and assessment in the college
- On the job training for the students in the work place.
- Job placement for students
- Memorandum of Understanding
- Representatives in the Governing Body of the college

Impact of the System

Profile of 55,214 Students from 184 Community College

1. Total No of Students

Year	Total No. of students
1996 – 1997	174
1997 – 1998	204
1998 – 1999	577
1999 – 2000	1,815
2000 – 2001	2,282
2001 – 2002	2,933
2002 – 2003	3,840
2003 – 2004	4,815
2004 – 2005	6,969
2005 – 2006	10,244
2006 – 2007	11,303
2007 – 2008	10,058
Total	**55,214**

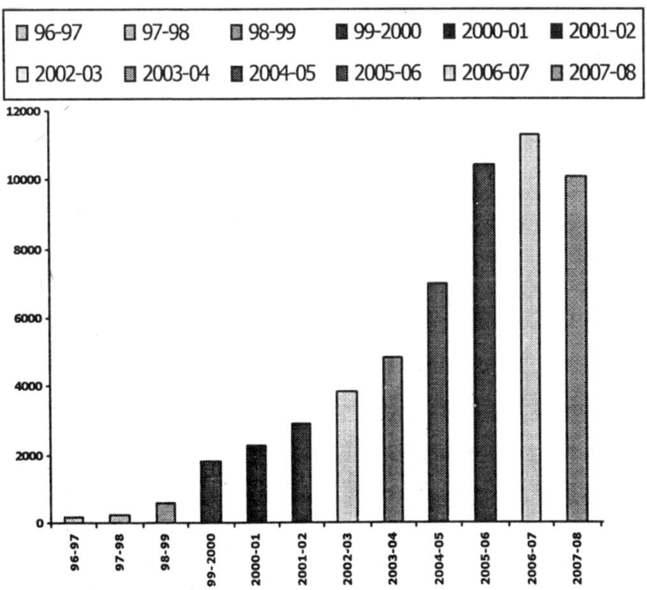

2. Students : Male / Female (in 184 Community Colleges)

Male	- 14,030
Female	- 41,184
Total	***- 55,214***

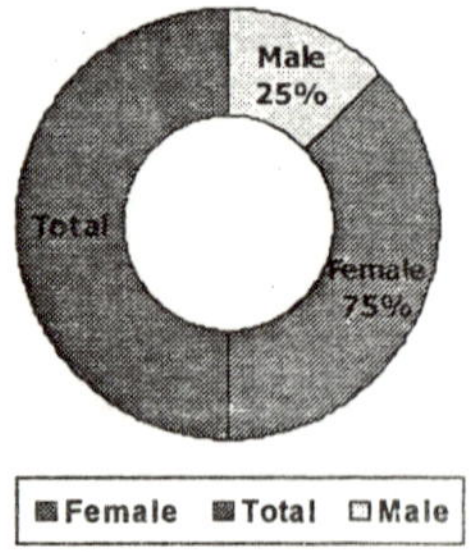

3. Students : Married / Unmarried (in 184 Community Colleges)

Married	- 4,445	8%
Unmarried	- 50,769	92%
	Total	***- 55,214***

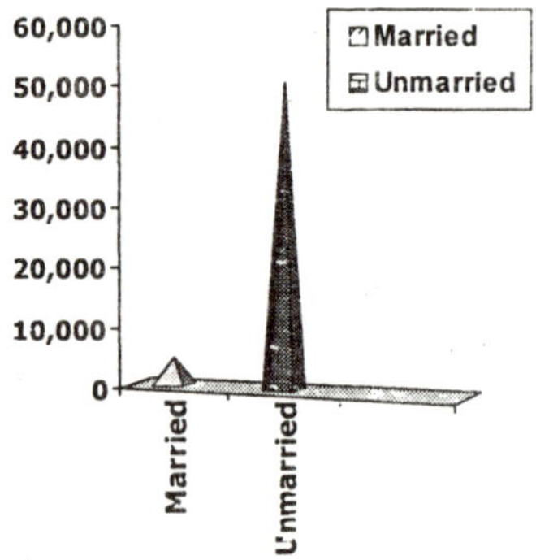

4. Student's : Age (in 184 Community Colleges)

16-18	- 21,478	39%
19-21	- 21,724	40%
22-25	- 7,210	13%
26-30	- 2,973	5%
31-34	- 1,254	2%
35 – above	- 575	1%
	Total	***- 55,214***

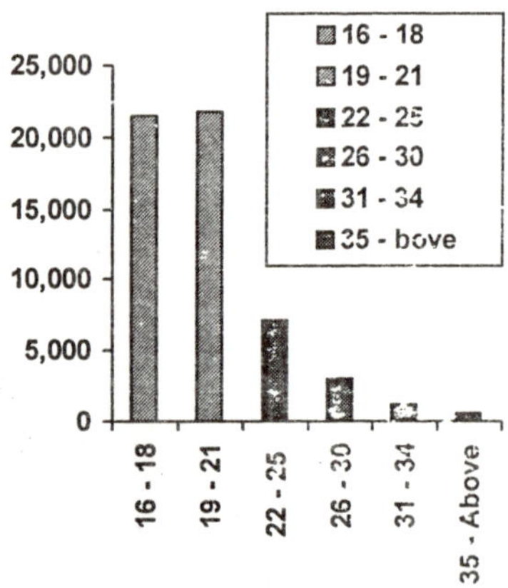

5. Student's Qualification (in 184 Community Colleges)

Below 10th	- 9,300
10th Passed	- 14,637
12th Passed	- 27,672
Degree	- 3,605
Total	***-55,214***

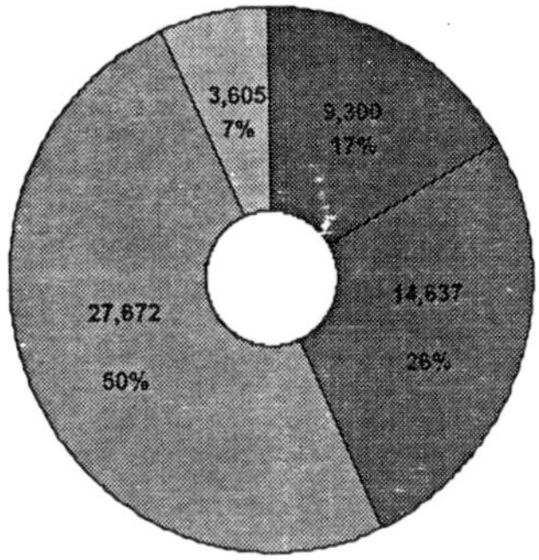

6. Distribution as per student Caste (in 184 Community Colleges)

SC	- 14,816
ST	- 4,837
MBC	- 8,081
BC	- 21,677
OC	- 5,803
Total	***- 55,214***

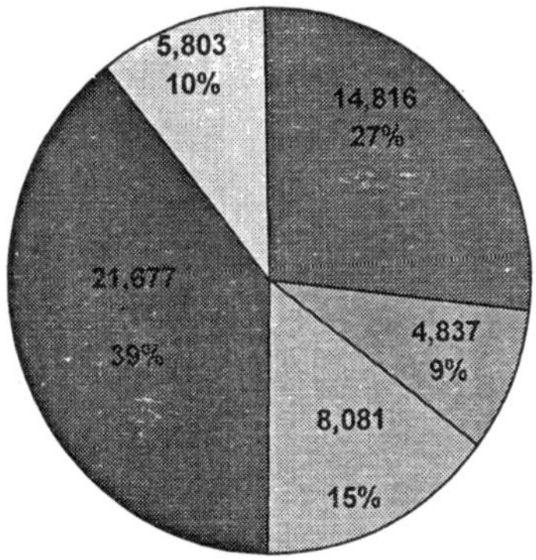

7. Monthly Family Income of students (in 184 Community Colleges)

Below Rs.1,000	- 18,916
Rs. 1,001 – Rs. 2,000	20,363
Rs. 2,001 – Rs. 3,000	9,829
Rs. 3,001 – above	6,106
Total	***- 55,214***

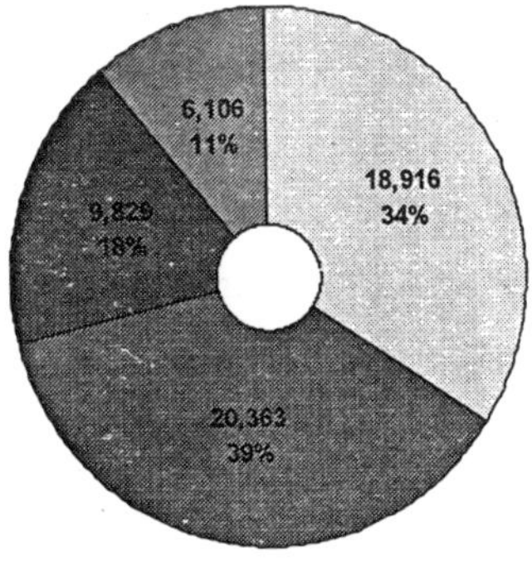

8. Student's Religions (in 184 Community Colleges)

Hindus	30,951	56%
Christians	22,416	40%
Muslims	1,803	3%
Buddhists	40	
Sikhs	4	
Total	*55,214*	

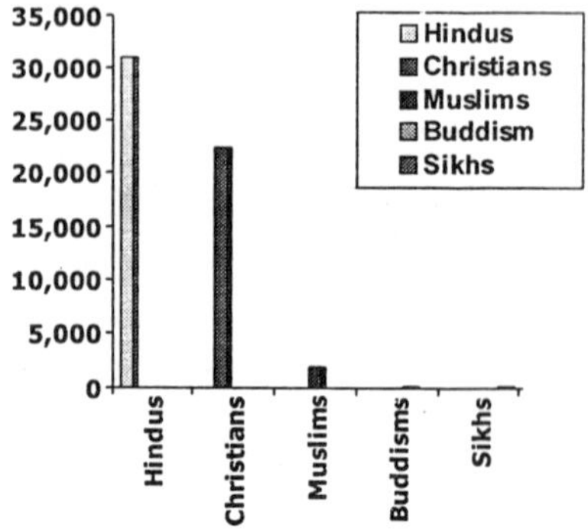

9. Job Placements of students

Year	**Job Placement%**	**Hr.Edu%**
1997-1998	- 81.26	- 9.37
1998-1999	- 75.04	- 22.49
1999-2000	- 66.26	- 20.49
2000-2001	- 72.84	- 15.16
2001-2002	- 78.72	- 16.14
2002-2003	- 74.75	- 12.19
2003-2004	- 76.54	- 12.61
2004-2005	- 70.68	- 14.41
2005-2006	- 73.01	- 13.12
2006-2007	- 76.57	- 1214
Total Average-	*74.44 -*	*15.11*

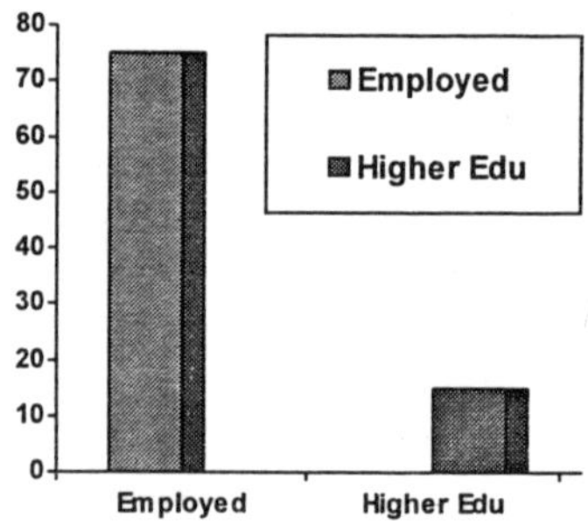

COURSES CONDUCTED BY THE COMMUNITY COLLEGES

Part I – Life Skills

(a) Life Coping Skills.

(b) Interpersonal Relations and Communication skills.

(c) Basic Computer Applications.

(d) Developmental English.

Part II – Diploma Courses

1. DTP Operator.
2. Computer System Technology.
3. Tally Accounting / Computerized Financial Accounting.
4. Computer Hardware Maintenance.
5. Information Technology.
6. Health Assistant / Nursing Assistant.
7. Medical Lab Technology.
8. Medical Radiographic Assistant.
9. Clinical Nutrition.
10. Physiotheraphy.
11. Veterinary Health Assistant.
12. Yoga and Health Science.
13. Refrigeration and Air Conditioning Technician.
14. House Electrician.
15. Four Wheeler Mechanism.
16. Plumbing Technology.
17. Two Wheeler Mechanism.
18. Printing Technology.
19. Leather Technology.
20. Carpentry.
21. Welding.
22. Masonry.
23. Radio and Television repair and maintenance.
24. Small Home Appliance Services and Repair.
25. Electronics and Electrical.
26. Fitter.
27. Motor Mechanism.
28. Crop Plant Maintenance.

29. Sustainable Agriculture Workers.
30. Integrated Farm Development.
31. Agro farming.
32. Naattu Vaidhyam.
33. Rural Marketing.
34. Orchids and Anthurium Cultivation.
35. Vermi Composting.
36. Sales and Marketing.
37. Travel Management.
38. Office Management and Secretaryship.
39. Cargo Management.
40. Hotel Management/ Catering Assistant.
41. Bakery and Confectionery.
42. Food Processing/ Food Preservation.
43. House Keeping.
44. Beautician and Health Care.
45. Tailoring and Embroidery/ Fashion Designing and Garment Making.
46. Small Business Development.
47. Pre School Teacher/ Early Childhood Care Education.
48. Multipurpose Rural Development Worker.
49. Micro Credit Management/ Community Enterprises.
50. Industrial and Labour Relations.

Publications

(a) Concept

1. Changing Track
2. Mismatch
3. Neglected Majority
4. Back to the Villages
5. Community Colleges in India – Education for Livelihood

(b) Implementation

6. Best to the Least
7. Reaching Beyond – Vol. I
8. Reaching Beyond – Vol. II

(c) Testimony

9. Miracles of Hope
10. Tears into Cheers

(d) Recognition and Accreditation

11. Including the Excluded
12. Marching with the Marginalised
13. Community College – Empowerment Endorsed
14. Best for the Community

(e) Propagation

15. People Building Business
16. Reaching Out
17. Power Within

(f) Life Skills – Text Books

18. We Shall Overcome
19. Walking the Extra Mile
20. English Made Simple
21. Computer Made Easy
22. Life Coping Skills – LCS I – TNOU
23. Communication Skills – CNS I – TNOU
24. African Book - We Shall Over Come
25. Hindi Book – We Shall Over Come

(g) Work Skills – Text Books

26. Health is Wealth – Vol. I
27. Health is Wealth – Vol. II

Recognition and Accreditation from the State and the Central Governments

- The Community College System has been working successfully with 75% Job Placement without getting Recognition from any Approved Educational Bodies of the Country. However most of the Community Colleges felt there is the need for Recognition from the State and Central Governments to facilitate the horizontal mobility and the vertical mobility of the students of the Community College.
- The ICRDCE has conducted Twelve Consultations to further this cause. It is for the first time in the educational history of the country, the agencies that run Community Colleges have devised Self-Regulatory and Autonomous Guidelines to ensure credibility and accountability of the system.
- The ICRDCE has succeeded in influencing the State and Central Governments for Recognition and Accreditation of the system and for Student Centered Funding. The issue of Accreditation was examined closely by the NIOS, New Delhi at the direction of the MHRD, Government of India, New Delhi.
- The NIOS has given accreditation so far to 18 Community Colleges in the country. Tamil Nadu Open University has recognised 119 Community Colleges in Tamil Nadu and it has extended its recognition to the Community Colleges in other States of India.

  Tamilnadu Budget 2008 – 2009

  Higher Education – Announcement No. 48

- Having regard to the fact that Community Colleges are playing a very important role in imparting employment oriented skills to poor dropouts who could not continue their education, Government will extend its support to them.

  From the Coming academic year onwards, these Community Colleges will be given student grant at the rate of Rs.1,000 per student through Tamilnadu Open University. **A sum of Rupees One Crore is allocated in the Budget for this purpose. 10,000 students will benefit from this scheme.**

- The Government of Tamilnadu has issued a G.O. dated 22.5.2008 recognizing the System.

Community College – Differs from other Systems of Vocational Education.

There are various formal systems of Vocational Education in operation in India such as:

- Apprenticeship Training.
- Plus Two Vocational System in Schools.
- Industrial Technical Institutes (ITI).
- Community Polytechnics.
- Vocationalisation of first-degree level education at the collegiate level.
- Teaching of Life Skills, Communication Skills and English.
- Also Personal, Social, Language, Communication, Work and Creative skills.
- They also undertake Evaluation and Assessment of Skills.
- Lessens the burden of Higher Education.

Index